Russian and
Soviet History

Russian and Soviet History

From the Time of Troubles to the Collapse of the Soviet Union

Edited by
Steven A. Usitalo
and William Benton Whisenhunt

ROWMAN & LITTLEFIELD PUBLISHERS, INC.
Lanham • Boulder • New York • Toronto • Plymouth, UK

ROWMAN & LITTLEFIELD PUBLISHERS, INC.

Published in the United States of America
by Rowman & Littlefield Publishers, Inc.
A wholly owned subsidiary of The Rowman & Littlefield Publishing Group, Inc.
4501 Forbes Boulevard, Suite 200, Lanham, Maryland 20706
www.rowmanlittlefield.com

Estover Road, Plymouth PL6 7PY, United Kingdom

British Library Cataloguing in Publication Information Available

Library of Congress Cataloging-in-Publication Data

Russian and Soviet history : from the Time of Troubles to the collapse of the
Soviet Union / edited by Steven A. Usitalo and William Benton Whisenhunt.
    p. cm.
Includes bibliographical references and index.
ISBN-13: 978-0-7425-5590-7 (cloth : alk. paper)
ISBN-10: 0-7425-5590-9 (cloth : alk. paper)
ISBN-13: 978-0-7425-5591-4 (pbk. : alk. paper)
ISBN-10: 0-7425-5591-7 (pbk. : alk. paper)
  1. Russia--History. 2. Soviet Union--History. I. Usitalo, Steven A. II. Whisenhunt,
William Benton.
  DK40.R8495 2008
  947—dc22   2007035203

Printed in the United States of America

©™ The paper used in this publication meets the minimum requirements of
American National Standard for Information Sciences—Permanence of Paper
for Printed Library Materials, ANSI/NISO Z39.48-1992.

For Margarita and Izabella
and
Donald W. and Betsy A. Whisenhunt

Contents

Preface

When your editors decided to compile this collection of essays embracing Russian history over the "modern" era, we also decided that rather than introduce a single theme, or set of themes, to bind the chapters together, which we concluded would attach an artificial framework onto a work that we hoped would be more wide-ranging, in fact eclectic, than roughly comparable products available, we approached some twenty-five scholars in the area of Russian history writ large whose work we admired, or in some manner found compelling, and asked for contributions from them in areas that they were working. Out of this process came the twenty essays that comprise *Russian and Soviet History*.

In selecting scholars, junior and senior, living in North America and abroad, whose research and writings we found noteworthy, we also asked they contribute pieces that would provoke, inspire questioning, and ask, if only implicitly, larger questions about the course of Russian history. Or more prosaically, pieces that explain what the author's observations (which in many cases are of a decades-long durée) tell us about Russia. Chester Dunning's introductory essay, for example, compellingly argues for the central role of the Time of Troubles in not only reinforcing many of the developmentally troublesome trends already present in Russian history (most of which eventually denoted "backwardness," at least in comparison to the states to which the Russians compared themselves), but also in providing the parameters within which Peter the Great had to work in his quite conscious efforts to "revolutionize" Russia.

The fate of Russia for the next two centuries, or until the Bolshevik takeover in 1917, was in some sense set down by the wrenching changes effected in the Russian polity by Peter the Great and his cohort/admirers. The editors believe that the Petrine revolution in Russian history was at its core a cultural revolution. In this vein, part I of this volume is devoted to offering a series of vignettes demonstrating the contours (richness, if you will) of Russian culture during the eighteenth century. Part II, which speaks to Russia in the nineteenth century, moves the study of political, economic, and social conditions onto the same rarefied area as culture. With the onset of Soviet power in 1917, the range of offerings becomes even wider; part III of the text provides what the editors believe is an introduction to some of the most intriguing historical work done on Soviet history in general, as well as a set of writings that will give the reader a taste of what made the Soviet Union such a beguiling, if also repellant, entity.

This reader's coverage includes four centuries of Russian history, a vast time frame that is often divided into three distinct periods in Russian history: the Muscovite (or at least in our case, the late Muscovite); the Imperial; and the Soviet. It would, however, be rather difficult for the reader to discern any strict periodization in our text (other than the artificial division of centuries into parts). This is not to say that we do not appreciate the very real presence of continuities and discontinuities in history, but rather we do not see the fundamental junctures in Russian history as occurring in 1917, or 1861 (the emancipation of the serfs), or even in 1700 (when Peter the Great began his reform/revolutionary efforts). Instead we maintain that if there is a fundamental episode that marked or represented a type of continuity and discontinuity in Russian history, than that "moment" (broadly drawn) is located in the span of time incorporating both the Time of Troubles and the later Petrine period, which combined to undermine many aspects of traditional Russia while reinforcing other, rather more stubborn aspects of "old" Russia. This "moment" in Russian history might, for want of a better term, be described as the beginning of a form of Russian modernization (the editors are sadly cognizant of the fact that one can only use modernization, or even more horrifyingly, westernization, with caveats so numerous that this preface would be far longer than space limitations allow).

The essays that make up this work cannot be subsumed under a rubric of Russian modernization or westernization; though if the editors have accomplished their task, this book will confront notions of innovation, backwardness, and yes, modernization and westernization throughout. What our text does most, however, is comprise a resonant set of glimpses into Russian history. Sixteen of the following twenty essays appear in print here for the first time, and the remaining have in some manner been rewritten or edited for this publication. This is not a collection of previously published articles. Each essay is based on extensive documentation, both primary and secondary. Some of the authors (and perhaps one of the editors), however, took more note than others of exhortations to keep references to a minimum. At the end of each essay the reader will find a list of suggested

English-language sources. This volume has been designed for a diverse audience, including Russian history undergraduates, graduate students in history generally, scholars in the field, and the interested reader.

With minor modifications, we have used the Library of Congress system of transliteration throughout the text. When referring to events in Russia, dates are given according to the Julian (or Old Style) calendar observed in Russia from the beginning of the eighteenth century until 1918, when the Gregorian (or New Style) calendar (dominant in Europe and elsewhere) superseded it. In the eighteenth century the Julian calendar trailed eleven days behind the Gregorian, in the nineteenth, twelve days, and was thirteen days behind in the twentieth.

For their assistance in getting this book to publication, the editors wish to thank the contributors to the volume, who not only submitted work of uniformly high quality, but whose patience throughout and willingness to make editorial changes, often abruptly, are deeply appreciated. Jessica Gribble at Rowman & Littlefield has advised us well and in a timely manner in developing this project, and we are grateful to her. Ben Whisenhunt offers his thanks and love to his wife, Michele, and to his children, Meredith and Matthew, who have been unstinting in their support of his work. Because this book was conceived as a teaching tool, Ben dedicates it to his parents, Donald W. and Betsy A. Whisenhunt. It was they (both academics in their own rights) who, more than any professor or mentor along the way, instilled in him a love of teaching. We deeply appreciate Donald W. Whisenhunt's preparation of the index to this work. Thank you! For Steven Usitalo, Horace Dewey and Valentin Boss were inspirations as historians and scholars of Russia. They were also kind interlocutors willing to spend many hours discussing all types of queries posed by a perhaps then-naive undergraduate (and later a less-naive, if equally inquisitive, graduate student). To Valentin Boss especially, thank you. Seija and Arnold Usitalo sustained Steven in many ways over many years (perhaps too many years), and no words of gratitude can express his thanks. Margarita and Izabella are his life, which they have made wonderful (and they know it!).

Introduction

THE SEVENTEENTH CENTURY

1

The Disturbing Legacy of the Time of Troubles

Chester S. L. Dunning

The Time of Troubles (1598–1613) was one of the darkest chapters in Russian history, but it has also been one of the least understood. From the era of Catherine the Great until the collapse of the Soviet Union, historians generally described the powerful popular uprisings that occurred during the Troubles as Russia's first social revolution against serfdom. Only at the beginning of the twenty-first century has that venerable but perverse interpretation been decisively overturned. We now know that instead of class war, Russia at the dawn of the seventeenth century endured and barely survived its first civil war—an extremely violent conflict that split Russian society vertically instead of horizontally and was so bitter and destructive that its impact reverberated for many generations.

The Time of Troubles began when the ancient ruling dynasty died out and Boris Godunov (1552–1605) defeated rival aristocrats to become tsar. Many questioned the legitimacy of the new ruler, whose sins supposedly included having Ivan the Terrible's youngest son, Dmitrii, killed in 1591 in order to clear a path to the throne for himself. During Tsar Boris's reign, Russia suffered a horrible famine (1601–1603) that wiped out up to a third of the population. The effects of the famine, coupled with serious long-term economic, social, demographic, fiscal, and political problems, contributed to the delegitimization of the new ruler in the eyes of many Russians. Then in 1604 the country was invaded by a small army headed by a man who claimed to be Tsarevich Dmitrii, miraculously saved from Godunov's plot. Many towns, fortresses, soldiers, and Cossacks of the southern frontier quickly joined Dmitrii's forces in the first popular uprising against a tsar. When Tsar Boris died suddenly in April 1605, resistance to "the pretender Dmitrii" (also known as "False Dmitrii") broke down and he became tsar—the only tsar

3

ever raised to the throne by means of a military campaign and popular uprisings. Tsar Dmitrii ruled for about a year before he was assassinated by a
small group of aristocrats, triggering a powerful civil war. The usurper, Tsar
Vasilii Shuiskii, denounced the dead Dmitrii as an impostor, but the former
tsar's supporters successfully put forward the story that Dmitrii had once
again miraculously escaped death and would soon return to punish the traitors. So energetic was the response to the call to arms against Shuiskii that
civil war raged for many years and produced about a dozen more pretenders
claiming to be Dmitrii or other members of the old ruling dynasty. In the
name of Tsar Dmitrii, Ivan Bolotnikov led more than fifty thousand rebels in
an unsuccessful siege of Moscow, and for almost two years the beleaguered
country had two tsars, two capitals, and two armies locked in mortal combat.
Russia's internal disorder prompted Polish and Swedish military intervention,
resulting in even greater misery and chaos. Eventually, an uneasy alliance was
forged among Russian factions and the Time of Troubles ended with the establishment of the Romanov dynasty in 1613. Tsarist Russia's first great state
crisis, its worst before the twentieth century, had been so severe that it nearly
destroyed the country.

The Time of Troubles left deep scars, but assessing its impact has puzzled
generations of scholars for at least two reasons. First, historians have usually evaluated the outcome of the Troubles primarily in terms of winners
and losers in a mythical class struggle. Second, the incredibly rapid recovery
of the autocratic regime and the spectacular expansion of Russia's empire
under the early Romanovs have obscured the impact of Russia's first civil
war and led some writers to minimize or even ignore it in their comments
about the development of autocracy, increasing social stratification, or the
growth of Russia in the seventeenth century. That view is just as mistaken as
the class war interpretation. In fact, the Time of Troubles produced a powerful consensus in favor of restoring and even enhancing the power of the
tsars. At the same time, however, the extraordinary success of Russian autocracy in the seventeenth century exposed deeply embedded elements of
opposition among the tsars' overburdened subjects—opposition that, ironically, found much of its origin, justification, tactics, and vocabulary in the
very same civil war that produced the consensus favoring a more powerful
autocracy. Such was the troubling and somewhat confusing legacy of the
Time of Troubles.

Without doubt, the real winner in Russia's first civil war was the autocratic
government represented by the new Romanov dynasty. Writers have, of
course, long noted that the Time of Troubles hastened centralization of authority and the strengthening of autocracy, but they have been unable to explain with any credibility how Russia, devastated by civil war and foreign intervention, could so quickly restore the essential components of its state
structure and bureaucratic administration, let alone develop them so breath-

takingly far beyond the precrisis order within just a few decades. Nor have they been able to account for the astonishing growth of Russia in the seventeenth century.

Under Tsar Mikhail (1613–1645), the Russian Empire reached the Pacific Ocean and became the world's largest country. In the next generation, his son, Tsar Aleksei (1645–1676), was able to shift forever the balance of power between Russia and Poland-Lithuania in the Thirteen Years' War (1654–1667), managing in the process to regain all territory lost to Poland in the Time of Troubles and adding the ancient capital city of Kiev and half of Ukraine to his domain for good measure. Within a century of the Troubles, Aleksei's son, Peter the Great (1689–1725), completed Russia's revenge against Sweden. Peter, of course, not only regained all territory that had previously been lost to the Swedes and once again gave Russia direct access to the Baltic Sea, but, in the process, he also transformed the Russian Empire into the "great power" so well known and feared since the eighteenth century. Although there is clearly no mono-causal explanation for the incredible success of the early Romanovs, one of the most important causes was the Time of Troubles itself.

Many factors related to the civil war contributed to the enhanced power of the autocratic regime of the early Romanovs. It is important to note that the Time of Troubles did not lead to political innovation or the emergence of any secular notion of a Russian "nation-state" independent of the tsar. Instead, the chaos and destruction of the civil war years produced a sharp political, social, and cultural reaction that rejected innovation in favor of restoring as much as possible of the precrisis order. As a result, the prestige and authority of the tsar—already very high in Russian political culture—actually increased in the seventeenth century. That, in turn, strengthened and sanctified the imperial ambitions of the early Romanovs and the quick reconstruction and growth of the central state bureaucracy, which soon resumed its coercive and large-scale allocation of Russia's human and capital resources for the purpose of exalting the ruler and expanding the state. The results were profound. The Russian Empire tripled in size over the course of the seventeenth century. In the same period, the tsarist bureaucracy grew at an even faster rate and produced a powerful "caste of professional civil servants" accustomed to interfering with the economy and regulating and controlling the lives of the Russian people.

It is well known that, even before the Time of Troubles, Russian culture placed a high value on the preservation of established order and the maintenance of traditional social hierarchy. Not surprisingly, that tendency was strengthened by the violence and uncertainty of the civil war years, and in the decades after the Troubles it combined with a sharp political and cultural reaction, a very weak economy, and zealous bureaucrats to greatly accelerate the regimentation and stratification of Russian society. Russia in the seventeenth century became even more of a "role prescriptive" society than it had been in the late sixteenth century. By the time Tsar Aleksei issued his famous law code, the *Ulozhenie*, in 1649, in which his regime took the final legal step in the enserfment of the peasants, the central government also attempted to force all other subjects into fixed positions in a "highly stratified, explicitly ordered society." The result was the legal codification of an eerily premodern, near–caste society dedicated to the service of Russia's "God-chosen" ruler. As elite and popular worship of the tsars increased, the emerging "orientalized" Russian political culture severely limited any possible modernization of society even as Russia emerged as a major player on the European and world stage. Although Russia's rather backward system was powerful enough to lay the basis for the country's emergence as a great power in the eighteenth century, that system also impoverished Russia and its people in many ways.

According to the traditional interpretation of the Time of Troubles, the winners included the townsmen. A brief look at the condition of the Russian economy and towns in the seventeenth century will demonstrate very quickly that almost nothing could be farther from the truth. Russia lay in ruins by the end of the Troubles. Large parts of the country had been destroyed; many towns and villages stood empty; several important towns had been lost to Poland-Lithuania and Sweden; and an already-declining economy had been seriously disrupted. In many places trade and industry simply disappeared and agricultural activity ceased altogether or continued its late sixteenth-century slide backward to a low-level focus on self-sufficiency rather than production for the marketplace. Several scholars have emphasized that the huge decline in production and the reversion to a "natural economy" caused by the Time of Troubles, coming on top of the late sixteenth-century economic crisis, delivered the "final blow" to the development of the early modern Russian economy along capitalist lines—with drastic consequences for the Russian people. Among other things, in spite of a return to relatively normal prices by the late 1620s, the "great ruin" contributed significantly to the relative backwardness of the economy and to the already-developing stratification and regimentation of Russian society.

The overall population of Russia recovered relatively quickly after the Time of Troubles; by mid-century, it had reached more or less the level of the late sixteenth century. That growth, however, was very uneven and did not favor the towns and taxpaying villages of central Russia. Towns in the far north and along the Volga River, which had been less adversely affected in the civil war years, tended to recover more quickly; some of them saw significant growth in population and economic activity in the seventeenth century. It was a very different story in the heartland, however, where a number of towns and more than half of all peasant villages had been completely abandoned by the end of the civil war.

Although the economic base of the country remained fragile and relatively unproductive, the cash-strapped central government's appetite for revenue grew in the years following the Time of Troubles. Unfortunately, that meant raising taxes on townspeople—still the most important source of revenue for the state's increasing military expenses. Just as the collection of taxes without concern about its impact on the economy had hurt Russian towns and trade activity in the sixteenth century, so too did overtaxing a struggling urban population in the seventeenth century seriously interfere with Russia's recovery from the Time of Troubles. It led to a further spiraling down of the urban economy, occasional outbreaks of violence, and further abandonment of towns by desperate, overtaxed subjects. Under those circumstances, it should really be no surprise that over the course of the seventeenth century the percentage of urban taxpayers in Russia relative to the overall population actually declined. Russian towns and commercial activity continued to stagnate for several generations; even a hundred years after the Time of Troubles, many towns had not recovered the population, vitality, and economic growth they had enjoyed in the mid-sixteenth century. Instead, in the towns, as elsewhere, a highly stratified society emerged—a clear sign of economic backwardness and trouble.

It is no exaggeration to state that, in the aftermath of the Time of Troubles, the failure of early modern Russian towns and capitalism to develop significantly until the eighteenth century had drastic consequences. It not only put Russia further behind the West economically, but it also helped push the country down an entirely different, decidedly illiberal path of political, social, legal, and cultural development—one in which wealth actually declined as a status symbol in favor of one's position in an increasingly rigid social hierarchy dedicated to the service of the tsar. While in the early modern West the rise of capitalism, towns, and an increasingly powerful and self-aware middle class laid the basis for the transition to modern states and societies, at the same time in Russia the economy remained extremely weak; the tiny and beleaguered Russian middle class merely constituted another relatively powerless stratum in a backward, highly regimented, near–caste society.

According to the traditional interpretation of the Time of Troubles, the gentry shared "victory" with the townsmen and were, in effect, a "rising class" during the seventeenth century. The gentry militiamen supposedly demonstrated their new power and self-awareness by participating in Tsar Mikhail's election and by working closely with him in the *zemskii sobor* (Assembly of the Land). In fact, however, it is well documented that gentry participation in the activities of the central government quickly faded as autocracy was reconstructed. Whatever sense of common identity had been forged among the gentry during the civil war did not in any way mark the emergence of a triumphant new interest group with budding political aspirations. Instead, what developed was a growing realization on the part of the economically and militarily weak gentry of their shared vulnerability to serious threats posed to them by greedy and influential "strongmen" at court on the one hand and by competent Cossack military forces on the other.

Contrary to the conclusions of some scholars, the extraordinary activity of the *zemskii sobor* in the early years of Tsar Mikhail's reign did not represent either a secular notion of the Russian state developing as something separate from the tsar, or groups of the tsar's subjects emerging as forces independent of and interested in sharing power with the ruler. On the contrary, the gentry representatives to the *zemskii sobor*—like the townsmen—were pleased to be invited to help the tsar restore order, and they asked few questions about whose interests were being served in the process. Looking ahead to the lobbying activities of unhappy cavalrymen during the 1630s and 1640s, however, one cannot help but conclude that the gentry's involvement in the *zemskii sobor* of Tsar Mikhail's early years did significantly raise their collective consciousness about how autocracy functioned, whose interests it served, and how to pragmatically and rationally protect gentry interests in the future.

It should be remembered that the gentry militia had been in deep crisis on the eve of the Time of Troubles. Needless to say, the destruction and dislocation associated with the famine, a prolonged civil war, and foreign intervention made things much worse. By the end of the Time of Troubles, the ranks of the gentry had been seriously depleted. Many militiamen remaining in service had lost most of their peasant labor force and were barely able to eke out a living. Many others had lost everything and by 1613 were truly desperate men. Perhaps even worse, the battered gentry had proven to be almost useless in the age of gunpowder technology, frequently being humiliated in battle by Cossacks and foreign troops. Because of that, the early Romanovs were forced to attempt significant military reforms in order to compensate for the weakness of the gentry and move beyond reliance on those nearly obsolete forces for defense and expansion of the realm. Nevertheless, Russia's ruling elite shared the gentry's fear of the militarily potent free Cossack forces as a threat to an increasingly rigid social hierarchy in which even a badly weakened gentry still had some role to play. Tsar Mikhail and his courtiers consciously shored up the gentry as Russia's exclusive warrior caste and made common cause with it to purge the Russian army of free Cossacks. In addition, and much to the relief of the gentry, the Romanovs more or less put a stop to the use of slaves in combat.

In spite of the new regime's efforts to shore up its traumatized gentry, however, the early seventeenth century did not see much improvement in its overall condition. As a result, the struggling gentry's complaints about its status and conditions grew louder and more frequent. Protests were especially strong against unfair and often illegal competition for land and peasant labor on the part of corrupt and greedy "strongmen," but the government usually ignored the gentry's complaints or failed to implement promised remedies. By the 1640s, many members of the gentry were actually so upset at being taken advantage of by the rich and powerful and at being ignored by an obviously corrupt government that they dared to vent their anger and frustration against Tsar Aleksei himself. In 1648, the demoralized gentry profoundly shocked the tsar and his ruling circle with its unwillingness to take the side of the central government against rioters in Moscow and other towns, whose ominous protests about the abuse of power by bureaucrats and "strongmen" echoed the gentry's own complaints. It was only then that the Romanov regime finally agreed to make fundamental concessions to the gentry, including specific language in Tsar Aleksei's *Ulozhenie* that formally codified the enserfment of peasants in ways favorable to the gentry. Thus, it was only after 1649, not at the end of the Time of Troubles, that the Russian gentry began to look and act like real "winners" and members of the "ruling class."

According to the traditional interpretation of the impact of the Time of Troubles, Russia's old aristocratic families were to be counted among the losers. That is an extremely faulty interpretation. As Robert Crummey and others have ably demonstrated, in the generations following the Time of Troubles, aristocrats must surely be counted among the biggest winners. Tsar Mikhail painstakingly restored as much as possible of the old aristocracy and court and showered gifts and privileges on most of the survivors. From the outset of his reign, the tsar forged a strong alliance with members of the reactionary aristocracy, and those "strongmen" took maximum advantage of their privileged position to secure greater wealth and power for themselves—even to the point of harming the country. Among other things, over the course of the seventeenth century many of them entrenched themselves in the top ranks of the rapidly expanding central state bureaucracy, further enriching themselves. Sometimes those aristocratic servitors performed their jobs well; often they badly misgoverned Russia in the name of the tsar.

According to the traditional interpretation of the Time of Troubles, the lower classes were the real losers. Even though Russia's first civil war was not a social struggle against serfdom, it is impossible to disagree with that general conclusion. The most significant impact of the Time of Troubles on the bulk of the Russian people, apart from sheer physical destruction and economic stagnation, may have been the harsh precedent set by Tsar Vasilii Shuiskii's 1607 decree on runaway peasants that strongly reinforced serfdom. In it Shuiskii "introduced a police element into what had largely been a civil matter," making local officials for the first time legally and materially responsible for returning runaway peasants to their rightful owners. Although the beleaguered Shuiskii was unable to enforce his decree in much of the country during the civil war, after the Time of Troubles his coercive approach to enforcement proved to be so successful that it became a permanent part of serf law. Moreover, Shuiskii's decrees began an ominous blurring of the distinction between peasants and slaves, an innovation that was also retained by the Romanovs. In the decades following the Troubles the legal rights of all peasants continued to decline as the government increasingly tended to equate peasants with slaves and began treating both groups less as subjects and more as mere property. As a result, in the highly stratified, near–caste society codified by Tsar Aleksei's *Ulozhenie*, not only were the bulk of the Russian people reduced to the status of serfs, but those unfortunate souls by law and custom were also well on their way to becoming something akin to chattel.

There has never been much scholarly controversy about the impact of the Time of Troubles on the Russian Orthodox Church. Instead, there has been general agreement that the church was a big winner. In fact, however, the growth of the church's power and wealth in the early seventeenth century helped set the stage for a traumatic schism among Russia's Orthodox population. During the Time of Troubles, the Orthodox faith, the patriarch, the clergy, and the monasteries had played crucial roles in stirring "patriotic nationalism" and in rallying the Russian people to resist foreign intervention. As a result, Orthodoxy and the Russian Orthodox Church emerged from that period with significantly enhanced stature. That was especially true for the relatively new office of patriarch. Its more exalted status was symbolically and powerfully expressed by the selection of Tsar Mikhail's father for the position and by Patriarch Filaret's immediate emergence as the real ruler of Russia. That was something no mere metropolitan could ever have aspired to, and it inadvertently established an awkward precedent that would later haunt Filaret's grandson, Tsar Aleksei.

The "great sovereign" Patriarch Filaret (1553–1633) presided over the development of a powerful clerical bureaucracy, an increase in the power of his own office in both secular and church affairs, and the rapid growth of the church's landholdings and wealth. Just as the enhanced prestige of the tsar sanctified and facilitated the unprecedented growth of the central state bureaucracy's interference in the lives of ordinary Russians, so too did the enhanced prestige and authority of the patriarch sanctify and facilitate the unprecedented growth of the clerical bureaucracy's aggressive, overbearing, and sometimes crude and violent efforts to expand the church's territory, wealth, and influence and to regulate and intrude into the lives of ordinary Russians. To cite just one example, during the Time of Troubles the church had managed to acquire by various means much additional land, and Filaret and other church leaders made sure it retained all those gains and acquired even more. Like the aristocrats at the tsar's court, the "strongmen" of the church took maximum advantage of their positions and influence to increase their holdings and to gain and retain valuable peasant labor. At the outset of Tsár Mikhail's reign, the church was able to secure the government's active assistance in recovering runaway peasants. From then on, powerful and wealthy church officials' successful ongoing efforts to acquire even more land and peasants put them in direct but uneven competition with the struggling gentry, who grew just as angry about the greed of spiritual "strongmen" as they were about predatory lay magnates. Needless to say, many peasants also deeply resented the church's insatiable appetite for acquiring them and exploiting their labor. It is worth noting that by the time Tsar Aleksei was forced to confront the imperious and unpopular Patriarch Nikon (1605–1681) at mid-century, the spiritual leader of the Russian people owned approximately thirty-five thousand serfs.

In the decades following the Time of Troubles, the Russian Orthodox Church followed many of the same general trends that Jack Goldstone detected in the religious establishments of other early modern agrarian societies recovering from severe state crises. In Russia, as elsewhere, as the power and authority of the church was strengthened, traditional religious Orthodoxy was reaffirmed and made more rigidly defined and conformist. Major efforts were made to purify a society (and clergy) perceived as corrupt and to purge all deviations from Orthodoxy—which were widely regarded as being responsible for the crisis in the first place. Russian society also became increasingly xenophobic and chauvinistic, and there emerged both elite and folk "ideologies of rectification." It is well known that Patriarch Filaret and his successors jealously guarded the church's control over the spiritual life of the tsars' subjects and in matters of faith demanded obedience from all of them. In addition, during the seventeenth century the church worked tirelessly to shield "true Christians" from evil foreign influences and ended up presiding over one of the more xenophobic and chauvinistic periods in Russian history. After the Time of Troubles the church also launched major efforts to purify a society viewed as corrupt and to reform the intellectual and moral life of the clergy. For many Russians, the resulting changes, such as the banning of the extremely popular minstrels or the requirement that the faithful stand for several hours in church, were annoying and almost as unpopular as the Orthodox Church leaders' lust to acquire land and peasants.

Historians have traditionally focused on Patriarch Nikon's zealous liturgical reforms as the primary cause of the development during the second half of the seventeenth century of the most traumatic and long-lasting schism in the history of the Russian Orthodox Church. In fact, in that era of extreme xenophobia, one group of deeply conservative and suspicious dissenters—known as Old Believers—did reject the patriarch's reforms (his reactionary attempt to "re-Byzantinize" the Russian church) as "foreign cultural innovations" that threatened the purity of their faith and their very souls. The response of the church and the tsarist regime was, not surprisingly, the brutal persecution of the Old Believers and harsh imposition of Nikon's unpopular reforms. In the cultural and emotional climate of the seventeenth century, there was simply no possible compromise between the radically differing "ideologies of rectification" represented by the equally stubborn Patriarch Nikon and Archpriest Avvakum (1620–1682). The shock of the resulting collision was profound. Recently, however, Georg Michels has demonstrated that at the heart of the rapidly developing split between the official church and many faithful Orthodox dissenters was not concern about the liturgy at all but instead a growing alienation from the powerful Romanov-era church's unprecedented, acquisitive, and aggressive intrusion into the countryside, the villages, and the lives of the tsar's ordinary lay and clerical subjects. Although most Russians, at least publicly, refrained from criticizing the brutal suppression of those spiritual dissenters, many Orthodox Christians were deeply impressed by the courage and passion of the schismatics, who remained a thorn in the side of the Romanov dynasty until 1917.

One of the most important legacies of the Time of Troubles was that Russian people at all levels of society were forced to take a closer look at their traditional faith and how it was practiced. In ways somewhat reminiscent of the impact of the Black Death on the fourteenth-century European mind, the Troubles profoundly shocked most Russians psychologically, emotionally, and spiritually. Some regarded the Troubles as God's punishment for the sins of the Russian people or their rulers and concluded that, if God allowed the country to survive, there would be need for significant moral and spiritual reform. At the same time, others who fought long and hard against an "evil" regime or against foreign intervention had their traditional faith reaffirmed and strengthened; many of them became utterly convinced that untainted Orthodox Christianity itself was primarily responsible for the country's survival. Under those circumstances, it should be no surprise that the early decades of the seventeenth century produced a resurgence of interest in religion and a considerable variety of official and personal commitments to defend, shore up, or reform Russian Orthodoxy. Many Russians apparently concluded that the Time of Troubles had been caused primarily by the "silence" of the Russian people—that is, by the failure of the Orthodox faithful to oppose an evil or false tsar. As a result, at least some resolved not to remain silent in the future if they saw a tsar deviate from or threaten the existence of "true Christianity."

The idea that the Russian people were themselves personally responsible for the fate of the realm and for Christianity itself made very significant progress during the Time of Troubles. The civil war saw tens of thousands of Russians who were willing to stand up to oppose false tsars; they set a powerful precedent and greatly reinforced the potentially destabilizing aspect of early modern Russian political culture that allowed even lowly Orthodox subjects to oppose erring or evil rulers. According to Paul Bushkovitch, the Time of Troubles actually undermined the older Orthodox notion of complete harmony between tsar and people and contributed to the growing split between the state and the nation. Moreover, when all national institutions failed during the Troubles, Russia's salvation came at the hands of the people themselves, adding to patriotic Russians' growing sense of personal responsibility to defend their homeland as the last refuge of true, untainted Christianity. According to Michael Cherniavsky, the Time of Troubles inevitably led to some separation in the minds of the faithful between the sacred mission of "Holy Russia" and the temporary, sometimes evil occupants of the tsarist or patriarchal thrones.

Scholarship on the intriguing notion of Holy Russia has traditionally focused on the sixteenth century or even earlier as its point of origin. The first usage of the term that can be precisely dated, however, was in 1619. It was, significantly, associated with Patriarch Filaret's return from Poland—a joyful event marking the symbolic end to the Time of Troubles. The term actually came into common usage only in the decades after the Time of Troubles and was associated especially with the Don Cossacks—those "Christian crusaders" who had played such an important role in the salvation of Holy Russia during the Troubles. All things considered, therefore, it seems highly probable that the term originated in the growing realization during the civil war that the Russian land and its people, not just the tsar, had important roles to play in safeguarding the country's sacred mission. In other words, if Russia was ruled by a sacred shepherd, then the shepherd's flock and land were sacred too. Daniel Rowland has demonstrated that the notion of the Russian people as a holy people or God's chosen people was already in play during the sixteenth century. In addition, Nancy Shields Kollmann has charted the increasing use of such terms as the Russian "state" and "land" during the Time of Troubles and has detected in them an intentional distinction from the tsar's authority and the central government. According to Cherniavsky, what remained in the Time of Troubles "after Tsar and State and Church hierarchy were gone" was nothing less than the "concentrated essence of Russia," or Holy Russia. After the Troubles, much of Russia's religious resurgence was apparently animated by such an idea. The early Romanovs, deeply fearful of this popular attitude, saw clearly enough the subversive potential of any notion of Holy Russia that was separate from the person of the tsar; it was a dangerous concept that might empower the ruler's otherwise devout subjects to dare to judge or even to oppose his actions. For that reason, the central government was careful to avoid use of the term.

Over the course of the seventeenth century, as many of the tsars' unhappy subjects periodically challenged the oppressive state and church's growing aloofness, rationalization, and bureaucratization in such outbursts as the 1648 riots, the Russian schism, and the Razin rebellion (1670–1671), an increasingly nervous ruling elite came to the conclusion that Russia's traditional, God-centered ideology was responsible for much of the unrest. As a result, starting with Peter the Great's father, Tsar Aleksei, most of the court and aristocracy (followed by the gentry once the *Ulozhenie* satisfied them) gradually abandoned the traditional ideology in favor of one that would compel the allegiance of all subjects and maintain stability. Not surprisingly, they gravitated toward a more Western-style ideology in which "the ruler was the sole judge alike of God's will and the public good" and in which "to advocate putting God's law above the law of the state" would be treated as "an act of treason."

It was Peter the Great, of course, who completed the transformation of Russia from a sacred realm to a secular empire and, in the process, completely replaced the old, potentially destabilizing ideology with his own vision of a "well-ordered police state" based on the impersonal rule of law. The bulk of the ruling elite and gentry saw for themselves the utility of that transition and went along with it without much protest. Try as they might, however, Peter and his successors were unable to eradicate all vestiges of the troublesome old nonsecular political culture. Religious dissent became the rallying point for many discontented elements of Russian society and seriously undermined popular loyalty to both church and state. Opponents of the Petrine empire and the very heavy burden it placed on its subjects frequently rose in rebellion in the name of the "true faith," the "true tsar," and "Holy Russia." In fact, the term "Holy Russia" had a very long life as what Cherniavsky called the "myth of enslaved masses."

The rapid reconstruction of a highly effective fiscal-military state in the years following the Time of Troubles further enhanced the status of the tsar and patriarch and led to the dizzying growth of the Russian Empire and its secular and clerical bureaucracies. Even more than in the sixteenth century, the ambitious new regime and its church grossly overburdened the Russian people and, in the process, helped produce a rigidly stratified, near-caste society. The rapid growth of state and church power also produced a widening split between the Russian people and the increasingly impersonal central government and church that intruded more and more into the lives of the tsar's subjects. Even before the schismatics broke with the official church and state, there were a number of sharp outbursts of popular violence directed against the growing bureaucratization, corruption, and arrogance of the autocratic government and the Russian Orthodox Church. Especially alarming to many Russians was the Romanov regime's determination to rationalize the state order and to remove the tsar from all vulgar contacts—in effect, abandoning the tsar's traditional role of "merciful ruler" and protector of his people. In such popular disturbances as the 1648 riots and the activities of

the spiritual dissenters, we can detect many Russian people stubbornly cling-
ing to their "traditional, highly personalized and theocratic ideological system" in spite of the regime's relentless efforts to create a more rational, impersonal, and ultimately secularized state order.

The growing split between the tsarist government and the official church
on one hand and the Russian people on the other, which was noticeable by
the mid-seventeenth century, became a permanent feature of the Romanov
era and had disastrous consequences, the effects of which were still being felt
in the twentieth century. As the state building of the Romanovs focused increasingly on meeting the needs of an expanding empire, the condition or
needs of the tsar's subjects were never seriously taken into account. Geoffrey
Hosking has reminded us that, in addition to overburdening the Russian
people and alienating many of them from church and state in the process,
the tsar's government failed utterly to nurture the development of "community associations which commonly provide the basis for the civic sense of nationhood." Instead, the rapid growth of the Russian Empire actually increased the huge gap between elite society and the Russian people and
impeded the formation of a Russian nation. Some of the origins of that
tragic split can be traced back to the sixteenth-century development of autocracy, imperialism, and enserfment. Nevertheless, Russia's first civil war
also played a critically important role. In addition to the tremendous boost
the traumatic Time of Troubles gave to the oppressive autocracy and the
heavy-handed church of the Romanovs, it ironically also helped give voice to
critics of the path being taken by the central government and the official
church. It is no exaggeration to say that the Troubles contributed significantly to the dissenting tradition which produced the 1648 riots and the
Russian schism and continued to haunt the Russian Empire until its demise.

Soviet scholars traditionally lumped the events of the Time of Troubles together with later Cossack-led frontier uprisings such as the Razin rebellion
(1670–1671) and the Pugachev rebellion (1773–1774), regarding them all
as "peasant wars" or social revolutions against serfdom. That faulty interpretation has, among other things, seriously distorted the study of the relationship of the so-called Bolotnikov rebellion and the Time of Troubles to those
later uprisings. A closer look at that relationship is worthwhile in trying to
assess the legacy of Russia's first civil war. We have already determined that
the civil war was not a social revolution, and Michael Khodarkovsky has
demonstrated that the Razin rebellion was also not a "peasant war" or a
struggle of the masses against serfdom. The Pugachev rebellion, on the other
hand, which occurred at a later time when the overburdened serfs really were
treated as little more than chattel, did see significant serf participation and
did take aim directly against serfdom and "evil" gentry masters. It contained
powerful elements of social revolution and thus was qualitatively different
from the earlier uprisings to which it is usually compared. Nevertheless, the

Pugachev rebellion did share certain characteristics with and was influenced by both the Time of Troubles and the Razin rebellion.

In ways similar to Russia's first civil war, the Razin and Pugachev rebellions both saw the southern frontier go up in flames as Cossacks and non-Russian minorities reacted violently to the relentless pressure of a central government determined to expand its control deeper into the frontier zone and to harness more tightly that region's population. Just as in the Time of Troubles, disgruntled Cossacks took the lead in the Razin and Pugachev rebellions, and those uprisings were to some extent anti-colonial in nature. Repetition of such patterns tells us something about continuing instability on Russia's southern frontier throughout the early modern period and something about Russian imperialism; but generalizations based on such comparisons have only limited value in assessing the period of the Time of Troubles. Even though Russia's first civil war also started out as a frontier rebellion, it quickly expanded into a huge, long-lasting civil war, whereas the Razin and Pugachev rebellions never overcame their frontier or sectional character, never seriously threatened the heartland, and were ruthlessly suppressed relatively quickly.

A far more revealing point of comparison concerns rebel consciousness. In ways strikingly reminiscent of the Time of Troubles, many Razin and Pugachev supporters were motivated to a great extent by their religious beliefs. We have already observed that the religious revival produced by the Troubles can be regarded as one of the sources of opposition to the Romanovs—from rioters in 1648 to religious dissenters to Cossack-led frontier uprisings. Although there are good reasons to be skeptical of the emphasis placed in traditional scholarship on Old Believers as the inciters, organizers, and leaders of the Razin and Pugachev rebellions, there is no denying the presence and energetic activity of Russian schismatics within the ranks of those powerful movements. Many early modern Russian rebels were undoubtedly just as troubled by the empire's lack of spiritual orientation as they were by its corruption and gross exploitation of the masses. Some rebels really did regard themselves as representatives of God's "chosen people," who had been betrayed by a wicked ruling elite that casually abandoned Russia's all-important spiritual mission in favor of the fleeting benefits and glory of a secular empire. In this context, it was certainly no coincidence that opponents of the Romanovs rallied so often behind pretenders masquerading as "true tsars" or their representatives.

The real source of Russian pretenderism, which became a chronic problem by the eighteenth century, was the miraculous story of the "true tsar" Dmitrii's multiple "resurrections" during Russia's first civil war. Emilian Pugachev was, of course, the most famous Russian pretender after the Time of Troubles. Interestingly enough, even though he claimed to be Catherine the Great's unfortunate husband, Peter III, some of Pugachev's followers regarded him as nothing less than the "second coming" of Stenka Razin. In fact, both Pugachev and Razin were, in a very real sense, spiritual reincarnations of Russia's original pretender, Dmitrii. It is quite striking that, just like Tsar Dmitrii, Razin and Pugachev were both regarded by many Russians as immortal, Christlike deliverers of the people from an overbearing and evil regime; and both were hailed, just as Dmitrii had been, as "resplendent suns" with magical powers who—even if defeated—would return again with God's help to champion the cause of Russia's faithful Orthodox masses.

Early modern Russia's ruling classes reacted with horror and incomprehension to the Razin and Pugachev rebellions and tried to dismiss them—in Aleksandr Pushkin's famous phrase—as "senseless and merciless." As a result, the lords came to fear the Russian people as irrational, uncontrollable, and sometimes even irreligious. To protect themselves from the violent and superstitious masses, much of privileged Russian society not only strongly supported harsh repression of all rebels but also became increasingly reactionary supporters of autocracy and serfdom. Try as they might, most of the Romanov empire's increasingly secularized elites utterly failed to comprehend the Russian people's mystical, nonsecular ideas about the meaning and purpose of the sacred realm they had so bravely defended against false tsars and evil foreigners during the Time of Troubles.

It is, of course, well known that some thoughtful members of imperial Russia's "ruling class" eventually recoiled from the harsh treatment and miserable conditions of the bulk of the tsar's subjects and formed an intellectual, conscience-based opposition to autocracy and serfdom. Ironically, that "revolutionary intelligentsia" also deeply misunderstood the source of much of the anger and alienation of the Russian people whose cause they so ardently championed. Inspired by what they believed had been the heroic resistance of the masses to serfdom under the leadership of Bolotnikov, Razin, and Pugachev, many radicals in the nineteenth century made energetic but ineffective (and very frustrating) efforts to stir the people against the imperial government by conjuring the memory of those past rebel leaders as champions of the lower classes. Fixated on purely secular notions of state, society, materialism, and class conflict, even the most sincere "friends of the people"—from Populists to Socialist Revolutionaries to Marxists—usually failed to bridge the huge gap in consciousness that separated many of them, as members of the elite, from the empire's long-suffering, faithful Orthodox masses. Sadly, that split between the Russian people and their "ruling class," which developed in the era of the Time of Troubles and deepened with each successive popular uprising, did not close in 1917 or during the "dictatorship of the proletariat" that followed the revolution. In light of that, it really should not be surprising that most Russian and Soviet historians who studied early modern popular uprisings could not bridge that gap, either.

The Time of Troubles left a profound, disturbing, and complex legacy. Even as memories of that nightmarish experience gradually faded away, its impact continued to reverberate for generations. Looking back, it is possible to trace many of the problems associated with Russia's historical "backwardness," as well as the poverty and oppression of its people under both the tsars and the commissars, to the aftermath of the civil war carried out in Tsar Dmitrii's name.

SUGGESTED READING

Bushkovitch, Paul. *Religion and Society in Russia: The Sixteenth and Seventeenth Centuries.* New York, 1992.

Cherniavsky, Michael. *Tsar and People: Studies in Russian Myths.* 2nd ed. New York, 1969.

Crummey, Robert O. *Aristocrats and Servitors: The Boyar Elite in Russia, 1613–1689.* Princeton, N.J., 1983.

Dunning, Chester S. L. "Does Jack Goldstone's Model of Early Modern State Crises Apply to Russia?" *Comparative Studies in Society and History* 39, no. 3 (1997): 572–592.

———. *Russia's First Civil War: The Time of Troubles and the Founding of the Romanov Dynasty.* University Park, Pa., 2001.

———. "Terror in the Time of Troubles," *Kritika* 4, no. 3 (2003): 491–513.

———. "Who Was Tsar Dmitrii?" *Slavic Review* 60, no. 4 (2001): 705–729.

———, and Norman S. Smith, "Moving beyond Absolutism: Was Early Modern Russia a 'Fiscal-Military' State?" *Russian History* 33, no. 1 (2006): 19–44.

Hellie, Richard. *The Economy and Material Culture of Russia, 1600–1725.* Chicago, 1999.

———. *The Muscovite Law Code (Ulozhenie) of 1649.* Irvine, Calif., 1988.

Hosking, Geoffrey. *Russia: People and Empire, 1552–1917.* Cambridge, Mass., 1997.

Hughes, Lindsey. *Sophia: Regent of Russia, 1657–1704.* New Haven, Conn., 1990.

Khodarkovsky, Michael. "The Stepan Razin Uprising: Was It a Peasant War?" *Jahrbücher für Geschichte osteuropas* 42 (1994): 1–19.

Kivelson, Valerie. *Autocracy in the Provinces: The Muscovite Gentry and Political Culture in the Seventeenth Century.* Stanford, Calif., 1996.

———. "The Devil Stole His Mind: The Tsar and the 1648 Moscow Uprising," *American Historical Review* 98 (June 1993): 733–756.

Kollmann, Nancy Shields. "Concepts of Society and Social Identity in Early Modern Russia." In *Religion and Culture in Early Modern Russia and Ukraine,* edited by Samuel H. Baron and Nancy Shields Kollmann. DeKalb, Ill., 1997.

Longworth, Philip. *Alexis, Tsar of All the Russias.* New York, 1984.

Michels, Georg. *At War with the Church: Religious Dissent in Seventeenth-Century Russia.* Stanford, Calif., 1999.

Rowland, Daniel B. "Moscow—the Third Rome or the New Israel?" *Russian Review* 55 (October 1996): 591–614.

Shusherin, Ivan. *From Peasant to Patriarch: Account of the Birth, Upbringing, and Life of His Holiness Nikon, Patriarch of Moscow and All Russia.* Edited by Kevin Kain and Katia Levintova. Lanham, Md., 2007.

Stevens, Carol Belkin. *Soldiers on the Steppe: Army Reform and Social Change in Early Modern Russia.* DeKalb, Ill., 1995.

I

THE RUSSIAN
EIGHTEENTH CENTURY

The eighteenth century was, at least for a small number of Russians (the elite, if you will), a time of enlightenment. As the century progressed, however, the dimensions of what constituted enlightenment and its effects widened in Russia, as elsewhere. Although much of the historiography in the former Soviet Union tended to vastly exaggerate the scale and reach of an apparently indigenous enlightenment (usually casting it as quite radical), it should in no way undermine the idea of a Russian Enlightenment. Histories of the Enlightenment in the West have tended to either ignore the Russian example or mention it in passing (with an aside to Catherine the Great as an "enlightened autocrat"). If we accept for the Russian case Immanuel Kant's protean definition of enlightenment as representing the expansion of reason, though not so far as to overturn established norms (or authorities); the ability to think freely, yes, but also temper any public expressions of said thought; in short, the encouraging of a wider use of the intellectual capacities of the individual, though not all at once, and perhaps not by every individual, then we have the Enlightenment as witnessed in Russia. Rapid cultural changes first launched by Peter the Great and his cohort and later admirers, initially most fruitfully cultivated and then assaulted (alas for later Russian rulers, too late to curtail its implications) by Catherine the Great, produced in eighteenth-century Russia an intellectual movement (or set of expressions) that can be described as enlightenment.

Commencing with James Cracraft's disquisition on the transformations initiated by Peter the Great (especially in the "cultural" arena), the authors of the chapters in part I are linked by a determination to demonstrate the significance of intellectual change in eighteenth-century Russia. Jelena Pogosjan's contribution (focusing on the court of Empress Elizabeth, Peter the Great's daughter) highlights the establishment of new forms of ruler imagery, inherited partially from Peter the Great, and perhaps more so from an incipient rococo style. Whatever the case, Russian rulers began to perform, officially and unofficially, in ways they never had to before, and to an audience they previously were unaware of—for it had not existed. By looking at the forging of Russia's "first scientist," a figure unimaginable in pre-Petrine Russia, Steven Usitalo examines the birth of a more modernized natural philosophy in Russia, and implicitly the origins of a Scientific Revolution in Russia. (If the Enlightenment remains difficult to define, the Scientific Revolution is no less elusive a subject.) Colum Leckey's portrayal of Andrei Bolotov, a prominent agriculturist and fascinating memoirist and critic, illustrates Catherine the Great's efforts to transform her realm (as Lomonosov earlier exemplified the reach of the Petrine revolution). Even more than Lomonosov he proved to be an enlightener, if not so powerful a symbol. Secret (or morganatic) marriages were courtly institutions of enormous importance, principally in absolutist Europe. Douglas Smith's account of the secret (or better said, publicly unacknowledged) marriage of Catherine the Great and Prince Potemkin not only exposes power relations at the Catherinian court, but due to the richly comparative texture of his research, he also situates the Russian imperial court more firmly in a pan-European context of absolutism.

2

The Revolution of Peter the Great

James Cracraft

Historians traditionally have viewed the reign of Peter the Great (1689–1725) as marking, or completing, the transition in Russia from medieval to modern times. To be sure, a minority of historians, specialists on earlier periods in Russian history, have scoffed at the suggestion that anything really new occurred during Peter's reign. All the really important developments, they argue, confusing opportunities with actualities, the swallow with the summer, took place in the decades and even centuries before Peter came to the throne. Such developments, they conclude, were at best accelerated under Peter rather than initiated or transformed. But this remains a minority view. Most historiographical debate centers on the question of how and in what ways the Petrine era witnessed the birth of modern Russia. And the debate has fostered new looks at the voluminous records surviving from the era, both visual and verbal, as well as renewed quests for fresh evidence.[1]

The most obvious answer to our question points to political (including diplomatic) events. Russia under Peter became, for the first time, a full member of the European system of sovereign states. The system itself arose on the Italian peninsula in the fourteenth and fifteenth centuries, and had spread from there to the rest of Europe. Dozens of principalities, dukedoms, and kingdoms (republics were few and far between) covered the continent by the end of the seventeenth century, the hereditary ruler of each area claiming "sovereignty" or absolute control of his territory and its governing apparatus or "state." Every such state supported an army and often a navy with which its ruler enforced his control and made war on his rival monarchs. Relations between these states were increasingly regulated by a budding "international law" and the related practice of "diplomacy," meaning the pattern of resident ambassadors, diplomatic immunity, and periodic peace conferences that we now take for granted. By the later seventeenth century the universal jurisdictional claims of the pope and the Holy Roman emperor, which went back to the early Middle Ages, had been decisively repudiated in Europe in favor of this system of sovereign states (only later, with the French Revolution of 1789 and the European revolutions of 1848, would these states begin to see themselves as "nation-states" as well).

Before Peter, Russia had not been an integral part of the European state system. By the late seventeenth century, the kingdom (*tsarstvo*) of Muscovy maintained only one ambassador abroad, in Warsaw, to keep a protective eye on fellow Orthodox Christians living in neighboring Polish territory and to promote the tsar's own interests at the Polish court. Muscovy, as it was usually called in Europe, was a vaguely charted land on the northeastern fringe of Europe, a valuable source of furs and other raw materials, to be sure, but otherwise of little political account. In the decades before Peter's active reign, Muscovy's rulers had striven without success to gain European allies against Ottoman Turkey; and Muscovy's periodic wars against Poland, Sweden, or the Baltic provinces controlled by German knights had been viewed with disfavor if not outright hostility by the rest of Europe's rulers. Under Peter, however, this situation changed dramatically. In Amsterdam in August 1717, a Franco-Prussian-Russian trade and political agreement was concluded which formally recognized Russia's role as a European power (not "Muscovy" now but "Russia" (*Rossiia*), the term that Russians preferred). And by 1728, with the convening of the Congress of Soissons, the first European peace conference with full Russian participation, Russia had become a permanent member of the European state system.[2]

The key to Peter's success in this regard was his military and naval victories over the kingdom of Sweden, which for a century or more had been the dominant power (along with Denmark) in the Baltic region, blocking Russia's direct access to its Western European trading partners. The kings of Sweden had been leading promoters of the military revolution that occurred in conjunction with the rise in Europe of the sovereign state. The revolution involved major innovations in weapons technology and related tactics and strategy, enormous increases in the size of armies and navies, and the ensuing bureaucratization by warring states of their armed forces.[3] Early in his reign Peter undertook a massive reorganization of the Russian army along the same lines in order to withstand a Swedish invasion of his kingdom and to gain, at last, a foothold on the Baltic, long a Russian objective. He also created a Russian navy. In short, he brought the military revolution of early modern Europe to Russia.[4]

Peter's passionate interest in military and naval matters went back to his boyhood in and around Moscow, where he was born in 1672. In the 1680s he learned to sail with the help of a Dutch shipwright and by the summer of 1693 he was exercising his "toy fleet" on the White Sea, where he witnessed the annual visit of the Dutch and British merchant ships that had sailed all the way around Norway to reach the Russian port of Archangel, a route necessitated by Swedish dominance of the eastern Baltic. In the summer of 1694 Peter took his fleet, some of whose ships were purchased in Holland, others built with Dutch help in Russia, for a three-week cruise on the Arctic Ocean—another wholly unprecedented venture for a Muscovite tsar. During these same years he built "play" fortifications in the contemporary European or modern style on the royal estates near Moscow, where he drilled his new-style "play regiments" composed of conscripted courtiers and servants together with regular soldiers and foreign mercenaries. In 1695 these regiments took the lead in his first real campaign, against the Turkish-held port of Azov located far to the south, on the approaches to the Black Sea, which was still a Turkish domain blocking Russia's unrestricted access to the rich trade of the Middle East. That first campaign was a failure. But Peter reorganized his forces and with the help of his fledgling navy they captured Azov in 1696, which caused a sensation in both Russia and Europe. It was the first Russian victory over Turkey in more than a generation and proof, or so Peter thought, that Russia could be a valuable ally against the mighty Ottoman Empire.

In 1697–1698 Peter and a "Grand Embassy" of some two hundred officials and attendants went to Europe, traveling through the Baltic provinces and northern Germany to Holland and England, where they spent a total of about twelve months before returning via Austria and Poland to Russia. It was an epic voyage, and generally recognized as such at the time. The ostensible purpose of the Embassy was to secure allies for a full-scale war against Turkey. But meanwhile Peter also hoped to acquire, at first hand, up-to-date military, naval, and related expertise. The Grand Embassy failed to achieve its diplomatic goal; the principal European powers were preoccupied with one of their incessant dynastic wars. But Peter did much to realize his other purpose, particularly in Holland and England, where he and selected attendants spent much of their time working in shipyards and observing naval maneuvers, meeting scholars and technical experts, and hiring specialists of various kinds to assist in upgrading the Russian army and navy. They also visited libraries, hospitals, schools, print shops, and picture galleries, and attended scientific lectures, theatrical performances, and musical concerts—experiences which would prove decisive in Peter's broader program of cultural modernization in Russia. These multifarious activities, propelled by his boundless energy and curiosity, only enhanced Peter's burgeoning reputation in Europe as one of the most remarkable monarchs of the age.[5]

When stopping in Riga on his way west in 1697, Peter supposedly was shown less than the customary courtesies by the commander of the Swedish garrison stationed there. At any rate, this alleged insult was later seized upon by Peter's government as a pretext for declaring war on Sweden in alliance with the rulers of Denmark and Poland-Saxony, who had their own quarrels with Charles XII, the Swedish soldier-king. Late in 1700, while Charles's main forces were campaigning in Poland, Peter's as yet only partially remodeled army laid siege to the Swedish-held Baltic port of Narva—and suffered ignominious defeat. It was the beginning of what proved to be a long and grueling war between Russia and Sweden for control of the eastern Baltic. The war drove Peter, with his characteristic determination, to complete the wholesale modernization of his army and the creation of a navy and then to take, whenever possible, the offensive. The decisive battles in the war, both Russian victories, were fought on land near Poltava in Ukraine in June 1709 and at sea off Hangö Head, on the Finnish coast, in July 1714. But peace was not finally concluded until August 1721 (the Treaty of Nystad), after Charles XII had been killed in battle and the Swedish mainland threatened with imminent invasion. By this time Peter had established a new Russian capital on territory conquered from Sweden, which he called St. Petersburg. There, in October 1721, in celebration of the Peace of Nystad, he was named Emperor, Father of the Fatherland, and the Great by his grateful government. His realm thus became known as the Russian Empire, and the Imperial or St. Petersburg period in Russian history had begun.

Peter soon discovered that creating a navy and a modern, standing army necessitated an extensive reorganization of the Russian state. In this he replicated, again, a process that had taken place all over Europe and particularly in neighboring Sweden and several of the German states, most notably Prussia. Bureaucratization in conformity with the theories of cameralism and mercantilism was the name of the game, the former understood as the science of rational, efficient government by trained professionals, the latter, as a doctrine calling for the state to play a leading role in the development of a country's economy. Peter's reorganization proceeded piecemeal until 1718, when, with the worst of the Swedish or Great Northern War (as it was called in Europe) behind him, he founded a series of "colleges" in St. Petersburg for administering foreign affairs, justice, commerce, mines and manufactures, finance, and the army and navy. The new offices were called colleges because each was run by a board of officials rather than a single minister. Each was given a governing statute based on Swedish, German, or French models and all were made subject to a "Senate" appointed by the monarch. A "Holy Synod" or college of clergy, also appointed by the monarch, was created to administer the Russian Orthodox Church in place of the patriarch, who had died in 1700; since then, at Peter's insistence, with his eye on the church's revenues and its potential for disruption, the patriarchal throne had been left vacant. A detailed *General Regulation* was promulgated in 1720 to guide the Senate and the colleges in their work (an *Ecclesiastical Regulation*, to guide the Holy Synod in its duties, in 1721); and a

Table of Ranks, framed to regulate promotion in the army, navy, civil, and court services, was published in 1722. At the same time, a regime of special prosecutors and fiscal inspectors was instituted to keep Russia's redesigned government honest and productive, and rudimentary educational standards were established for its subordinate personnel, whose numbers were greatly increased by comparison with the old government offices in Moscow. The empire was divided into provinces, each governed by a similarly reformed administration, and new taxes were levied—especially the notorious capitation or "soul" tax based on a universal census of male subjects (a first for Europe as well as for Russia) and from which only the nobility, the clergy, and men on active military service were exempt. Finally, a new doctrine of absolute monarchy was elaborated to justify it all—most notably in the tract *The Right of the Monarch's Will,* first published in 1722. Peter had brought the bureaucratic revolution of early modern Europe to Russia, too, and with comparably mixed results.[6]

Thus the Petrine era in Russia witnessed military and naval revolutions, the emergence of a modern, bureaucratic state, and the birth of the Russian Empire as a major European power. But it cannot be said that either an economic or a social revolution took place at this time as well. True, society was newly regimented as a result of Peter's policies: the noble elite, with few exceptions, was drafted into permanent state service, and new military, labor, and tax burdens were imposed on the mostly peasant masses. It is also true that both industry and foreign trade underwent a sharp upsurge, the former mainly to supply the armed forces without relying on imports, the latter, to provide luxuries for the elite as well as advanced technical equipment. Yet none of these changes produced a fundamental reordering of society or the economy.[7] On the other hand, it *can* be said that a cultural revolution occurred in Russia during Peter's time, a revolution that issued from but also transcended all the concurrent changes in the political, economic, and social arenas of contemporary Russian life that he initiated. And it is on this transcendent or culminating aspect of Peter's reign in Russia, one which historians have hitherto largely ignored, that we will dwell.[8]

Each of Peter's grand projects—his creation of the navy, massive reorganization of the army, bureaucratization of the state, and injection of Russia into Europe, all justified by the invention of a new theory of monarchy—entailed the adoption by Russians of countless new cultural practices, values, and norms: how to build and sail, and to engage in battle, a fleet of modern warships; how to uniform, train, equip, provision, deploy, and command in war a modern military machine; how to organize and operate a new-style bureaucracy, one capable of financing and directing the new navy, modernized army, and reformed state; how to conduct diplomacy on equal terms with the *other* European states; and how to rationalize the new governing system in appropriate conceptual terms. All this had to be learned by Russians—by some Russians anyway—within a single generation if the new Petrine state, the Russian Empire, which had replaced Sweden as the great power of northern Europe, was to survive the death of its founder. New ways of dress, deportment, communication, navigation, building, gardening, gunnery, drawing, computing, measuring, sculpting, writing, visualizing, indeed of thinking had to be adopted along with all the new vocabularies needed for naming these activities and all the new weapons, tools, devices, clothes, furniture, tableware, and other things involved. A cultural revolution thus underlaid and ultimately linked up all of Peter's projects, "culture" being our common word for the innumerable ways human beings have of making and doing things and of thinking and talking about them—or about such natural phenomena as the wind and the weather, both of which were newly conceptualized and in part renamed by Russians in Peter's time in connection with his creation of the navy.

The Petrine revolution in Russian culture is most readily apparent in architecture, broadly understood. From early in his reign Peter promoted revolutionary changes not only in fortification and shipbuilding (which contemporary Europeans called military and naval architecture) but also in "civil" architecture, which included palaces and mansions, churches and government buildings, formal parks and gardens, and Renaissance principles of town planning. He did so by hiring dozens and then hundreds of architects, builders, and decorators in Europe for service in Russia, by requiring them to train Russians in their various specialties (some of whom he sent to Holland, France, or Italy to complete their studies), by encouraging architectural schools to be opened in St. Petersburg, and by acquiring Italian, Dutch, French, and German architectural treatises and manuals to be translated and printed in Russia. St. Petersburg, founded in 1703, rapidly became the center, indeed the embodiment, of this revolution in Russian architecture, a revolution that affected every aspect of the building art and sooner or later reached into every part of the Russian Empire, working transformations in the built environment unimaginable in an earlier age. The extent of the transformation is especially obvious when we compare St. Petersburg as Peter left it with the Moscow of his father, the latter a medieval maze of crooked lanes and wooden structures centered on its picturesque citadel or Kremlin, the former a grid of straight streets and broad boulevards lined with masonry mansions and centered on its sleekly bastioned Peter-Paul fortress. Existing Russian cities, starting with Moscow, were partially rebuilt as occasion permitted in accordance with the new architecture and new towns were designed to resemble St. Petersburg. Under Empress Catherine II (1762–1796), Peter's enthusiastic successor in this as in so many other respects, a central building commission directed the razing and renovation of some two hundred older towns as well as the planning and construction of more than two hundred new ones. This gigantic enterprise was directed by architectural graduates of the St. Petersburg Academy of

Fine Arts, founded in 1757 by Peter's daughter, Empress Elizabeth; and its purpose was to give the Russian built environment, in Catherine's words, a "more European appearance."[9] Indeed making Russia more like Europe, the Europe of the Renaissance and the Scientific Revolution as well as that of the military, naval, diplomatic, and bureaucratic revolutions discussed above, was the dominant motive of the long reigns of both Elizabeth (1741–1761) and Catherine, both of whom consciously modeled their policies on those of Peter the Great.

Peter simultaneously promoted a revolution in imagery, or the other visual arts. Before his time these arts were practiced in Russia, when practiced at all, in a typically medieval or "Byzantine" fashion—as witness the ubiquitous holy icons painted in egg tempera on wood that prompted the recurrent disdain of contemporary European visitors. But under Peter, again, visual art in the naturalistic Renaissance tradition along with the allied techniques of image making—of drawing, engraving, etching, and painting in oils, of portraiture, true fresco, and metalwork, of three-dimensional sculpture in marble and bronze—were all vigorously propagated in Russia, utterly transforming Russians' depictions of themselves, their rulers, and their world. This revolution in Russian imagery largely followed the course of Peter's concurrent architectural revolution, not surprisingly, as the two were at many points closely interrelated. Dutch, German, French, and Italian artists were recruited to work and teach in Russia; sizable collections of paintings, prints, and sculptures executed in the European Renaissance tradition were assembled in the Moscow, St. Petersburg, and suburban or country residences of the monarch and leading grandees, their example soon followed by lesser nobles and their kin; print shops and studios were set up; Russian art students were sent to the Netherlands, France, and/or Italy to complete their training; and the collections of Peter and his immediate successors, especially Catherine II, were converted into the first public art galleries in Russia, accessible for viewing and study by both art students and the elite public. Within half a century of Peter's death, St. Petersburg contained one of the largest assemblages of such art in Europe and an art school, the Imperial Academy of Fine Arts, of European-class distinction. From its founding in 1757, the Academy was the center of an enormous expansion of the new art in Russia, having produced within fifty years more than seven hundred painters, sculptors, architects, and graphic artists whose work was disseminated from one end of the empire to the other. In the words of one Russian art historian, the Academy "directed the entire artistic life of the country in the eighteenth and first half of the nineteenth centuries."[10] And in this respect, as in architecture, Russia had entered the European mainstream.

Nor was the Petrine revolution in Russian imagery restricted to fine or elite art. The cult art of the Russian Orthodox Church was more or less directly affected too, though again, as in church architecture, less so than

other forms of imagery. After Peter the church retained its religious traditions intact; only its governance had been changed and its educational standards raised. A somewhat analogous development took place in popular or
folk art. Over the centuries after Peter, until it largely expired in Soviet times,
Russian folk art produced a fascinating fusion of traditional peasant forms
(suns, flowers, birds, animals, mermaids) and new-art or high-art elements,
whether in ornament, in new genre scenes (tea drinking, promenading, rid-
ing in carriages or sleighs), or in details of dress, gesture, and background.[11]
Yet more important perhaps than either of these was the revolution's effect
on what might be called official imagery, or the visual representations of
their status and power projected by Peter and his successors for the purpose
of enhancing their prestige in Europe and reinforcing their rule at home.
Such imagery included, in addition to innumerable painted or engraved
portraits and sculpted statues, symbolic representations of themselves and
their state produced on seals and medals and coins, on flags and banners,
on the insignia of new knightly orders and in a new noble heraldry, and in
porcelain (the famous dinner sets manufactured by the imperial china factories) and tapestry (produced, again, by an imperial factory established under Peter with the help of Gobelins in France). Under Peter, to take an obviously important example of this official imagery, a regular decimalized
coinage was minted for the first time in Russia in unprecedented quantities;
and along with the coins thus dispersed to the far corners of the realm went
the image of the tsar in the guise now of a Roman caesar, a symbolic visage
very like that of the contemporary Austrian emperor on his coins or those
of the kings of England and France on theirs. Equally significant, under Peter Russia was properly mapped for the first time, the size of its empire and
all of its borders, hitherto vague or unknown except in the west, now plain
for all to see.

The core of any human culture worthy of the name is not visual, however,
but verbal. Drastic changes in language also occurred in Russia in Peter's
time, a result both of his linguistic policies and of his many other innovations and reforms. Mapping Russia, for instance, entailed the hiring of
French astronomers and cartographers and the learning, by their Russian
students, of all the new technical terms involved. Creating a navy, to take a
bigger and still more obvious case, required the recruitment of Dutch, Italian, and British shipwrights and officers to teach the appropriate skills to
Russians, the translation into Russian of Dutch, Italian, and English manuals on navigation and shipbuilding, and the adoption by Russians of the related technical vocabularies—hence another, much bigger increase in the
Russian lexicon. The same may be said for Peter's modernization of both
the army and the state. Yet more, to expedite the translation of all the European technical manuals and legal, historical, scientific, and other works
required to implement Peter's various projects and to facilitate the assimi-

lation by Russians of their contents, Russian spelling, syntax, and punctuation had to be standardized in keeping with contemporary European norms. A new system of numbering (the standard European one) also had to be adopted in place of the ancient Slavonic system and a new alphabet devised, an alphabet that would be more suitable for printing all the new texts than were the cumbersome letters of traditional Cyrillic. In fact, the European print revolution, which as much as anything else had marked the transition from the medieval to the modern era in Europe itself,[12] had to be established at last in Russia, as did the necessary paper mills. All of this Peter somehow also accomplished, thus laying the foundations of the modern Russian literary language.[13]

The St. Petersburg Academy of Sciences was in many ways the epitome of this verbal revolution—indeed, of the Petrine cultural revolution more generally. Its genesis can be traced to Peter's visit to the Royal Society of London in 1698, which was generally considered the most distinguished of the new scientific societies springing up in Europe. The great Isaac Newton (whom Peter may well have met) was the Society's longtime president and it was to Newton, in that capacity, that the St. Petersburg Academy of Sciences addressed its first formal communication, in Latin, on October 11, 1726.[14] But the idea of founding such an institution in Russia certainly had other sources, too, most notably Peter's correspondence from 1697 and several subsequent meetings with another prominent figure of the Scientific Revolution, Gottfried W. Leibniz, the father of the Berlin Academy of Sciences. Then there were Peter's visit to the Paris Academy of Sciences in 1717, in the course of a second extended tour of Europe, and his ongoing contacts with that famous institution of royal science. His gradual buildup, from early in his reign, of a scientific library and collection of scientific specimens and instruments along with his ever-expanding cartographic projects also pointed to the necessity of creating an academy both to house and administer it all and to plan for the future—not to mention the desirability of establishing parity in this respect, too, with the "other" European monarchs. Equally relevant here were Peter's multifarious activities as "the Father of Russian medicine,"[15] since several of the Dutch, German, and Scottish physicians whom he appointed to create a Russian medical service were instrumental in creating his academy of sciences.

The founding of the Imperial Academy of Sciences was proclaimed in St. Petersburg on January 28, 1724. A special office was promptly set up to handle the relevant correspondence, the groundwork was laid for a permanent building designed in the new, classical style (it would be ready in 1726), and announcements of the Academy's establishment were circulated in Europe along with invitations to join it. By the end of 1725 sixteen German, Swiss, and French scholars, all highly qualified, some even distinguished, most still quite young, their interests typical of the science of the times, had settled in St. Petersburg and taken up their appointments. Informal meetings of the new Academy were held in the summer of 1725 and its first formal gathering took place in November. By this time Peter himself, the Academy's first patron, had died (January 28, 1725). But there was no turning back. His wife and successor, Empress Catherine I, soon ratified the project and formally nominated the Academy's first president and secretary-librarian, both of whom had worked closely with her late husband in creating it.[16]

It is common knowledge that the St. Petersburg Academy of Sciences, from its birth a European rather than narrowly Russian institution, went on to achieve international fame in mathematics, physics, chemistry, psychology, and other fields of scientific endeavor. Less well known is the role it played in disseminating science and modern European culture within Russia itself. Its use of Latin in its formal proceedings and related publications during its first decades, for one thing, introduced Russian students to the language still used by the European learned world, and thereby facilitated the assimilation in Russian of current scientific and other scholarly concepts and terms. Its press was the single most important publisher of scientific, literary, and other secular works in Russia until the end of the eighteenth century, just as its staff included, for many years, the ablest translators working in Russia and the compilers of the first grammars and dictionaries of Russian. Its print shop was the most important center of the new graphic arts in Russia until the Academy of Fine Arts was founded, nearby, in 1757. Several of its first academicians, Germans though they originally were, served in the Academy with distinction for many years, and laid the foundations in Russia not only of the natural sciences but of archeology, geography, and history as well. Dozens of Russian youths were trained in science and foreign languages in the Academy's subordinate schools during those first years and by 1733, less than a decade after its establishment, one of them, V. E. Adodurov, had been appointed adjunct (teacher) in mathematics. He was also an accomplished translator from German, taught Russian to the future Catherine II (German by birth), in 1762 was appointed by Catherine to be the administrator of the recently founded Moscow University, and in 1778 was named an honorary academician. He was followed by another twenty-eight Russians (along with sixty foreigners) appointed to senior positions in the Academy in the remaining years of the eighteenth century, one of whom, Gregorii Teplov, wrote the first philosophy textbook in Russian (published by the Academy's press in 1751), while two others, Mikhail Lomonosov and Vasilii Trediakovsky, contributed importantly to the creation of modern Russian literature and the standardization of the modern Russian literary language.[17] Lomonosov, sometimes called the Ben Franklin of Russia, was also a scientist of renown and a co-founder of Moscow University.

The St. Petersburg Academy of Sciences, in other words, was not only Russia's first fully fledged research center and one that rapidly took its place among the similar institutions already or subsequently established all over Europe. It also represented the apex of Peter's many and varied educational initiatives, which included primary and secondary naval and military schools, programs for advanced training in visual art and architecture, and a network of diocesan seminaries and parochial schools for the training of clergy. In this respect, yet once more, his reign was revolutionary in Russia above all in the cultural sphere. Historians in Russia itself, abandoning the restrictive Marxist historiography of the Soviet era as well as their nearly exclusive focus on military and political developments, are at last fully recognizing this fact.

NOTES

1. Nicholas V. Riasanovsky, *The Image of Peter the Great in Russian History and Thought* (New York: Oxford University Press, 1985) is the most complete survey of the debate. See also Lindsey Hughes, *Russia in the Age of Peter the Great* (New Haven, Conn.: Yale University Press, 1998), the most comprehensive study of Peter's reign in English which adduces, as well as much fresh evidence on the subject, various aspects of the historiographical debate.

2. For the more recent scholarship on these topics, see the essays by various historians in Euan Cameron, ed., *Early Modern Europe* (New York: Oxford University Press, 1999).

3. Geoffrey Parker, *The Military Revolution: Military Innovation and the Rise of the West, 1500–1800* (Cambridge, UK: Cambridge University Press, 1999; first published 1988) is a good introduction to this subject.

4. For a concise account of these developments, see James Cracraft, *The Revolution of Peter the Great* (Cambridge, Mass.: Harvard University Press, 2003), chap. 2.

5. See for example Anthony Cross, *Peter the Great through British Eyes: Perceptions and Representations of the Tsar since 1698* (Cambridge, UK: Cambridge University Press, 2000), chaps. 1–3.

6. For a largely critical account of Peter's bureaucratic revolution, see Evgenii V. Anisimov, *The Reforms of Peter the Great: Progress through Coercion in Russia*, trans. John T. Alexander (Armonk, N.Y.: M. E. Sharpe, 1993), 143–263. A more concise as well as more positive account, emphasizing the broader European context, is in Cracraft, *Revolution of Peter the Great*, chap. 3.

7. On the importance of Peter's reign in Russian economic history, see the detailed study by Arcadius Kahan, *The Plow, the Hammer, and the Knout: An Economic History of Eighteenth-Century Russia*, ed. Richard Hellie (Chicago: University of Chicago Press, 1985). For society as well as the economy, see Hughes, *Age of Peter*, chaps. 5, 6.

8. The following draws on Cracraft, *Revolution of Peter the Great*, chap. 4. For much more detailed accounts see James Cracraft, *The Petrine Revolution in Russian Architecture*

(Chicago: University of Chicago Press, 1988); Cracraft, *The Petrine Revolution in Russian Imagery* (Chicago: University of Chicago Press, 1997); and Cracraft, *The Petrine Revolution in Russian Culture* (Cambridge, Mass.: Harvard University Press, 2004), which focuses on verbal culture.

9. Quoted in Cracraft, *Revolution in Architecture*, 249. For the striking architectural contrast between Moscow and St. Petersburg, visible even today, see Cracraft, *Revolution in Architecture*, chaps. 2, 3, 6, 7, extensively illustrated.

10. Quoted in Cracraft, *Revolution in Imagery*, 257.

11. Alison Hilton, *Russian Folk Art* (Bloomington: Indiana University Press, 1995).

12. See Elizabeth L. Eisenstein, *The Printing Revolution in Early Modern Europe* (Cambridge, UK: Cambridge University Press, 1984), a digest of her earlier two-volume, now classic work on the subject.

13. A story told, in great detail, in Cracraft, *Revolution in Culture*; see also, for some aspects of the story, Gary Marker, *Publishing, Printing, and the Origins of Intellectual Life in Russia, 1700–1800* (Princeton, N.J.: Princeton University Press, 1985), chaps. 1, 2.

14. Valentin Boss, *Newton and Russia: The Early Influence, 1698–1796* (Cambridge, Mass.: Harvard University Press, 1972), 93–96.

15. John T. Alexander, "Medical Developments in Petrine Russia," in *Peter the Great Transforms Russia*, ed. James Cracraft, 193–208 (Boston: Houghton Mifflin, 1991).

16. Alexander Vucinich, *Science in Russian Culture: A History to 1860* (Stanford, Calif.: Stanford University Press, 1963), 71–76. See also J. L. Black, *G.-F. Müller and the Imperial Russian Academy* (Kingston, Ontario: McGill-Queen's University Press, 1986), 7–13. Müller was a history graduate of Leipzig University and one of the first scholars to be appointed to the St. Petersburg Academy, where he worked from 1725 until his death in 1783, compiling a distinguished record as a geographer and ethnographer as well as a historian.

17. See Wallace L. Daniel, *Gregorii Teplov: A Statesman at the Court of Catherine the Great* (Newtonville, Mass.: Oriental Research Partners, 1991); and, for Lomonosov and Trediakovsky (Trediakovskii), Harold B. Segel, ed. and trans., *The Literature of Eighteenth-Century Russia*, 2 vols. (New York: Dutton, 1967), 1:53–68, 165–220.

SUGGESTED READING

Anisimov, Evgenii V. *The Reforms of Peter the Great: Progress through Coercion in Russia*. Translated by John T. Alexander. Armonk, N.Y., 1993.

Boss, Valentin. *Newton and Russia: The Early Influence, 1698–1796*. Cambridge, Mass., 1972.

Bushkovitch, Paul. *Peter the Great: The Struggle for Power, 1671–1725*. Cambridge, UK, 2001.

Cracraft, James. *Peter the Great Transforms Russia*. Boston, 1991.

———. *The Revolution of Peter the Great*. Cambridge, Mass., 2003.

Cross, Anthony. *Peter the Great through British Eyes: Perceptions and Representations of the Tsar since 1698*. Cambridge, UK, 2000.

Hughes, Lindsey. *Russia in the Age of Peter the Great*. New Haven, Conn., 1998.

Kahan, Arcadius. *The Plow, the Hammer, and the Knout: An Economic History of Eighteenth-Century Russia*. Edited by Richard Hellie. Chicago, 1985.

Marker, Gary. *Publishing, Printing, and the Origins of Intellectual Life in Russia, 1700–1800*. Princeton, N.J., 1985.

Riasanovsky, Nicholas V. *The Image of Peter the Great in Russian History and Thought*. New York, 1985.

Wortman, Richard S. *Myth and Ceremony in Russian Monarchy.*, Vol. 1, *From Peter the Great to the Death of Nicholas I*. Princeton, N.J., 1994.

3

Masks and Masquerades at the Court of Elizabeth Petrovna (1741–1742)

Jelena Pogosjan

In Russian culture, masks and masking were closely associated with the traditions of the pagan past up to the beginning of the eighteenth century. The Russian Orthodox Church strictly prohibited wearing masks, and, naturally, there was no place for masks at the court of the Russian tsars: wearing a mask was understood as a great sin and an utmost dishonor. When Ivan the Terrible, known for his eccentricities and paroxysms of blasphemous behavior, forced his boyars to put on masks, while being drunk and dancing under a mask himself, Prince Mikhail Repnin preferred death to the disgrace of wearing one.[1]

The *Synopsis* (1674), the first printed history handbook, which describes events from the time of the early Slavs to the mid-seventeenth century,[2] specifically stated:

> Some people cover their faces and their human beauty, which was created in God's own image, with larvae,[3] which is a terrifying contrivance constructed in the devil's own image. They do so to scare a crowd, or to entertain it, but by this, they reproach their own Creator, as if these people are displeased or scorned by the creation of God's hands. Every Christian man should shun this [attitude], and should be satisfied with the image that God created for him.[4]

In the seventeenth century, two major terms for "mask" in Russian were *lichina* and *kharia*. *Lichina* belongs to a string of three semantically related words—*lik, litso, lichina* (image on an icon, face, mask or spurious face). *Kharia* refers to a mask or an ugly mug, muzzle. In the beginning of the eighteenth century, the new term "mask" came into use. Together with this term, a new concept was introduced: if *lichina* and *kharia* were understood as masks that depicted ugly and deceitful ("the devil's") images, the new term "mask" was used mainly as a reference to a "black covering worn on the face, which has openings for the eyes." Instead of the Russian pagan past, it was associated with contemporary European fashion, elegance, and luxurious court entertainments. By the reign of Elizabeth Petrovna (1741–1761), the mask as a cultural object with strong symbolic potential assumed its rightful place in Russian official culture.

Elizabeth ascended the throne by a coup d'état on the night of November 25, 1741. The circumstances of the coup are known primarily from the diplomatic dispatches of Marquis de la Chétardie, the French ambassador to the Russian court. Chétardie knew that the coup was being planned and was trusted by the empress, so can therefore be considered one of the most informed observers. The reports of other foreign ambassadors and the notes of eyewitnesses confirm and complete Chétardie's observations.[5] The coup had not appeared to contemporaries as being a well-planned arrangement. Yet Elizabeth, seemingly acting spontaneously, conducted this coup as if she was following the instructions of the most experienced political plotters, who had planned her every step in advance.

Mikhail Vorontsov, Elizabeth's chamberlain, her physician Lestocq, and her music teacher Schwartz were with the empress on the night of November 25. Elizabeth, according to Chétardie's words, having decided to carry out the coup, "first prayed to God in the presence of the three above-mentioned persons," afterwards "put on a cuirass over her casual dress," and over the cuirass she put on the Order of Saint Catherine "as a sign of bravery of the Emperor's scion, the lawful heir."[6]

The Order of Saint Catherine was supposed to "awaken" qualities in Elizabeth that her mother had possessed: Peter the Great, Elizabeth's father, founded this order for his wife after the Prut campaign in order to recognize her personal courage and decisiveness. The holiday of the order fell on November 24, Saint Catherine's Day according to the Orthodox calendar; it coincided with the eve of the coup.

Elizabeth's prayer also had great significance. Field marshal Burkhart Christoph Munnich points out that Elizabeth prayed that night "before the *image of the Mother of God*." However, the account of the coup presented by the Russian resident at the English court (the account is dated from Elizabeth's birthday on December 18) indicated that Elizabeth prayed, "bowing her head to the ground before the *Savior's image*."[7] And so it may be assumed that on the night of the coup there were two miracle-working icons before Elizabeth. Thus, on the Triumphal Gates, which were erected by the Holy Synod, and dedicated to Elizabeth's coronation, she was depicted in the form of the Greek empress Irena, "holding in one hand *the icon of the Savior*, in the other hand *the icon of the Mother of God*."[8]

The details of the coup were extremely meaningful, and Elizabeth intended to incorporate them into the official routine of everyday life.[9] It can be assumed that other gestures of the empress from the night of the coup also made an ideological statement, although at first glance this might be less apparent.

In the course of the coup, after praying, as Chétardie informs us, Elizabeth immediately set out for the barracks of the Preobrazhenskii regiment. There she addressed the members of that regiment: "Do you know who I am?"[10] Other contemporaries of these events describe this scene in similar terms. Elizabeth's wording had a double meaning. It is known that on the night of the coup the empress was masked. A contemporary observer wrote: "Princess Elizabeth . . . *stood masked* with a sword in her hands in front of her armed contingent."[11] This mask was to a certain extent a cautionary measure so that the people whom she might meet by chance could not identify her.[12] When she arrived at the barracks, Elizabeth asked the guards if they had recognized her under the mask. On the night of the coup this traditional "masquerade question" gave her followers the opportunity to reveal themselves and to declare that before them was the lawful heir to the throne.[13]

The mask that was on Elizabeth's face was not intended so much to hide her identity as to force those around her to "remove their masks" and declare their intentions. Elizabeth's mask was no less an important symbolic element of her costume than the Order of St. Catherine, her "casual" dress, or the cuirass.

The empress did not invent this "test" on the night of the coup. Somewhat earlier Elizabeth visited Feofilakt Lopatinskii, the former archbishop of Tver, when he was dying. Under Anna Ioannovna (1730–1740), primarily through the efforts of Feofan Prokopovich, the archbishop of Novgorod, many priests were stripped of their rank, often defrocked and exiled, having been accused of insufficient loyalty to the government; they had "great censure towards her Imperial Majesty."[14] Feofilakt Lopatinskii was among them. After the arrest of Ernst Johann Biron, Anna's favorite, the government wanted "to isolate the memory of the empress Anna by burdening her favorites with everything negative that had occurred during her reign,"[15] and declared the return of those who had been exiled. At the very end of 1740, Feofilakt was released from Vyborg Fortress and brought to St. Petersburg. The bishop of Novgorod, Amvrosii Iushkevich, executing the directive of the Holy Synod, dressed Feofilakt in a monk's and bishop's vestments. Elizabeth Petrovna secretly visited Feofilakt. She asked if he knew her, and Feofilakt answered: "You are the spark of Peter the Great."[16] A. Kartashev offers the following explanation for Elizabeth's "strange" question: "The exhausted Feofilakt was barely able to turn in bed and speak. Therefore Elizabeth Petrovna asked him if he knew her."[17] It is possible, however, that Elizabeth, just as on the night of the coup, was masked out of caution, and therefore asked Feofilakt this question. Feofilakt, however, answered the question as if Elizabeth had asked him, not if he had recognized her under the mask, but rather if he knew who, in essence, she really was.

The "test" very quickly became a part of the official culture. The first court celebration following the coup occurred on December 18, 1741, Elizabeth's birthday. Archbishop Amvrosii, in the empress's presence, gave a sermon that was immediately printed. The sermon introduced the story of the recognition of Elizabeth by the guards into regular use. "The Lord," stated Amvrosii, "sent her a courageous heart, infused her with Peter's spirit . . . she went to the soldiers, upon whom she could rely on and who had long desired this, . . . and deigned to say to them briefly: '*Do you know, lads, who I am?* Whose daughter I am?'"[18]

Besides Amvrosii's sermon, three other panegyrics were dedicated to this event. Jakob Stählin, a professor at the Academy of Sciences, wrote an ode and a scenario for fireworks. In addition, a second sermon was composed and presented by Kirill Florinskii, the rector of the Moscow Academy.

Jakob Stählin's ode was printed on December 8, 1741, under the authority of the Academy of Sciences. The theme of recognition of the new empress by her subjects dominates this ode. The ode begins with an account of the surprise of the academicians, represented in the ode by the Muses. The academicians see the light after a long period of darkness, and try to discern, "Whose gaze shines that is so pleasant?" They call the source of light *Hope*, and Hope informs them:

> *My look* is *covered* by such a dawn
> So as to gladden you and Russia.

It is already in the second stanza that the audience is introduced to the concept of mask through the figurative expression "*My look* is *covered*." In the closing verse of the third stanza, Elizabeth is openly named as the source of the unusual light (she is the one whose appearance is covered).

The next theme is that of the unmasking after the accession to the throne. The subjects really do want to see their empress, who finally opens her face:

> Everyone elbows his way to *look* upon you,
> To everyone you generously *show* your *sight*.

Even if Elizabeth had "concealed" herself, and even if she had concealed her name, her loyal subjects would have recognized her:

> No matter where You had *concealed* Yourself . . .
> Even though You *hid* Your name,
> Our *love would have discovered it*.[19]

The subjects' love allows them to recognize their true ruler.

In the fireworks scenario, which was printed simultaneously with the ode, Stählin reinterprets the same subject matter. However, here several additional shades of meaning appear in the interpretation of the theme of the empress's concealed identity. First, the program explains why Elizabeth had to hide her face. "Her Imperial Majesty, who was destined from birth to be our Sovereign," writes Stählin, "was from Her very infancy endowed with a face that holds much greatness and importance." Majesty was "*depicted on her most pleasant face.*" That is, on Elizabeth's face was "displayed" her right to her father's throne, which is why she had to conceal it. Secondly, according to Stählin, not only Elizabeth hid her face, but also Russia. Russia, which embodied the subjects of the Russian Empire, was supposed to cover her face in order to hide her adoration of Peter's daughter. "Now," Stählin writes, "peaceful Russia can meet the joyous day of the Imperial birthday with a *bright and free face.*"

The prevailing idea in the theme of masks as interpreted by Stählin is that of recognition. The ability to recognize Elizabeth under the mask as the true empress is depicted as "seeing," whereas the inability to recognize (to "see") is depicted as blindness. God's design ("foresight") is juxtaposed by Stählin to "*blind* chance."[20]

Kirill Florinskii did not turn to the subject of the events of the coup itself in his sermon. However, the theme of "the recognition of the true ruler by her loyal subjects" is developed in his speech in a very detailed and well-considered manner. Kirill starts the sermon with the words "His seed will be strong on earth," and, in this way, attunes the listener to the fact that the speech will be about the "seed" of Peter the Great. However, the image of the seed gives the preacher the possibility of turning to the Gospel parables about the sower, and unexpectedly alters the course of the argumentation. Kirill recalls the episode in which the disciples ask Jesus why he speaks in parables. Jesus answers that the reason is the hardening of human hearts: people have shut their eyes, so as not to see; they do not want to hear with their ears or understand with their hearts.[21]

This episode allows Kirill to very shrewdly set forth the question of the guilt of Peter's subjects before his daughter: after all, it is they who allowed her to be kept from power. While Elizabeth was "growing," remaining forgotten and neglected, all of Russia "slept . . . in lethargy." The word "lethargy," seldom used, was a reference to the well-known speech of Feofan Prokopovich, given at Peter's burial: "This very sorrowful loss may be through *lethargy, a certain deathlike sleep,* which it is impossible for us to forget."[22] It turns out that Russia, having fallen into a "deathlike sleep" at Peter's death, did not awaken until Elizabeth ascended the throne. Kirill returns to this theme often. Thus he writes, "Longer than a decade all we were more unfeeling than a tree," being "slumbering and sleeping," "our eyes have become shut."[23]

This theme receives yet another treatment by Kirill. He turns to the third parable about the sower: among the seeds, sown by Peter, the devil scatters "weeds." These "weeds"—"emissaries" of the devil—are clever, and it is difficult to recognize them, especially for those of Peter's subjects who have fallen into "lethargy." These "emissaries" appear "in the form of sons of the fatherland." In order to see through them, Kirill suggests turning to a *"theoretical microscope"* to see more clearly. "Until now we have slept," Kirill continues, *"but now we see* that Ostermann and Munnich,[24] with their mob, have crawled into Russia like emissaries of the devil . . . *in the form* of . . . faithful service to the Russian State." In direct connection with the theme of understanding and recognition, Kirill juxtaposes the activities of the enemies of Russia with "a crafty *masquerade.*"[25]

Masquerades planned and conducted at the court were a continuation of the trend, which was triggered by Elizabeth's mask on the night of the coup. In fact, the empress intended to prepare a masquerade that would be a mockery of Russia's "internal enemies." Thus, an order was issued in which the empress demanded that she be provided, by the time of her coronation, with "masquerade dress and various attire from both the confiscated *property of Count Ostermann* and that remaining from *the wedding of Prince Golicyn.*"[26]

The "attire" remaining from the wedding of Prince Golicyn, one of Anna Ioannovna's jesters, were the costumes of the participants of the well-known "Jester's Wedding in the Ice Palace," arranged during the celebration of the peace with Turkey in February 1740. The French ambassador, who witnessed this wedding, provided a speedy account of the unusual event to his government on February 19, 1740: "Only this country might deliver an amusement of the sort organized by the Tsarina. . . . Prince Gallitzin, one of her pages . . . gave a reason for it, by wanting to marry [an Italian commoner] against the Tsarina's wishes. . . . For the wedding some Lopars, Samoyeds, Kalmyks and Kazaks were brought [to St. Petersburg]. More than 200 of them appeared wearing masquerade costumes and joining the wedding procession. The newlyweds were locked in a cage, which was placed on the back of an elephant. They were followed by buggies pulled by mules, wild and domestic pigs, goats, and dogs. The Lopars and the Samoeds stood out because of their fur costumes and sleds pulled by reindeer. The wedding dinner was followed by the ball, and each group performed an ethnic dance. Soon after, the newlyweds were taken to the Ice Palace . . . and spent their wedding night in the Palace."[27]

This masquerade was also oriented toward political problems: while celebrating the peace with Turkey, Anna found it appropriate to design the masquerade as a mockery of the Crimean Khan, the ally of Turkey. Prince Golicyn represented "the Khan's son," and his bride—"the khaness." Representatives of exotic peoples played the role of guests at the wedding: several of them had long been "kept" in St. Petersburg (for example, the

Samoyeds and Japanese); several were ordered specially for the masquerade. It was a mockery because the role of the Khan was performed by a jester surrounded by "savages" (special costumes were prepared so that the "guests" were reminiscent of monsters from the accounts of Herodotus). This masquerade was created in the tradition of the masquerades of Peter I, particularly the procession that was included in the celebration of the Poltava victory and in which a mock "Samoyed king" represented Charles XII of Sweden.[28]

The second category of "attire" that Elizabeth requested consisted of items "from the confiscated property of Count Ostermann." It is unlikely that the attire had included masquerade costumes, remaining, for example, from some celebration or another. First, because during Anna's reign, Ostermann, suffering from "podagra," could not walk and moved around only on stretchers. Secondly, Ostermann was not a fop, someone who would carefully preserve masquerade costumes. "The domestic form of his life," writes a contemporary observer, "was exceptionally strange: he was even more untidy than Russians or Poles; his rooms were very poorly furnished and his servants were dressed like paupers. His silver dishware, which he used every day, was so dirty that it resembled lead. . . . His clothing in later years, when he only left his study to go to the table, was so dirty, that it evoked disgust."[29] If one assumes, nevertheless, that Elizabeth specifically ordered Ostermann's masquerade costumes, then she most likely needed them, not because they stood out due to some special exquisiteness or inventiveness, but because they belonged to the man who was, according to her, a true villain. However, it is most likely that this attire was simply the recognizable clothing of her enemy,[30] since the jester, dressed in Ostermann's attire, was supposed to be easily recognizable by the public.

Ostermann was famous not only because of his intellect and incorruptibility but also for his craftiness and mastery of hypocrisy, which all memoirists emphasized. Contemporaries wrote about his "talent for falsification," "falsified illnesses" at moments when it was necessary to take the side of one or another party, and noted that he was called "cunning Count Ostermann."[31] Even Ostermann's interrogation was arranged according to a special scenario "for the better exposure of his falsity."[32]

It is not by chance that, in one of the speeches in praise of Elizabeth in 1742, Ostermann was described as the "cunning fox."[33] Ostermann's hypocrisy was emphasized as well in the speech of Markell Radyshevskii that was delivered before the empress on Christmas of 1741. Markell called Ostermann "a shameful owl, who *pretended to be* a hawk or eagle," and emphasized the inability of contemporaries to see his true essence: "And the entire world *shut their eyes and closed their lids* to the most foul and blasphemous wonder, hated by God." The one thing that indicated Ostermann's hidden nature was his lameness: "*he is lame in his soul, lame in con-*

science, and he is lame in his legs." Only Elizabeth, according to Markell, was able to see Ostermann's true nature, and because of this Ostermann was so much afraid of her ascension to power.[34]

Against the background of such characterizations of Ostermann as the "cunning fox" and his lameness, which appeared to be an external manifestation of a certain "lameness of the soul," it can be assumed that Ostermann's staged execution was, in a certain sense, the first act of a masquerade invented by the empress. Ostermann, together with Munnich and other "internal enemies," was first sentenced to death, then led to the scaffold, and only then was pardoned. Witnesses of this scene emphasized Ostermann's strange attire. "Before everyone else," reports, for example, the Saxon ambassador, "appeared Count Ostermann, who already for several years could not stand on his feet due to illness, and sat on a simple . . . sleigh, drawn by one horse. On his head were a small wig and a traveling cap made from black velvet. He was wearing *an old reddish fox-hair coat,* which fell halfway down his legs, the clothes in which he was usually seen at home."[35] It can be surmised that Ostermann's fox-like attire was designed by Elizabeth to symbolize his true foxlike and sly nature.

For contemporaries of the coup, the real masquerade was the reign of Anna Ioannovna. Elizabeth, as the true ruler, was compelled to hide under a mask, and the "internal enemies" of Russia hid under their masks of "true sons of the fatherland." The wedding of jesters in the Ice Palace could not but recall the masquerades of Anna. The lame jester, dressed in Ostermann's fox-hair coat, surrounded by Samoyeds and Lopars in buckskin coats, was supposed to, without any doubt, comprise not only an amusing spectacle, but also represent the hypocrisy of the recently concluded era.

A whole series of court masquerades took place at the beginning of May 1742 as a part of the coronation festivities in Moscow. Two "masquerade halls" were constructed in six weeks especially for this occasion. *Vedomosti,* a St. Petersburg newspaper, announced that the principal hall was upholstered in "Chinese silks," all the columns were covered with mirrors and chandeliers, and in the center of the hall was placed a "handsome grotto" with a fountain, cascades, and statues. On the evening of May 8, "masquerade amusements" were conducted in both halls, with the usual division of masks into "court" and "town." These masquerades lasted for more than two weeks. On each of these occasions "it was possible to see a lot of rich and curious attire," and the empress herself always appeared "in the variable and different dresses."[36] Unfortunately, no existing sources—the court journal, *Vedomosti,* diplomatic dispatches, or contemporary memoirs—contain detailed descriptions of this "curious attire." It can be assumed that these masquerade costumes were not unusual for either Russians or their foreign observers.[37] Nothing particularly special, which would shed light on the conception of these masquerades, is found in the decorations of the halls (just mirrors, silks, and fountains). However, some assumptions regarding masquerades can be made.

In the "Coronation Album,"[38] prepared by the Academy of Sciences under the strict supervision of the empress herself and published in 1744, an engraving of the court masquerade was included (it was engraved by Ivan Sokolov based on a drawing by I.-E. Grimmel). Only one costume was depicted in detail in this picture. It belonged to a male figure on the right. His large nose, goatee, costume, and very distinctive pose indicated that this was a costume of Pantaloon, depicted in exactly the same way as it was depicted by Jacques Callot. It is obvious that Grimmel used Jacques Callot's *Pantalone* (1618) as his model. Some other masks in the "Coronation Album," which were less detailed, could be identified as traditional characters of *Commedia dell'Arte*.

Italian comedy was first introduced in Russia in the time of Anna Ioannovna. The first troupe arrived in St. Petersburg in 1731, and its opening performance pleased the empress so much that she "got up from her chair and was applauding facing the public." In the 1730s there were three alternating Italian troupes working in St. Petersburg. During this time, the performances were held at court on Tuesdays and Fridays.[39] Actors performed in Italian, and special translations were then made for the empress. In many cases these translations were published by the day of a performance and distributed among the Russian public.

The unmasking of masked characters is one of the major "situations" in *Commedia dell'Arte*. In almost every Italian play which was performed at Anna's court, masking and unmasking was included as a part of a plot. In the *Escapades of Harlequin*, for instance, the main character appeared as a captain; the real captain exposed him, "taking off his false goatee"; and later Harlequin dressed up as a Turk. In the comedy called the *Four Harlequins* all the characters disguised themselves under the mask of Harlequin, and it took almost the entire play to clarify who was the real Harlequin. In *Harlequin as a Statue*, Harlequin appeared in the image of a deserter, a chimney sweep, an astrologer, a statue of a negro, a "moving statue," and finally as one of the zodiac signs. Each time he was recognized and beaten. In other performances Harlequin played, for example, an ape and a "pregnant woman."[40]

The influence of *Commedia dell'Arte* on court life was not limited only to regular performances. Soon after his arrival in St. Petersburg, one of the Italian artists, Pietro Mirra, a buffoon and a violin player, "changed his profession for a position as the empress' court jester," under the new name Pedrillo. Anna loved Pedrillo's jokes and made her courtiers participate in his "performances." Once, for instance, Ernst Johann Biron said in jest that Pedrillo was married to a goat. Pedrillo made a low bow and replied that it was true, and that his wife was due to deliver a baby. He then invited the empress with all the court to honor his newborn, noting that he was expecting a lot of expensive gifts from such a refined crowd. On the day of the "delivery," on the stage of the court theater, a bed was set, and on this bed a goat was placed. When the curtain rose, Pedrillo appeared lying in the bed with his "wife." Anna was very amused, and granted her jester a large amount of money and made her courtiers follow her example.[41] The empress staged this farce in the theater, making it look like a spectacle, but the funniest, and most telling, part of it lay in the forcing of her courtiers to act in this comedy side by side with Pedrillo and the goat. This joke, as well as a number of similar ones, followed traditional comic plots and created the specific atmosphere of *Commedia dell'Arte* at court.

The concept of the mask and masquerade in official culture at the beginning of Elizabeth's reign, along with the exceptional role of Italian comedy at the court of Anna Ioannovna, clearly seem to indicate that Italian masks of the coronation masquerade in 1742 were supposed to represent Anna's time. That Elizabeth's accession to the throne was the end of a dismal theatrical performance is articulated in a poem, written by the empress's physician Lestocq for the coronation:

> The Divine Intent was *sleeping*, the Civil arts were *slumbering*,
> The All-Russian Empire was a *theater*. . . .[42]

The deliberate obliteration of the barrier between stage and court life was not a feature unique only to Anna's reign.

A well-known episode that took place around 1750 serves as an example of the "theatricalization" of Elizabeth's court life. A contingent of students from the cadet corps performed a tragedy by Alexander Sumarokov, a neoclassical poet and dramatist. Elizabeth dressed the cadets herself. "Young Beketov played the lead role. He appeared in a magnificent costume, started by performing well, but then . . . under the influence of overwhelming fatigue, he fell into a deep sleep on stage. The curtain began to be lowered, but, according to a sign by the empress, it was again raised, the musicians began to play a tender melody and Elizabeth, with a smile, admired the sleeping actor."[43] Elizabeth's gesture apparently violated the theatrical conditions of the situation, and the result was that the viewers saw on the stage, not a hero of Sumarokov, but Beketov, the empress's favorite, and the entire hall watched what was no longer a tragedy but the private life of the empress, which became a theatrical spectacle.

The absence of a border between the private and public life of the empress was the result of Elizabeth's understanding of her imperial power. Elizabeth did not find it necessary to put on the "mask of empress" when entering the throne room and take it off while in her private quarters: she *was the empress*.

If one is to believe the memoirs of Catherine II, Peter Fedorovich, Elizabeth's nephew and heir, also tried "to play at theater." Catherine described how, after Easter of 1746, he set up a marionette theater in his room and invited guests.

> One day the Grand Duke, occupied in his rooms with preparations for the so-called spectacle, heard a conversation from the neighboring room and, due to his frivolous liveliness, took a carpentry tool . . . and made a hole in the boarded-up door, and saw everything happening there, specifically how the empress dined, and with her dined . . . Razumovskii in his brocade robe. . . . His imperial majesty, not satisfied that he himself enjoyed the fruits of his skilful labor, called all who were around him so that they could enjoy looking through the hole.[44]

It is not important if this really was the Grand Duke's enterprise or if Catherine herself invented this episode. What is important is that here, too, the conditional nature of performance is violated in order to make a scene from the empress's private life into an object of the audience's attention. However, in the instance with Beketov the empress's feelings were projected onto the heightened passions of tragic heroes; here the tragedy was replaced by a marionette comedy.

Unlike Empress Anna, who played scenes from *Commedia dell'Arte* at court, Elizabeth chose a different, "higher" genre of "performances." Catherine II, by describing the court of her "aunty," once again lowered the genre of the "performance" by making Elizabeth's court life not a tragedy, but a theater of marionettes.

Anna held to Peter I's tradition, according to which a masquerade was a show of a political nature, staged for and performed in front of the emperor or empress. Both Peter I and Anna made the courtiers perform for them. Elizabeth, on the contrary, wanted to play the lead role herself. In that, she was disposed towards the theatricalization and aestheticization of her daily court life, of not only that which was festive and ritualized, but of the private and everyday.

The premier of the Italian opera *La Clemenza di Tito* (*Tito's Charity*) accompanied one of the coronation masquerades. It took place on May 29, 1742, and, according to *Vedomosti*, "all the spectators of the opera were to wear masks, and after the performance a masquerade was to be held at court."[45]

This opera was supposed to "represent all the charitable commissions of Her Imperial Majesty." An allegorical prologue of this opera, called "Russia after Her Sorrows Is Gladdened Again," was intended to depict the coup. In the beginning of this prologue, Ruthenia (Russia) sat with her children in the darkness, surrounded by ruins (all that was left of Peter I's legacy), then the Sun rose, and the ruins miraculously changed into magnificent buildings. The opera itself not only presented the happy present state of the Russian Empire, but followed some quite peculiar and personal details of Elizabeth's life.

Toward the end of the prologue, Astrea encouraged Ruthenia and her children to raise a "public monument" in honor of the empress. The inscription read: "Long live Elizabeth, . . . Mother of her fatherland, the amusement of the human race and Tito of our times." This episode foreshadowed the beginning of the opera itself, when the Senate presented Tito with the title of "Father of the Fatherland" and wanted to build a temple in his honor. Tito accepted the title, but rejected the idea of a temple. Soon after, Tito decided to abandon his beloved Berenica because she was hated by the people of Rome. However, his new bride, Servilia, confessed that she was in love with another man. At the end of the opera Tito announced his final decision:

> Besides Rome I won't have another bride,
> And my subjects shall be my children,
> All of whom I love equally.[46]

Being father of the nation, Tito decided to renounce marriage and dedicate himself to his people. Similarly, Elizabeth's celibacy was an important issue in the precoronation and coronation panegyric literature. Mikhail Lomonosov, a rapidly rising young poet, for instance, in an ode written in February 1742, gave the description of his "prophetic vision," which was incorporated in the ode. He opened this description with the line: "I see the *Virgin* standing in the Sun." This line appealed to both Christian[47] and classical[48] mythology. Amvrosii, in his coronation sermon, compared Elizabeth to Judith "adorned in her *virginity*," and called the empress "a miraculous star in a *virginal* body shining."[49] Elizabeth, as Tito, chose to be a "Mother" for her subjects over marriage.

The opera *Tito's Charity* was held by the empress as part of her masquerade and, therefore, the audience was masked during the performance. This shows that these two forms of entertainment, the opera and the masquerade, were associated in the empress's mind. The masquerade was meant to symbolize the rule of Anna Ioannovna, a time when all hid their true nature behind masks, as in Anna's favorite Italian comedy. The opera was a representation of the present, in which Elizabeth had taken her place as the rightful ruler of Russia. During the opera the audience was still masked in the darkness of the past, and could gaze upon the splendid light of the present rule of Elizabeth.

The "masquerade theme" is evident in G. Ch. Groot's portrayal of Elizabeth: *A Portrait of Elizabeth Petrovna in a Black Domino with a Mask in Her Hand*. It was painted in 1748 by the direct order of the empress. In this full-length portrait, Elizabeth is shown in entirely black attire. The mask in her hand was a full mask of a woman's face, so detailed that it even possessed two black beauty spots. It was on this face that a black half-mask was carefully painted. Elizabeth's face and her hand with the mask stand out on the dark background, and therefore appear significant. Taking into consideration the masquerade theme in court culture, with its two dominant motifs of "hiding a face" and "unmasking," this portrait should be understood not only as a depiction of the empress in her masquerade costume, but also as a symbolic composition as well. Elizabeth was represented in this portrait as a ruler who had freed herself from the necessity of hiding her face, and "generously showed her sight" to her subjects.

A Portrait of Elizabeth Petrovna in a Black Domino with a Mask in Her Hand, together with *A Portrait of Elizabeth Petrovna as Flora*, belonged to a series of Groot's two so-called chamber portraits. These two portraits of Elizabeth were kept in the empress's private Amber Room.[50] A "chamber portrait" was, in its essence, the result of a peculiar interplay between different genres. On the one hand, this type of portrait still preserved its relation to official portraits. On the other hand, it was a "pleasant ornament," typical for rococo style, aimed to reduce the official to the intimate, the serious to the amusing, and the symbolic to its outer shell.[51]

A Portrait of Elizabeth Petrovna as Flora was truly remarkable in this respect. As Flora, Elizabeth was first depicted by Louis Caravaque. By the order of Peter I, Caravaque painted the tsar's children in the images of Flora, Diana, Cupid, and Apollo.[52] The nude body of the Roman goddess Flora served as a "costume" for the princess Elizabeth for this painting.

The first anniversary of Elizabeth's coronation was celebrated in St. Petersburg with great pomp. Masquerades played an important part in this festival. The empress was dressed for this event as Flora.[53] Her choice of costume was significant, as she made a decision to dress as Flora to remind everyone of her effigy.

Groot made a replica of Caravaque's painting. However, this second portrait was created in a totally different context, and obviously had a different meaning. It was a nude portrait of a fully grown woman, famous for her beauty. Moreover, it was a portrait of the empress. It was therefore impossible to completely detach the nude image on the portrait from the royal persona of Elizabeth.

Groot's two paintings, *A Portrait of Elizabeth Petrovna in a Black Domino* and *A Portrait of Elizabeth Petrovna as Flora*, were connected by more than the masquerade theme. On both paintings Elizabeth was depicted "uncovered": on the first her face was uncovered, on the second—her "magnificent body," "a body shining with the *virginity.*"[54] Therefore, both masquerade costumes of the empress were meant to represent Elizabeth's understanding of her own status. The notion of "being an empress" for

Elizabeth was "natural" and was "embodied" in her own real, "natural" body. According to the well-known concept of *The King's Two Bodies*, natural and political,[55] her "nuditas naturalis" was, therefore, equal to her "nuditas virtualis."

Elizabeth in her accession manifesto named herself "the natural sovereign."[56] The idea of being "the natural sovereign" was probably internalized by Elizabeth at a very early age. Her birth, for instance, coincided with the celebration conducted by Peter I in honor of his Poltava victory. Peter I understood Russia's war with Sweden as a "great flood," and the victory as "God's covenant" with him—his "rainbow in the clouds." Elizabeth's name, which meant "God's covenant" or "rainbow," was intentionally chosen by Peter as a symbol of his victory. God gave Peter I a daughter as a "covenant," together with Peter's victory, which became "the resurrection of Russia."[57] Elizabeth believed that she was given to Russia by God as an "embodiment" of Peter's "covenant" and that her natural bodily beauty was a sign of her destiny. Therefore, Elizabeth was the "natural" ruler of Russian Empire.

The theme of masks and masquerades or, more precisely, of "taking off the mask" in the beginning of Elizabeth's rule represented the concept of Russia's "natural" ruler. This concept undoubtedly defined "the face" of Elizabeth's court life with its highly significant corporeality and unexpectedly ideologized rococo culture.

NOTES

1. D. S. Likhachev, ed., *Biblioteka literatury drevnei Rusi* (St. Petersburg: Nauka, 2001), 11:414.

2. *Synopsis* was extremely popular in Russia in the eighteenth century. Its first printings were in Moscow in 1714 and 1718, and then it went through six additional editions in St. Petersburg between 1735 and 1798.

3. Larvae (Latin for "masks").

4. Hans Rothe, ed., *Sinopsis. Kiev, 1681. Fascimile mit einer Einleitung* (Cologne, 1983), 195–196.

5. P. Pekarskii, ed., *Markiz de-la Shetardi v Rossii 1740–1742 godov* (St. Petersburg, 1862), 396–425; *Sbornik imperatorskogo russkogo istoricheskogo obshchestva*, vol. 91 (St. Petersburg: Tipografiia Akademii nauk, 1894), 338–352; *Perevoroty i voiny* (Moscow: Fond Sergeia Dubova, 1997), 196–197, 310–312; L. Levin, *Rossijskii generalissimus gertsog Anton Ulrih, Istorija "Braunshveiskogo semeistva" v Rossii* (St. Petersburg: Peterburgskii pisatel, 2000), 314–315.

6. Pekarskii, *Markiz de-la Shetardi*, 39, 432.

7. *Perevoroty i voiny*, 312, 431.

8. *Materialy dlja istorii Imperatorskoj Akademii nauk*, vol. 5 (St. Petersburg: Tipografiia Akademii nauk, 1889), 815. Italics here and in all following quotations have been added.

9. The image of the Mother of God, before which Elizabeth prayed, had belonged to her father. Later, at the end of August 1742, the Saxon ambassador reported: "Last Thursday [August 19—*J. P.*] a church celebration took place for the first time throughout the entire state by the order of Her Majesty the empress in honor of the miracle-working icon that *the Emperor Peter I raised above his palace in times of important or dangerous undertakings and which was carried before the empress on the night when she personally led the soldiers of the guard from their barracks and then occupied the throne.* Her Majesty, accompanied by the court, set out to pray at *the Don Monastery church,* where the icon had been placed for safekeeping, and she offered for its decoration, among other things, a diamond bought for thirty thousand rubles" *Sbornik imperatorskogo russkogo istoricheskogo obshchestva,* vol. 6 (St. Petersburg: Tipografiia Akademii nauk, 1871), 442. This testimony about Elizabeth's visit of August 19 to the Don Monastery is also affirmed in the court journal (*Pridvornyj zhurnal, 1741–1742 gg.* St. Petersburg, 1883, 30), and in the *Monastery Chronicle* (I. Zabelin, *Istoricheskoe opisanie Moskovskogo stavropigialnogo Donskogo monastyria* [Moscow: T-vo Tip. A. I. Mamontova, 1865], 72). Another new official holiday dedicated to the icon of Jesus Christ, "Not Made with Hands," appeared in the calendar printed for 1743 on the sixteenth of August (*Sanktpeterburgskij kalendar na leto ot Rozhdestva Hristova 1743.* [St. Petersburg: Tipografiia Akademii nauk, 1742]).

10. *Perevoroty i voiny,* 399, 405.

11. Levin, *Rossijskii generalissimus,* 314.

12. Even though St. Petersburg was to some extent a "Northern Venice," it was not customary for the Russian nobility to wear a mask on a daily basis. A masked person on St. Petersburg's streets would certainly be noticed, especially since it was not a "masquerade day" at the court (the last masquerade before the coup was held on October 31, 1741, the first anniversary of Ivan IV's accession to the throne).

13. Elizabeth herself later was very suspicious toward those who put on masks without an obvious reason. Thus, on March 17, 1746, the empress gave General Police Commissioner Tatishchev her personal orders "about the investigation and arrest in Moscow of persons taking part in secret companies that have gathered in well-known houses *in masks* for malevolent purposes" (Baranov, no. 9532).

14. A. Kartashev, *Ocherki po istorii russkoi tserkvi,* vol. 2 (Moscow: Nauka, 1991), 415.

15. S. Solovev, *Istoriia Rossii s drevneishih vremen,* vol. 21, bk. 11 (Moscow: Mysl, 1963), 46.

16. I. Chistovich, *Feofan Prokopovich i ego vremia* (St. Petersburg: Tipografiia Akademii nauk, 1868), 668–674.

17. Kartashev, *Ocherki,* 420–421.

18. Amvrosii [Iushkevich]. *Slovo v vysokotorzhestvennyi den rozhdenia . . .* (St. Petersburg: Tipografiia Akademii nauk, 1741), 12.

19. M. Lomonosov, *Polnoe sobranie sochinenij,* vol. 8 (Moscow: Izdatelstvo AN SSSR, 1959), 54–56.

20. *Primechania k vedomostiam* (St. Petersburg: Tipografiia Akademii nauk, 1741), 139–147.

21. Matthew 13:13–15.

22. V. Grebeniuk, ed., *Russkaia staropechatnaja literatura, XVI—pervaia chetvert XVIII v.,* vol. 4, *Panegiričeskaja literatura petrovskogo vremeni* (Moscow: Nauka, 1979), 279.

23. Kirill [Florinskii]. *Slovo v vysokotorzhestvennyj den rozhdeniia . . .* (St. Petersburg: Tipografiia Akademii nauk, 1741), 12, 14.

24. Vice chancellor Andrei Ivanovich Ostermann and field marshal Burkhart Christoph Munnich were the major political figures during the reign of the empress Anna Ioannovna and the brief regency of Anna Leopoldovna (October 1740–December 1741).

25. Kirill, *Slovo*, 8.

26. P. Baranov, ed., *Opis vysochaishim ukazam i poveleniiam, hraniashchimsia v Sanktpeterburgskom Senatskom arhive za XVIII v.*, vol. 3, *1740–1762* (St. Petersburg, 1878), no. 8794.

27. Pekarskii, *Markiz de-la Shetardi*, 224–226.

28. Jelena Pogosjan, "I nevozmozhnoe vozmozhno: Svadba shutov v Ledianom dome kak fakt oficialnoi kultury," *Trudy po russkoj i slavjanskoj filologii. Literaturovedenie.* Novaia seria 4 (2001): 90–109.

29. *Perevoroty i voiny*, 203, 174.

30. Elizabeth knew well of what sort her enemies' belongings were. After the arrests of Ostermann and Munnich, Elizabeth confiscated their property and ordered it brought to her palace (Munnich's possessions were brought with some delay—the empress decided to go to Munnich's house herself and examine them) (Baranov, nos. 8662, 8675). Of course, what she was looking for was not masquerade costumes, but compromising documents.

31. *Perevoroty i voiny*, 36, 27, 384, 409, 461.

32. Pekarskii, *Markiz de-la Shetardi*, 470.

33. Petr [Grebnevskii]. *Slovo v vysokotorzhestvennyi den koronatsii . . .* (St. Petersburg: Tipografiia Akademii nauk, 1742), 15.

34. Markell [Rodyshevskii]. *Slovo v den rozhdestva . . .* (St. Petersburg: Tipografiia Akademii nauk, 1741), 11–12.

35. *Sbornik* (1871), 405.

36. *Sankt-Peterburgskie vedomosti* (St. Petersburg: Tipografiia Akademii nauk, 1742), 191, 356, 362.

37. In the case when the masquerade costume of the empress was (or better yet understood as) significant, a description was usually provided. On the last week before the Great Lent in 1743, for example, Elizabeth, according to the Saxon minister, was dressed as a Dutch sailor (*Sbornik* [1871], 482). The minister mentioned this costume probably because Peter I especially loved to wear a similar outfit, and because of the fact that Elizabeth decided to discuss Russia's foreign policy in the middle of a masquerade, while wearing "Peter I's favorite costume." Thus Elizabeth's gesture had (or could have had, as the Dutch minister assumed) a political meaning.

38. *Obstoiatelnoe opisanie torzhestvennykh poriadkov . . . koronovaniia . . . Elisavet Petrovny . . .* (St. Petersburg: Tipografiia Akademii nauk, 1744).

39. V. N. Vsevolodskii-Gerngross, *Teatr v Rossii pri imperatritse Anne Ioannovne i imperatore Ioanne Antonoviche* (St. Petersburg: Tipografia Imperatorskih St. Petersburg. Teatrov, 1914), 3, 5, 18.

40. V. N. Perets, ed., *Italianskie komedii i intermedii, postavlennye pri dvore Anny Ioannovny v 1733–1735 gg. Teksty* (Petrograd, 1917), 94, 99–106, 107–117, 199–203.

41. Vsevolodskii-Gerngross, *Teatr v Rossii*, 14–15.

42. *Primechania k vedomostiam* (St. Petersburg: Tipografiia Akademii nauk, 1742), 193.

43. V. N. Vsevolodskii-Gerngross, *Teatr v Rossii pri imperatritse Elisavete Petrovne* (St. Petersburg: Giperion, 2003), 199.

44. Ekaterina II, *Sochinenia* (Moscow: Sovremennik, 1990), 282–283.

45. *Sankt-Peterburgskie vedomosti*, 371.

46. *Miloserdie Titovo* (Moscow: Tipografiia Akademii nauk, 1742), 6–8, 13, 47.

47. Jelena Pogosjan and M. Smorzhevskih, "'Ia Devu v solnce zriu stoiashchu . . .': Obraz apokalipticheskoi Zheny v russkoi oficialnoi kulture 1695–1742 gg.," *Studia Russica Helsingiensia et Tartuensia* 8 (2002): 9–37.

48. V. Proskurina, "Mif ob Astree i russkii prestol," *Novoe literaturnoe obozrenie* 63 (2003), nlo.magazine.ru/scientist/112.html.

49. *Obstoiatelnoe opisanie*, 64.

50. L. A. Markina, *Portretist Georg Khristof Groot I nemetskie zhivopistsy v Rossii serediny XVIII veka* (Moscow: Pamiatniki Istoricheskoi Mysli, 1999), 165.

51. O. S. Evangulova and A. A. Karev, *Portretnaia zhivopis' v Rossii vtoroi poloviny XVIII v.* (Moscow: Izd-vo Moskovskogo universiteta, 1994), 56.

52. Markina, *Portretist*, 163.

53. *Sbornik imperatorskogo russkogo istoricheskogo obshchestra*, vol. 105 (St. Petersburg: Tipografiia Akademii nauk, 1899), 8–9.

54. Lomonosov, *Polnoe sobranie sochinenij*, 55; *Obstoiatelnoe opisanie*, 65.

55. Marie Axton, *The Queen's Two Bodies* (London: Royal Historical Society, 1977); Ernst H. Kantorowicz, *The King's Two Bodies: A Study in Mediaeval Political Theology* (Princeton, N.J.: Princeton University Press, 1981).

56. *Polnoe sobranie zakonov Rossijskoj imperii*, 1, vol. 11. (St. Petersburg: Gosudarstvennaia Tipografia, 1830), no. 8473.

57. Jelena Pogosjan, *Petr I—arhitektor rossiiskoi istorii* (St. Petersburg: Iskusstvo—St. Petersburg, 2001).

SUGGESTED READING

Anisimov, Evgenii V. *Empress Elizabeth: Her Reign and Her Russia, 1741–1761.* Edited, translated, and with a preface by John T. Alexander. Gulf Breeze, Fla., 1995.

Baehr, Stephen L. *The Paradise Myth in Eighteenth-Century Russia: Utopian Patterns in Early Secular Russian Literature and Culture.* Stanford, Calif., 1991.

Brennan, James F. *Enlightened Despotism in Russia: The Reign of Elisabeth, 1741–1762.* New York, 1987.

Hughes, Lindsey. *Russia in the Age of Peter the Great.* New Haven, Conn., 2000.

Naumov, V. P. "Empress Elizabeth I, 1741–1762." In *The Emperors and Empresses of Russia: Rediscovering the Romanovs,* edited by Donald J. Raleigh and compiled by A. A. Iskenderov, 66–100. Armonk, N.Y., 1996.

Whittaker, Cynthia H. *Russian Monarchy: Eighteenth-Century Rulers and Writers in Political Dialogue.* DeKalb, Ill., 2003.

Wortman, Richard S. *Scenarios of Power: Myth and Ceremony in Russian Monarchy.* Vol. 1, *From Peter the Great to the Death of Nicholas I.* Princeton, N.J., 1994.

Zitser, Ernest A. *The Transfigured Kingdom: Sacred Parody and Charismatic Authority at the Court of Peter the Great.* Ithaca, N.Y., 2004.

4

Russia's "First" Scientist

The (Self-)Fashioning of Mikhail Lomonosov

Steven A. Usitalo

For more than two hundred years the eighteenth-century polymath Mikhail Vasil'evich Lomonosov (1711–1765) has been heralded in Russian culture as the "father" of Russian science, literature, and, more generally, learning. The outlines of his biography have long been familiar in his own country. Heroic tales describing the emergence of this son of a fisherman from the far northern periphery of Russia (he was born in a village not too distant from Archangel, near the White Sea) and his indefatigable acquisition of knowledge, culminating in many productive years of activity at the St. Petersburg Academy of Sciences (an organization conceived by Peter the Great and set up following his death in 1725, it remains to this day the fundamental scientific and cultural institution in Russia), were recited, albeit hardly voluntarily, by generations of Russian schoolchildren. An accomplished physicist, chemist (his chair at the Academy of Sciences was in chemistry), poet, historian, linguist, and geographer, he is the most celebrated personage identified with the Russian Enlightenment.[1]

As was often typical for a natural philosopher in the eighteenth century, the scope of Lomonosov's interests and activities was protean. Aside from dissertations on chemistry, physics, metallurgy, mining, geology, astronomy, and the administration of science in Russia,[2] he composed several literary and linguistic treatises, including a manual on rhetoric, a Russian grammar, and a proposed series of reforms for Russian versification. Lomonosov is also remembered for being one of Russia's most notable poets, a less remarkable dramatist, and the author of once widely disseminated historical works. For a time he directed the Academy of Sciences's gymnasium and university, oversaw its geographical department, helped supervise the Academy's publishing activities, founded Russia's first chemical laboratory, assisted in establishing Moscow University, opened a factory devoted to glass production, expended enormous energy in developing the mosaic arts in Russia, and worked on devising scientific instruments, perhaps most conspicuously in the area of those that might aid Russian navigational endeavors.

Lomonosov has been uniformly extolled within Russia as one whose contributions to science,[3] undeservedly neglected though they might be outside of Russia, do not pale in comparison with those of such scientific, cultural, and ultimately national icons as Newton, Copernicus, Galileo, and Benjamin Franklin. Analogies to Newton and Franklin especially are inscribed in the historiography on Lomonosov, and tellingly underscore the lofty stature assigned to him in Russian cultural discourse. But unlike the above "worthies of science," there are no sure discoveries or paradigm-shattering insights universally attributed to him. Russian scholars have taken great pains to correct this apparent deficiency, and their efforts to broadly inculcate the notion that Lomonosov's fertile scientific speculations demonstrate profound originality and prescience have proceeded at an escalating pace over the past two centuries.[4]

A commonplace in the historical literature on Russian science is the ostensibly commensurate assumption that Lomonosov's research in chemistry, physics, geography, and wherever else his manifold work habits led him can be concretely linked to the work of successive generations of scientists. The highly speculative nature of Lomonosov's scientific papers, in addition to the unfinished state he left many of them in, allowed scholars working in the shadow of the expansive renown his name achieved in the decades after his death to engage in extraordinary inferences in regard to his apparent connection with the conjectures and discoveries of later scientists.

Although any attempt to delineate direct intellectual influence is fraught with pitfalls, avowals such as that of the historian Mikhail Sukhomlinov that "Rumovskii, Kotel'nikov, and Protasov received their scientific education under Lomonosov; Lepekhin and Inokhodtsev were the students of Rumovskii and Kotel'nikov; Ozeretskovskii, Sokolov, and Severgin had their views formed under the beneficial influence of Lepekhin, etc.,"[5] have exerted a tenacious hold on Russian and Soviet scholars evaluating Lomonosov's place in the history of science. While the aforementioned natural philosophers, active in the late eighteenth and early nineteenth centuries, were all certainly aware of Lomonosov's scientific work, and several of them knew him personally, there is no evidence of a common lineage between Lomonosov's scientific treatises and the substance of their respective studies. This is true of his eighteenth-century contemporaries, and markedly true of any presumed line of descent, uninterrupted or not, between Lomonosov and later generations of scientists.

In the more easily delimited area of whether Lomonosov created a school or community of students who carried on his work in the sciences, it can be categorically stated that he left none. The only pupil trained by Lomonosov who determinedly attempted to follow in his footsteps, Vasilii Klement'ev, served as his assistant in chemistry, but unfortunately predeceased him by more than five years (Klement'ev died in 1759). Moreover, Lomonosov had largely abandoned active work in his chemical laboratory and the training of students by the early 1750s. Despite the assertions of many Russian and Soviet scholars, such esteemed eighteenth-century natural philosophers as Rumovskii and Kotel'nikov assiduously avoided Lomonosov's embrace. Rumovskii, in particular, was scathing in his view of Lomonosov's scientific abilities, and can scarcely be classified as a follower of his.

While the elevation of scientists to secular sainthood with the accompanying inaccuracies, exaggerations, or falsehoods that mark their received biographical lives is, of course, hardly unique to Russian culture, there are singularities that characterize the birth of any myth. The pervasive mythmaking temper of eighteenth-century Russia, which enabled Lomonosov's reputation to develop to astounding proportions, seems to have derived its strength from the more momentous, indeed quite omnipotent, historical presence of Peter the Great, whose reign was invested with commensurately apocalyptic meanings by many Russians.

Central to conceptions of the Petrine epoch was that the old Russia, and its attendant culture, had been thoroughly vanquished. With the result, according to the cultural historians Iurii Lotman and Boris Uspenskii, that "the 'new' was identified with all that was good, valuable and worthy of emulation;" while "the 'old' was thought to be bad, due for destruction and demolition."[6] From this belief was generated the resolute conviction, widespread among elites, that commencing with the era of Peter the Great, Russians had experienced not merely a cultural reawakening, but nothing less that an entirely "new beginning" that had reoriented their very thinking.

Certainly the latent, and hence disturbing, potentialities of science and the scientist were pivotal to why Peter's rule was perceived as such a transformative break with tradition. Motivated only by a selfless desire to further learning among his countrymen, Lomonosov, who so clearly appeared to personify the ideals of the Petrine era, served initially as a vehicle to induce acceptance of this new type of knowledge, and then to propagate it. Both in his personal qualities and in his professional attainments, his biography signified an individual of superhuman (indeed of Petrine) dimensions. The eventual conflation of his life with both the myth of Peter the Great, albeit in a distinctly supporting role,[7] and the complementary notion of a revolutionary pace of change that seemingly characterized the entire eighteenth century broadly reveal the genesis of what he came to mean historically.

Mikhail Lomonosov's reputation as a natural philosopher grew exponentially in the years immediately following his death. This is not to imply that prior to this posthumous devotion, which took shape most distinctly through a plethora of biographical encomiums, Lomonosov's name was in danger of falling into obscurity in Russia. It must be noted, though, that the exact mechanisms whereby such renown originally became attached to his life are unclear.[8] The quite discernible mythogenic features in eighteenth-century Russian culture can partially explain it. But it is Lomonosov's zealous and skillful advocacy of his own image that is especially interesting. This aspect of the creation of his biography in many senses still determines how parts of his life are perceived, and it will be defined, with deference to Stephen Greenblatt, as Lomonosov's self-fashioning.

Transposing Greenblatt's claims that to a degree literary life in Renaissance England was marked by the "increased self-consciousness about the fashioning of human identity as a manipulable, artful process" to eighteenth-century Russia,[9] it is evident that the paths pursued by Lomonosov resemble nothing so much as the advancement strategies adopted by a "profoundly mobile," educated outsider, who, lacking high social status and desirous of succeeding in a hierarchical society, sought always association with and the protection of powerful figures close to the locus of authority, the court. Mario Biagioli cautiously employed Greenblatt's idea(s) in his study of Galileo's shaping of his "socioprofessional" persona as both a philosopher and a mathematician, or rather as a "philosophical astronomer," a decidedly new and fragile combination, at the court of the Medicis and at the Vatican.[10] Although Biagioli concentrates on revealing Galileo's manipulation of patronage mechanisms, he also shows, often strikingly, how Galileo's self-presentation structured later accounts of his life.

Lomonosov's use of patronage is laid bare in this analysis of the origins of the heroic imagery that surrounded him, for it was in order to situate himself more firmly at the Academy of Sciences that he composed what passed for an autobiography and communicated it to pertinent authorities. His most valued patron was Ivan Shuvalov, while Leonard Euler (a pioneering Swiss mathematician who spent many productive years in Russia) and Christian Wolff (Lomonosov's former teacher in Marburg; he was a renowned German natural philosopher), by dint of both real and exaggerated association, were cherished patronage resources. It is, however, the characteristics that Lomonosov chose when fashioning his identity as a Russian scientist, along with the permutations that identity underwent after his death, that are mainly relevant to attempting to understand what he signified in Russian culture.

Seventeenth- and eighteenth-century natural philosophers—irrespective of country—revealed maddeningly little information about their inner lives for future biographers to utilize. Lomonosov left a few direct references in his writings that later memoirists, litterateurs, historians, and scientists would use to great advantage in constructing an image of an extraordinarily diligent polymath, quite unique in time and place. Significant autobiographical reflections were conveyed in Lomonosov's letters to his well-placed Maecenas, Ivan Shuvalov (1727–1797), a member of one of the more powerful families of the day, and a longtime favorite of the Empress Elizabeth.[11]

Lomonosov and Shuvalov are perhaps most famously joined in historical accounts by their efforts, largely led by Shuvalov, to found Moscow University in 1755.[12] He was also persuaded by Shuvalov, or forced by the nature of his dependence on his patron, to abandon his science for long periods of time to engage in such work as assisting Voltaire in his writing of the *Histoire de l'empire de Russie sous Pierre le Grand* (which came out in two volumes in 1759 and 1763),[13] as well as in writing two historical tracts of his own—*A Short Russian Chronicle with a Genealogy* (1760) and *Ancient Russian History from the Beginning of the Russian Nation to the Death of the Great Prince Iaroslav I, or to 1054* (1766). Lomonosov dedicated several works to Shuvalov; perhaps his best known is the *Letter on the Usefulness of Glass* (1752).

Lomonosov wrote more often and in greater detail to Shuvalov than he did to any other correspondent—between 1750 and 1764 at least thirty-two letters. Through these letters, many of which were first published in the six-volume 1784–1787 Academy of Science's edition of Lomonosov's collected works, Lomonosov established the vague outlines of what would become constants in the historiography: tales of a mythic youth in the far north of Russia; his journeying for education to Moscow and then to Marburg, where he followed a winding path in his search for the intellectual benefits that he might receive; and ending with his long years of heroic toil at the Academy of Sciences. Most interesting in these letters are those themes that would become biographical tropes in the elaborate mythology devoted to Lomonosov: his obstacle-strewn path to the sciences, and the arduous, yet historically triumphant, nature of his labors once he arrived. Struggles are present throughout Lomonosov's representation(s) of his life.

In Lomonosov's writings to Shuvalov there are two direct references of substance pertaining to his childhood, his journey from Kholmogory to Moscow, and to his time spent at the Slavo-Greco-Latin Academy. These letters are stylistically complex, even turgid, and personal details conveyed by Lomonosov were, as is to be expected, heavily bound up in questions of patronage and his own evolving self-identification. That contemporaries knew the content of both letters—they were among those published in the first volume of Lomonosov's 1784–1787 collected works—makes them particularly valuable.

In a letter of 1753 to Shuvalov, much of which was concerned with outlining some of his research on electricity and experiments with a thunder machine *(gromovaia mashina)* together with fellow Academician Georg Richmann, Lomonosov began by profusely thanking Shuvalov, who, unlike the "patrons" of apparently unworthy fellow scientists, always asked for and received work of the highest quality from him. But for him, presumably as opposed to many others at the Academy of Sciences, the desire to learn, the need for hard work, and the obligation to search for the truth were characteristics that he had exhibited since his youth, and he declared that

> although my father was by nature a kind man, he was without learning while my stepmother was wicked and jealous, and at every opportunity she sought to anger him against me by saying I was lazy, satisfied only to waste away my time with books. Therefore, I found it necessary, again and again, to find a place to read and study in dark and desolate places, to suffer cold and hunger, until the time I was able to leave for the Spasskii school [the Zaikonospasskii Monastery, the home of the Slavo-Greco-Latin Academy].[14]

He insisted that despite these deprivations, there was nothing to be ashamed of in his childhood. Quite the contrary, it would seem. Considering the hardships into which Lomonosov was born, his present standing was even more astounding.

Lomonosov's miraculous rise from humble beginnings on the periphery of Russia; his early love of learning; his attraction to books, the titles of which later biographers would adduce with some creativity; and his journey to enlightenment, or at least what passed for that in eighteenth-century Russia—all staples of his biography—make their appearance for the first time. Lomonosov's passage from Kholmogory to Moscow and the Slavo-Greco-Latin Academy has the aura of legend both in Russian and Soviet historiography. The enemies, even of a familial variety, are also present in Lomonosov's remembrances. Omnipresent adversaries and obstacles overcome are a constant in the narratives.[15] From such thin autobiographical lore were myths constructed.

Due to Lomonosov's strenuous efforts to garner imperial backing to begin work on a glass factory near St. Petersburg—which were finally recognized by the court in early 1753—his financial situation had become complicated, and the insufficiency of support conferred by the state on scientific endeavors, or rather to their organizers, was at the forefront of his thinking. He signaled his disquiet at this parsimoniousness to Russian science in a May 1753 letter to Shuvalov, in which he also responded to his benefactor's belief, or jest, apparently conveyed in an earlier note, that having been granted his request for a factory by the government, he might now pursue his other scientific activities with less passion than he had previously demonstrated.

Lomonosov pointed out that if, despite his many past travails, his pursuit of knowledge had never been unfavorably affected, then how could it be so now, "for even when I lived in the utmost poverty, which for the sciences I willingly endured, I could not be deterred." He informed Shuvalov that

when studying at the Spasskii school there were very strong influences from all
sides to turn me away from learning, and these proved to be nearly irresistible.
On the one hand, father, not having any other children than myself, said that
I, being his only child, had deserted him and all of the property and income
(according to local conditions) which he had built up for me by his own sweat
and blood. All of it, he said, would be seized after his death by strangers. On
the other hand, in the Academy, I had to endure the most extreme poverty: I
had only one *altyn* per day stipend and could not spend more than half a
kopeck for bread and half a *kopeck* for *kvas*, the rest was for paper, shoes, and
other necessities. In this way I lived for five years and never gave up on learning. On the one hand, knowing my father's means, the people at home hoped
to marry their daughters off to me, just as they had when I lived there. On the
other hand, at the school many of the other pupils, who were young children
after all, would yell and point at me: "Look at what a blockhead to start studying Latin at twenty."[16]

Lomonosov was also thankful for the opportunity to travel abroad to continue his studies, where he held that support for the sciences, and the individual scientist, was munificent by comparison.

Referring to the comfortable professional lives enjoyed by Isaac Newton,
Robert Boyle, Hans Sloane, and Christian Wolff, he suggested that these scientists succeeded so spectacularly in part because they had been freed, in
varying manners, from financial worry. These and other eminent and well-
rewarded worthies (Leonard Euler must be included on the list) were models to Lomonosov of people whose commitment to science was sustained
by society.[17] He not only held up their achievements for his patrons to examine, but he explicitly connected himself to their attainments. Although
Lomonosov greatly exaggerated the level of state or regime maintenance
available to his archetypal natural philosophers in Western Europe, which
was arguably no greater than in Russia, it was a useful rhetorical device. He
was arguing for elevating the status of the natural philosopher in Russia;
implicit also in his plea is the supposition that few could hope to match
Lomonosov's skills in surmounting the obstacles he had faced.

In a letter to Shuvalov on January 4, 1753, a time when he was engaged
in historical studies at the apparent expense of his scientific labors,
Lomonosov wrote of his many obligations:

As for my other occupations in physics and chemistry, there is neither the
need nor the possibility that I forsake them. Every man requires relaxation
from his labors; for that purpose he leaves serious business and seeks to pass
the time with guests or members of his household at cards, draughts, and
other amusements, and some with tobacco smoke, which I had given up long
ago, since I find nothing but boredom in them. And thus I hope that I shall
be allowed several hours a day to relax from the labors which I have expended

on the collection and composition of Russian history and on the beautifica-
tion of the Russian tongue so that I may use these hours, rather than for bil-
liards, for experiments in physics and chemistry; they serve not only as a re-
placement for amusement, but furnish exercise instead of medicine and can
bring no less benefit and honor to my native land, than my first occupation.[18]

This passage became one of the most frequently reprinted extracts from all
of Lomonosov's writings. Indeed, it would be difficult to find an account of
him over the past two centuries that does not either quote it or allude to it.
The tension between Lomonosov's work in chemistry and physics and the
manifold other duties imposed on, and sought by, him is the ostensible
subject of this letter. Many later examinations of Lomonosov explain the
unfinished quality of his scientific labors as resulting less from his undisci-
plined work habits or gaps in his theoretical knowledge than from the oner-
ous requirements of patronage, which prevented him from completing his
research in chemistry and physics.[19]

It would then seem to follow that untold discoveries were never made, or
were postponed for later generations to make, because Lomonosov was
forced to engage in nonscientific work. Such beliefs are, of course, far too
speculative to be subject to serious scrutiny. What is unmistakable is that
Lomonosov attained Shuvalov's support for his chemical and physical science exertions by completing any commission, in any domain, that Shuvalov required of him. That Shuvalov deigned to subsidize and encourage
his scientific activities indicates that an association with science brought
some adornment to its sponsors. Patronage and Lomonosov's molding of
his specific scientific self were inextricably bound together.

Conspicuous in Lomonosov's letter is the image of his selfless devotion to
the sciences, a calling that served as a glorious respite from the toils that ab-
sorbed his daily life. His eighteenth-century biographers would greatly am-
plify this perception of his disinterest in any activities that might distract him
from his intellectual pursuits. Eventually, the mantra in studies of
Lomonosov as a scientist would be that his primary work—his real "first occupation"—was physics and chemistry and not the composition of history,
the writing of odes and oratorical prose, linguistic investigations, or the
sundry other ventures that competed for his attention. Although for a scientist to be active in multiple fields was not viewed as unusual in Lomonosov's
era, it became untenable in the nineteenth century, and Lomonosov's brief
comments concerning the division of his day would serve as a rationale to
later chroniclers for severing his activities into, principally, either science or
literature. In the eighteenth century, however, his citing of his multiple roles
should be viewed mainly as augmenting his idealized self-portrait.

Lomonosov's entreaties to Shuvalov soliciting greater respect for the scientist were also attempts to bring shape to a new and ill-defined social category

in eighteenth-century Russia, that of the scientific practitioner. Lomonosov's declaration that his work would bring honor and benefit to his "native land" was one that would have considerable appeal to later nationalist-minded historians of Russian science. His strong assertion of his worth to Russia, however, is better interpreted as an attempt to prescribe firmly his own position within the Academy of Sciences. He was the first indigenous Russian scientist to be made a full member of the Academy, and this nascent vocation was, initially through his own efforts, utterly conflated with his drive to elevate his self-representation. This was a crucial element in the ascription of honor to his calling, be it chemist, physicist, litterateur, or historian. Those aspiring to any of these new socioprofessional identities would not be priests in the temple, as it were, but rather would aim for systematized recognition of a wholly new kind.

That Lomonosov's status, and that of the scientist, was still quite fragile in Russia, however, is seen in two subsequent missives that he sent to Shuvalov. In 1754, he petitioned his patron to assist him in obtaining either a transfer out of the Academy of Sciences or a promotion to directing it himself. If granted the latter, which he obviously would have preferred, he could then put a stop to the "crafty undertakings" that were plainly damaging its operations.[20] If he did leave, though, he was convinced that posterity would regard him, and the Academy, as the victims, and he predicted

> that all should say: "The stone that the builders rejected has become the chief cornerstone, this is the Lord's doing" . . . [and] in my departure from the Academy it will become perfectly clear what it is losing, when it is deprived of such a man, who for so many years has embellished it, and has always fought against the persecutors of learning, despite the dangers to himself.[21]

Lomonosov's supplication, as far as can be ascertained, was ignored. It is unlikely that he meant it to be seriously considered; his strategy was to call attention persistently to his plight, and, whenever possible, to tie his fate securely to the perceived fortunes of the Academy of Sciences, and moreover, to that of the sciences in Russia themselves.

Some years later, incensed at a presumed slight, or "insult," by Baron Aleksandr Stroganov (later president of the Academy of Arts), Lomonosov wrote to Shuvalov that

> highly-placed people scorn me for my low origins, seeing me as if I were an eyesore, even though I won my honors not by blind chance, but by my talent, diligence, and tolerance for suffering in extreme poverty, [all of which] were granted to me by God, and willingly endured for science.[22]

These two letters are remarkable illustrations of Lomonosov's laying claim to rank. He believed that his achievements were such that men of lesser

accomplishment, even a noble like Stroganov, owed him a level of deference. To enforce this required that the position of professor of chemistry at
the Academy of Sciences, occupied by this humble fisherman's son, be fash-
ioned into one held in some esteem. The style of the letters is familiar; they
resonate with similarities to memoirs of journeying and discovery. Obstacles and enemies, as in Lomonosov's recollection of his younger days, are
prominently displayed. Tacit in his writing is his faith in his eventual as-
cendancy over his rivals.

The letters to Shuvalov are not of consequence as guides to the minutiae
of Lomonosov's scientific labors; rather they are rare autobiographical
sources portraying his ascent to scientific heights. One further letter is interesting in that it combines some detail of Lomonosov's actual science
with an incident in his biography that added immeasurably to the legend
that grew up around him. Georg Richmann, his collaborator in experiments
on electricity with a thunder machine, was killed on July 26, 1753, by a bolt
of lightning. This event attracted enormous attention throughout Western
Europe and America.[23] Lomonosov conveyed a poignant description of
Richmann's death, composed on the day of the accident, to Shuvalov.[24] His
plea that this tragedy "should not be interpreted in a way that is injurious
to the augmentation of the sciences," together with his professed determination to preserve Richmann's memory, was tailor-made for hagiography.
Lomonosov was quite successful in tying his name closely to that of the
martyred, and better-known, Richmann.

Lomonosov's work on electricity was the scientific research to which his
early admirers (or biographers/hagiographers) most often referred. It was
perhaps less theoretically weighty than most of his other writings, and had
a definite potential for practical application. Lomonosov's continuation of
his and Richmann's experiments, dangerous though they had proven to be,
fit perfectly into the heroic image expected of, and being written for, these
early natural philosophers. In Lomonosov's autobiography, and in the accounts of his contemporary biographers, the details of his scientific work
were not yet as important as his path toward, and devotion to, science.

The introduction of natural philosophy into eighteenth-century Russia, a
development initiated by Peter the Great, inarguably brought about a revolutionary alteration in the lives of a number of Russians; and the images of
natural philosophers, with that of Lomonosov as the primary signifier, were
among the heroic myths which gave assistance to those attempting to negotiate a new age. The details of their scientific work were projected onto the
life stories of natural philosophers beginning in the mid-nineteenth century,
a time when an emergent scientific community and the interested public
sought the science in the lives of these representative subjects. Prior to that,
it was the practitioner's biography—composed of certain stock heroic features—which was of principal import. Lomonosov's work in physics, chem-

istry, et alia was subject to substantive appraisals in his lifetime by highly regarded arbiters; these assessments, however, were more often adapted in a
manner, then and later, that highlighted his character rather than the value
of his theoretical suppositions. The mythology of Lomonosov developing
out of this process became ever more central to Russian cultural and scientific pretensions.

The chemist and historian of science Boris Menshutkin (1876–1938),
Lomonosov's most accomplished "modern" biographer, spent nearly four
decades in Russian and Soviet archives laboring to "discover" ever more evidence demonstrating the prescient nature of Lomonosov's scientific work. In
bringing to light Lomonosov's previously unpublished or seemingly forgotten chemical and physical manuscripts, along with adding extensive com-
mentaries to them (he produced some twenty studies on Lomonosov), Menshutkin strove to superimpose an extensive scholarly apparatus onto the
already impressive scientific legacy ascribed to Lomonosov. Even so, he
wisely concluded his most thorough study of Lomonosov not with a
strained attempt to demonstrate the continuing importance of Lomonosov's
scientific labors, but rather by quoting from Lomonosov's translation of Horace's *Exegi monumentum*:

> I have reared myself a monument of immortality
> Higher than the pyramids, and stronger than brass,
> Stormy Aquilon cannot break it,
> And it will not be overwhelmed by the passage of centuries.
> I shall never wholly die, and death will leave aside
> The greatest part of me, when my life is at an end.[25]

Horace's ode (it was later more famously rendered into Russian by the poet
Alexksandr Pushkin) beautifully allegorizes not only Lomonosov's apparently successful quest for earthly honors, but also his desire to be immor-
talized by succeeding generations of his compatriots. The great praise with
which Russian culture has long endowed Lomonosov's name suggests that
his goals were achieved. As is the case with Pushkin's,[26] Lomonosov's fame
has far surpassed any realistic association with the known details of his biography; Lomonosov's monument is his mythology.

NOTES

1. Discussions over not only the nature, but also the very concept, of a Russian Enlightenment (*russkoe prosveshchenie*) became deeply colored by contemporary ideological dictates at times during the Soviet period. Especially commencing with the
rise of a more assertive Russian nationalism in the 1940s and 1950s, many scholars
began to insist that eighteenth-century Russian society experienced a rather expansive

indigenous enlightenment that at its apogee was marked by a thoroughgoing materialism. If Russia underwent enlightenment, then the requisite presence of enlighteners (*prosvetiteli*) is obvious (as noted by David Griffiths in his "In Search of Enlightenment: Recent Soviet Interpretations of Eighteenth-Century Russian Intellectual History," *Canadian-American Slavic Studies* 16, nos. 3–4 [Fall–Winter 1982]: 317). Lomonosov, as the "first Russian scientist," was a clear candidate for canonization. His modest, non-noble background harmonized well with the quasi-Marxist tenets that many Soviet historians and literary specialists were forced to pay obeisance to in their studies of the Russian eighteenth century. Equally impressed, however, by the seemingly stark contrast between Lomonosov's plebian upbringing and his attainments were eighteenth- and nineteenth-century writers who made his childhood struggles to surmount all manner of social and economic impediments so central to their reverent accounts of his life.

2. The majority of Lomonosov's writings were in natural philosophy, widely defined. See the latest and arguably definitive version of his collected works: M. V. Lomonosov, *Polnoe sobranie sochinenii* (hereafter *PSS*), vols. 1–11 (Moscow-Leningrad, 1950–1983) (especially vols. 1–5; in addition vols. 9–11 contain extensive official documentation and correspondence related to his scientific work).

3. *Nauka*, which is the Russian word for science, has a broader meaning than its English equivalent and is better compared to the German *Wissenschaft*, which connotes a somewhat diffuse pursuit of knowledge not confined to natural philosophy.

4. The "Lomonosov industry" has been a fantastically prolific one—by my count some four thousand published items and growing.

5. M. I. Sukhomlinov, *Istoriia Rossiiskoi Akademii*, vol. 4 (St. Petersburg, 1878), 2. Stepan Rumovskii (mathematician), Semen Kotel'nikov (mathematician), Aleksei Protasov (anatomist), Ivan Lepekhin (explorer), Petr Inokhodtsev (astronomer), Nikolai Ozeretskovskii (naturalist), Nikolai Sokolov (chemist), and Vasilii Severgin (chemist and mineralogist) were among the most illustrious figures of early Russian science.

6. Iu. M. Lotman and B. A. Uspenskii, "The Role of Dual Models in the Dynamics of Russian Culture (Up to the End of the Eighteenth Century)," in Iu. M. Lotman and B. A. Uspenskii, *The Semiotics of Russian Culture*, ed. Ann Shukman, trans. N. F. C. Owen (Ann Arbor: University of Michigan, 1984), 18.

7. A recent article by Aleksandr Portnov, "Nu, Mikhailo Vasilich, zadal zagadku. Byl li Lomonosov vnebrachnym synom Petra I?" *Trud* 65 (April 13, 1995), speaks to a tale that holds Lomonosov to have been Peter's illegitimate son. This piece is cited by Lindsey Hughes in *Russia in the Age of Peter the Great* (New Haven, Conn.: Yale University Press, 1998), 331. Hughes, of course, dismisses the "legend" that Lomonosov was Peter's issue, as does Portnov, while also noting that Lomonosov "was undoubtedly Peter's spiritual offspring."

8. Richard Yeo makes a similar point about the "precise origin and development of the elements that constitute the Newtonian mythology" (Richard Yeo, "Genius, Method, and Morality: Images of Newton in Britain, 1760–1860," *Science in Context* 2, no. 2 [Autumn 1988]: 258–259). Despite uncertainty regarding the inception of that mythology, his subsequent emphasis on its enveloping ubiquity throughout eighteenth-century England is convincingly presented.

9. Stephen Greenblatt, *Renaissance Self-Fashioning: From More to Shakespeare* (Chicago: University of Chicago Press, 1980), 2.

10. Mario Biagioli, *Galileo, Courtier: The Practice of Science in the Culture of Absolutism* (Chicago: University of Chicago Press, 1993).

11. Lomonosov's use of patronage to advance his professional objectives has not yet been subjected to a thorough study. E. V. Anisimov, Walter J. Gleason, and, most trenchantly, Viktor Zhivov have, however, begun the discussion with the following: Anisimov, "M. V. Lomonosov i I. I. Shuvalov," *Voprosy istorii estestvoznaniia i tekhniki*, no. 1 (1987): 73–83; Gleason, *Moral Idealists, Bureaucracy, and Catherine the Great* (New Brunswick, N.J.: Rutgers University Press, 1981), 24–33; Zhivov, "Pervye russkie literaturnye biografii kak sotsial'noe iavlenie: Trediakovskii, Lomonosov, Sumarokov," *Novoe literaturnoe obozrenie*, no. 25 (1997): 47–53.

12. Stepan Shevyrev, *Istoriia imperatorskogo Moskovskogo universiteta, 1755–1855* (Moscow, 1855), 7–22. Shevyrev's remains the best study of the university's founding and early years.

13. See Carolyn H. Wilberger, "Voltaire's Russia: Window on the East," in Theodore Besterman et al., eds., *Studies on Voltaire and the Eighteenth Century*, vol. 164 (1976): 23–133, for an examination of Voltaire's composition of *Histoire de l'empire de Russie sous Pierre le Grand*.

14. Lomonosov, *PSS*, vol. 10, 481–482.

15. Iurii Lotman and Boris Uspenskii compellingly argue that a Manichean opposition was both present in and in fact necessary to the formation of Russian myths. The positive, almost godlike, qualities invested in the hero permitted no intermediary ground that might be shared with the antithetical anti-hero. See their "Role of Dual Models."

16. Lomonosov, *PSS*, vol. 10, 479.

17. Lomonosov and his biographers from the eighteenth century to the present day have also made repeated analogies between his reputation and that of Benjamin Franklin.

18. Lomonosov, *PSS*, vol. 10, 475; *Polnoe sobranie sochinenii Lomonosova*, vol. 1 (1784), 322–324.

19. This theme is reiterated in the most recent biographies of Lomonosov. See Evgenii Lebedev, *Lomonosov* (Moscow: Molodaia Gvardiia, 1990) (Lebedev's book, which came out in an enormous print run—150,000 copies—was aimed at a general audience); G. E. Pavlova and A. S. Fedorov, *Mikhail Vasil'evich Lomonosov, 1711–1765* (Moscow: Nauka, 1986); Il'ia Z. Serman, *Mikhail Lomonosov: Life and Poetry*, trans. Stephany Hoffman (Jerusalem, 1988); and Valerii Shubinskii, *Mikhail Lomonosov: Vserossiiskii chelovek* (Moscow, 2006). Serman judiciously makes note, however, of the tangible rewards that patronage brought to Lomonosov (p. 42). Henry Leicester (*Mikhail Vasil'evich Lomonosov on the Corpuscular Theory*, translated by Henry M. Leicester [Cambridge, Mass.: Harvard University Press, 1970], 10) assigns partial blame for his peripatetic ways to his famous tendency to get bogged down in bitter disputes with other academicians. See also Alexander Vucinich, *Science in Russian Culture: A History to 1860* (Stanford, Calif.: Stanford University Press, 1963), 112–113. Conflict is, of course, part and parcel of the workings of patronage (as well as of institutionalized academic life).

20. Lomonosov, *PSS*, vol. 10, 518–519 (the letter is dated December 30, 1754); *Polnoe sobranie sochinenii Lomonosova*, vol. 1 (1784), 338–339.

21. Lomonosov, *PSS*, vol. 10, 519. Following Catherine II's ascension to the throne in 1762, and with Ivan Shuvalov—who was soon to leave Russia—no longer in a position to assist him in his undertakings, Lomonosov, possibly wishing to test his support at Catherine's court, applied to be discharged from the Academy of Sciences. In his application, reminiscent of the above letter, he reminds the empress of his valuable years of service to the Academy and of the great renown he has brought to it in wider scientific circles (Lomonosov, *PSS*, vol. 10, 351). Lomonosov's request was, after much to and fro, dismissed; indeed, in 1764, to much fanfare, Empress Catherine II even visited the scientist in his laboratory on the Moika. There, she viewed his mosaic art and "observed physics instruments that he had invented as well as several experiments in physics and chemistry." *Sankt-Peterburgskie vedomosti*, no. 48 (1764).

22. Lomonosov, *PSS*, vol. 10, 539. Lomonosov wrote this letter on April 17, 1760.

23. For an example of the reaction to Richmann's death, see Charles Rabiqueau's *Lettre èlèctrique sur la mort de M. Richmann* (Paris, 1753).

24. Lomonosov, *PSS*, vol. 10, 484–485. Lomonosov's letter concerning Richmann was originally published in *Polnoe sobranie sochinenii Lomonosova*, vol. 1 (1784), 330–333.

25. Boris Menshutkin, *Zhizneopisanie Mikhaila Vasil'evicha Lomonosova*, 2nd ed. (Moscow-Leningrad, 1937), 236. Lomonosov's translation of Horace is from his *Kratkoe rukovodstvo k krasnorechiiu* [*Brief Guide to Eloquence*] (1748). See Lomonosov, *PSS*, vol. 7, 314.

26. Abram Tertz [Andrei Sinyavsky], *Strolls with Pushkin*, trans. Catharine Theimer Nepomnyaschy and Slava I. Yastremski (New Haven, Conn.: Yale University Press, 1993); and Stephanie Sandler, *Commemorating Pushkin: Russia's Myth of a National Poet* (Stanford, Calif.: Stanford University Press, 2004) are fascinating studies of the veneration accorded Pushkin in Russian history.

SUGGESTED READING

Boss, Valentin. "Lomonosov, Mikhail Vasil'evich." In *Encyclopedia of the Enlightenment*, edited by Alan Charles Kors, 2:431–433. Oxford, 2003.
——. *Newton and Russia: The Early Influence, 1698–1796*. Cambridge, Mass., 1972.
Chant, Colin. "Science in Orthodox Europe." In *The Rise of Scientific Europe, 1500–1800*, edited by David Goodman and Colin A. Russell, 333–360. London, 1991.
Gordin, Michael D. "The Importation of Being Earnest: The Early St. Petersburg Academy of Sciences." *ISIS* 91, no. 1 (March 2000): 1–31.
Jones, W. Gareth. "The Image of the Eighteenth-Century Russian Author." In *Russia in the Age of Enlightenment: Essays for Isabel de Madariaga*, edited by Roger Bartlett and Janet M. Hartley, 57–74. New York, 1990.
Lomonosov, M. V. *Mikhail Vasil'evich Lomonosov on the Corpuscular Theory*. Translated and with an introduction by Henry M. Leicester. Cambridge, Mass., 1970.

McClellan, James E. III. *Science Reorganized: Scientific Societies in the Eighteenth Century.* New York, 1985.

Menshutkin, B. N. *Russia's Lomonosov: Chemist, Courtier, Physicist, Poet.* Translated by Jeannette Eyre Thal and Edward J. Webster. Princeton, N.J., 1952.

Reyfman, Irina. *Vasilii Trediakovsky: The Fool of the 'New' Russian Literature.* Stanford, Calif., 1990.

Schulze, Ludmilla. "The Russification of the St. Petersburg Academy of Sciences and Arts in the Eighteenth Century." *British Journal for the History of Science* 18 (1985): 305–335.

Serman, Il'ia Z. *Mikhail Lomonosov: Life and Poetry.* Translated by Stephany Hoffmann. Jerusalem, 1988.

Vucinich, Alexander. *Science in Russian Culture: A History to 1860.* Stanford, Calif., 1963.

5

Andrei Bolotov

Portrait of an Enlightened Seigneur

Colum Leckey

For students of eighteenth-century Russia, the image of the enlightened seigneur poses a riddle of great human interest. Like its better-known counterpart, enlightened absolutism, it defies any single definition. The label itself presents some difficulty, for the Russian language has no exact equivalent for it. Probably the most commonly used term was *razumnyi domostroitel'*, which translates rather clumsily into English as "rational housekeeper" or "rational estate manager." Contemporary writers applied it in a wide variety of circumstances: absentee landowners in possession of thousands of serfs; service nobles in cities employing large domestic staffs; and mid-level provincial squires personally managing their holdings. None of these usages are necessarily linked to the cultural and intellectual movement known as the Enlightenment, or even to education in the broadest sense of the word. What they are linked to is basic administration—of people, resources, and finances.

Yet there is much more to the enlightened seigneur than this. Andrei Bolotov—provincial landowner, writer, publicist, and the focus of this chapter—certainly felt this way. A young landowner from the central province of Tula, Bolotov retired from military service at the age of twenty-four upon hearing of the nobility's "emancipation" in 1762 and returned to his ancestral estate to manage its operations. Over the course of Catherine II's reign, he built a reputation as one of Russia's most prolific and versatile literary celebrities. His publications of the 1760s and 1770s in particular present a nobleman whose lived experience in the countryside synthesized the mundane practices of estate administration with a cultural mission to westernize and enlighten rural dwellers. Bolotov did not merely manage his properties and try to turn a profit from them. In his view, enlightened seigniorialism was above all an agrarian way of life that required noble residency in the provinces as well as active participation in Russia's rising public culture under the leadership of Catherine II. Thanks to Bolotov's published writings of the 1760s and 1770s, the enlightened seigneur constitutes an essential piece of Russia's cultural landscape in the eighteenth century and merits much more attention than it has hitherto received.

It should be stressed that images of the enlightened seigneur emerged long before Bolotov set pen to paper in the mid-1760s. In peeling off its layers we find four distinct levels. First is the profit motive. It was this thirst for higher revenues that inspired landowners to attempt streamlining managerial practices on their demesnes and experimenting with alternative farming techniques. Governmental legislation and long-term economic growth encouraged these trends. With the dismantling of the empire's domestic tariffs in 1754, the elimination of the state's monopoly on alcohol production in the 1750s, and the opening of new ports in the Baltic and Black seas under Catherine, Russia's grand seigneurs capitalized on many new economic opportunities. Rising prices on the domestic and international markets boosted Russia's grain exports to record levels by the 1790s and spurred a new wave of settlement and cultivation of the fertile black-earth lands of New Russia, Ukraine, and the southeastern regions. All this crowned the enlightened seigneur with the fuzzy aura of illusory profitability, at least in the short run. Russia's agrarian prospects seemed so bright that in 1765 one writer boldly proclaimed "our century [to be] the economic century."[1]

Of course, economic factors alone explain very little. Equally significant was the nobleman's inclination to apply Petrine rationalism to the country estate and impose a "moral order" on a seemingly chaotic agrarian world. According to Edgar Melton, it was precisely this ideal that constituted "an essential element of enlightened seigniorialism—the belief that laws, properly formulated and carried out, could regulate and direct human behavior toward desired social and economic ends."[2] Consider, for instance, the views of Vasilii Tatishchev, a leading civil administrator and intellectual of the mid-eighteenth century and one of the most renowned defenders of the Petrine reforms. In an instruction dating from 1742 written for the manager of his estate, Tatishchev seems concerned primarily with controlling his peasants and reforming their material and moral condition. Aiming to eliminate "lawlessness," "disorder," and the influences of outside forces, he kept close track of all economic activities on his estate and expressly forbade most of his peasants from selling anything or working outside the village "since from this [they] will fall into poverty, sell off all their belongings, and through this enrich other villages."[3] Equally striking is Tatishchev's conviction that peasants could learn to excel at agriculture just as the Russian nobleman had once learned to serve Peter the Great with zeal and competence. Tatishchev believed that peasant weaknesses and vices were the product of custom and

could be supplanted by strong morals and virtues. His program of moral improvement required parents to raise their children in a virtuous environment, which, he assumed, would accustom the peasant to hard work, teach
him to "know and fear God's law," and enable him "to call himself a true
man and to distinguish himself from cattle."[4]

The urge to forge a "moral order" on the estate coexisted with the
seigneur's desire to reassert personal dominion over his patrimony after
years of state service. In a testament written for his son in 1733, Tatishchev
condemned the "domestic manners and willfulness" of private life, which,
without a patriarch at the helm, invariably disintegrated into idleness and
disorder.[5] Similar hankerings for patrimonial authority surfaced in the periodical literature of the 1750s and early 1760s. Russian journals began to
envision the numerous benefits to the individual and society of a rational,
virtuous, and paternalistic seigneur at home on his estate. Just as the "good
peasant" was obliged to obey his master and work diligently,[6] so his lord
was expected to exercise reason and humanity in administering his
demesne. As one journal put it, the "good master" possessed knowledge of
science, medicine, the mechanical arts, accounting, and, naturally, modern
agriculture. He selected a wife to assist him on the basis of her virtue and
education, not wealth or physical appearance. And above all he knew his
place in the larger social hierarchy, serving his God and ruler with the same
loyalty and deference that the "good peasant" displayed for him.[7]

This fixation on noble self-improvement reflected the rising influence in
Russia of European modes of "moral instruction" (*nravouchenie*).[8] After
1762, the discourse of *nravouchenie* merged with the aspirations of many
nobles to retire from service, producing the final dimension of the enlightened seigneur's persona—the tendency to equate life in the country with a
pastoral ideal of peace, virtue, and rationality. One story in particular captures this critical development. Translated from German and published
shortly after the nobility's emancipation from obligatory state service in
1762, it was no doubt intended to serve as a cautionary tale for petty and
middling nobles, who, like Bolotov, desired to return home and reassert
their patriarchal authority. Its protagonist, Mr. Hans, belongs to an impoverished branch of an old aristocratic lineage. After serving in the military for
several years, he resigns and returns to his small estate where he races his
coach, carouses with friends, steals from neighbors, and brutalizes his peasants. Upon the death of his father eight years later, he promptly fires the
current estate manager and replaces him with a young sycophant who es-
tablishes a new regime marked by ceaseless work and cruel punishments.
Mr. Hans's life takes a dramatic turn for the better when he becomes fixated
on a local girl whose humility and good looks make her the ideal candidate
for a wife. Unlike the peasant girls he had conquered previously, however,
this one declares that "she loves virtue, good morals, and a peaceful, orderly

life; her chief enjoyments consisted of the management and care of domestic tasks and in reading useful books."[9] In drawing a visible line between permissible and unacceptable behavior, Mr. Hans's future wife inspires his eventual rebirth as an exemplary country gentleman: "His only pleasure came in reading useful books, in experiencing nature, and in the company of rational and virtuous individuals. Nothing was as pleasing to him as the country life, and every day he found a new theater of endless enjoyment, courtesy of the wise creator."[10]

Bolotov deftly integrated into his writings all of these themes—profit, Petrine rationalism, patriarchy, and pastoral bliss. However, we must also bear in mind two points regarding his work. First, as popular agronomical literature, his writings belong to a different genre than the estate records and journalistic fare that preceded them. In contrast to the grand seigneurs whose economic instructions historians have studied so closely, Bolotov wrote for a national public in the empire's first agricultural journal, *Trudy Vol'nago Ekonomicheskago Obshchestva* (*Transactions of the Free Economic Society*). And unlike other writers of journalistic literature in the 1750s and 1760s, Bolotov had real agronomical expertise.[11] Although his readership was small—it probably numbered in the hundreds at the most—the fact that he even had an audience demanded that he convert his private experiences into an accessible narrative that his readers could assimilate. Secondly, in stressing the need for the provincial nobility to improve and enlighten the Russian countryside, Bolotov is inseparable from the cultural milieu that produced Catherine's reform program in the opening years of her reign. According to Alexander Kamenskii, the empress sought "to realize the idea of the 'general welfare' through a developed legal system that ensured in full the rights and mutual obligations of the sovereign and the people."[12] Arguably the main obstacle confronting Catherine in her efforts was the legal ambiguity of the landlord-peasant relationship, particularly after the abolition of mandatory state service for the nobility. Although Bolotov remained a staunch advocate of serfdom and noble privilege to the end of his days, he certainly shared Catherine's agrarian vision for Russia, in which peasants carried out their duties as farmers while nobles performed the tasks of public service and leadership. It was this combination of Catherinean reformism, voluntary noble service, and transparency before Russia's reading public that made Bolotov the exemplary enlightened seigneur of his times.

Translating Catherine's vision into reality hinged on involving educated Russians in her reform program, and it was primarily to the Free Economic Society that she entrusted this task. Founded in 1765 by a small group of academicians, aristocratic magnates, and service nobles, its mission was to promote agriculture and the benefits of a useful rural life. Operating under the protection of its prized royal charter, the Society summoned the fledgling public, and provincial dwellers like Bolotov in particular, to embrace the values of enlightened citizens—patriotism, constructive criticism, and reciprocity. As it turned out, few provincial nobles responded to the call, either as correspondents or journal subscribers. We can only imagine how few actually became real agricultural improvers. Bolotov, however, jumped at the chance. His memory of discovering the *Trudy* at a Moscow kiosk in 1766 makes this quite clear:

> The booklet's title sparked my curiosity. To many, such an economic society was foreign and the booklet might as well have been written in Double Dutch; but to me, who had already read a sufficient number of foreign economic works, these matters were already known. I had enough understanding of economic societies in other lands and all their statutes that, seeing from this booklet that now we too had established such a [society], and moreover that it was distinguished to have been taken under the special protection of the empress herself, I nearly jumped for joy, reading it with enormous greed from cover to cover; my satisfaction deepened still more when I saw that all of us nobles who resided in villages, regardless of title, were invited by the Society to send in economic observations after the fashion of foreign [societies]; in order to guide us along this most suitable path there was attached at the end of the booklet 65 questions of such a kind and about such matters that required neither great intelligence nor strain to answer, if only someone who had an understanding of the rural economy and knew how to write would pick up a pen.[13]

Bolotov's excitement in recollecting this singular episode starkly contrasts with the bleak intellectual landscape of rural Russia. His decision to retire from service and reside in the country baffled even his colleagues in the Society, who praised him for a job well done and thanked him for "his detailed observations over the course of his three-year residence in the country."[14] Three years in the country! From the Society's perspective, it appeared strange for a person of such intelligence and ability to spend so much time in the provinces milling around his fields and pastures. Here was a man who clearly broke the mold—but which one?

The answer is both. Like all seigneurs, Bolotov sought to increase profits and maximize control over his administration, an objective summed up in his "basic rule" of rural economics: to increase the lord's profits without bringing harm to the village.[15] But he also knew estate management required exemplary noble leadership, hard work, and a good measure of audacity. Such a combination was rare. Taking a broad view of his district, he admitted that most landowners "do not care at all about the rural economy or about its improvement, nor are bothered by the decline of agriculture."[16] Their apathy and negligence knew no bounds. For the typical landowner, estate management consisted of knowing how much land was sown and if the peasant had stolen anything from him. Nobles lacked knowledge of basic agronomy and regarded even low-risk experiments in gardens as incapable of being duplicated in the field and a waste of time. Instead of taking measures to end deforestation, for instance, landowners exhausted their forest reserves and feuded with each other over the few remaining scraps. On the rare occasion when nobles did display some inventiveness, they refused to divulge their secrets to the community.[17] The root cause of the "decline of agriculture" was not the peasantry, but the laziness and obstinacy of his fellow nobles.

While critical of nobles, Bolotov saved most of his venom for the peasantry's blind adherence to economic custom: "Our common people come with such an inclination for the old customs, and are so attached to them, that . . . when [the peasant] sees and praises the great use from something new, and admits that he might derive no small profit from it, he still looks upon it with a critical eye and in no way considers applying it."[18] "Custom" was a catchall term that explained everything mysterious and irrational in peasant behavior. For Bolotov, its pervasiveness also blurred the social and cultural distinctions between nobles and peasants. In one of his most astute observations, Bolotov demonstrated how the peasant practices of communal land tenure and strip farming necessarily became noble practices. "Nowhere have I found that the peasant has all his land enclosed around his own house, or at least close to it," he began, "but everywhere it is generally scattered across all the fields which belong to the village."[19] The thorough intermingling of strips between separate villages and even landowners hindered the individual peasant (and the lord) from using the land "according to his wishes," for everywhere he looked he beheld a bewildering mishmash of strips belonging simultaneously to everyone and no one:

> [The] peasant cannot walk one step away from his house without being cramped on two sides by other houses, on the third side by a river, brook, or hill, and on the fourth by a house belonging to another landowner. Owing to this he not only has no place where he can set up a garden, orchard, or something else that is useful to his household economy, but he does not even have enough space for a vegetable garden which is so essential for his sustenance. . . . [He remains] silent over the land belonging to outside households that surround his [own], and [says nothing] about the cattle and fowl overrunning his own land which he is powerless to stop.[20]

In delegating managerial tasks to peasants, landowners not only gave a critical leadership role to what Bolotov regarded as the most conservative elements in Russian society, but perpetuated obsolete farming techniques which then percolated up to the commanding heights of the rural economy.[21] It should come as little surprise that all the negative qualities that Bolotov perceived in his fellow nobles—apathy, obstinacy, negligence, idleness—also appeared in his peasant types.

Bolotov's solution to this thicket of problems was to increase administrative control over the peasantry and establish a distinct culture of noble enlightenment in the countryside. In his best-known work of these years, "model instruction" written for an imaginary estate manager, he envisioned a managerial system for country estates inspired by European practices. Bolotov's manager sounds remarkably like the person Bolotov imagined himself to be: "prudent," "honorable," "upright," "virtuous," "goodhearted," "God-fearing," "observant," and immune to "vice, banditry, drunkenness, and hypocrisy."[22] He is the perfect foil to the lazy, apathetic, and superstitious bumpkins that dot Bolotov's social landscape. More importantly, he functioned as a transmitter of Western values, in the process replicating the enlightened social order that Catherine was attempting to institute for the empire as a whole. Just as the empress knew her realm, so did the enlightened seigneur possess all the facts about his own demesne. And just as the Society co-opted the finest provincial nobles into its network, so did Bolotov seek out the "most responsible men in the village" to assist him. The key player here was the peasant elder, whose chief duties included overseeing the orderly execution of plowing, sowing, harvesting, carting, threshing, and grinding of grain.[23] Working in tandem with the elder, the manager enforced a maximum of three labor days per week (*barshchina*), and permitted a limited migration within the general vicinity of the estate. At the same time, the manager was expected to take the usual measures to stave off peasant destitution: assigning misfit peasants to the strongest and most efficient households; distributing free grain in times of crisis; and spreading the tax burden equitably.[24] Managing an orderly estate resembled governing an empire upon rational and activist principles. Even the rewards were similar. Like the participants in Russia's service culture, who measured success and status in terms of their personal proximity to the empress, so did Bolotov's manager earn the "love and trust of the seigneur" for his "indefatigable diligence, sincere heart, and inviolable faith in his master."[25] The payoff for distinguished service to the seigneur belonged to the same category of intangible "virtue" that motivated Bolotov to offer his services to the Society.

Did enlightened seigniorialism produce any of the desired effects—greater profits for the lord, a "moral" order on the estate, the breaking of economic custom, or an enlightened noble culture in the provinces? Regarding profitability, the answer is decidedly no. To paraphrase Michael Confino, Bolotov attempted to reach "El Dorado" simply by tightening the reins of management, hardly a formula for striking it rich.[26] As for establishing a moral order and the breaking of economic custom, the answer is also negative. Although Bolotov's system granted peasants much more autonomy than did other projects for enlightened estate management, the fact remains that the structural inequalities inherent in serfdom invariably turned a basically decent person like Bolotov into a despot and his system into a "police regime."[27] His peasants regarded his improvements as foreign frippery with no real application to their everyday lives. In one article, for instance, he described a strategy for increasing emergency grain reserves—a praiseworthy objective to be sure. There was little to it: he had young boys and old men retrieve the ears of grain which littered the fields in the wake of the harvest with a special rake imported from Pomerania. "I saw," he concluded, "that all this work could be done with . . . very little labor, and with such productivity that it was approved by even the local *muzhiki*, who, as we all know, regard such novelties with a sidelong glance."[28] More grain at no extra expense—who could argue with such a scheme? As it turned out, he learned that no one wanted to use his method for fear of being branded an "upstart" by his neighbors. Peasants also informed him that the rake disturbed the stubble that they used as supplementary cattle fodder. "Have you ever heard a more stupid and baseless excuse?" Bolotov asked his audience in disbelief.[29] It is not difficult to visualize peasant reactions to such high-handed interference in their domain: silence, stonewalling, eye rolling—anything to make their master go away.

The question of Bolotov's success in promoting enlightened noble culture is more problematic because there is no real consensus on what "enlightenment" signified in the context of eighteenth-century rural Russia. Obviously, Bolotov was an "enlightener" in the sense that he subscribed to what Olga Glagoleva calls "a fully defined system of sociopolitical views founded on rationalism." Although he accepted social inequality as a fact of life, his tireless promotion of rational and humane estate management bears witness to a lifetime full of "enlightened activity," to use Glagoleva's phrase.[30] Yet recent scholarship has unearthed other aspects of provincial culture that clarify Bolotov's understanding of enlightened seigniorialism. In her study of Russian country estates, Priscilla Roosevelt has shown how the estate offered nobles the only real venue for expressing their privileged status. Given their close identification with the autocracy, estate owners tended to emulate the court rituals and service culture of the capital through elaborate and theatrical displays of power for their neighbors and peasants.[31] On a related note, Thomas Newlin has suggested that Bolotov's renowned pleasure gardens of the 1780s, filled with sham medieval ruins and "echoing walls" that spoke in French, reflected their designer's awareness that pastoral bliss was an illusion—knowledge he had gained from years spent rubbing shoulders with his peasants and neighbors.[32] The luxurious flights from reality that typify eighteenth-century provincial noble culture reflected a deep-seated insecurity caused by the elite's dependence on the autocracy, fear of a hostile peasantry, and bitter disillusionment with real life in the provinces.

There was a good deal of histrionics to Bolotov—a certain literary Potemkinism in fact—that compensated for his inability to penetrate the thick walls of "custom." This was no ordinary correspondence between a "representative" nobleman in the provinces and his editors, but an imagined salon in which Bolotov and the reading public gathered to vent their frustrations and commiserate with each other. As he said in a landmark piece on the uses of potatoes, he wrote for a discriminating audience of "curious and experimental people . . . who care about the general welfare," people who, "out of love for the fatherland," have justifiably earned the praise of enlightened society.[33] Bolotov's ambition to be included in this exclusive club necessitated that he portray the daily grind of agricultural improvement as a morality play pitting virtue and reason against vice and tradition. His self-image calls to mind Oldwise in Fonvizin's *The Minor*, another enlightened protagonist who similarly serves as a beacon of wisdom against a backdrop of provincial indolence and corruption. Like Oldwise, Bolotov was fond of sermonizing: peasants plow too deeply and scatter grain seeds indiscriminately; they have no understanding of soil quality; they fail to increase cattle and then wonder why they have no manure for fertilizing their fields. His model instruction reads like an agricultural syllabus of errors— peasants spend too much money on alcohol; they steal at any given opportunity; they fight, shirk, and complain; they cuss too much.[34] And although at times he gave credit to a few hardworking peasant families and open-minded *muzhiki*,[35] the longer he lived in the country, the more convinced he became of the "stupidity and ignorance of our peasants."[36] The overlap between Fonvizin's Oldwise and Bolotov should come as no surprise—the dramatist wrote for the same audience as did the agronomist. Yet in contrast to Oldwise, whom Fonvizin mercifully freed from the entanglements of landownership and family obligations, Bolotov was really stuck in the provinces. The incongruity between his public identity and his everyday surroundings must have turned him into a terrible crank.

After a decade of futility, Bolotov began to lose hope. Ever since his return to the country in 1762, he had experimented with "particular things" within the perimeters of the three-field system, the traditional method of crop rotation, and the bête noire of the rural economy. Experience had convinced him that "tradition" and "custom" would undermine all his efforts so long as the "fundamental basis" of agriculture remained untouched. Permanent improvement, he concluded, had to be geared towards "the establishment of a completely different order in the economy."[37] In lieu of the traditional three-field division, he recommended an ambitious seven-field system that promised to put an end to the nagging problems of dwindling pasturage, mediocre soil quality, and small harvests. His utopian blueprint called for a drastic reduction in plow land in order to increase pasturage, generate more manure, and enhance the soil's fertility in the long run.[38] While consistent with certain aspects of Russian agrarian custom—no artificial grasses or year-round stabling of livestock were necessary—requiring farmers to leave more than half of their fields unsown was unrealistic, to put it mildly. One can only imagine how his neighbors, managers, and peasants—the same ones who refused to plant potatoes—would react to such a scheme. The point, however, is that Bolotov no longer cared what they thought. For the first time in all his economic writings, Bolotov's debating partner was no longer the bearded *muzhik* or narrow-minded neighbor, but the educated public—particularly the academicians and literati in the Free Economic Society.

Bolotov often spoke with an imaginary interlocutor in his public and private writing, a polyphonic tendency characteristic of many of his Russian contemporaries and which Newlin has suggested denoted a "certain quiet madness" in him.[39] It is also likely that Bolotov was simply wrestling with the profound and interminable boredom that derives from being completely alone. In a few transparent moments he dropped all pretense of enlightened zeal. Rural economics, he discovered, provided "fun entertainment which will prevent the lord from lapsing into idleness" while "alleviating the monotony of rural life." Even his beloved hops garden served as something for his envious neighbors to talk about.[40] Having accepted the limitations of his projects for provincial enlightenment, Bolotov gravitated back towards Russia's urban-based service culture. After 1775 he earned renown as the empire's foremost authority on gardens, orchards, and landscaping—the sort of amusements that had inspired leisure classes ever since the ancient Persians. At least someone was listening. In a letter to the Free Economic Society from 1778, just as he was embarking on his first independent publishing enterprise, *Sel'skii zhitel'* (*Rural Dweller*), he thanked his colleagues for "instilling in him the desire to write about economics," which placed him on the "very unusual path . . . of rural housekeeping (*sel'skoe domostroitel'stvo*)." Fittingly, he signed the letter not as "Captain A. Bolotov" as he did all his previous pieces, but as "Editor, *Sel'skii zhitel'*." His apprenticeship with the Society had earned him passage out of provincial isolation and into the inner circles of Russia's educated public.[41] Enlightened seigniorialism had its uses, just not for seigneurs and certainly not for peasants.

Enlightened seigniorialism in Russia was a cultural phenomenon as much as the landowning nobility's attempt to wring greater profits from their estates. At its core lay the Petrine impulse to institute a rational social order in the service of an abstract general welfare. In no way did it imply greater personal freedom for peasants or the limiting of seigniorial privileges. Most enlightened minds of the eighteenth century took human inequality for granted and regarded their task as one of eliminating abuses of noble power and encouraging peasants to work more diligently at farming—their "natural occupation."[42] For Bolotov, this meant demonstrating to the emancipated nobility the virtues and profitability of enlightened noble leadership in the countryside. Others shared Bolotov's assumptions and exercised their leadership by applying many of his recommendations to the administration of their own demesnes. As one historian has suggested, many of Russia's most powerful families came to regard enlightened seigniorialism as an ideological reinforcement for serfdom. And just as Bolotov learned that the complex thicket of communal land tenure and peasant farming systems obstructed his own reforms, so did the Gagarins, Sheremetevs, and Kurakins eventually see their efforts snap under the same leaden realities of subsistence and servility. By the 1820s and 1830s, enlightened seigniorialism had exhausted itself, a victim of the fundamental contradiction of "improving" the condition of serfs by forcing them to work harder.[43]

Bolotov's significance extends well beyond the parameters of the manorial economy and the famous "peasant question." In his writings for the *Trudy*, he constructed for the reading public a new cultural type—the westernized rationalist endeavoring to break agrarian "custom" and failing miserably. Bolotov chronicled this dilemma in maddeningly prosaic detail—all the way to its dead end. In terms of measurable and tangible accomplishments, he was an abject failure. Still, his gentle polyphonic "madness" may have provided a template for the superfluous anti-heroes of nineteenth-century Russian literature and for the readers who consumed it.[44] It is not what Bolotov wanted to be remembered for, but it is a failure for which admirers of Russian culture can nonetheless be grateful.

NOTES

1. Timothy von Klingstedt, "Preduvedomlenie," *Trudy Vol'nago Ekonomicheskago Obshchestva* (hereafter *Trudy*) 1 (1765): 1–2.

2. Edgar Melton, "Enlightened Seigniorialism and Its Dilemmas in Serf Russia, 1750–1830," *Journal of Modern History* 62, no. 4 (1990): 691–692.

3. V. N. Tatishchev, "Kratkaiia ekonomicheskiia do derevni sleduiushchiia zapiski," *Vremennik imperatorskago moskovskago obshchestva istoriia drevnostei rossiskikh*, vols. 1–2 (1852), 24.

4. Tatishchev, "Kratkaiia ekonomicheskiia," 27–28.

5. V. N. Tatishchev, *Dukhovnaia* (St. Petersburg, 1773), 30.

6. Tatishchev, "Kratkaiia ekonomicheskiia," 27–28.

7. "Vseobshchiia o khoziaistve nemetskom pravila," *Ezhemesiachniia sochineniia* (January 1760), 84–90; see also "Uveshchanie umiraiushchago otsa k synu," *Ezhemesiachniia sochineniia* (April 1756): 316–317, 320, 321–322.

8. Douglas Smith, *Working the Rough Stone: Freemasonry and Society in Eighteenth-Century Russia* (Dekalb: Northern Illinois University Press, 1999), 42–52.

9. "Zhizn' sel'skago dvorianina Gospodina Gantsa," *Sobranie lushchikh sochinenii*, vol. 4 (Moscow, 1762), 224.

10. "Zhizn'," 228.

11. See for example, "Pis'mo o uprazhnenii v derevenskom zhitii," *Ezhemesiach-niia sochineniia* (November 1757): 405–406.

12. A. Kamenskii, "Znachenie reform Yekateriny II v russkoi istorii," in *A Window on Russia*, ed. Maria di Salvo and Lindsey Hughes (Rome, 1996), 60.

13. *Zapiski Andreia Timofeevicha Bolotova*, vol. 1 (Tula, Russia: Priokskoe Knizh-noe Izd-vo, 1988), 436–437.

14. Rossiiskii Gosudarstvennyi Istoricheskii Arkhiv (RGIA), fond 91, opis' 1, delo 3, list 12.

15. "Nakaz upraviteliu ili prikashchiku, kakim obrazom emu pravit' derevniami v nybytnost' svoego gospodina," *Trudy* 16 (1770): 72.

16. Bolotov, "Primechaniia o khlebopashestve voobshche," *Trudy* 11 (1768): 37. Compare Bolotov's views on this matter with those of Prince Shcherbatov in Wallace Daniel, "Conflict between Economic Vision and Economic Reality: The Case of M. M. Shcherbatov," *Slavonic and East European Review* 67 (1989): 4750.

17. Bolotov, "Primechaniia," 41; "Primechaniia i opyty, kasaiushchiesia do poseva semian khlebnykh," *Trudy* 9 (1768): 105–106; "O rublenii, popravlenii i zavedenii lesov," *Trudy* 4 (1766): 72–73; "O udobrenii zemel'," *Trudy* 15 (1770): 28–30.

18. "O sposobe k polucheniiu sel'skim zhiteliam nekotorago kolichestva vsiak-ago khleba sverkh obyknovennago urozhaia," *Trudy* 30 (1775): 178.

19. Bolotov, "Opisanie svoistva i dobroty zemel' Kashirskago uezda," *Trudy* 2 (1766): 162.

20. Bolotov, "Opisanie svoistva," 171–172.

21. Bolotov, "Opisanie svoistva," 172–173; see also "Primechaniia," 41–42.

22. "Nakaz upraviteliu ili prikashchiku," 69–71.

23. "Nakaz upraviteliu ili prikashchiku," 88–89.

24. "Nakaz upraviteliu ili prikashchiku," 185–186, 200–203.

25. "Nakaz upraviteliu ili prikashchiku," 209.

26. Michael Confino, *Domaines et Seigneurs en Russie vers la fin du XVIIIe siècle* (Paris: Institut d'études slaves de l'Université de Paris, 1963), 136.

27. V. Aleksandrov, *Sel'skaia obshchina v Rossii (XVII–nachalo XIX vv.)* (Moscow, 1976), 67. See also Esther Kingston-Mann, *In Search of the True West: Culture, Economics, and the Problems of Development* (Princeton, N.J.: Princeton University Press, 1999), 50–51.

28. "O sposobe k polucheniiu," 172.

29. "O sposobe k polucheniiu," 177–179.

30. O. Glagoleva, *Russkaia provintsial'naia starina: Ocherki kul'tury i byta Tul'skoi gubernii XVIII–pervoi poloviny XIX vv.* (Tula, Russia: Ritm, 1993), 82.

31. Priscilla Roosevelt, *Life on the Russian Country Estate: A Social and Cultural History* (New Haven, Conn.: Yale University Press, 1995), 148–150.

32. Thomas Newlin, "Rural Ruses: Illusion and Anxiety on the Russian Estate, 1775–1815," *Slavic Review* 57, no. 2 (1998): 298–299, 304–305, 307.

33. "Primechaniia o tartofele," *Trudy* 14 (1770): 2–3.

34. "Primechaniia i opyty," 93; "Primechaniia," 40–41; "O udobrenii zemel'," 19–22, 42–45. "Nakaz upraviteliu ili prikashchiku," 188–197.

35. Bolotov, "Opisanie svoistva," 210–211; "O sposobe k polucheniiu," 180–181.

36. "Ekonomickeskiia primechaniia o khmelevodstva, i opyty kasaiushchiiasia do zavedenii i razmnozheniia khmelia," *Trudy* 24 (1773): 61–62.

37. Bolotov, "O razdelenii polei," *Trudy* 17 (1771): 176–177.

38. Bolotov, "Prodolzhenie o razdelenii zemli na semi polei," *Trudy* 18 (1771): 51–53, 76.

39. Thomas Newlin, "The Return of the Russian Odysseus: Pastoral Dilemmas and Rude Awakenings," *Russian Review* 55 (1996): 472.

40. Bolotov, "O istreblenii kosteria iz pshenitsy, i nekotoryia drugiia, kasaiushchiiasia do vychishcheniia khlebov, ekonomicheskiia i opyty," *Trudy* 23 (1773): 214; "O novom rode sazhdeniia derev," *Trudy* 29 (1775): 263.

41. RGIA, fond 91, opis' 1, delo 394, listy 124–125.

42. See, for example, the views of Catherine II and Jacob Sievers on this matter: David Griffiths, "Catherine II's Charters: A Question of Motivation," *Canadian-American Slavic Studies* 23 (1989): 68; and Roger Bartlett, "J. J. Sievers and the Russian Peasantry under Catherine II," *Jahrbücher für Geschichte Osteuropas* 32 (1984): 20–21.

43. Melton, "Enlightened Seigniorialism," 692–695, 702–704.

44. Thomas Newlin, *The Voice in the Garden: Andrei Bolotov and the Anxieties of Russian Pastoral, 1738–1833* (Evanston, Ill.: Northwestern University Press, 2001), 66–67.

SUGGESTED READING

Augustine, Wilson R. "Notes toward a Portrait of the Eighteenth-Century Russian Nobility." *Canadian-American Slavic Studies* 4 (1970): 373–425.

Dukes, Paul. *Catherine the Great and the Russian Nobility.* London, 1967.

Gleason, Walter. *Moral Idealists, Bureaucracy, and Catherine the Great.* New Brunswick, N.J., 1981.

Jones, Robert. *The Emancipation of the Russian Nobility.* Princeton, N.J., 1973.

Kahan, Arcadius. *The Plow, the Hammer, and the Knout: An Economic History of Eighteenth-Century Russia.* Edited by Richard Hellie. Chicago, 1985.

Melton, Edgar. "Enlightened Seigniorialism and Its Dilemmas in Serf Russia, 1750–1830." *Journal of Modern History* 62 (1990): 675–708.

Newlin, Thomas. *The Voice in the Garden: Andrei Bolotov and the Anxieties of Russian Pastoral, 1738–1833.* Evanston, Ill., 2001.

Raeff, Marc. *Origins of the Russian Intelligentsia: The Eighteenth-Century Nobility.* New York, 1966.

Roosevelt, Priscilla. *Life on the Russian Country Estate: A Social and Cultural History.* New Haven, Conn., 1995.

Smith, Douglas. *Working the Rough Stone: Freemasonry and Russian Society in the Eighteenth Century.* DeKalb, Ill., 1999.

6

Did Catherine the Great and Grigorii Potemkin Wed?

Some Myths, Facts, and Observations on Secret Royal Marriages

Douglas Smith

On October 5, 1791, Prince Grigorii Aleksandrovich Potemkin-Tavricheskii died at the age of fifty-two while on his way to Nikolaev in southern Russia. When word of his death reached Catherine II (the Great) in St. Petersburg a week later, the empress broke down in tears, was bled by her doctors, and was put to bed. Unable to sleep, she arose in the middle of the night to pour out her grief in a letter to Baron Melchior Grimm:

> A terrible, crushing blow struck me yesterday. After dinner around six in the evening, a courier brought me the mournful news that my pupil, my friend, one might say my idol, Prince Potemkin-Tavricheskii has died! . . . You have no idea the extent of my affliction. . . . No one led him, but he had a rare ability to lead others. In a word, he was a man of state, who could both advise and execute. He was passionately, fervently devoted to me, . . . we always understood each other and paid no heed to the talk of those whose thoughts did not measure up to ours. In my opinion, Potemkin was a great man, who did not accomplish even half of what he was capable.[1]

Through her tears, Catherine complained to her secretary Aleksandr Khrapovitskii that there was now no one she could lean upon.[2]

With the death of Potemkin, Russia lost one of its greatest statesmen and Catherine one of her most devoted subjects and trusted advisors. Potemkin had been among the officers who put Catherine on the throne in 1762 and had served her ever since. She raised him up from obscurity to become president of the War College, field marshal and commander in chief of the Russian armed forces, grand admiral of the Black Sea and Caspian fleets, grand hetman of the Black Sea and Ekaterinoslav Cossacks, and governor-general of several provinces—New Russia, Azov, Astrakhan, Saratov, Ekaterinoslav, and Tauride.

Their bond was more than that of a sovereign and a subject, however, and this explains the depth of her grief. In the spring of 1774, Catherine appointed Potemkin her official favorite and for roughly the next two years they were lovers. While this fact is well known, there remains much about their intimate relations from these years that is not. At the center of this black hole lurks one question that has long intrigued observers and spawned considerable speculation: namely, were Potemkin and Catherine actually husband and wife?

Secret marriages are part and parcel of the mythology of the European royalty. To delve into the subject is to enter a labyrinth of legend and rumor through which it is difficult to make one's way with any certainty. Every promising path seems to lead to a dead end of dubious evidence, destroyed documents, and silent witnesses. What is more, the scholar tends to feel a bit uneasy about the undertaking itself; there is something unseemly about it all—hunched over, hands on knees peering through keyholes and eavesdropping, ear to the door, on intimate conversations—that seems beneath his dignity. Nevertheless, one must trudge on, for references to secret marriages are forever being made, and who best to investigate them and their validity if not the professional scholar?

Historians differ on the subject of Catherine's marriage to Potemkin, some answering with a resounding "yes," others inclined to a more circumspect "possibly" or an emphatic "no." Members of the first camp include the empress's first biographer, Jean-Henri Castéra, writing in the eighteenth century, as well as today's two leading Potemkin specialists, Viacheslav Lopatin and Ol'ga Eliseeva.[3] Recent Western biographers of Catherine have tended to hedge their bets, echoing John Alexander's assessment that they "may have been secretly married."[4] And a small minority rules out the matter altogether or simply chooses to ignore it.[5] It warrants noting that those who focus on Potemkin (Lopatin, Eliseeva, Montefiore) have tended to be strong proponents of the notion, while historians of Catherine have typically taken a more equivocal stand (Madariaga, Alexander, Troyat). Works published in Russia in the nineteenth century had to pass over the question in silence due to tsarist censorship, although once the subject could be openly discussed, following the Revolution of 1905, the prevailing sentiment was in favor of the marriage.[6]

The best evidence for Catherine and Potemkin having married is to be found in the letters she wrote him during their affair. In her billets-doux, Catherine refers to Potemkin as her "husband" and "spouse" thirty times and calls herself his "wife" four times:[7]

[After June 8, 1774]

Grishenok, priceless, rarest and sweetest in the world, I love you madly, extraordinarily, my dear friend, I kiss and embrace you with all my body and soul, *dear husband.* [emphasis here and below mine—DS]

[After June 8, 1774]

My good man, my dear, as if there could be anything awkward about your asking me to come and snuggle. This is all quite natural for me, sweet and priceless darling, *husband dear.*

[July 22, 1774. Peterhof]

Darling dearest, *cher Epoux* [dear spouse], pray come cuddle with me. I find your caress both sweet and pleasing. And I thank you for it. . . . *Priceless husband.*

[March–December 1774]

My dear, I shall write my answer tomorrow, but today my head aches. I am not cross and beseech you too not to be angry and not to pine. In short, *I shall remain to the grave your true wife*, should you so desire; if not, then you are a Giaour, Muscovite, Cossack.

[February–March 1776]

Mon mari m'a dit tantôt [My husband said to me earlier]: "Whither should I go, where should I hide myself?" *Mon cher et bien aimé Epoux, venés chez moi. Vous serés reçu à bras ouverts* [My dear and beloved spouse, come to me. You will be received with open arms].

While the meaning behind such terms appears straightforward, it might be argued that Catherine used them not in any literal sense, but metaphorically. Here one could note that Potemkin, like all Russian subjects, called Catherine *matushka* (usually translated as "Little Mother") although he obviously did not mean to imply any biological connection between them. There is reason to believe, however, that Catherine meant precisely what she wrote Potemkin. First, there is no literary tradition of Russian sovereigns referring to favored subjects as "spouse" or "husband," and, second, Catherine apparently (for few of her letters to other favorites have survived) never used these terms with anyone but Potemkin.

Another letter of Catherine's from this period lends further support to this interpretation and provides more evidence of their secret marriage:

[February–March 1776]

My Lord and *Cher Epoux* [dear husband]! I shall begin my answer with that line which touches me most of all: Who ordered you to cry? Why do you give greater weight to your lively imagination than to the proofs that speak in *your wife's favor? Was she not joined to you two years ago in the bonds of Holy Matrimony?* My dear, you deign to suspect the impossible in regard to me. Have I changed my tune, could you be unloved? Believe my words—*I love you and am attached to you by all bonds.* So now, consider for yourself: were my words and deeds in your favor stronger two years ago than now?[8]

The letters, however, represent only part of the evidence, albeit the most persuasive. Also significant is the way Catherine treated Potemkin and the way he behaved after his official tenure as favorite ended in 1776. Far from diminishing, Potemkin's authority grew over time as Catherine came to increasingly rely on him as an advisor, administrator, and later commander in chief. While it is true that other former favorites returned to state service (e.g., Grigorii Orlov, Piotr Zavadovskii), none did so in a manner remotely comparable to Potemkin's. No single individual, save the empress herself, possessed greater authority—authority given by Catherine—and Potemkin knew it. He acted like a monarch, or at least a prince consort, setting up his own elaborate court in the south and flouting the habits of the status-conscious Russian nobles in a way intended to signal his unassailable position. His arrivals to and departures from the capital were treated with no less ceremony than those of Catherine herself.[9]

Their intimate affairs following their romance are also significant for what they reveal about Potemkin's place with Catherine. First of all, despite the fact that Catherine had several subsequent favorites, almost all of whom, it warrants noting, were chosen with Potemkin's involvement, none were able to usurp his position of authority. This is even true of Platon Zubov, Catherine's final favorite, who came closest to supplanting Potemkin. Even he had to admit, in a revealing choice of words, that although Catherine did love him, Potemkin she both loved and "feared . . . as if he were an exacting husband."[10] If Potemkin were the husband and Catherine the wife, then her subsequent favorites were, paradoxically, simultaneously her lovers and their children. Being the favorite meant accepting Catherine and Potemkin's greater bond and adopting him as a surrogate paternal figure. The favorites Aleksandr Lanskoi and Aleksandr Dmitriev-Mamonov spoke of Potemkin as their "father," and Catherine referred to Zubov as "our Child."[11] This most unusual of families was completed by Potemkin's nieces, whom Catherine accepted at court and treated as if they were her own.[12]

Rumors of a secret marriage were prevalent during their lifetimes, and while whispered about at court, all knew to be cautious in discussing the matter. Count Louis-Philippe Ségur, the French ambassador, wrote Versailles in 1788 in veiled terms that Potemkin "takes advantage of . . . certain sacred and inviolable rights which secure the continuance of his privilege. The singular basis of these rights is a great mystery, which is known only to four people in Russia; a lucky chance enabled me to discover it, and when I have thoroughly sounded it, I shall, on the first occasion which presents itself, inform the King."[13]

The four people mentioned by Ségur most likely refer to the individuals believed to have participated in the wedding: Ioann Pamfilov, the empress's confessor; Mar'ia Perekusikhina, her trusted chambermaid; Evgraf Chertkov, court chamberlain and Potemkin's adjutant; and Aleksandr Samoilov, his nephew and an officer in the Semenovskii Life Guards Regiment. All of them kept quiet about the wedding for the rest of their lives, except Samoilov, who, while organizing his valuables as an old man, is reported to have shown Count Orlov-Davydov a memento "given to me by the Empress in remembrance of her marriage to my dear late uncle."[14]

Samoilov reportedly also possessed a document testifying to the marriage, which was placed inside his coffin and buried along with him in 1814. A second such certificate is believed to have been inherited by Potemkin's beloved niece, Countess Aleksandra Branitskaia. Upon her death Branitskaia left it to her daughter, who for unknown reasons gave it to Count Aleksandr Stroganov sometime in the middle of the nineteenth century, instructing him to toss it into the Black Sea on his way from Odessa to the Crimea.[15]

The mysterious and macabre fate of these certificates, combined with the fact that those belonging to Perekusikhina and Chertkov have yet to be found, lends a certain implausibility to their existence. Such tales, while they cannot be ruled out, have a whiff of nineteenth-century romanticism about them that challenges their veracity. It is quite possible that given the marriage's secret nature, nothing was ever written down to commemorate it. It stands to reason that no banns were read aloud before the ceremony or that it was ever recorded in any church register as is usually the custom. This was a most extraordinary affair and was treated as such. Here one might recall the secret wedding of the Prince of Wales (the future George IV) to the Catholic widow Maria Anne Fitzherbert in December 1785. Since the marriage could not be recognized for dynastic reasons, no certificate of marriage was drawn up; however, the prince did draft a statement testifying to the marriage, signed by him and the two witnesses, for Maria to keep.[16] It is possible that Catherine too produced such a document for Potemkin at the time of their marriage.

Although historians have proposed several dates for the marriage (1774, 1775, 1784), the most likely was June 8, 1774. It has been suggested—though this remains conjecture—that late that night, Catherine, accompanied by Perekusikhina, left the Summer Palace and climbed aboard a waiting boat that took them down the Fontanka River to the Neva. After a short ride, they landed at an isolated corner of the city where a carriage took them to the Church of St. Samson. There they met Potemkin, Samoilov, and Chertkov. Ioann Pamfilov presided over what was most likely a brief ceremony. Within minutes, Catherine and Potemkin were married. All the witnesses were sworn to secrecy.[17]

Catherine would have had her reasons for keeping the marriage a secret. She knew that her marriage to Potemkin would arouse jealousy and factions among the powerful clans at court. Years before, her lover Grigorii Orlov had pushed Catherine to marry him. Catherine appears to have considered it and discussed it with some of her leading courtiers, one of whom, Count Nikita Panin, reportedly warned that "a Mrs. Orlov would never be Empress of All the Russias." Part of the resistance to the idea emanated from a concern for what such a marriage would do to the succession rights of Catherine's son and heir to the throne, Grand Duke Paul. Word of the proposed marriage incensed many of the guard's officers, and in 1763 a plot was uncovered to unseat Catherine and murder Orlov should the marriage take place. Catherine prudently denied Orlov his wish.[18]

The hostile reaction to the proposed marriage provided ample cause for Catherine's desire to keep her marriage to Potemkin a closely guarded secret. What is particularly shocking is that she was even willing to consider it in light of the danger this presented. We may never know all the reasons why Catherine would have decided to marry. One reason was the intense love she felt for Potemkin, as her letters from this period so movingly show. Another appears to have been the gratitude she had for his helping her through two major crises of her reign: the First Russo-Turkish War (1768–1774) and the Pugachev rebellion (1773–1774). In an undated letter written late in their affair, Catherine makes a suggestive reference to his having given her "the means to reign whilst taking away the powers of my soul."[19] As for Potemkin, the reasons are quite clear: marriage to the empress would solidify his position and establish an incomparable bond with the sovereign.

In evaluating this evidence, it is worthwhile to take a look at two other secret royal marriages. The first is that between Empress Elizabeth (reigned 1741–1761) and Count Aleksei Razumovskii. Of uncertain Ukrainian origin, Razumovskii (né Rozum) was a singer in the court choir when he caught Elizabeth's eye in the early 1730s. They became lovers and, after ascending the throne, Elizabeth made Razumovskii her favorite and showered him with wealth and titles.

Historians generally agree that Elizabeth and Razumovskii secretly wed, although the details are sketchy, at best, and there is no documentary proof. The ceremony is considered to have taken place either at Razumovskii's estate at Perovo outside Moscow or at the Church of the Presentation of the Virgin on Moscow's Pokrovka Street, either in 1742 or 1744. None of the witnesses are known and accounts differ on who married them. The claim that they married is constructed out of a few shards of dubious evidence. A list of guards officers, for example, contains information on the marital status for all of the officers except Razumovskii, an omission which has been interpreted as a sign that his personal situation (i.e., the empress's secret spouse) was too delicate to mention.[20] A descendant of Razumovskii has recently produced a small silk pillow belonging to the family depicting the pair beneath the words "Blessed is this secret" in Russian, which she offers as the best proof of the marriage.[21] True, the diplomatic rumor mill was full of the story of their marriage in the 1740s, although given the noted inaccuracy of much of what passed among diplomats as truth and the lack of written proof to corroborate the rumors, these should not be given too much weight. An old legend has it that when Orlov was pressuring Catherine to marry him, she dispatched a messenger to Razumovskii to inquire about his marriage to the late empress. An aged Razumovskii, so the story goes, produced a document proving the marriage, and then tossed it into the fire in a gesture to Catherine. While undeniably colorful, the legend is no longer considered to be true.[22]

A second secret marriage is that of Louis XIV of France and Madame de Maintenon, the Sun King's confidante and mistress when his wife, Marie-Thérèse of Austria, died in 1683. Little is known about the specifics of this wedding as well. While most accounts place it on the night of October 9–10, 1683, other dates have been proposed (1684, 1685, 1686, and 1697).[23] There is also no solid evidence on who attended, and the number of possible witnesses varies by a few individuals depending on the account. Both Versailles and the château de Maintenon have been proposed as sites for the ceremony. The marriage was kept a secret, and although many at court suspected it, only a few could actually claim to know of its existence.[24]

What evidence is there to support the story of the marriage? Like Catherine and Potemkin's marriage, there is no irrefutable proof. The Vatican archives supposedly contain the marriage certificate, although not unlike those from Catherine's marriage, it has never been produced.[25] Louis and Madame de Maintenon exchanged letters from this period, though they contain nothing to suggest they ever married.[26] Rather, the evidence is all circumstantial. It was noticed that the king began paying much more attention to Madame de Maintenon after his wife's death, for example, and that she was then seen at court sitting in an armchair in the presence of the royal family (the prerogative of the late queen) and attending mass seated in the queen's box.[27] The memoirs of court figures, most notably those of Saint-Simon, speak of a marriage as having taken place.

Much significance has been given to what can be surmised concerning their psychological states at the time. Louis, subject to a growing religiosity, suffered from the sinfulness of his relations with Madame de Maintenon and possibly sought relief through marriage. For her part, Madame de Maintenon wrote in her letters from this period that the "vapeurs" and "indispositions" she had suffered after the queen's death, thought to be the result of stress over her relationship with Louis, had of late given way to a new sense of "happiness." The cause for this happiness, historians assert, was her marriage.[28]

Another reason the marriage has been accepted is that certain powerful social groups, most notably the church, wanted Louis to remarry, even if secretly and morganatically, so as to lead a moral, regular life in the eyes of God. The situation was quite different in Catherine's Russia where the church lacked any comparable influence on the monarch and her court and where the powerful noble clans that formed the country's ruling class all opposed the idea of the empress marrying. These differences may have something to do with the greater willingness to accept Louis's secret marriage than Catherine's, despite the evidence.

Who she married may be another factor. Since his days as Catherine's favorite, Potemkin has been the subject of much calumny: few figures in Russian history have been so unfairly demonized by their contemporaries, or by posterity. The Potemkin of myth—corrupt, debauched, and lazy—seems unworthy of Catherine, and the possibility of their being married a stain on her proud reign. Perhaps this explains why historians of Potemkin, who have done the most to dispel the myths and recover the true Potemkin, have been more apt to recognize the marriage than have students of Catherine. This appears to be changing, however, as two recent works on Catherine by respected scholars that fully support the marriage suggest.[29]

Did Catherine and Potemkin wed? In light of the evidence, the answer must be yes. Secret marriages are, by definition, "secret": they attempt to hide and fear making themselves known. It is not surprising, therefore, that the archives have yet to give up any document in Catherine's (or Elizabeth's or Louis's) hand testifying to the marriage. The historian is forced to rely on more indirect proof, and Catherine's letters to Potemkin provide what must be considered the best possible proof, proof made even more convincing by the other supporting evidence.

Recognizing Catherine and Potemkin's marriage is important for several reasons. First, a basic task of the historian is to establish the historical record, to find out what has been and what has happened. More than two hundred years after the fact, it is time to set the record straight. Second, the marriage is a vitally important fact in their lives, the significance of which we are only now beginning to appreciate. As Lopatin and Montefiore have suggested, Potemkin's secret marriage to Catherine was partially responsible for his turbulent emotional life and, consequently, erratic behavior; it is an intriguing, though still dimly understood notion that future biographers will most likely explore further. The same might be said of Catherine: what new findings about or deeper understandings of her life and reign might the recognition of her marriage reveal to researchers?

Finally, secret royal marriages remind us of an important fact about absolutism, namely that even at the apogee of royal power in Europe, rulers were never free to do whatever they desired. All monarchs were enmeshed within webs of interdependence that bound them to the nobility, church, and other social groups and that presented real constraints on their actions. This was especially true for female rulers like Elizabeth and Catherine, raised to the throne on the backs of their noble male supporters. Marriage, even if later in the ruler's life after the birth of an heir, was always of considerable political significance and was to be entered into only after a careful calculation of the possible political ramifications had been made. If, despite the danger, rulers decided to marry, then it often had to be a secret. Few images convey this fact better than that of Catherine and Potemkin sneaking off to exchange their wedding vows, in hushed voices, their ears pricked up to the faintest noise beyond the chapel door.

NOTES

1. *Sbornik imperatorskogo istoricheskogo russkogo obshchestva*, vol. 23 (1878), 561.

2. *Pamiatnye zapiski A. V. Khrapovitskogo*, ed. G. N. Gennadi (1862; reprint, Moscow: Soiuzteatr, 1990), 252.

3. Jean-Henri Castéra, *The Life of Catherine II, Empress of Russia*, trans. and revised by William Tooke, vol. 3 (London: T. N. Longman and J. Debrett, 1800), 14–15, 253; V. S. Lopatin, *Ekaterina II i G. A. Potemkin. lichnaia perepiska, 1769–1791* (Moscow: Nauka, 1997), 479–483, 513–515; O. I. Eliseeva, *Geopoliticheskie proekty G. A. Potemkina* (Moscow: Institut rossiiskoi istorii RAN, 2000), 6, 53–57; and O. I. Eliseeva, *Perepiska Ekateriny II i G. A. Potemkina perioda vtoroi russko-turetskoi voiny (istochnikovedcheskoe issledovanie)* (Moscow: Vostok, 1997), 26–30. Also, Simon Sebag Montefiore, *Prince of Princes: The Life of Potemkin* (London: Weidenfeld and Nicolson, 2000).

4. John T. Alexander, *Catherine the Great: Life and Legend* (New York: Oxford University Press, 1989), 204; Isabel de Madariaga, *Russia in the Age of Catherine the Great* (New Haven, Conn.: Yale University Press, 1981), 344; Isabel de Madariaga, *Catherine the Great: A Short History* (New Haven, Conn.: Yale University Press, 1990), 209; Zoé Oldenbourg, *Catherine the Great*, trans. Anne Carter (New York: Pantheon, 1965), 319; Henri Troyat, *Catherine la grande* (Paris: Flammarion, 1977), 310–311. Vincent Cronin is a bit more convinced of the marriage in his *Catherine, Empress of All the Russias* (New York: William Morrow and Co., 1978), 216.

5. In his review of Montefiore's *Prince*, A. G. Cross refers to the wedding as a "rumour." "Round and About Montefiore's Potemkin," *Study Group on Eighteenth-Century Russia, Newsletter* 29 (2001): 91. Ian Grey expresses the same view in *Catherine the Great, Autocrat of All the Russias* (Westport, Conn.: Greenwood Press, 1975), 177, 184–185n19. Aleksandr Kamenskii, Russia's leading expert on Catherine, strangely avoids the subject in his various works on the empress. See, for example, the chapter "Liubov' i vlast'" in *Zhizn' i sud'ba imperatritsy Ekateriny Velikoi* (Moscow: Znanie, 1997), and his chapter on Catherine in Donald J. Raleigh, ed., *The Emperors and Empresses of Russia: Rediscovering the Romanovs*, comp. A. A. Iskenderov, *The New Russian History Series* (Armonk, N.Y.: M. E. Sharpe, 1996).

6. A. G. Brückner's books on Catherine and Potemkin published in Russia are silent on the matter. *Istoriia Ekateriny Vtoroi* (1885; reprint, Moscow: Terra, 1996);

Potemkin (1891; reprint, Moscow: Terra, 1996). For post-1905, see P. Bartenev, "Iz zapisnoi knizhki izdatelia 'Russkogo arkhiva'," *Russkii arkhiv* bk. 3 (1906): 613–616, and Ia. L. Barskov, ed., "Pis'ma Ekateriny II k G. A. Potemkinu," *Voprosy istorii* 7 (1989): 121. Barskov's work was actually prepared in the early decades of the twentieth century.

7. Lopatin, *Perepiska*, 513.

8. Lopatin, *Perepiska*, 31, 34, 64, 94–95.

9. Montefiore, *Prince*, 137–139; Marc Raeff, "In the Imperial Manner," in *Catherine the Great: A Profile*, ed. Marc Raeff (New York: Hill and Wang, 1972), 233–236.

10. Quoted in *Russkii biograficheskii slovar'*, s.v. "Zubov, Platon Aleksandrovich."

11. Lopatin, *Perepiska*, 271, 370, 721n5; and letters of Lanskoi to Potemkin in Rossiiskii Gosudarstvennyi Arkhiv Drevnikh Aktov, fond 11, opis' 1, delo 914, listy l, 6.

12. See chapters 11 and 12 in Montefiore, *Prince*.

13. Kazimierz Waliszewski, *The Story of a Throne*, vol. 1 (1895; reprint, Freeport, N.Y.: Archon, 1971), 189; Montefiore, *Prince*, 139–140; Lopatin, *Perepiska*, 482.

14. Bartenev, "Iz zapisnoi knizhki," 615.

15. Bartenev, "Iz zapisnoi knizhki," 613–614; Castéra, *Life*, 3:253 and note.

16. E. A. Smith, *George IV, Yale English Monarchs* (New Haven, Conn.: Yale University Press, 1999), 36–39.

17. P. Bartenev, "Iz zapisnoi knizhki," 613–615; Lopatin, *Perepiska*, 513–514; Montefiore, *Prince*, 136–139. On the sources relating to the possible marriage, see Lopatin, *Perepiska*, 479–483.

18. Alexander, *Catherine the Great*, 73–76; David L. Ransel, *The Politics of Catherinian Russia: The Panin Party* (New Haven, Conn.: Yale University Press, 1975), 124–126.

19. Lopatin, *Perepiska*, 87.

20. Evgenii Anisimov, *Elizaveta Petrovna* (Moscow: Molodaia gvardiia, 1999), 197–199.

21. Maria Razumovsky, *Die Rasumovskys: Eine Familie am Zarenhof* (Köln, Germany: Böhlau, 1998), 6 and photograph between pages 20–21.

22. Anisimov, *Elizaveta*, 197–199; Evgenii Anisimov, *Rossiia v seredine XVIII veka: Bor'ba za nasledie Petra* (Moscow: Mysl', 1986), 186; Tamara Talbot Rice, *Elizabeth, Empress of Russia* (London: Weidenfeld and Nicolson, 1970), 76–77.

23. François Bluche, *Louis XIV* (Paris: Fayard, 1986), 588, 709–715; André Castelot, *Madame de Maintenon: La reine secrète* (Paris: Perrin, 1996), 133; Charlotte Haldane, *Madame de Maintenon: The Uncrowned Queen* (Indianapolis: Bobbs-Merrill, 1970), 154–155; Louis Hastier, *Louis XIV et Madame de Maintenon* (Paris: Arthème Fayard, 1957), 77–86, 219–223; anon., *Histoire de Mme de Maintenon, fondatrice de Saint-Cyr*, vol. 2 (Paris, 1814), 31; Jean-Christian Petitfils, *Louis XIV* (Paris: Perrin, 1995), 311–312, 312n1; John B. Wolf, *Louis XIV* (New York: W. W. Norton, 1968), 332.

24. Prince Michael of Greece, *Louis XIV: The Other Side of the Sun*, trans. Alan Sheridan (London: Orbis, 1979), 239; Haldane, *Madame*, 155; *Histoire*, 2:31; Wolf, *Louis*, 333, 335.

25. Bruno Neveu, ed., *Correspondence du nonce en France Angelo Ranuzzi (1683–1686)*, vol. 1 (Rome: École Française de Rome, 1973), 63n11; Petitfils, *Louis*, 312n1.

26. Wolf, *Louis*, 334.

27. Olivier Bernier, *Louis XIV: A Royal Life* (New York: Doubleday, 1987), 225–226.

28. Prince Michael, *Louis,* 238–242; Haldane, *Madame,* 152–154; Wolf, *Louis,* 331–334.

29. Simon Dixon, *Catherine the Great* (Harlow, UK: Longman, 2001), 54, 57; N. I. Pavlenko, *Ekaterina Velikaia* (Moscow: Molodaia gvardiia, 1999), 367.

SUGGESTED READING

Alexander, John T. *Catherine the Great: Life and Legend.* New York, 1989.

———. "Favourites, Favouritism and Female Rule in Russia, 1725–1796." In *Russia in the Age of the Enlightenment: Essays for Isabel de Madariaga,* edited by Roger Bartlett and Janet M. Hartley. New York, 1990.

Dixon, Simon. *Catherine the Great.* Harlow, UK, 2001.

Elliott, J. H., and L. W. B. Brockliss, eds. *The World of the Favourite.* New Haven, Conn., 1999.

Herman, Eleanor. *Sex with Kings.* New York, 2004.

Madariaga, Isabel de. *Russia in the Age of Catherine the Great.* New Haven, Conn., 1981.

Montefiore, Simon Sebag. *Prince of Princes: The Life of Potemkin.* London, 2000.

Raeff, Marc. "In the Imperial Manner." In *Catherine the Great: A Profile,* edited by Marc Raeff. New York, 1972.

Scott, H. M. "The Rise of the First Minister in Eighteenth-Century Europe." In *History and Biography: Essays in Honour of Derek Beales,* edited by T. C. W. Blanning and David Cannadine. Cambridge, UK, 1996.

Smith, Douglas, ed. and trans. *Love and Conquest: Personal Correspondence of Catherine the Great and Prince Grigory Potemkin.* DeKalb, Ill., 2004.

II

THE RUSSIAN NINETEENTH CENTURY

The Napoleonic conflict and the development (or further development) of a Russian national identity; Russia's first revolution and the emergence of the intelligentsia; Russia's status as a great power and the paradox of its apparent economic weaknesses at the same time that its rulers also attempted to exercise the prerogatives of empire; the rise of a revolutionary movement; and the flowering of a nascent "civil society"—these are only a few of the issues that predominated in nineteenth-century Russia. When a Russian national consciousness or Russian nationalism began to form is, in view of the obvious importance of national identity in a multinational state such as imperial Russia, an intriguing question. By delving into three seemingly distinct areas: the origins of the modern Russian literary language, the makeup of the social order in late eighteenth- and early nineteenth-century Russia, and Russians' view of their role in Europe (again in late eighteenth- and nineteenth-century Russia), Alexander Martin asserts that by the early decades of the nineteenth century a distinct idea of "Russianness" was evident among "Russia's educated elite." Much has been written about imperial Russia's relationships with the European great powers, but considerably less on early Russian-American interactions. This lacuna in the historiography is addressed in Ben Whisenhunt's account of the fitful early years of Russian-American "friendship." (The experiences of John Paul Jones and John Quincy Adams in St. Petersburg are more than a bit revealing, particularly the former's.) Russia's first revolution, the failed Decembrist revolt of 1825, attracted vast attention from Soviet scholars, who inflated both the heroics of the Decembrist plotters and their possibilities for success. That said, Patrick O'Meara's study of the Decembrist Pavel Pestel, arguably Russia's most politically compelling revolutionary until 1917, is not only a thoughtful intellectual critique of Pestel's political ideals, but a cautionary tale about the limits of potential reform in nineteenth-century Russia.

Susan McCaffray attempts to debunk still-prevailing notions of Russian economic "backwardness" in the late Imperial era. Thus, she argues against any notion (still prevalent in the historiography) that the revolutions in early twentieth-century Russia were due, perhaps inevitably, to Russia's desperately weak economic foundations. The trial of Vera Zasulich was one of the most celebrated public spectacles emerging from the rise of the revolutionary movement during the 1870s and 1880s. Ana Siljak revisits the trial to paint a multifaceted picture of post–Great Reform Russia, underlining not only the development of more formalized legal procedures (even of a legal ethos, however tenuous), but also the contempt for such a development by many within the regime and the revolutionary movement. The concept of a civil society is explored in Thomas Porter's analysis of the role of the *zemstvo* (a form of local governance). Porter offers new arguments and reinterprets older evidence to demonstrate that *zemstvo* institutions, which acted as an intermediary between the center (the St. Petersburg- and Moscow-based authorities) and rural or provincial Russia, were beginning to more and more resemble a nascent civil society. McCaffray's, Siljak's, and Porter's essays outline an economically and socially vibrant late imperial Russia; whether it was also an anachronistic anomaly fated for destruction is for the reader to decide.

7

The Invention of "Russianness" in the Late Eighteenth–Early Nineteenth Century

Alexander M. Martin

Russia's Westernization during the eighteenth century had utopian elements that grew out of centuries of European cultural development. Christianity had long encouraged the faithful to look forward to Christ's Second Coming, while the absolutist rulers of the baroque era and the Freemasons of the eighteenth century held that an all-powerful monarch or the secret wisdom of Masonic orders held the keys to the creation of a better world. In each case—Christian, absolutist, Masonic—there was a common belief that the world could become better in some vague yet truly life-transforming way if only history followed the correct path. In Russia, beginning with the reign of Peter the Great—which came at the end of a seventeenth century scarred by devastating civil strife and unprecedented religious violence—the official ideology of the imperial regime linked such utopian dreams with the empire's Westernization. Anxious to remove any doubts about the radical character of the changes he was seeking, Peter ordered the nobles to abandon beards and styles of clothing and architecture that were hallowed by centuries of tradition; he ordered the adoption of the Julian calendar to coincide with the symbolic dawn of a new century (January 1, 1700) and called himself Peter *the First* (not, as his forebears would have, Peter *Alekseevich* ["son of Aleksei"]) to suggest that his reign marked the beginning of a new era; and he called his deliberately foreign-looking new capital city of St. Petersburg, at that time still a muddy frontier outpost in the northern marshes, his "paradise," a term with unmistakable religious overtones. Beyond copying specific features of Western Europe, his aim was for Russia to blend its own national genius with the best of Western societies to create a superior new civilization.[1]

Like the totalitarian states of modern Europe, Peter's regime believed that this program offered breathtaking vistas of future greatness, and he had little patience for those who did not share his vision or who objected to the methods employed in its pursuit.[2] This enforced Westernization created a profound split in Russian society. The vast, largely powerless majority remained outside the Westernization process, their attitude ranging from reserved skepticism to outright hostility, and their culture growing ghettoized and ossified as the Westernized elite continually skimmed off the wealthiest and most educated individuals.[3] However, the tiny eighteenth-century ruling minority embraced the transformation and acknowledged the monarch's exclusive power to guide it; aside from the succession crisis of 1730, neither churchmen, intellectuals, property owners, the judiciary, nor ancient aristocratic families—usually the most politically assertive groups of early modern society—seriously questioned the monarch's supremacy.[4]

Faced with the glaring discrepancy between its grandiose ambitions and limited resources for achieving them, the regime often had to settle for merely rhetorical or symbolic gestures; the Christian way of thinking, which placed high value on publicly proclaiming one's faith, thus lived on in secularized form.[5] One consequence was that the regime founded institutions and announced policies that dramatically advertised its commitment to Westernization but were out of touch with Russian realities. For example, it created a magnificent, imitation-European capital, St. Petersburg, when most Russian cities and towns were still small settlements of log cabins; it founded an academy of sciences (in 1724) before it had universities to train scientists to staff it; it established its first university (in 1755) before it had the necessary schools to train potential applicants; and it attempted (in 1767) to create a law code based on Enlightenment notions of individual rights, at a time when half the population were serfs with hardly any rights at all. Much like the Russian Communists of the twentieth century, who began by proclaiming the existence of a "proletarian dictatorship" and only later tried to industrialize the country and actually create the industrial proletariat whose representatives they claimed to be, Peter and his heirs hoped that once Russia had the visible symbols of an advanced European society, the social realities that elsewhere gave rise to these symbols in the first place would appear as well.

Similarly, the high culture of Russia's educated elite was, to a large extent, driven by the belief that if Russians imported the styles and artifacts of European culture, the social underpinnings of that culture would also arise. For example, literary salons—social gatherings of writers and their readers, frequently hosted by ladies of the aristocracy, where ideas could be exchanged freely and informally—were important features of European upper-class life in the early eighteenth century; writers often carried on their salon conversations in their published poetry or fiction, such as the French author Paul Tallement's 1663 novel *Le voyage de l'Isle d'amour*,[6] that were filled with oblique references to salon discussions and acquaintances. The Russian writer Vasilii Kirillovich Trediakovsky hoped to popularize salons in Russia, where they did not exist, to help foster a public opinion that would be independent of the imperial court. So, in 1730, he published a Russian translation of Tallement's novel, hoping that Russians who read the book would be inspired to establish salons. In this case, as the Russian scholar Iurii Mikhailovich Lotman put it, in France "the salon (a literary milieu) had given rise to the novel, whereas in Russia the novel was expected to give rise to a particular cultural milieu. There [in France], reality created the text; here [in Russia], the text was supposed to create reality."[7]

This changed in the late eighteenth–early nineteenth century, when the regime was increasingly able to influence society's everyday existence— thanks to its expanding administrative apparatus, education system, judiciary, and so on—even while a growing minority of non-noble Russians became receptive to the Westernized culture of the nobility. As a result, the gap between the regime's utopian Westernizing rhetoric and the anti-Western traditionalism of the population gradually narrowed; in its place, there emerged, among the educated classes, a sense of Russian national identity that drew on pre-Petrine traditions as well as Western influences and that has been central to Russian thinking ever since. The remainder of this essay will explore the emergence and significance of this sense of "Russianness" in three contexts: the creation of the modern Russian literary language; changing conceptions of the social order; and Russians' thinking about their place in Europe.

LANGUAGE

The new sense of national identity was inconceivable without a proper national literary language. Pre-Petrine Russia had experienced a situation known as *diglossia*, that is, the simultaneous use of two distinct languages that were employed for different purposes and perceived as mutually complementary. The everyday *spoken* language was Russian, but lexicographers and grammarians had not fully developed the distinctions between formal and informal or between standard and substandard speech, or the specialized vocabularies of legal and political theorists, scientists, philosophers, and so on. The basis for the *written* language, on the other hand, was Old Church Slavonic, used in the Russian Bible and liturgy (like Latin in the medieval West) and generally associated with the church and religion. Officials and others writing on nonreligious themes—a comparatively rare occurrence before 1700—used a hybrid of the two languages.[8] The Russian–Old Church Slavonic diglossia faithfully mirrored pre-Petrine Russia's self-perception as a Slavic nation rooted in the Byzantine Orthodox tradition.

This diglossia was transformed in the eighteenth century, when the rapid expansion of nonreligious publishing reflected the shift away from pre-Petrine cultural traditions, while the primacy of Old Church Slavonic was challenged by the languages of the Protestant and Catholic countries that now served as models for Russia's Westernization; the effect of these developments, as the Russian statesman and scholar Pavel Nikolaevich Miliukov noted, "was to deprive the language used by the educated Russians of any firmly established foundation."[9] Foreign words and phrases were imported pell-mell into Russian. Thus, terms associated with new institutions of government were often taken from the German: for instance, the titles *Polizeimeister* ("police master") and *Oberhofmarschall* ("chief court marshal") were Russianized as *politseimeister* and *obergofmarshal*, even though to Russian ears these were meaningless strings of awkward syllables. Russians also translated, and sometimes mistranslated, foreign idiomatic expressions. For example, the French *ne pas être dans son assiette* means "not be in one's proper position," that is, feel awkward or out of kilter. *Assiette* here means "proper position," but in other contexts it can mean "plate" or "bowl," so Russians adopted the garbled translation *byt' ne v svoei tarelke*— "not to be in one's bowl." However, many genuinely valuable words and phrases—"development," "concentrate," "theory," "fashion," "actor," "soldier," "university," and countless others—entered the language as well, enriching its storehouse of concepts and enhancing its expressive powers. At the same time, writers began using Old Church Slavonic vocabulary as a stylistic device for evoking a religious or patriotic mood, while folk expressions were used to add an earthy flavor to one's writing. Russian thus became a sophisticated literary language, capable of expressing a vast range of feelings and ideas in a variety of literary styles and levels of speech. However, in an era that regarded the language as the core of a nation's identity, the heterogeneity of Russian's linguistic roots—both (Orthodox) Old Church Slavonic and (Catholic or Protestant) West European, both aristocratic and peasant—made it unavoidable that discussions about language would become ideologically charged.

Russia's literary elite (poets, prose writers, playwrights, journalists, literary and theater critics) was a tiny minority within the already small nobility, but its members—who, in addition to their literary work, were generally government officials, military officers, landowners, or members of the aristocracy of St. Petersburg and Moscow—were fully integrated into the mainstream of noble society. This allowed them both to observe and to influence the values and everyday conduct of their upper-class readers, whose style of living and thinking was, in turn, the model for the ever-expanding population of Russians who obtained an education and aspired to a genteel way of life over the course of the next century. The literary elite thus had a long-term impact that was entirely out of proportion to its small numbers.

By about 1800, this literary world had become divided into two camps. Both agreed that Russians' ability to think creatively and take their place among the great cultures of Europe depended on the subtlety and expressiveness of their language. Furthermore, they took for granted—as did most educated Europeans of their time—that each nation had a distinctive personality that needed to be expressed in its own language; under this theory, a nation that relied on another's language was condemned to produce sterile imitations of that other nation's thought patterns. (Not coincidentally, it was in this same period that Noah Webster worked to codify an *American* form of English, in the hope of thereby cementing culturally the American people's independence from Great Britain.) Authors writing in Russian, it was agreed, needed to achieve European levels of intellectual and aesthetic sophistication while preserving distinctly Russian ways of thinking and feeling.

The linguistic debate of the early 1800s, while fundamentally about national identity, concretely took the form of a dispute about vocabulary, grammar, literary and rhetorical style, and everyday behavior. On one side were the advocates of the "New Style," so called because they sought Russia's integration into the mainstream of Enlightenment Europe. They were open to borrowings from Western languages and regarded the spoken Russian of educated nobles as the proper model for the written language. Like the ideal noblewoman, the Russian language and the corresponding sentimentalist style of literature—exemplified in the highly popular writings of Nikolai Mikhailovich Karamzin—were supposed to be "delicate," "pleasant," sensitive, consciously aristocratic, cosmopolitan in outlook, and not pompous, pedantic, servile, or overly religious; the writers associated with this style cultivated a refined sense of irony, informality in their personal relationships, and a critically minded individualism. This vision of the world was rejected by the champions of the "Old Style," which was actually quite new but whose advocates saw themselves as the upholders of Russia's Slavic, Orthodox, and monarchical tradition. In contrast to the "feminine" literary sentimentalism of the New Style, the Old Style, whose chief exponent was Admiral Aleksandr Semenovich Shishkov, favored the more "masculine" literary style of classicism and stressed such qualities as "gravity," hierarchy, decorum, and stoicism. Whereas the New Style borrowed from European languages, the Old drew its vocabulary and style from Old Church Slavonic and Russian folk sources. The New Style was accused of ignoring Russia's heritage, fawning over Europe, and favoring "feminine" private emotions rather than "masculine" public ones (e.g., patriotism); the Old Style, on the other hand, was accused of being dull and rejecting the beneficent influence of Europe while idealizing Russia's medieval past. Reflecting these philosophical differences, the pro–Old Style "Symposium of Lovers of the Russian Word" was a large organization that held decorous public readings and was hierarchically structured under the leadership of older writers and statesmen, while the pro–New Style "Arzamas Society of Obscure People" was an intimate gathering of young writers who, as their group's very name indicated,[10] delighted in irony and satire, such as delivering mock eulogies for Old Style writers whom they deemed intellectually "dead."

Both the Old and New Style embraced Russia's eighteenth-century Westernization. Within that framework, however, the Old Style wanted to strengthen the elite's frayed ties to the Orthodox, pre-Petrine, and folk traditions, and keep out what it considered the frivolous, caustic French Enlightenment spirit that challenged all inherited beliefs and ultimately corroded decency and the bonds of society. The New Style, by contrast, hoped to lead Russian society toward "enlightenment" by combating superstition, tyranny, servility, ignorance, and the general coarseness of manners; this meant looking to Enlightenment Europe (including France) as a role model and adopting a critical distance toward many national traditions. Against the background of the Napoleonic Wars and Alexander I's intermittent reform efforts, the debate had political overtones—the advocates of the Old Style were accused of being authoritarian enemies of "enlightenment," while the supporters of the New Style were charged with being unpatriotic and serving the interests of Napoleonic France, Russia's enemy.[11]

By the 1820s–1830s, the two currents merged. The end of the Napoleonic Wars and of Alexander I's reform efforts had removed the principal earlier sources of domestic political discord, but more broadly, Russian writers had achieved a greater consensus on what "Russianness" meant. The premier writer of the New Style, Karamzin, spent the years after the traumatic 1812 war against Napoleon writing a patriotic and immensely popular history of medieval Russia; this reflected his entire generation's deepening sense that Russia's past, long extolled by the Old Style, was indeed central to the national identity. The Old Style's openness to Church Slavonicisms and folk expressions likewise found acceptance as ways to express the national character. On the other hand, the crusade against linguistic borrowing conducted by the Old Style's main champion, Shishkov, came to be seen as quixotic and unproductive, while the Old Style's orientation toward classicism produced a literature that seemed anachronistic, wooden, and uninspired. More generally, the Europe-wide fashion of romanticism—which encouraged a cosmopolitan outlook, individual introspection, and attention to the uniqueness of each nation's history and folk culture—was conducive to a synthesis of the two styles.

The embodiment of that synthesis was Aleksandr Sergeevich Pushkin. His prose remains to this day the gold standard of "good" Russian, monuments to his memory adorn streets and squares across the country, and Russians memorize his verse and speak of him with quasi-religious reverence. Equally important, his turns of phrase, the moods created by his poetry, and the characters who populate his stories have powerfully contributed to shaping Russians' sense of what it means to be "Russian," while Pushkin's own life—he is remembered as a romantic lover who died tragically in a duel, an ardent advocate of liberty, a prickly individualist, and a proud yet melancholy aristocrat and patriot—remains a touchstone for Russian national ideals.

The conception of the national character popularized by Pushkin, Nikolai Vasil'evich Gogol', Sergei Timofeevich Aksakov, and other writers of the first half of the nineteenth century became accepted by educated people and has played an important role ever since in shaping how Russians see themselves and are seen by others. Fundamental to this conception is the idea that "Russianness," like the character traits popularly attributed to American regions and ethnicities (such as southerners or Italian Americans), is a quintessentially personal attribute that manifests itself in how an individual thinks, feels, and interacts with other individuals. (It is therefore quite different from the conception of American *national* identity that sees Americans as being "diverse" individuals who reveal their "Americanness" mainly by adhering to certain values, such as respect for the rights of others, when they interact with society at large.) By contrast with stereotyped notions about the frivolous French, the pedantic Germans, or the treacherous Poles, ideal Russians were supposed to be easygoing, tolerant, warmhearted, communal, spiritual, sincere, and loyal; the shortcomings attributed to them by Russian writers—superstitiousness, drunkenness, corruption, laziness, disregard for rules—were deemed logical, even endearing corollaries to these favorable qualities. While earlier stereotypes had focused on differences between social groups, such as peasants and nobles, the *national* stereotype applied to both sexes and all classes of society.[12]

THE SOCIAL AND POLITICAL ORDER

This conception of the Russian national character crystallized in tandem with evolving ideas about the social and political order. Eighteenth-century upper-class Russians generally took their rigidly hierarchical social order for granted as a natural fact of life that was justified by the superiority of the "enlightened" nobles over the "benighted" peasants and by the nobles' duty to serve the monarch. Reading the autobiographies of such thoughtful nobles as Ekaterina Romanovna Dashkova, Anna Evdokimovna Labzina, Gavriil Romanovich Derzhavin, Aleksandr Semenovich Shishkov, Ivan Vladimirovich Lopukhin, and others, one rarely senses any unease with the social or political order.[13] At the same time, as Richard Wortman and others have pointed out, the eighteenth-century monarchs' "scenarios of power"—that is, the ideological constructs that justified their rule—typically argued that the current monarch represented a break with his or her predecessor's policies and that the goal of his or her reign was to implement changes that would make Russia more similar to Europe.[14] The idea of regime-sponsored Westernizing change, starting at the top of society and gradually spreading downward—along with an attitude of fear and contempt toward the peasant masses—lay at the core of the regime's ideology for most of the eighteenth century.

These ideas changed around the turn of the century. In part, educated Russians underwent the same influences as their counterparts elsewhere: the Enlightenment and romanticism made folk culture appear as a virtuous repository of national tradition, not brutish primitiveness;[15] the French Revolution caused many to lose faith in the ability of traditional social and political structures anywhere to maintain order; and the participation of lower-class soldiers in the wars against Napoleon inspired many nobles with a new respect for the peasants' bravery and patriotism. As a consequence, post-Napoleonic elites across Europe made greater efforts than had their predecessors to create an emotional bond between themselves and the common people.

In Russia, this development exhibited several peculiarities. The notion of "folk" (*narod*) society was interpreted in light of Russia's eighteenth-century history of Westernization, the weakening influence of the Orthodox Church, the expansion of serfdom, and the absence of significant urbanization: the "folk" hence was defined as a monarchical, communal, Orthodox world of non-Western peasant villagers, whose heyday was situated between the Time of Troubles and the reforms of Peter the Great. (The "folk" tradition was defined variously in different countries: for example, Germans often associated it with the semi-feudal communalism of late medieval towns, while Americans identified it with the individualistic, democratic farmers of the early republic.)[16] This vision of the folk appears repeatedly in the Russian high culture of the early nineteenth century, in such disparate sources as Shishkov's polemical *Treatise on the Old and New Styles of the Russian Language* (1803), Sergei Nikolaevich Glinka's nationalistic journal *The Russian Messenger* (1808–1825), Aleksei Gavrilovich Venetsianov's 1820s paintings of rural life, or Mikhail Ivanovich Glinka's opera *A Life for the Tsar* (1836).

Ideas about Russian national identity, which took shape gradually during the eighteenth century, affected Russian politics in a variety of sometimes contradictory ways. On the one hand, the reigns of Peter III (1761–1762) and Paul I (1796–1801) were discredited among the nobility, and cut short by coups, in part because their oppressive, militaristic authoritarianism was perceived as too "German."[17] On the other hand, when Alexander I and his advisors mooted liberal reforms in 1801–1812, both Karamzin and Derzhavin (leading exponents of, respectively, the New and the Old Style) roundly denounced these efforts as driven by an un-Russian—in this case, French and Polish—spirit of liberalism, while the nationalist writer and statesman Fedor Vasil'evich Rostopchin argued that Russian serfdom was uniquely benign because it reflected the essential benevolence of the national character.[18]

During the reign of Alexander I's brother and successor, Nicholas I (1825–1855), the highly influential minister of education, Count Sergei Semenovich Uvarov, defined the regime's ideology as "Orthodoxy, autocracy, nationality"—in other words, the Orthodox faith (favored over other religions mainly because it was historically Russian, not for theological reasons), the absolute monarchy, and the spirit of the folk.[19] The absolutist implications of this doctrine were not universally accepted by educated Russians, but the underlying premises were widely shared. Not only did the Slavophiles of the 1840s broadly hold this view[20]—even the early socialist Aleksandr Ivanovich Herzen (a Westernizer and vehement critic of the Slavophiles), who denounced Nicholas I's regime as a form of German bureaucratic authoritarianism imposed on the Russian people, nonetheless agreed with the basic assumption that bourgeois capitalism and liberal politics were alien to Russia, that the Russian peasantry lacked the capitalistic impulses of its Western counterparts, and that radical changes were possible in Russia that would be unthinkable elsewhere in Europe.[21] Even though Uvarov was a conservative monarchist, and Herzen a revolutionary socialist, the emerging consensus on what constituted "Russianness" profoundly influenced both of them. This sense of Russia's greatness, its irrationalism, and its vast yet mysterious potential was captured by one of its best-known poets, Fedor Ivanovich Tiutchev, who wrote in 1866 that "The mind cannot grasp Russia / Nor can the common yardstick measure her / She has a stature all her own / All you can do is believe in Russia."

The emerging conception of a Russian identity fostered the belief in a great national destiny and the existence of shared values and behaviors that made all Russians fundamentally alike and different from foreigners. During the second quarter of the nineteenth century, this strengthened educated Russians' sense of kinship with the peasantry and thereby undermined their support for serfdom; while Aleksandr Nikolaevich Radishchev's searing 1790 indictment of serfdom (*A Journey from St. Petersburg to Moscow*) still appealed to nobles to empathize with the serfs on the grounds of their shared *humanity*, in the 1840s Ivan Sergeevich Turgenev's *Hunter's Sketches* went a significant step farther and emphasized the enserfed peasants' inherent *Russianness*. The significance of this shift is apparent when we consider the experience of the United States, which also had a large servile population but where the educated classes developed no comparable sense that their slaves were members of the same American nation and therefore had claims on the respect and solidarity of their fellow Americans.[22] However, the deepening sense of national distinctiveness also encouraged educated Russians after mid-century to think that Russia could dispense with the liberal industrial capitalism that increasingly dominated Western societies, and it made them generally intolerant of the aspirations of their empire's minority nationalities. Thus, key features of post-1850s Russian history—the educated classes' reaching out to the peasantry, the failure of Western-type liberalism to make inroads in Russian public opinion, and the empire's worsening ethnic tensions—were all related to the concept of "Russianness" that had taken shape by the mid-nineteenth century.

RUSSIA'S ROLE IN EUROPE

A third area where the notion of "Russianness" played a role was Russia's relationship with other European powers. Of course, international relations are always influenced by pragmatic considerations—as Great Britain's foreign secretary Lord Palmerston famously declared in 1848: "We have no eternal allies and we have no perpetual enemies. Our interests are eternal and perpetual, and those interests it is our duty to follow."[23] The Russian Empire in the eighteenth century likewise had "eternal and perpetual" interests: hence its abiding rivalry with its neighbors Sweden, Poland, and Turkey, its lasting alliance with their enemy, Austria, and its enmity toward their patron, France. However, ideology helps shape international relations by suggesting ways to interpret one's own and others' long-term interests and strategies. For example, the belief among mid-nineteenth-century German nationalists that Germans could protect themselves against French aggression only by creating their own nation-state was a sweeping ideological vision undergirded by complex beliefs about the two nations' characters and destinies, not merely a response to self-evident facts. As public opinion became increasingly influential in politics in the mid to late eighteenth century, as an ideological split opened up between liberal and conservative states after the Napoleonic Wars, and as states became increasingly identified with their dominant nationality's culture and ethnic identity, the importance of the ideological component in foreign policy steadily increased.

As in so many things, it was Catherine II, ironically a French-speaking, German-born usurper on the Russian throne, who recognized and fostered the deepening sense of Russianness among the elite. She played a crucial role in creating a nationalist ideological framework for Russian foreign policy with her "Greek Project," whose core was the ambition to revive the long-defunct Byzantine Empire, its capital once more in Constantinople, in what was presently the Balkan and Anatolian heartland of the Ottoman Empire. This Greek empire would be ruled by Catherine's grandson (who was therefore given the name Constantine), and would serve as a junior ally of the Russian Empire. The Greek Project linked concepts that had not hitherto been connected in Russian ideology: Russia's *strategic* interest in the Black Sea region; its supposed *religious* mission to liberate the Orthodox Balkan peoples and the city of Constantinople (Orthodoxy's historic capital) from the Muslim Turks; and the novel claim that, as the successor to *medieval* Greco-Byzantine *Christianity*, Russia was somehow also the rightful heir to the *pagan classical* Greek culture that educated Europeans everywhere celebrated as the mother of Western civilization and that predated Byzantium by over six hundred years.[24] (In the nineteenth century, the notion of Russia's *ethnic* kinship with the Slavic Serbs and Bulgarians would be added to this mix.) In pursuing this plan, Catherine hoped to appeal to Russian public opinion, enhance Russian prestige in Europe, and win allies in the Balkans. While the Greek Project itself ultimately failed for military reasons, it helped to foster a Russian nationalist interest in the Balkans that continued when the Russians fought the Ottomans in 1828–1829, 1853–1856 (the Crimean War), and 1877–1878—thereby helping to secure the independence of Greece, Bulgaria, Serbia, and Montenegro—as well as when they entered World War I in defense of Serbia in 1914, and, most recently, vehemently opposed NATO's war against Yugoslavia in 1999.

The second element of a self-consciously "Russian" view of European affairs that we see appearing in the late eighteenth century is hostility to Poland. To be sure, the strategic and religious hostility between Orthodox Russia and Catholic Poland had been a prominent feature of sixteenth- and seventeenth-century European politics, but the relationship had changed fundamentally by the early eighteenth century, when Russia's religious antagonism toward the West dwindled and its power steadily increased while Poland entered a long-term decline. In this context, Poland and Russia were allies in the Great Northern War (1700–1721), and the increasingly feeble Polish state posed no serious threat to Russian security for the remainder of the eighteenth century.

Nevertheless, Catherine II joined Prussia and Austria in partitioning Poland. The partitions created a huge practical problem: how to control the restive Poles and prevent them from supporting Napoleonic France against Russia, as well as the ideological challenge of justifying the complete destruction of a large, sovereign European state, an act that contradicted the most elementary notions of international law. The Russian elite's response was twofold. On the one hand, the authors of poems, plays, novels, and operas depicted the Poles as a devious, pompous, anarchic, arrogant nation that served as a bridgehead for French revolutionary influences and continually sought to harm Russia; Poland's intervention in seventeenth-century Russia's Time of Troubles was frequently recalled, as were intrigues by Polish aristocrats at the Russian court under Catherine II and Alexander I, and the participation of Polish troops in Napoleon's 1812 invasion of Russia.[25] (In his 1870 novel *The History of a Town*, a mordant satire of Russian government set in an imaginary provincial backwater, Mikhail Evgrafovich Saltykov-Shchedrin describes a hilarious, weeklong mini civil war among female pretenders to local power that recalls both the Time of Troubles and eighteenth-century Russian court politics; among the instigators of the mischief are, of course, "Polish conspirators.") Russia itself, by contrast, was depicted as a magnanimous conqueror whose generosity the Poles continually repaid with treachery and rebellion, especially during their uprisings of 1830–1831 and 1863–1864. Once established, this antagonism toward the Poles—whom Russians pointedly excluded from the family of Slavic "brother nations" for which they exhibited such solicitude—remained in place at least until the Romanov monarchy collapsed in 1917.[26]

Finally, a third important ideological current emerged in late eighteenth- to early nineteenth-century Russian thinking about international relations: a moralistic, frequently religious, and usually conservative impulse that was often associated with fantasies about a vast international plot against Russia; the villains of these conspiracy theories at various times included Western governments, Western radicals, Protestants, Jesuits, Jews, and Freemasons, among others. The roots of this way of thinking stretch back to Muscovite ideas about Moscow being the beleaguered Third Rome, but its modern incarnation originated in the late eighteenth century, when Russia's aggressive expansion gave rise simultaneously to grandiose Russian ambitions (e.g., the Greek Project) and growing European fears of Russian power. Russians' sense that envious Europeans were obstructing Russia's imperial destiny fueled the suspicion that Russia was the target of an international conspiracy. These concerns were reinforced by the French Revolution and the Napoleonic Wars, which encouraged the belief that foreign enemies were in league with subversive elements within Russia;[27] in various guises, such conspiracy theories continued to flourish throughout the tsarist and Soviet periods of Russian history and remain widespread even now.

The element of ideological conservatism first becomes prominent in Russian foreign-policy thinking during the brief reign of Paul I (1796–1801). Unlike his mother, Catherine II, who had treated the French Revolution and its international repercussions primarily as a foreign-policy issue, Paul regarded it as a threat to the survival of monarchical society as such. His response was to demand that Russians renounce any aspects of European culture that might encourage ideological sympathy for the revolutionaries, and he was outraged when his British and Austrian allies seemed to place national self-interest ahead of the anti-French crusade during their joint War of the Second Coalition against France in 1798–1799. Paul's son, Alexander I, pursued a more stable foreign policy than his mercurial father, yet he likewise saw his mission as going beyond the defense of specifically Russian interests to include the restoration of "order" in Europe as a whole. To that end, he pursued Napoleon's armies from Moscow all the way to Paris in 1812–1814; persuaded the other powers to join him in a "Holy Alliance" that committed European monarchs to uphold Christian principles in their conduct of domestic and foreign affairs; urged other European states to adopt constitutions after 1815; and considered sending Russian troops to suppress revolutions in Italy in 1820. His successor, Nicholas I, continued this role of "policeman of Europe," though in a more explicitly conservative spirit: thus, he was prepared to send Russian troops in 1830 to prevent Belgium from seceding from the Netherlands, and in 1849 his armies came to the Habsburg Empire's rescue by crushing the rebels in Hungary.

Many educated Russians disapproved of the foreign policies of Paul, Alexander, and Nicholas, whether because they saw no practical benefit to Russia or because they disagreed with their ideological orientation. However, these policies also reflected growing sentiment that Russian society had a unique moral character that ought to find expression in its foreign policy; though there was no consensus on just what policies should embody this "Russianness," it seemed clear that it entailed maintaining Russia's status as a great power and was neither capitalist nor liberal. In various guises—Nicholas I's anti-revolutionary conservatism, the pan-Slavist leanings of his successors (and much of Russian public opinion) until 1917, the revolutionary socialism of the Soviets, and many post-Communist Russians' suspiciousness toward the West—this legacy has lived on from the late eighteenth century to the present.

CONCLUSION

For most of the eighteenth century, Westernizing ideas in Russia were bold and sweeping yet frequently touched only the surface of the everyday world in which most Russians lived, but by the early to mid-nineteenth century, an emerging notion of "Russianness" increasingly formed the basis for institutions, practices, attitudes, and behaviors that gradually spread through society and remained stable for generations, in some cases down to the present. As "Russianness" crystallized into this particular form, it naturally failed to take other forms that would also have been imaginable from the vantage point of the eighteenth century, such as a stronger impetus toward liberal capitalism or a consensus that Russia was an integral part of Western civilization and should aspire to follow the same historical path. The notion of "Russianness" thus helped give stability and cohesiveness to society but discouraged Russians from pursuing what might otherwise have been promising paths of development for their country.

NOTES

1. See, for example: Lindsey Hughes, *Russia in the Age of Peter the Great* (New Haven, Conn.: Yale University Press, 1998), 96, 211–213, 249, 280–288, 388–389, 452–453.

2. The parallel between Peter and Stalin is developed most forcefully in Evgenii Viktorovich Anisimov's *The Reforms of Peter the Great: Progress through Coercion in Russia*, trans. John T. Alexander (Armonk, N.Y.: M. E. Sharpe, 1993).

3. Marc Raeff, *Comprendre l'Ancien régime russe: Etat et société en Russie impériale— essai d'interprétation* (Paris: Editions du Seuil, 1982), 66–68. English translation: *Understanding Imperial Russia: State and Society in the Old Regime*, trans. Arthur Goldhammer (New York: Columbia University Press, 1984).

4. On the importance of public opinion in eighteenth-century Russian politics, see Cynthia Hyla Whittaker, *Russian Monarchy: Eighteenth-Century Rulers and Writers in Political Dialogue* (DeKalb: Northern Illinois University Press, 2003).

5. Viktor Markovich Zhivov, "Kul'turnye reformy v sisteme preobrazovanii Petra I," in *Iz istorii russkoi kul'tury. T. III (XVII–nachalo XVIII veka)*, 2nd ed., ed. A. D. Koshelev (Moscow: Iazyki russkoi kul'tury, 2000), 574–578.

6. Translated into English as *Lycidus; or, The Lover* (London, 1688).

7. Iu. M. Lotman, "Ocherki po istorii russkoi kul'tury XVIII–nachala XIX veka," in *Iz istorii russkoi kul'tury. T. IV (XVIII—nachalo XIX veka)*, 2nd ed., ed. A. D. Koshelev (Moscow: Iazyki russkoi kul'tury, 2000), 97.

8. See, for example, Pavel Miliukov, *Outlines of Russian Culture*, 3 vols. (New York: A. S. Barnes and Company, 1960), 2:19–21.

9. Miliukov, *Outlines of Russian Culture*, 2:20.

10. Arzamas is a small provincial town and, in this case, the subject of a humorous literary allusion.

11. Anthony G. Cross, *N. M. Karamzin: A Study of His Literary Career (1783–1803)* (Carbondale: Southern Illinois University Press, 1971), 223; Alexander M. Martin, *Romantics, Reformers, Reactionaries: Russian Conservative Thought and Politics in the Reign of Alexander I* (DeKalb: Northern Illinois University Press, 1997), 29–31, 113–120, 187–188, passim.

12. On the role of literature in forming a conception of Russian national identity, see Geoffrey Hosking, *Russia: People and Empire* (Cambridge, Mass.: Harvard University Press, 1997), 291–294.

13. Of these memoirs, two are available in English translation: *The Memoirs of Princess Dashkova: Russia in the Time of Catherine the Great*, trans. Kyril Fitzlyon (Durham, N.C.: Duke University Press, 1995); and *Days of a Russian Noblewoman: The Memories of Anna Labzina, 1758–1821*, trans. and ed. Gary Marker and Rachel May (DeKalb: Northern Illinois University Press, 2001).

14. Richard Wortman, *Scenarios of Power: Myth and Ceremony in Russian Monarchy*, 2 vols. (Princeton, N.J.: Princeton University Press, 1995–2000), 1:5–6.

15. On the romantic "discovery" of folk culture (with case studies about Great Britain), see Eric Hobsbawm and Terence Ranger, eds., *The Invention of Tradition* (Cambridge, UK: Cambridge University Press, 1983).

16. Jean-Luc Pinol, *Le monde des villes au XIXe siècle* (Paris: Hachette, 1991), 52; Richard Hofstadter, *The Age of Reform: From Bryan to FDR* (New York: Vintage Books, 1955), 24–25.

17. See, for example, Isabel de Madariaga, *Russia in the Age of Catherine the Great* (New Haven, Conn.: Yale University Press, 1981), 24–25.

18. Martin, *Romantics*, 40, 105; Richard Pipes, *Karamzin's Memoir on Ancient and Modern Russia: A Translation and Analysis* (New York: Atheneum, 1966), 184.

19. Andrei Zorin, *Kormia dvuglavogo orla . . . : Literatura i gosudarstvennaia ideologiia v Rossii v poslednei treti XVIII—pervoi treti XIX veka* (Moscow: Novoe Literaturnoe obozrenie, 2001), 359–368.

20. Andrzej Walicki, *A History of Russian Thought: From the Enlightenment to Marxism*, trans. Hilda Andrews-Rusiecka (Stanford, Calif.: Stanford University Press, 1979), 93–99.

21. Abbott Gleason, *Young Russia: The Genesis of Russian Radicalism in the 1860s* (New York: Viking Press, 1980), 55–56; Martin Malia, *Alexander Herzen and the Birth of Russian Socialism* (New York: Grosset & Dunlap, 1961), 393, 402–403.

22. See Peter Kolchin, *Unfree Labor: American Slavery and Russian Serfdom* (Cambridge, Mass.: Belknap Press of Harvard University Press, 1987), 190–191.

23. *Hansard*, March 1, 1848, col. 122 (cited in www.xrefer.com/entry/249231).

24. Zorin, *Kormia*, 34–37; Franco Venturi, *The End of the Old Regime in Europe, 1768–1776: The First Crisis*, trans. R. Burr Litchfield (Princeton, N.J.: Princeton University Press, 1989), 121.

25. Zorin, *Kormia*, 154–156, 163–167, 173–179.

26. See, for example, the views of Mikhail Nikiforovich Katkov, in Edward C. Thaden, *Conservative Nationalism in Nineteenth-Century Russia* (Seattle: University of Washington Press, 1964), 46–48.

27. See, for example: Zorin, *Kormia*, 67–94, 198–237; Martin, *Romantics*, 100–102, 107, 183, 198.

SUGGESTED READING

Flynn, James T. *The University Reform of Tsar Alexander I, 1802–1835*. Washington, D.C., 1988.

Hartley, Janet M. *Alexander I*. Profiles in Power Series. London, 1994.

Karamzin, Nikolai. *Karamzin's Memoir on Ancient and Modern Russia: A Translation and Analysis*. Translated, edited, and with an introduction by Richard Pipes. Ann Arbor, Mich., 2005.

Lincoln, W. Bruce. *Nicholas I: Emperor and Autocrat of All the Russias*. DeKalb, Ill., 1989.

Martin, Alexander M. *Romantics, Reformers, Reactionaries: Russian Conservative Thought and Politics in the Reign of Alexander I*. DeKalb, Ill., 1997.

Riasanovsky, Nicholas V. *Nicholas I and Official Nationality in Russia, 1825–1855*. Berkeley, Calif., 1959.

Schrader, Abby. *Languages of the Lash: Corporal Punishment and Identity in Imperial Russia*. DeKalb, Ill., 2002.

Treadgold, Donald W. *The West in Russia and China: Religious and Secular Thought in Modern Times.* Vol. 1, *Russia 1472–1917.* Cambridge, UK, 1973.

Walicki, Andrzej. *A History of Russian Thought: From the Enlightenment to Marxism.* Translated by Hilda Andrews-Rusiecka. Stanford, Calif., 1979.

Wirtschafter, Elise Kimerling. *The Play of Ideas in Russian Enlightenment Theater.* DeKalb, Ill., 2003.

8

Starts and Stops

The Development of Official Diplomatic Relations between Russia and the United States

William Benton Whisenhunt

As Russia experienced a type of "Europeanization" begun by Peter the Great (1682–1725), it also expanded its diplomatic and commercial ties to Europe and beyond. Russia's developing relationship with Great Britain proved to be one of its most important and beneficial diplomatic and commercial connections by the time of Catherine the Great (1762–1796). Therefore, by extension, the British American colonies were also growing in importance for Russia. However, the turmoil that turned into the American Revolution (1775–1783) left Russia's official relationship with the rebellious colonies and later the new nation in a precarious position. Russia wanted to honor its traditional relationship with Great Britain, but the United States offered opportunities for Russia that the former could not. The United States desired official recognition from as many nations as possible to secure its fragile position as an independent nation. France had aided the rebellious colonies in the revolution and also extended official recognition, but many nations, including Russia, were hesitant to take such a bold step in the face of the military and commercial strength of Great Britain. This chapter analyzes the difficult and inconsistent development of official and unofficial relations between Russia and the United States, culminating in official recognition by Russia of the United States in 1809 and the establishment of missions in the respective countries.

Many historians claim that the first contact between Russia and America began in 1763, but relations between these two parts of the world began well before this. As early as 1698, Peter the Great met with American colonist William Penn during the emperor's trip to London. They discussed Quakers, religious tolerance, tobacco, and trade. The two certainly did not reach any official agreements, but new commercial relations were established between

Russia and England for tobacco trade.[1] Up to the Seven Years' War (1756–1763), little contact existed between the British American colonies and Russia, but as the war ended, more concrete relations between the two began to appear.

Some of the most profound contacts were between American and Russian natural philosophers. The most famous association was between Benjamin Franklin and Mikhail Lomonosov. Even though the two never met and never had direct correspondence, they were familiar with each other's work. Clearly, the letters Franklin and Ezra Stiles (American clergyman and scholar) drafted to Lomonosov illuminated the nature of their interests, which included electricity, temperature, and trade routes between Siberia and North America. However, Lomonosov's death in 1765 prevented a closer connection between the Russian and American scholars from being developed.[2] As the American Revolution approached, the First Turkish War and the rebellion led by Emilian Pugachev preoccupied the attention of Catherine II. By the time Catherine could turn her attention to the situation in America, the conflict had already begun. Pressing commercial and naval issues with Great Britain contributed to the empress's reluctance to establish direct ties with the American colonies. It was no secret that while the empress was interested in enlightened ideas, she was not necessarily sympathetic to the colonists' cause nor did she feel threatened by it as she would later by the French Revolution.[3]

During the American Revolutionary War several Russians supported the colonists' cause, even though Catherine II's official stance was neutrality. Some of these Russians played minor roles in the revolution, though very little record remains of the encounters. However, Fedor Karzhavin (a Russian trader) spent more than a decade in America, and it is widely believed that he had significant contacts with such prominent American revolutionaries as John Hancock and James Madison. Upon his arrival in the 1770s, he offered his services as a translator of French, but he was not used immediately. He spent much of his time in America writing about his travels, associating with as many notable Americans as possible, and working as a translator at the French consulate.[4]

The American Revolution placed great strain on relations between Russia and Great Britain. As early as 1775, King George III of Great Britain asked Catherine for help in suppressing the American rebels, but the Russian empress refused to send the twenty thousand troops to Canada as requested by George III. Catherine further reduced the possibility of aiding the British when she issued the Declaration of Armed Neutrality in 1780, and she even offered to serve as a mediator between the two sides. Catherine noted that she did not have an ample supply of soldiers to deal with Russia's military concerns with Sweden and Poland. Also, many of Russia's troops were suffering from fatigue after a lengthy war with the Turks. She concluded that without speaking of the disadvantages of employing so considerable a corps in another hemisphere, living there under a power almost unknown to it, and deprived almost entirely of all correspondence with its sovereign, my own assurance of my peace, which has cost me so many efforts to acquire, absolutely requires that I not strip myself so soon of so considerable a part of my forces.[5]

In the later days of the American Revolution, colonial officials sought support and recognition from more than just France. American officials periodically debated the prudence of seeking at most recognition and at least support from Catherine for their independence movement from Great Britain, which was still allied with Russia. In the early 1780s, the American diplomatic mission in France sent Francis Dana of Massachusetts to St. Petersburg with the charge of establishing some sort of relationship with Russia. The nature of the ties to be forged by the Americans was unclear. Dana received cautionary and contradictory instructions from the American officials in France about his status and duties in Russia. Dana traveled privately to "test the waters." Catherine, however, due to the importance of Russia's relationship with Great Britain, could not and would not recognize Dana as an official American representative, let alone support the American independence movement.[6]

It was evident that many in the Russian government were concerned with the commercial implications that an association with America would bring them. Dana tried to convince several Russian officials that an association with America would only enhance Russia's commercial prospects. Dana proved to be a controversial figure during his brief tenure in Russia. He was sent there with the knowledge that he would quite likely not receive official recognition; however, he was charged with the duty of establishing some kind of relationship. Many American officials criticized Dana for making too many pleading, and direct, advances to Catherine for recognition and thereby jeopardizing the possibility of a future relationship with Russia. Dana was quickly recalled as the American Revolutionary War officially ended in 1783, without having established a clear formal or informal relationship with Russia. Even before the war ended, however, high officials in the Russian government like Ivan Osterman were open to discussing a more formal relationship with the new United States.[7]

During the 1780s, the relationship between the two nations continued to develop in starts and stops, although there was no official diplomatic recognition. Some of the encounters were in naval and commercial developments in the Pacific. One of the most interesting involvements came at the end of the 1780s when former Revolutionary War hero John Paul Jones received a commission in the Russian navy. In late 1787, Thomas Jefferson and the Russian envoy in Paris, I. M. Simolin, arranged for Jones to enter service in the Russian navy. The official order came from Catherine II in February 1788, and Jones arrived in Russia in April of that year at the rank of rear admiral (*kontraadmiral*). Even though Jones and Simolin disagreed initially about his rank, the agreement was reached and Catherine, not wanting to damage Russia's ties to Great Britain, but also more than willing to needle the British, was happy to have an anti-British servitor on hand. He was well received by Catherine in St. Petersburg and Russian society seemed to be intrigued by him. Unlike his predecessor, Francis Dana, Jones was outspoken and bold in Russia. He spoke in support of the Declaration of Armed Neutrality and gave Catherine a copy of the American Constitution. Jones, however, also made inappropriate personal statements about the empress. He wrote to the Marquis de Lafayette, of American Revolutionary fame, that "If her Imperial Majesty were not the Empress of all Russia (not to mention her other great qualities), in my eyes she would have been the most amiable of all women."[8]

By June 1788, Jones was leading a naval operation in the Dnieper Liman under the command of Prince Charles Nassau-Siegen, a French naval adventurer. The two knew each other from 1778 when Jones refused to serve under Nassau-Siegen during the American Revolution. The initial battles of June 1788 went well for Jones, but much of the credit went to the Frenchman. Jones criticized Nassau-Siegen's role in the battles with the Turks. Even though Nassau-Siegen's role was publicly lauded, Jones gave credit to himself and his men for defeating the Turks and saving the war effort. Jones took his criticism of Nassau-Seigen higher, to Grigorii Potemkin, who did not receive such bold violations of protocol well. Jones received the Order of St. Anne, but Nassau-Seigen received the Cross of St. Sergei, the highest military honor in Russia. Potemkin dismissed Jones's criticism as being inappropriate, but the American decided to launch new criticisms of Potemkin himself to one of his subordinates, General Alexander V. Suvorov. The two men had developed a friendship, and the Russian general showed some sympathy for Jones's views, but was wise enough not to express them publicly. Soon after this conflict began, Potemkin asked Catherine to remove Jones from his duties in the south. By December 1788, Jones was back in St. Petersburg, though he had no official assignment. However, he outlined in early 1789 a plan for an alliance between Russia and the United States that would be applied "in the Mediterranean against the attacks on commercial shipping by the Barbary corsairs."[9] This proposal did not receive serious attention, however, no doubt because of Jones's abrasive personality and the incident in which he was involved later that year.

On March 30, 1789, Jones allegedly raped a twelve-year-old German butter peddler in his home. On April 2, 1789, the girl, Katerina Stepanova Koltzwarthen, submitted a statement to the head of St. Petersburg police, Nikolai Ryleev, claiming that she had been called to the house of a man she did not know to sell him some butter. She was ushered into the master's room by a manservant and was left alone there. She sold the man butter, but when she tried to leave the man, "in a white uniform, in front of which was embroidered in gold and decorated with a crimson ribbon and a gold star," grabbed her and stuffed a handkerchief in her mouth that cut her lip. Then he carried her into a different room and raped her "until she lost her memory." The girl claimed that the man, who spoke Russian very badly, threatened more violence if she told anyone. She left and told no one of the incident until she arrived home. This incident swirled out of control during the next few weeks. Jones was questioned repeatedly, but charges were never brought against him, despite the fact that he appeared quite guilty.[10]

In the end, the allegation against Jones was neither tried in court nor proven. Ultimately for Russian-American relations, the truth of the allegation itself was not important, though the incident might have temporarily damaged relations between the two countries. By the 1790s, however, Russia had developed a strong trading relationship with the United States. The Jones affair left the admiral in disgrace as he left the country in the summer of 1789 to join the revolutionary forces in France, but it did not seem to undermine the relationship between the two nations. Between 1790 and 1807 trade relations expanded between the two countries by more than five times. In 1795, John Miller Russell arrived in St. Petersburg to take up the post of American consul in Russia. Catherine II refused to recognize him because his appointment had not been approved by England. This was an odd decision, considering American independence had been achieved more than a decade earlier. This failure was the first serious attempt at gaining official recognition since Francis Dana, but the results were much the same. Nonetheless, American ships continued to visit the port of St. Petersburg, even though official relations remained ambiguous.[11]

During the 1790s, several prominent and lesser-known Russians visited the United States. In particular, naval officer Iurii Lisianskii traveled and wrote about his time in America. His travel narrative was simple, blunt, and generally positive about the United States. He noted that "many see Philadelphia's lack of hospitality as coming from the Quakers, who make up a large part of the city. But, on the contrary, I found that these people are much more courteous to foreigners than others."[12] In the last years of the 1790s, the new emperor, Paul I, and American officials found common ground in commercial interests in the Mediterranean and an emerging fear of potential French aggression. Sporadic discussions took place under Paul, but the chaotic nature of his government, which in any case was rather attenuated in duration (1796–1801), did not produce any concrete agreements or resolutions with the Americans.[13]

At the turn of the century, relations between the United States and Russia were intertwined with British commercial interests, fears of radicalism in France, and the ambition of Napoleon Bonaparte. By 1801, two dramatic changes helped shape the future of relations. First, court servitors and supporters of his son, Alexander I, deposed and assassinated Paul I. Second, Thomas Jefferson took office as president of the United States after winning the contentious and controversial election of 1800. Even though Levett Harris of Philadelphia was the first official American consul in Russia, the direct and indirect personal relationship between Alexander I and Jefferson provided much of the foundation for the furthering of Russian-American relations. These two leaders exchanged letters on such matters as constitutionalism and land settlement. Such issues were timely for both countries. The United States was testing and amending its new constitutional system and trying to settle its newly acquired (1803) Louisiana Territory. Alexander I and his close group of young advisors, known as the Unofficial Committee, were entertaining ideas of constitutionalism. They were also trying to incorporate vast amounts of new land as a result of successful conquests in the south.[14]

It was evident that the unofficial relationship that developed between Alexander and Jefferson helped open the way for the establishment of official diplomatic recognition. It was also evident that the activity of the Russian-American Company, chartered in 1799 by Paul I, had created numerous commercial and cultural contacts between the two expanding countries in the Pacific. Both countries were interested in furthering trade in the Pacific, settling more territory, trading with China, and limiting British influence generally. Even though the two countries agreed on these ideas, however vaguely drawn, there were still points of contention between Russians and Americans. One of these areas was each country's interaction with the native peoples of the Pacific. The Russians were particularly upset about the sale of liquor and guns to many native groups. In addition, the Russians and the Americans were at odds over supplies. Russians were reliant on American ships, primarily from Boston, for supplies, while American ships often used Russian ports for transportation. After 1803, and the purchase of the Louisiana Territory, the tensions continued to rise over land. Americans were moving westward and Russians eastward, with the latter reaching the port of San Francisco in 1806 and establishing Fort Ross about sixty miles to the north in 1812.[15] Despite these tensions, or perhaps because of them, Russia and the United States agreed to establish official relations and to the exchange of diplomats. In 1809, the first American minister to Russia, John Quincy Adams, arrived in St. Petersburg. In the same year, Andrei Dashkov arrived in Philadelphia to head the first Russian diplomatic mission to America.

THE AMERICAN MISSION IN RUSSIA

William Short had been nominated to the post of minister to Russia by the outgoing president, Thomas Jefferson, in early 1809, but his rejection by the Senate left the position in the hands of the future president, James Madison, who then appointed John Quincy Adams to the position. In July 1809, Adams received a cordial letter from Andrei Dashkov, head of the Russian mission in America, just before he left for his post in St. Petersburg.

Dashkov assured Adams that he was confident that good commercial and diplomatic ties could be developed between the two nations.[16] Once in Russia, Adams faced internal and external problems. First, partisan fighting over the election of James Madison in 1808 and the selection of Adams had left some in the American mission uneasy about their positions in Russia. One official in the mission noted how solemn and distant Adams was, with others noting that he was outright aloof, especially during social gatherings. Second, to add to Adams's melancholy disposition, after two years in St. Petersburg, his infant daughter died.[17]

Not all associations between Russians and Americans were cold and distant. Many American traders, merchants, and visitors had been resident in Russia for many years. Most of the Americans in St. Petersburg mingled with Russian society through the auspices of the English Club. Established in 1770, the English Club provided a lively forum for resident foreigners and interested locals to discuss social, commercial, and political issues. The relationship between Russians and Americans in St. Petersburg at the time has been characterized thusly:

> The Russians tolerated well the American traits of frugality, plainness of dress, and smattering of the court language, French, and many even seemed to enjoy the opportunity to be at ease with friendly Americans at social occasions and to practice their English. In turn, Americans were impressed with the formality, luxury, and ostentation of Russian society, but did not find it particularly to their liking.[18]

Clearly, the beginning of official relations and the first American mission in Russia began with complications. One of the most difficult periods was when Europe, Russia, and the United States were engulfed in conflicts between 1812 and 1815. Despite the fact that the two nations were on opposing sides in the war(s), relations remained as close as they could as Washington, D.C., was captured and burned by the British and as Moscow suffered the same fate at the hand of French emperor Napoleon Bonaparte. After four years of difficult political, personal, and cultural relations, Adams summed up his feelings by writing that "[we] have formed no social attachments that can make us regret the Country; and I have no employments here which even afford the consolation of being useful to my own."[19] The difficulties faced by the American mission were serious, but the problems faced by the first Russian mission in America nearly jeopardized the future of relations between the two nations.

THE RUSSIAN MISSION IN AMERICA

The Russian diplomatic mission arrived in the United States in July 1809 under the leadership of Andrei Dashkov. He, like Adams, was not the original choice for the position. He was appointed to serve in Philadelphia, which was the diplomatic location that oversaw the Russian delegations in Boston, Charleston, and other cities. Ironically, there was not a diplomatic contingent in Washington, D.C. Most of Dashkov's early official interaction with the American government concerned trade in the Pacific. While commerce was a primary interest for both countries, personal, legal, and cultural difficulties persisted here as they did in St. Petersburg.

Dashkov's overall duties entailed oversight of the Russian consuls in other cities. One consul in Boston, Aleksei G. Evstaf'ev, gave a toast at a public occasion in 1813 in which he endorsed the policies of the Federalist opposition to the current president, James Madison. American officials openly criticized Evstaf'ev and petitioned Dashkov for an explanation and a redress of grievances. Apparently, the Boston consul had criticized America's policy in the War of 1812 and had been positive toward the British, with whom the United States was still at war. Evstaf'ev explained that he meant no offense and that he was actually supporting "the politics and morals of Boston." However, secretary of state James Monroe noted that the statement was offensive and that "the impropriety of it is the more evident when it is compared with the spirit of impartiality with which the Emperor, his Sovereign, has offered his mediation between the United States and Great Britain."[20] Only a year into the mission, armed violence broke out between some citizens of Philadelphia and the Russian diplomatic mission. In 1810, Dashkov displayed imperial symbols and crowns in the windows of his residence to mark the anniversary of Alexander I's coronation. This drew criticism from some Philadelphians who passed by his home. At a social gathering with much of the Philadelphia elite in attendance, a mob arrived and demanded the removal of the imperial symbols. As Dashkov was removing the symbols, someone in the mob fired two shots through the windows. No one was hurt, and Dashkov was later satisfied that authorities in Philadelphia were investigating the matter. American officials were more embarrassed by the incident than Dashkov was outraged.[21]

Despite some tension between the diplomatic missions in each country, there were also positive political and cultural relations. Pavel P. Svin'in's (1787–1839) arrival as a secretary and translator for the Philadelphia mission in 1811 opened a more extensive and detailed dialogue between the two nations. Svin'in spent about twenty months in America, but because he had few official duties, he took the time to travel widely (this included journeying from Maine to Niagara Falls to Virginia). He saw more of America than most Americans had seen at that time. He left America in 1813 in order to escort exiled French general Jean Victor Moreau back to Europe. However, he left three important works detailing his time in America. While residing in Philadelphia, he published—in English—*Sketches of St. Petersburg and Moscow* in order to give Americans a glimpse of what Russians were like. He illustrated the book with sketches and gave Americans much information about Russian customs, traditions, cities, and the like. Soon after he left the United States he published *An Attempt at a Picturesque Journey across North America*. This travel narrative discusses, among other things, the American political system, slavery, religion, Niagara Falls, and steamboats. He also painted more than fifty watercolors that depicted many of the scenes described in the narrative. This is the earliest known account of America by a Russian official, but it opened a greater cultural connection than it did a diplomatic one.[22]

Not long after, a serious incident further jeopardized Russian-American relations. In November 1815, a Russian consul in Philadelphia, Nikolai Kozlov, was accused of raping a twelve-year-old servant girl in his home. He was immediately arrested and held and since the girl swore an oath, he was, in accordance with the laws of the time, sent to jail without the possibility of bail. Dashkov immediately came to his defense by stating that a foreign diplomat could not be charged and should be released. This request was not granted, but they did convince the judge that rape was not a crime tried by federal courts, so Kozlov was released by the summer of 1816. Even though the charges were dropped, he was not determined to be innocent, nor did Dashkov let things lie. Dashkov sent inflammatory letters on the matter with the desire to clear Kozlov's name and character. He received little response from American officials in Philadelphia, but American officials like Levett Harris in St. Petersburg were working to remedy the situation. Frustrated by the perceived lack of cooperation in Philadelphia, Dashkov broke official diplomatic relations with the United States by the fall of 1816, which, of course, made it extremely difficult to negotiate in St. Petersburg. Earlier, American officials had issued charges against Evstaf'ev in Boston for withholding British property during the war. Clearly, relations were at a breaking point. For weeks, Harris and Russian officials in St. Petersburg attempted to resolve the dispute. The Americans held firm to the notion that Kozlov had committed an offense and should be held accountable. Russian officials felt that the Americans had not followed "the law of nations" (basically forgiveness of offenses by diplomats) and had insulted Kozlov and Alexander I by this treatment. Many historians believe that in a different time, this conflict might have brought the two nations to war. However, the agreement reached by the end of 1816 placed the primary blame on Kozlov. Both nations appointed new diplomats, and the Russians moved their primary diplomatic mission to Washington, D.C.[23] The stark difference in how these respective events were addressed in the United States and Russia reveals the emerging sense of legality in each country. The United States, especially, broke new ground in foreign relations and in working with foreign residents on American soil. Events that appeared to threaten Russian-American relations, after many decades of sporadic contact, now seemed to introduce a new era in relations between the two nations.

The establishment of official Russian-American relations did not come easily. The process of starting and stopping periodically jeopardized the creation of a lasting relationship. Despite the difficulties, both countries recognized the mutual benefit in having official diplomatic, commercial, and cultural relations with the other. The number of travel accounts, especially of Americans in Russia, greatly increased from the 1850s through the end of the century. Although through the nineteenth century, Russia and the United States did not become allies or even primary trading partners, the official relationship helped open up greater travel for a number of curious Russians in America and Americans in Russia.

NOTES

1. Norman E. Saul, *Distant Friends: The United States and Russia, 1763–1867* (Lawrence: University Press of Kansas, 1991), 1–2; Eufrosina Dvoichenko-Markov, "William Penn and Peter the Great," *Transactions of the American Philosophical Society* 97, no. 1 (February 1953): 12–20; Jacob M. Price, "The Tobacco Adventure to Russia: Enterprise, Politics, and Diplomacy in Quest for a Northern Market for English Colonial Tobacco, 1676–1722," *Transactions of the American Philosophical Society*, n.s., 51, no. 1 (1961): 19–27.

2. Eufrosina Dvoichenko-Markov, "Benjamin Franklin, the American Philosophical Society, and the Russian Academy of Science," *Proceedings of the American Philosophical Society* 96, no. 3 (August 1947): 250–258; Nina N. Bashkina et al., eds., *The United States and Russia: The Beginning of Relations, 1765–1815* (Washington, D.C.: United States Department of State, 1980), 3–10. This source will hereafter be referred to as *USR*.

3. David M. Griffiths, "Catherine the Great, the British Opposition, and the American Revolution," in *The American Revolution and "A Candid World,"* ed. Lawrence S. Kaplan (Kent, Ohio: Kent State University Press, 1977), 85–110.

4. Saul, *Distant Friends*, 7–10; A. I. Startsev, "F. V. Karzhavin i ego amerikanskoe puteshestvie," *Istoriia SSSR* 3 (1960): 132–139.

5. "Letter from Catherine II to George III, September 23/October 4, 1775," in *USR*, 34.

6. Saul, *Distant Friends*, 13–18; David M. Griffiths, "American Commercial Diplomacy in Russia, 1780 to 1783," *William and Mary Quarterly* 27, no. 3 (July 1970): 338.

7. David M. Griffiths, "Rise and Fall of the Northern System: Court Politics and Foreign Policy in the First Half of Catherine II's Reign," *Canadian Slavic Studies* 4, no. 3 (Fall 1970): 547–569.

8. Quoted in Nikolai Bolkhovitinov, *The Beginnings of Russian-American Relations, 1775–1815* (Cambridge, Mass.: Harvard University Press, 1975), 149; Isabel de Madariaga, *Russia in the Age of Catherine the Great* (New Haven, Conn.: Yale Univer-

sity Press, 1981), 383–386; "From a Letter of John Paul Jones to the Marquis de Lafayette, June 15/26, 1788," in *USR*, 254–256.

9. Saul, *Distant Friends*, 24; "Letter from John Paul Jones to Ivan A. Osterman, January 31/February 11, 1789," in *USR*, 264–266.

10. Lincoln Lorenz, *The Admiral and the Empress: John Paul Jones and Catherine the Great* (New York: Bookman Associates, 1954), 123–124.

11. Saul, *Distant Friends*, 28; Bolkhovitinov, *Beginnings*, 107.

12. "From the Diary of Lieutenant Iurii F. Lisianskii," in *USR*, 301.

13. Norman Saul, *Russia and the Mediterranean, 1797–1807* (Chicago: University of Chicago Press, 1970), 61–77.

14. V. M. Kozlovskii, "Tsar' Aleksandr I i Dzhefferson: Po arkhivnym dannym," *Russkaia mysl'* 10 (1910): 79–95; N. Hans, "Tsar Alexander and Jefferson: Unpublished Correspondence," *Slavonic and East European Review* 32 (December 1953): 215–225.

15. See Edward Mornin, *Through Alien Eyes: The Visit of the Russian Ship* Rurik *to San Francisco in 1816 and the Men behind the Visit* (Oxford: Peter Lang, 2002).

16. "Letter from Andrei Ia. Dashkov to the United States Minister-Designate to Russia, John Quincy Adams," in *USR*, 575.

17. Saul, *Distant Friends*, 61–63.

18. Saul, *Distant Friends*, 62.

19. Quoted in Saul, *Distant Friends*, 63.

20. "Letter from Russian Consul at Boston, Aleksei G. Evstaf'ev, to Andrei Ia. Dashkov," in *USR*, 953; "Note from James Monroe to Andrei Dashkov," in *USR*, 961.

21. "From a Letter to Charles Jared Ingersoll to Rufus King," in *USR*, 644–645; Saul, *Distant Friends*, 65–66.

22. Marina Swoboda and William Benton Whisenhunt, *A Russian Paints America: Pavel P. Svin'in's Impressions of Early Nineteenth Century America* (Montreal-Kingston: McGill-Queen's University Press, forthcoming).

23. John C. Hildt, *Early Diplomatic Negotiations of the United States with Russia* (Baltimore: Johns Hopkins University Press, 1906), 91–107.

SUGGESTED READING

Bolkhovitinov, Nikolai. *The Beginnings of Russian-American Relations, 1775–1815.* Cambridge, Mass., 1975.

Griffiths, David M. "American Commercial Diplomacy in Russia, 1780–1783." *William and Mary Quarterly* 27, no. 3 (July 1970): 379–410.

——. "Rise and Fall of the Northern System: Court Politics and Foreign Policy in the First Half of Catherine II's Reign." *Canadian-American Slavic Studies* 4, no. 3 (Fall 1970): 547–569.

Hildt, John C. *Early Diplomatic Negotiations of the United States with Russia.* Baltimore, 1906.

Madariaga, Isabel de. *Britain, Russia, and the Armed Neutrality of 1780.* New Haven, Conn., 1962.

Prince, Sue Ann, ed. *The Princess & The Patriot: Ekaterina Dashkova, Benjamin Franklin, and the Age of Enlightenment.* Philadelphia, 2006.

Saul, Norman E. *Concord and Conflict: The United States and Russia, 1867–1914.* Lawrence, Kans., 1996.

———. *Distant Friends: The United States and Russia, 1763–1867.* Lawrence, Kans., 1991.

———, and Richard D. McKinzie, eds. *Russian-American Dialogue on Cultural Relations.* Columbia, Mo., 1997.

Swoboda, Marina, and William Benton Whisenhunt. *A Russian Paints America: Pavel P. Svin'in's Impressions of Early Nineteenth Century America.* Montreal-Kingston, forthcoming.

9

The Decembrist Pavel Pestel and the Roots of Russian Republicanism

Patrick O'Meara

THE IDEA OF A RUSSIAN REPUBLIC

In February 1917 the streets of Petrograd (St. Petersburg) erupted with the most serious rioting since January 1905, culminating with the abdication of Tsar Nicholas II. Thus came to an end the Romanov dynasty, which had only four years earlier celebrated its three hundredth anniversary. The resultant power vacuum was now filled with revolutionary organizations and political parties championing a variety of models for the future government of Russia. These ranged from a constitutional monarchy to a liberal parliamentary democracy to a socialist republic. The struggle continued until October, when Vladimir Lenin and his Bolshevik party seized the initiative, stormed the Winter Palace, the stronghold of the Provisional Government, and proclaimed a republic. It was to be based on workers' and peasants' soviets (councils) and shaped by the Communist ideology of Karl Marx and Friedrich Engels as refracted through Lenin's Russifying lens.

This historical watershed was the culmination of the Russian revolutionary movement which had effectively started with the assassination of Tsar Alexander II in 1881, but whose intellectual and ideological roots can be traced back to the Decembrist movement in the post-Napoleonic era of the reign of Tsar Alexander I. Republicanism as a system of government had a number of international precedents. The best known of them were the short-lived English Commonwealth under the Great Protector Oliver Cromwell following the execution of King Charles I in 1649, the confederated republic established in the United States after the Declaration of Independence of 1776 and the American Revolution, and the Directory, which replaced the House of Bourbon after the French Revolution of 1789. Nor

121

was the idea of a Russian republic unknown before Lenin, though, to be sure, precedents lay in the distant past. It had been the basis of the political system of medieval Novgorod until that city-state's conquest by Ivan III of Moscow in 1478. Republicanism subsequently emerged in Russia, albeit only vaguely, in the late eighteenth century in the Sentimentalist indignation of Alexander Radishchev's writings. However, it was first properly developed as a real political and ideological goal only around 1816 in the secret societies of the Decembrist movement, chiefly by Pavel Pestel, Russia's first republican.

A Russian republic was as precocious and improbable an aspiration in the early nineteenth century as it would be in the early twentieth. The French Revolution, it is true, had shown that the unthinkable could happen and that old regimes could be swept away. In early nineteenth-century Russia, however, the tsarist regime's immunity from such elemental upheaval seemed assured, particularly as the relatively youthful Tsar Alexander I (1801–1825) appeared willing to move with the times. He commissioned projects for constitutional reform which were drafted by prominent ministers Mikhail Speranskii and Nikolai Novosiltsev. Following Napoleon's defeat and the shattering of his continental system, Alexander showed his determination to rebuild Europe in harmonious holy alliance with the emperors of Austria and Prussia. Further evidence of his understanding of modern politics and society came with the constitutional arrangements he introduced to two nation-states within his Russian Empire: Poland (1815) and Finland (1818). The impact of these measures on Russia itself, however, was negligible. If Alexander ever really had any serious intentions of fundamental reform on his accession in 1801, then by 1815 he had abandoned them. Yet, increasingly, young Russians dreamed of a new order in Russia, too, and one which would see an end to traditional autocratic despotism and the slavery of the enserfed peasantry.

THE DECEMBRIST SECRET SOCIETIES

The Russian Empire at the beginning of the nineteenth century extended from the Vistula and eastern Poland, across the whole of northeast Asia to the Bering Strait and beyond to Alaska. In the space of fifty years from around the time of the French Revolution, the population of this huge landmass doubled from 30 million to almost 60 million. In 1812 it stood at 41 million, compared to 18 million in Great Britain and 8 million in the United States.[1] Yet for all its size and large population, Russia was economically underdeveloped. This was largely due to its political and social structures. The peasantry accounted for some 96 percent of the total population, with over half being privately owned serfs. It was the enserfed peasantry which formed the basis of Russia's rigid social structure, enfeebled her economy, and stifled the development of her still-primitive political culture.

Nevertheless, Tsar Alexander I's accession prompted widespread confidence in imminent reform. The tsar's political course, however, soon proved hesitant and conservative. It eventually provoked the impatience and disappointment that were among the main sources of the growth from 1816 of the Decembrist secret societies. Their activity culminated in the first armed political rising in Russian history, named after the month in which it occurred in St. Petersburg in 1825. The Decembrist movement's secret societies were modeled on Masonic lodges and officers' dining clubs. The first of these, the Union of Salvation, was led by young army officers Sergei Trubetskoi, Nikita Muraviev, and his cousin Alexander Muraviev. Recently returned from the post-Napoleonic European wars of liberation, they were typical of the patriotic and idealistic sons of the gentry, anxious to see Russian politics and society modernized. In 1818 a new Decembrist society, the Union of Welfare, recruited more than two hundred members. From it in 1821 there emerged the Northern Society, based on the guards' regiments in St. Petersburg, and the Southern Society, at the Second Army's Tulchin garrison in Ukraine.

Both the Northern and the Southern societies developed constitutional projects for a new Russia based on the abolition of tsarist autocracy and serfdom. The acknowledged leader of the Southern Society, Colonel Pavel Pestel, was the author of *Russian Justice* (*Russkaya pravda*), which envisaged a dictatorial revolutionary government as the first step toward a strictly centralized Russian republic. However, a very different future for Russia was set out in the constitution of the leader of the Northern Society, Nikita Muraviev. While this document proposed the convocation of a constituent assembly to determine the future institutions of state, it actually already defined Russia as a constitutional monarchy with a federal structure similar to that of the United States. Russia was to be divided into fifteen states regulated by a state duma (assembly) and an elected chamber of peoples' deputies.

The Northern and Southern societies' negotiations for joint action made negligible progress, even though in St. Petersburg a small "cell" of Southern Society members mediated between their respective directorates. Nor was disagreement between Pestel and Muraviev over their visions for Russia's future settled by the former's visit to St. Petersburg in 1824. They agreed only to meet again in 1826, and that the signal for action would be the death of Tsar Alexander, who in 1824 was still only forty-five years old. Meanwhile, from 1822 to 1825 the Southern Society's directors convened at the January (Epiphany) trade fair in Kiev. It was at the 1823 "congress" that Pestel first presented his republican platform, placed regicide firmly on the Decembrists' agenda, and outlined his revolutionary plans for the transformation of Russia's rural economy.

Inexorably, rumors began to spread and spies informed the authorities of the secret societies and named many of their members. However, it was not betrayal alone that ended the nine-year-old movement, but the unexpected death of Tsar Alexander on November 19, 1825. It was assumed that he would be succeeded by the next in line, his brother Constantine. But in 1823, at Alexander's insistence, Constantine had renounced his right of succession in favor of their younger brother, Nicholas. The latter, however, was never informed of this, with the result that, on hearing the news of Alexander's death, he and Constantine immediately swore allegiance to each other.

THE DECEMBRISTS' CHALLENGE

The succession crisis which produced two apparent emperors but no actual ruler precipitated a two-week interregnum during which the Decembrists in St. Petersburg made their move. The death of Alexander I was, after all, the agreed signal for action. They discovered that the ruling elite had resolved the crisis by deciding that all regiments in St. Petersburg were to swear the traditional loyal oath to Nicholas rather than Constantine on December 14. By that afternoon, three thousand troops commanded by thirty officers and directed by six civilians, conspirators all, were assembled on Senate Square awaiting further instructions. Nicholas and his generals at first nervously imagined there to be four times the actual number of mutinous troops. Indeed, it seemed likely that the rebels might be about to seize the Winter Palace and arrest the imperial family. However, their elected commander, Colonel Prince Sergei Trubetskoi, failed to appear, thus enabling Nicholas to take advantage of the insurgents' confusion. A few salvos of artillery scattered them before the early onset of darkness. There followed a wave of arrests and on December 17 the Investigating Committee into the Decembrist Affair convened for the first of 145 sessions over the next six months. January 1826 saw the failure of the second Decembrist uprising, that of the Chernigov Regiment in Ukraine, led by Sergei Muraviev-Apostol and Mikhail Bestuzhev-Ryumin. It held out for six days but was eventually overwhelmed by troops loyal to Tsar Nicholas. Pavel Pestel played no part in either uprising, having been escorted from Tulchin to St. Petersburg on December 26 following his arrest two weeks earlier. In June 1826, the Investigating Committee passed its findings in respect to 121 of the 579 prisoners it had interrogated to the Supreme Criminal Court, which imposed sentences of hard labor and Siberian exile according to eleven categories of culpability. Five prisoners, placed "beyond category," were sentenced to death and hanged on July 13, 1826. Among them was Pavel Pestel.

The Decembrists are held to be the founding fathers and first martyrs of the Russian revolutionary movement because they combined an unprecedented ideologically based assault on autocracy and serfdom with the resolve to achieve their goals by force. The executions and the protracted sufferings of those exiled to Siberian lead mines only added to their aura of martyrdom. The Decembrists' failure, however, also cost Russia dearly. As well as sacrificing many of her brightest and best sons to the scaffold and Siberia, the Decembrist conspiracy impelled Tsar Nicholas I along a reactionary path from which for thirty years he never veered. It thus accelerated the "parting of the ways" between the court of Nicholas I and many members of the nobility, whose loyalty had hitherto been unwavering but who now felt increasingly alienated. Autocratic power in Russia became more than ever suspicious of proposals for modernization and change. Paradoxically, therefore, the result was to delay long-overdue social reforms, such as the abolition of serfdom, for which the Decembrists, and Pestel in particular, had agitated, for over forty years before Alexander II at last decreed it in 1861.

PESTEL'S REPUBLICAN MANIFESTO: RUSSIAN JUSTICE

Although Pestel never completed it, *Russian Justice* was the most outstandingly original and radical of the Decembrists' various projects and manifestos. Only the Northern Society's relatively modest proposal for a constitutional monarchy and a federated Russian state, drafted by Nikita Muraviev, came anywhere close to matching the importance and stature of Pestel's manifesto. The completed sections dealt with the territorial extent of the Russian republic, its constituent nationalities, the class composition of its population, and the administrative structure of postrevolutionary Russia. It may well be that Pestel himself destroyed some of the most important sections of *Russian Justice* on the eve of his arrest, as he claimed to the Investigating Committee, or that subsequently his friends in the Southern Society did so.

Pestel worked on versions of *Russian Justice* for over seven years, from 1817 to the winter of 1824–1825. Some key ideas, such as the ending of serfdom and autocracy, were present from the outset. But, crucially, the type of state governance he proposed changed from a constitutional monarchy to a republic as his own political ideas developed. Scholars have identified two versions of *Russian Justice*, the first dating from 1822–1823 and the second from 1824 to early 1825. Strictly speaking, *Russian Justice* is not just a constitutional project but a directive for the future provisional revolutionary government's implementation of the Decembrists' Russian revolution. Pestel referred to it himself variously as his "plan for the constitution" or "instruction" (*nakaz*), thus invoking the famous precedent of Catherine the Great's *nakaz* to the Legislative Assembly of 1767. In 1824 he named *Russian Justice* after the Kievan legislative document initiated in the eleventh century by Yaroslav the Wise, which had marked the first attempt in Russian history to draw up a regulating code of law.

Pestel's political thought was influenced by such Western European thinkers as Jeremy Bentham, Saint-Simon, and Destutt de Tracy. He was further impressed by the brutal pragmatism of the Jacobins in the French Revolution, especially Robespierre. Pestel's vigorous criticism of all privilege whether conferred by wealth or birth, his condemnation of the social disparity generated by modern economics, and his overt anti-clericalism are all reminiscent of the eighteenth-century tradition of Sismondi, whose *Nouveaux principes de l'économie politique* (1819) Pestel read early in 1820. Above all, however, he was influenced by Destutt de Tracy's *Commentary*, written about Montesquieu's "On the Spirit of the Laws." His committed republican stance at the meeting of the Union of Welfare's executive board in January 1820 indicates that he had already fallen under de Tracy's spell. As he made clear to the Investigating Committee, once he had reached this republican position he became irrevocably committed to it: "I became a republican at heart and could see no greater welfare and no higher blessing for Russia than a republican system of government."[2] According to Pestel's agenda, autocracy was to make way for the supreme power of the people on the grounds that "the Russian people are not the property of any one individual or family. On the contrary, the government is the property of the people and it is established for the good of the people." A republic based on popular representation was Pestel's proposed solution, which he had been led to by reading de Tracy.[3]

Russian Justice declared that the old class distinctions were to be swept away and replaced by just one "civil" estate (*grazhdanskoe soslovie*) with guaranteed equality before the law. All Russian males would be enfranchised from the age of twenty without any property or educational qualifications. Freedom of worship, speech, and occupation would be guaranteed and serfdom, "the vile privilege of owning other people," abolished entirely. Similarly, those who dared oppose such emancipation were "monsters" to be subjected to the severest punishment as "enemies of the Fatherland." Pestel stipulated that the serfs were to be emancipated with immediate effect. They were to be granted a landholding of around 10 *desyatiny* (10.9 hectares), which would be obtained by halving the landowners' own holdings.

Pestel's equally controversial proposals for the future of the peoples of the Russian Empire and the definition of the Russian republic's borders amount to what was, in effect, the first serious consideration of the nationalities problem in modern Russian history. Here Pestel exhibited unmistakable signs of great Russian chauvinism. In his view, the "right to nationhood" (*pravo narodnosti*) was only meaningful where a people were capable of preserving its independence or else restoring it. He considered that small, weak peoples would be better off merging with their larger neighbor and adopting its national identity and language. This category of weak peoples included Finland, Estonia, Lithuania, Bessarabia, Crimea, Georgia, and Ukraine; Pestel regarded them all as part of one Russian nation. For the Grand Duchy of Finland this designation represented a considerable downgrading of its national status, but Pestel wanted to see Finland Russified as it had been in the eighteenth century. Poland, however, Pestel considered viable enough as a nation to proceed to a "new life" of independence, but only on the basis of a binding treaty with Russia by which Poland's army would join Russia's in time of war, and the adoption of social and political institutions identical to Russia's, including the abolition of the Polish aristocracy.

Pestel's overarching concern was that the new government should make one Russian nation out of all the peoples who inhabited the territory of the republic, throughout which "the Russian language alone should hold sway." The very names of all the other tribes and peoples should be obliterated and united under "the one common Russian designation." This presumably would have included the Chechens, the Ingush, the Ossetians, and other troublesome ethnic minorities. Finally, the capital of the Russian republic was to be relocated eastward to the ancient city of Nizhnii Novgorod and renamed Vladimir "in memory of the Great Man who introduced the law of Christianity into Russia."

In general, the Russian republic was to bear a remarkable geographical resemblance to the then existing Russian Empire, retaining territory on the Black Sea littoral and in the Far East. Although Pestel was undecided as how best to settle Russia's Jewish question, he devoted a significant section of *Russian Justice* to a consideration of it. He bemoaned the Jews' rejection of Christianity, their failure to assimilate with the indigenous population, and their exemption from certain laws, such as the recruitment levy. He maintained that Jews actually enjoyed more rights than Christians, apart from the right to live where they liked in Russia. Ultimately, he favored resettling the Jews in their own state in Asia Minor.

The new revolutionary government was to immediately dismantle the military colonies which had been established by Alexander I. They had been devised to facilitate the maintenance of a huge standing army by transforming villages into barracks where troops were garrisoned and provisioned by the local serfs. In some of the most animated pages of *Russian Justice* Pestel subjected those responsible for these colonies to sustained criticism. He castigated the system as "the cruelest injustice" devised by a spiteful and evil regime, and one which had failed to meet any of its declared objectives. Its removal was envisaged as part of a wider military reform which included a maximum ten-year term of service and the abolition of corporal punishment.

The process of transition from the old regime to the new order was to be overseen by a provisional government with dictatorial powers which would be replaced by the National Assembly (*narodnoe veche*). Executive power was to be vested in the State Duma (*derzhavnaya duma*) while supreme judicial authority would be assumed by the Supreme Council (*verkhovnyi sobor*). This body was to comprise 120 members, called boyars, elected for life. The voice of the people at the local level was to be expressed through the annually convened regional people's assemblies (*zemskoe narodnoe sobranie*). These assemblies were to directly elect deputies to the next provincial tier of representative political institutions. To support the provisional government, Pestel envisaged a hugely expanded police force totaling around 113,000 men.[4] This figure dwarfs the 4,000 men in Nicholas I's Third Department in 1835. And just as Alexander I decreed the closure of secret societies and Masonic lodges in 1822, so Pestel at around the same time called for their suppression in *Russian Justice*. The dictatorial power of the revolutionary provisional government would brook no Decembrist-style opposition!

The age of majority was fixed at fifteen, and on attaining it, girls as well as boys would be required to take the oath of loyalty to the state. This was a major innovation, as in tsarist Russia women had been excluded from political life to the point where they were not even called upon to take the loyalty oath. The right to vote, however, even in Pestel's new republic, was to remain a male preserve, and *Russian Justice* makes no further proposals in relation to political equality for women.

Taken as whole, *Russian Justice* held out better prospects for Russia's transition to a constitutionally regulated state than the officially commissioned and discarded projects of Mikhail Speranskii or Nikolai Novosiltsev. And even though, to the certain relief of most of his contemporaries, it never came close to implementation, it retains its historical significance as the first republican constitutional project in Russian history.

ASSESSMENTS OF PESTEL

Pestel has been described by a recent commentator as "the most impressive Russian revolutionary before Lenin."[5] Many Decembrists blamed Pestel's influence for their involvement in the Southern Society. The Investigating Committee accepted that Pestel's persuasive readings from *Russian Justice* had proved hard to resist. Northern Society members, too, turned against him under interrogation. Sergei Trubetskoi claimed that "he horrified me," and that Nikita Muraviev had warned him that the Southern Society's leader was "dangerous and ambitious." Similarly, Kondratii Ryleev considered that Pestel posed a dangerous threat to Russia. Evgenii Obolenskii testified that Pestel's efforts to achieve unity within the Decembrist movement were doomed because "none of us personally trusted Colonel Pestel, whom we considered a dangerous individual."[6] Other views, however, were more positive. Ivan Yakushkin wrote that Pestel was a man of outstanding brilliance. And even Obolenskii was impressed by Pestel's lucid presentation of the most abstract issues, which, combined with his oratorical skills, made him very persuasive.

An emphatically positive view of Pestel was taken by the father of Russian Populism, Alexander Herzen. He hugely admired the Decembrists and especially Pestel. When, in the summer of 1826 as a thirteen-year-old in Moscow, he heard the news of the executions, he vowed to avenge them. In due course he became the main architect of the potent Decembrist legend. For Herzen, Pestel was neither a dreamer nor a utopian, but a man in close touch with reality and with "the spirit of his nation" who realized that to leave the land in the hands of the nobility would be to perpetuate an oligarchic elite. Pestel was a prophet and the first to think of involving the people in revolution, while the Decembrist movement as a whole was "a vastly important school for the modern generation."[7] For Herzen, the most important lesson to be drawn from Pestel's legacy was that "the wall which split Russia in two could only be breached by means of an *economic* revolution." Herzen famously went so far as to dub Pestel "a socialist before socialism" largely because of the radicalism of the agrarian reform set out in *Russian Justice* and because of his revolutionary aspirations. He was particularly impressed by Pestel's foresighted view of land distribution and credited him with expressing the view that the Decembrists' revolution would not succeed until the landowning gentry's property rights were fundamentally changed to the advantage of the land-hungry peasant.

It is undeniable that Pestel's "premature socialism" was decidedly agrarian in character. In fact, his agrarian proposals amounted to a potential revolution in that they posited a fundamental shift in rural relationships, anticipating, but actually far exceeding, the outcome of the 1861 Emancipation Act. They were based on the principle of common ownership of the land, half of it being assigned to the peasant communes. The Emancipation Act, in contrast, was based on the landlords' ownership of the land, with the peasants buying back their allotments from them. The historian R. V. Ivanov-Razumnik contended that Pestel's agrarian project as outlined in *Russian Justice* was some fifty years ahead of its time when Pestel wrote it and still made remarkable reading early in the twentieth century. In it "we see the first birth pangs of socialism which from the second half of the nineteenth century became the predominant viewpoint of the Russian intelligentsia" and Pestel himself was "the first representative of emergent Russian socialist thought."[8] Ultimately, it is this achievement which makes Pestel, despite all his flaws and contradictions, the most significant, controversial, and interesting Decembrist, and numbers him among the major political figures of nineteenth-century Russia.

SETTLING OF ACCOUNTS

Theorizing about agrarian reform within a republican framework was, however, a very different matter from implementing it. Pestel was found culpable by the Investigating Committee and convicted by the Supreme Criminal Court of intent to assassinate the entire imperial family as the first step toward the establishment of a Russian republic. The evidence against him on this charge was overwhelming and he admitted his guilt in a series of full and detailed written confessions. Indeed, the depth of his remorse and his abject plea for forgiveness, coupled with his pledge of loyalty to the new tsar and full cooperation with the Investigating Committee, raise the question of the genuineness of his intention to commit so heinous a crime as regicide. The balance of probability must be that Pestel was guilty more of rhetorical bravado than actual intent.

From the time of the St. Petersburg meeting of the Union of Welfare in January 1820, Pestel had become a committed republican. Over the next four years he would strive to unite the Decembrist movement as a whole under the banner of republicanism as set out in *Russian Justice*. When Pestel outlined the main ideas of *Russian Justice* at the Kiev congress of Southern Society leaders in 1823, he laid particular emphasis on the need for a constitution which the future revolutionary provisional government would be obliged to implement. But Pestel did not immediately have his own way. The Southern Society's leadership was so taken aback by his political audacity that they postponed a decision about *Russian Justice* until the next Kiev meeting. They clearly needed a whole year to think through the enormous implications for Russia of Pestel's proposed new deal: a republican system, the temporary dictatorship of a provisional government, the fate of the overthrown imperial house, the abolition of the existing class structure, and the redistribution of land. Thus it was not until the 1824 Kiev congress a year later that Pestel's proposals were finally adopted as the Southern Society's program.

He was so completely convinced of the absolute correctness of his own program and of his ability to "sell" it to the Northern Society that he had simply not prepared himself psychologically for the possibility of defeat. But the crushing failure of his mission to St. Petersburg in 1824 precipitated his crisis the following year. During 1825, therefore, as his energy and drive seemed to desert him, initiative and leadership increasingly passed to Sergei Muraviev-Apostol. Pestel's main problem was that he had not understood just how controversial his idea for a Russian republic would be. Moreover, while there was general acceptance among the Decembrists for the abolition of serfdom, there was much less sympathy for Pestel's agrarian revolution, which many found difficult to understand. And furthermore, the nettle which Pestel grasped—the ending of all class-based privilege and distinction—was too painful for most to handle. Worse still, the suggestion of regicide at a time when terrorist acts of political assassination were unknown in Russia was beyond the comprehension of most of Pestel's confederates. Russia was by tradition wedded to Orthodoxy and to rule by God's anointed tsar. For most Decembrists, the transformation of the tsar from an absolute autocrat to a constitutional monarch was the limit of their goals and expectations. "Those who think otherwise do not know Russia," as Sergei Trubetskoi expressed it. The hugely divisive issues of regicide and republicanism would thus remain unresolved and were to be the main stumbling blocks in St. Petersburg in 1824. Pestel's cause was not helped by the perceived scale of his personal ambitions; some thought these ambitions were a match for those of Napoleon, whom the Decembrist was said even to physically resemble.

Significantly, it was for his proposals rather than any insurrectionist activity that Pestel was executed. Specifically, these included regicide as the prerequisite for establishing a Russian republic within newly defined borders, the abolition of class-based privilege and distinction, revolutionary agrarian reform, and the dictatorship of a provisional government of a self-selected elite while the key demands of *Russian Justice* were implemented across the former Russian Empire. These were all prototypes of ideas common to the manifestos of Russian revolutionary groups later in the nineteenth and early twentieth centuries. Indeed, it is no exaggeration to contend that they are all recognizable precursors of elements of Lenin's program for the revolutionary transformation of Russia's political, social, and economic order after October 1917. They include the assassination of the Romanovs, the abolition of class distinction, a territorial redefinition of the boundaries of the former Russian Empire, and the collectivization of agriculture, all to be achieved through the dictatorship of the *nomenklatura* on behalf of the proletariat. As a British historian of Russia has wryly put it, "Thus a century before the October Revolution Pestel thought up the one-party state as the means of achieving happiness in Russia."[9] In addition, the crucial role played by the secret police throughout the years of Soviet power was also prefigured in Pestel's idea for an enforcement agency whose proposed manpower, as we have noted, far exceeded that of Nicholas I's own much-reviled Third Department and Corps of Gendarmes.

Pavel Pestel, then, had the intellectual courage and the political audacity to conceive of a Russian republic. To be sure, his conception raises serious doubts about his understanding of democratic, pluralistic society, of the right of nations within the Russian Empire to self-determination, and of civil rights generally. Yet, given that these are issues which have not been fully resolved in Russia right up to the twenty-first century, it seems unreasonable to expect Pestel to have succeeded in doing so early in the nineteenth. Nevertheless, Pestel's republican ideas were well ahead of their time, just as were his proposals for agrarian reform. It was for the startling temerity of his republican vision that on July 13, 1826, on a hangman's scaffold outside the Peter-Paul Fortress, the autocratic Russian state exacted its terrible revenge.

NOTES

1. J. N. Westwood, *Endurance and Endeavour: Russian History, 1812–1992*, 4th ed. (Oxford: Oxford University Press, 1993), 9.
2. From Pestel's statement of January 12, 1826, to the Investigating Committee into the Decembrist Affair, *Vosstanie dekabristov* (Moscow-Leningrad: Gosizdat, 1927), 4:91.
3. Testimony of the Decembrist A. V. Poggio, quoted in Franco Venturi, "Destutt de Tracy and the Liberal Revolutions," in *Studies in Free Russia* (Chicago: University of Chicago Press, 1982), 83.
4. *Vosstanie dekabristov*, 7:341, 69–73. One commentator has even suggested that Count Benkendorf actually got the idea of establishing a dedicated corps of gendarmes from reading these pages of *Russian Justice*, citing as evidence the speed with which the Third Department was set up under Nicholas I. See M. Ol'minskii, *Gosudarstvo, byurokratiya i absolyutizm v istorii Rossii*, 3rd ed. (Moscow-Leningrad, 1925), 184.
5. J. Gooding, *Rulers and Subjects: Government and People in Russia* (London: Arnold, 1996), 39.
6. Quoted in P. F. Nikandrov, *Revolyutsionnaya ideologiya dekabristov* (Leningrad: Lenizdat, 1976), 83, 85.
7. A. I. Gertsen, "O razvitii revolyutsionnykh idei v Rossii," in *Sobranie sochinenii v tridtsati tomakh*, ed. V. P. Volgin (Moscow, 1956), 7:200.
8. R. V. Ivanov-Razumnik, *Istoriia russkoi obshchestvennoi mysli* (St. Petersburg, 1911), 1:122–126.
9. Gooding, *Rulers and Subjects*, 40.

SUGGESTED READING

Fyodorov, Vladimir. *The First Breath of Freedom*. Moscow, 1988.
Gooding, John. *Rulers and Subjects: Government and People in Russia, 1801–1991*. London, 1996.
Keep, J. H. L. *Soldiers of the Tsar: Army and Society in Russia, 1462–1874*. Oxford, 1985.
Leighton, Lauren G. *The Esoteric Tradition in Russian Romantic Literature: Decembrism and Freemasonry*. University Park, Pa., 1994.
Mazour, A. G. *The First Russian Revolution, 1825: The Decembrist Movement; Its Origins, Development and Significance*. Stanford, Calif., 1962.
O'Meara, Patrick. "The Decembrist Pavel Ivanovich Pestel: Some Questions of Upbringing." *Irish Slavonic Studies* 9 (1988): 6–20.
———. *The Decembrist Pavel Pestel: Russia's First Republican*. Basingstoke, U.K., 2003.
———. *K. F. Ryleev: A Political Biography of the Decembrist Poet*. Princeton, U.K., 1984.
———. "Vreden Sever: The Decembrists' Memories of the Peter-Paul Fortress." In *St. Petersburg, 1703–1825*, edited by Anthony Cross, 165–189. Basingstoke, N.Y., 2003.
Raeff, Marc. *The Decembrist Movement*. Englewood Cliffs, N.J, 1966.

10

Economic Backwardness in Geographical Perspective

Russia's Nineteenth Century

Susan P. McCaffray

Economic backwardness is one of the most common images in Russian history. Both foreigners and native reformers have long agreed that Russia lagged behind what is commonly called "the West" in important ways. As long ago as 1591, English visitor Giles Fletcher wrote to Queen Elizabeth that "the commodities of Russia . . . grow and go abroad in far less plenty than they were wont to do, because the people, being oppressed and spoiled of their gettings, are discouraged from their labors."[1] Three and a half centuries later Joseph Stalin exhorted his people to redouble their efforts because "we are fifty to one hundred years behind advanced countries. We must cover this distance in ten years. Either we do this or they will crush us."[2]

At the same time, Russian and Soviet military power has often surprised and impressed outsiders and insiders as well. In the years following the expulsion of Napoleon's and Hitler's armies, observers on all sides recognized that Russia was a major military power in Europe. Between 1945 and 1989 the rich and mighty United States apparently had no more dangerous rival than this very same rude, barbarous, and backward country. The twin images of backwardness and power contributed profoundly to foreigners' propensity to consider Russia a great riddle.

Twentieth-century commentators often took Russia's economic backwardness as a point of departure. Marxist writers such as V. I. Lenin, Leon Trotsky, and J. V. Stalin dwelt much on the consequences of Russia's backwardness for the revolution they were pursuing. They accounted for it by referring to the slow growth of commercial capital and the resulting persistence of "feudalism." Nonetheless, the Marxists did agree that capitalism had begun to develop in late nineteenth-century Russia, indicating that Russia was following a universal path to economic development, if admittedly several paces behind the "advanced countries."

Many non-Marxist scholars shared this view of Russia following several steps behind on the same path that West Europeans had trod previously, although they naturally did not construe the Communist revolution as either inevitable or desirable. The most influential of these writers undoubtedly was Alexander Gerschenkron, who carefully described the peculiar features of late-blooming economies.[3] While Gerschenkron's point of departure was the assumption that economic backwardness was the best framework for understanding Russia's nineteenth century, he did implicitly undermine the notion of a universal pattern by showing how this backwardness pushed Russia toward experiences and policies not embraced in the advanced West.

In recent decades, economic historians of the "long nineteenth century" (from the French Revolution in 1789 to the outbreak of World War I in 1914) have tried to quantify and characterize the extent of Russia's economic backwardness. They have tackled many aspects of the questions "How was Russia backward?" and "How backward was Russia?" The effort to undertake concrete comparisons with the economic experiences of other European countries is the most fruitful new approach to Russian economic history. Not surprisingly, this endeavor is revising our picture of Russia's nineteenth century. Some of the assumptions of backwardness turn out to rest on misunderstandings of the situation in Western European countries. In other cases, the more careful examination of more complete data indicates a level of economic growth and sufficiency above what has generally been appreciated. Another approach, the close examination of the economic situation in specific regions or industries—that is, disaggregation of data—presents an impression that there were pockets of significant economic progress in late imperial Russia. Taken together, these efforts indicate that a number of Russian economic policies and projects achieved significant success in the decades before the First World War.

In spite of progress in some areas, however, the Russian standard of living remained quite low. Moreover, the Russian Empire failed the great test of the First World War and succumbed to revolution. These facts lend credence to the long-standing image of Russian economic backwardness and failure. How can we reconcile recent conclusions about Russian economic progress with these undeniable weaknesses? This is the challenge confronting historians of late imperial Russia today. Arriving at a satisfactory new framework with which to replace the increasingly suspect image of simple backwardness will require disentangling economic, political, and social aspects of Russia's nineteenth century, finding meaningful ways to compare Russia and the "advanced countries," and, above all, coming to grips with the extraordinary size and diversity of the Russian Empire.

In a short chapter, it is not possible to survey more than a few aspects of late imperial Russia's economic history, but the effort will illustrate some of the interpretive challenges posed by new questions and new data. To that end, let us briefly examine agricultural output and productivity; banking and supply of credit; growth of railroads and heavy industry; and indicators of personal well-being and standard of living.

In the history of Russian agriculture under the Old Regime, there is one great dividing line: the emancipation of the serfs that was announced in 1861. The emancipation changed bound peasants' legal situation profoundly. Before 1861 peasants on private landlords' lands and those on state lands were bound to the place of their birth. They could not move away without the permission of the master, who would sometimes permit peasants to go away to factories or towns for work, as long as they made monetary payments to the master from their wages and returned to plant in the spring. After emancipation, peasants did not have to ask permission from the landlord to move away or to seek seasonal employment in a factory. However, emancipated peasant communities were obliged to repay the state bank for money advanced them to "redeem," or buy, the land they were allotted from the noble landowner. It has long been assumed that these redemption payments were burdensome to peasants and reflected overvaluation of the land they received.[4] The redemption payments continued until 1905, when the government cancelled them.

But if the legal situation of peasants changed profoundly in 1861, many other aspects of their lives did not. For the most part, peasants continued to farm as they had done for generations, under the tutelage of their own village leaders or heads of households. There was nothing about the emancipation process that immediately led to increases in productivity or technological advance.

It has been common to see Russian agriculture as among the most backward in Europe.[5] Undoubtedly Russian peasants could be characterized as overwhelmingly poor compared to noble landowners and urban merchants. But were they poorer than peasants elsewhere in Europe? Although many scholars say yes, their assessments rest on two practices that have been questioned in recent work: relying on Russian government statistics and generalizing about the Russian Empire as a whole. One challenge to tsarist agricultural statistics comes from Stephen L. Hoch. Hoch demonstrates that provincial governors, from whom official data about grain production are drawn, had good reason to underreport output so as to minimize military requisitions. Moreover, the reports were due each January 1, so they omitted the sizable quantity of grain threshed after the New Year. Hoch's investigation, supported by archival evidence, suggests that in the heart of the Russian black-earth country, grain yields equaled those in France, Denmark, and Germany in the late eighteenth and early nineteenth centuries.[6] Not only were yields comparable, but the structure of Russian village society, with its periodic land redistribution, prevented the kind of rural vagrancy that was so common in technologically superior England.

Peter Gatrell has challenged the practice of taking the Russian Empire as an aggregate when trying to evaluate relative economic backwardness or progress. He finds that in the period after emancipation there was great variety in agricultural improvement throughout the vast country. In the central black-earth region he sees little evidence of growth in capital stock or adaptation to market-oriented agriculture. But in Siberia, the Baltic, New Russia (in the south), and the southwest, he finds great expansion in production of cereals for market, concluding that, "in the centre, progress was peripheral, but on the periphery there was progress."[7] The growth of grain surpluses in Ukraine and Siberia, along with expansion of the railroad network, meant that in the last twenty-five years of the tsarist regime the periodic harvest failures in the agricultural heartland did not become general famines.[8] Gatrell also suggests that the greatest share of investment in agriculture came from individual peasants, who financed improvements from their profits and savings.[9]

Gatrell's point about regional diversity is crucial. Although the practice is almost irresistible, it is not meaningful to summarize the economic condition of the Russian Empire as a whole. Russia was the size of eighty-eight Britains. If only half of them were making progress, does that make Russia's agriculture a failure, compared to Britain's? In terms of impact on the lives of real people it is certainly more appropriate to consider changes within Russia's various regions than to pursue aggregate figures. Moreover, just as regional variation was marked, so, increasingly, was economic differentiation among the peasants themselves. Tax receipts from peasants suggest that a significant proportion of them saw household income rise over the decades after emancipation.[10] Taken together, Hoch and Gatrell suggest that we should be cautious in accepting the famously pessimistic descriptions of both pre- and postreform Russian agriculture. Although Russia was a relatively poor country within Europe, its nineteenth-century crop yields were well within European norms. After the mid-century, new cultivation in peripheral regions produced significant gains in total national output, alleviating the effects of persistently unpredictable rainfall and the short growing season. Peasant agriculturalists, the vast majority of the empire's food producers, showed themselves sensitive to market demand for increased grain production and overall agricultural investment. It seems likely that the extent and effect of rural Russia's economic backwardness have been overstated.

Turning to manufacturing, Russia's textile industry flourished in the 1840s, its railroad boom came in the 1870s and 1880s, and a full-fledged industrial revolution in heavy industry and steel was under way by the 1890s. This chronology puts Russia a full century behind England, three decades behind the continental leaders, France and Germany, contemporaneous with Austria, and ahead of Italy.[11] Among the factors offered by way of accounting for this lag (which is often exaggerated), a shortage of capital and credit take pride of place. Government officials often decried the shortage of liquid capital in Russia and looked for ways to generate more of it. Their efforts produced a distinctive Russian banking system that was originally dominated by state banks to the virtual exclusion of private banks. The assumption that capital shortage restrained industrial development suggests to many historians that this Russian banking system was either backward, or a failure, or both. In order to shed light on this matter, several strands of this argument must be disentangled. First, was Russia behind other European countries in the creation of banks? Second, did Russia create the wrong kind of banks? Third, did Russian banks fail to supply adequate credit for industrial and agricultural investment? Finally, did weaknesses in Russian banking account for capital shortages in nineteenth-century Russia?

Was Russia behind in the development of banks? It is true that Russia was not first. The very first banks were private banks of deposit that arose in Italian cities at the end of the Middle Ages. The first public bank was the Bank of Amsterdam, founded in 1609. The first to issue banknotes was Sweden's Riksbank, founded in 1656. The Bank of England, founded as a private concern in 1694, eventually became a quasi-public institution with central bank functions.[12] Private joint-stock banks arose in England and France in the 1710s and 1720s, but collapsed in a sea of scandal. Thereafter formal banking virtually ended in France for many decades. Empress Elizabeth launched the Russian State Loan Bank in 1754, from which various incarnations developed in the following decades. The situation in the German lands varied widely. Thus the general pattern of commercial activity flowing from west to east across Europe at the rate of roughly a century seems to hold up in the case of banking, except that Russian banking was more developed than that of France and several of the smaller German states in the middle of the eighteenth century.

Some commentators contend that Russia's early preference for state as opposed to private banking institutions accounted for their general inadequacy. However, as the chronology above indicates, public banks were more the rule than the exception in seventeenth- and eighteenth-century Europe. Early private banking was often quite informal, and arose in conjunction with a quickening of commercial activity. Thus Renaissance Italian cities saw the first private banking, followed at length by Scotland and England, where the dense commercial activity of the eighteenth century gave rise to a multitude of country banks, each issuing their own banknotes. In Russia, both vast and far removed from the commercial quickening produced by access to the Atlantic and American silver, the demand for banking services was more limited, but it did grow steadily. Wealthy landowners and officials lent money to merchants via promissory notes, which were widespread by the late eighteenth century.[13]

Joint-stock banks had a bad reputation throughout Europe after the Mississippi and South Sea bubbles of the early eighteenth century. The precocious British, with their well-developed provincial and central banking institutions, did not permit joint-stock banks until the 1830s. The first German joint-stock bank was founded in Cologne in 1841, and the first French one in the mid-1850s.[14] In a general reform of Russian banking institutions that accompanied the period of the Great Reforms, a reorganized state bank was created out of existing state institutions in 1860 and joint-stock banking was legalized. In 1865 Russian joint-stock commercial banks held 1.4 million rubles in deposits and current accounts; by 1914 these accounts amounted to over 2.5 billion rubles.[15] Thus the lag in corporate banking was considerably shorter than in establishment of the first formal banking institutions. Moreover, it is not correct to argue that Russian banks were of a fundamentally different type than banks elsewhere in Europe.

Did Russian banks supply adequate credit for economic activity in the nineteenth century? The imperial government supported private economic activity not only through state bank policies, but also in such direct ways as conferring sizable land and resource grants to promising entrepreneurs. Besides these state efforts, much prereform manufacturing, especially textiles, was supported by family savings. In short, it is likely that there was sufficient credit in early nineteenth-century Russia to support the kinds of merchant-based enterprises that prereform Russians sought to establish.[16]

After mid-century in Russia, as in other European countries, the creation and expansion of joint-stock banks responded to demand for investment capital in quantities previously unneeded. More than anything else, it was the combined state and private interest in building railroads that triggered this expansion. Russia was no exception. In the mid-1890s, when demand for industrial capital really expanded, Russian banks responded enthusiastically. Many, but by no means all, Russian banks had significant foreign participation by the early twentieth century, but foreign bankers tended to allow the Russian bankers to manage investments and oversee investment decisions.[17] Moreover, Moscow and St. Petersburg commercial banks expanded their discounting operations in response to increased interregional trade, solving short-term credit problems exacerbated by the vast distances and harsh climate through which goods often had to travel. In fact, Russian total commercial bank deposits as a proportion of the gross national product (GNP) exceeded those of Germany in 1914.[18] Besides bank capital, Russian industry also had access to foreign and domestic stock markets as well as government subsidies. As Gatrell argues, although the development of the Russian credit system was a decade or two behind those of leading European powers, it expanded in proportion to demand, and was not a deterrent to the growth of heavy industry.[19]

Finally, did failures in the banking system account for capital shortages in Russia? Officials, reformers, and critics agreed that the country needed more capital, particularly for rural improvements. Innovative banking institutions, including mutual credit associations and savings banks, proliferated in response to slowly increasing demand for credit from both rural and industrial producers. Large corporate banks in the major cities attracted significant foreign investment by the turn of the century and foreign banks opened branches in Russia. Thus it does not seem to be the case that Russians were unable to create or attract modern banking institutions. If capital continued to be in short supply, the shortage almost certainly reflected the relatively low incomes of savers. Again, however, there was significant regional variation in income levels, especially in rural districts.

In developing the industries that most characterize the nineteenth century, Russia followed the general European pattern. The first widespread use of mechanized technology occurred in the textile industry, which was flourishing in Moscow and other towns in the central industrial region by the 1840s, despite the persistence of serfdom. Indeed, the most famous textile manufacturers were themselves serf or former serf entrepreneurs, and the cotton industry developed most in a part of the country where peasants needed to supplement their agricultural income with other occupations. Although the domestic demand for manufactured yarn and cloth did not increase rapidly, it did increase steadily, through population increases and the growth of that part of the peasant population that had disposable income, especially after emancipation. Kahan calculated that between 1890 and 1910 domestic demand for cotton goods increased 65 percent.[20] When the government decided to protect Russian industry with modest tariffs during the last two decades of the nineteenth century, both technological investment and total output of textiles increased significantly. Between 1879 and 1913 the total number of spindles and the number of power looms operating in Russia nearly tripled while total production of raw cotton cloth more than tripled.[21]

In Russia, as in other countries, the growth of domestic manufacturing and the domestic market for manufactured goods, as well as military requirements (in Russia's case after the losses in the Crimean War of 1852–1855), stimulated interest in railroad construction. Thus, industries associated with railroads, such as coal, iron, and steel, expanded in a "second" industrial revolution. Russia followed this pattern, experimenting with a few railroad lines in the 1840s, but investing, originally via private firms, in rapid expansion of the rail network beginning around 1860. The greatest periods of expansion were in the early 1870s, when the country added 1,656 kilometers of track, and the late 1890s, when it added 2,820.[22] The expansion in the last two decades before World War I was especially impressive, and changed Russia's ranking among European powers. Whereas in 1890 Russia's total railroad track placed it behind the United Kingdom, France, and Germany, by 1913 the only country that exceeded Russia in kilometers of track was Germany, and in terms of the increase between 1890 and 1913, Russia far exceeded any other country, adding over 31,000 kilometers in that period.[23]

The most significant measure of the adequacy of a railroad network, however, is not total kilometers of track, but density. How well did the rail network service commerce, industry, and the other needs of the population? In this category, no matter how much rail Russia added in the prewar years, the vast country would remain firmly in last place among European powers. Although the fact of Russia's immensity is well known, the numbers still impress. To give the size in square kilometers of just a few European countries in 1914, the United Kingdom encompassed 241,169; France, 531,044; Austria-Hungary, 674,046; and the Russian Empire, over 21.2 million. Thus, despite truly impressive gains in the last prewar decades, and despite possessing a 62,200-kilometer network in 1913, Russia ranked last among European powers in density, with only one kilometer of track per hundred square kilometers of territory. The United Kingdom, on the other hand, with 37,700 kilometers of track, boasted twelve kilometers per hundred square kilometers of territory. Even Spain, with fewer than 10,000 kilometers of track, boasted a network three times as dense as Russia's.[24]

In Russia, as throughout Europe and the United States, the growth of railroads generated vastly increased demand for coal, iron products, and steel. The powerful combination of demand for these products and the expansion of joint-stock investment banks produced the boom in heavy industry characteristic of late nineteenth-century Europe. Russia's boom came in the 1890s, following a decade of significant construction of rail lines and industrial plants. In the 1880s the southern industrial region, or Donbass, replaced the older Urals iron industry, becoming the center of coal and steel production in the empire. Table 10.1 summarizes the stages of growth in output of coal, pig iron, and steel.

Thus Russia experienced the highest average annual rates of growth in industrial output among European countries between 1880 and 1900, and the second highest between 1900 and 1913.[25] While it is common in many accounts to attribute most of this growth in heavy industry to foreign investment, this is a misleading characterization. Belgian and French investment in the Donbass was substantial, but several studies now demonstrate that virtually all Donbass firms were managed by native managers and guided by boards with substantial or dominant Russian participation. For-

Table 10.1.   Coal, Iron, and Steel Production in Russia, 1860–1913
(millions of poods)

Year	Coal	Pig Iron	Steel (all products)
1860	18.3	20.5	—
1880	200.8	27.4	—
1890	367.2	56.6	48.4
1900	986.3	179.1	163.0
1913	2,200.1	283.0	246.6

Source: P. A. Khromov, *Ekonomicheskoe razvitie Rossii v XIX-XX vekakh* (Moscow, 1950), 452–457.
Note: 1 pood equals 36.11 pounds.

eign banks tended to leave to Russians the management of the Russian banks in which they were invested, while Russian banks deferred to industrial managers in guiding the investment and production decisions of coal and steel firms.[26] The presence of foreign capital in Russian heavy industry does not distinguish Russia from other European countries or the United States. The British are the one exception, as the initial industrializers and initial suppliers of capital to virtually all other industrializing countries, particularly for railroad construction.

Nor was industrialization in Russia disproportionately dependent on the government for its market, as is sometimes alleged. While the government was a key consumer of the products of coal and steel firms, particularly for the state-owned railroads (which had been repurchased from private companies in the 1870s) and for defense industries, domestic demand for fuels as well as iron products steadily grew. In consumer industries, moreover, private demand was the most important, and in fact determining, factor in increasing output.[27] Domestic demand grew steadily after 1860, if not spectacularly. The total sales at fairs in European Russia, the traditional sites of commerce outside of the capital cities, more than tripled between 1868 and 1904, while the number of trading establishments of all kinds doubled between 1885 and 1912.[28]

It is clear, then, that the backwardness that persisted in the Russian economy in 1914 did not result from a lack of growth. The Russian economy grew in significant ways after the emancipation of the serfs in 1861 and especially after 1880. Moreover, Russia was not far behind most European powers, except England, in the timing of its turn toward such modern economic practices as joint-stock banking, railroad building, and the development of related industries such as coal and steel. The lag in these key indicators of a turn toward modern economic development was not much more than three or four decades, again, with the exception of England. It is clear that England's development is the outlier, not Russia's. While an earlier generation of historians characterized Russian economic development as substantially late, dominated by the state, devoid of a domestic market and credit institutions, and technologically backward, the studies cited here, along with many others, demonstrate that, without heavy qualification, all of these characterizations are so misleading as to give an impression of Russia's nineteenth-century economy that is mostly wrong.

And yet contemporary Russians as well as careful historians are not wrong in their persistent sense that the generally modest chronological differences between Russian and Western European development produced significant differences in the lives of people. If many indicators of backwardness are not present to the degree once thought, which ones are? Trebilcock cites figures indicating that Russia ranked at the bottom of the European scale in health and education of its population throughout the last half of the nineteenth century. While Russia's birthrate was much higher than the others', more than doubling the Russian population between 1850 and 1910, so was its death rate. At 27.4 deaths per thousand of population in 1914, Russia far outdistanced the next highest country, Hungary at 23.4. England, France, Germany, and Italy all had death rates between 14 and 18.5 per thousand in 1914.[29] Likewise, Russia also lagged far behind the others in numbers of students. Just 5.19 percent of Russians attended primary schools in 1910, compared to 9.7 in Italy, 14.9 in the United Kingdom, and 15.9 in Germany. The proportion of Russians attending university roughly equaled that of France in 1914, but was outdistanced by Italy, Austria, the United Kingdom, and Germany, the European leader by a significant proportion.[30] Although the 1874 *zemstvo* reform had created local government boards empowered to levy land taxes to support construction of schools and clinics, progress was slow. In the last years before World War I the empire's constitutionally weak legislature, the Duma, made considerable progress in both areas, outlining a plan for universal primary education by 1922 and creating national sickness and accident insurance in 1912.

What can we conclude about Russian economic development in the nineteenth century? Clearly, while Russia's experience in agricultural productivity, banking, and industrial development ranks it most often with Austria-Hungary, Italy, and Spain rather than with the more precocious England and Germany (with France occupying a fascinatingly ambiguous position), Russian experience is well within the European, or "Western" framework. To the extent that backwardness is understood chronologically, Russia is not consistently behind European leaders in all indicators or at all points.

It appears clear, for example, that in the early part of the nineteenth century serf agriculture was as productive as that of continental leaders. Serfdom did not prevent entrepreneurial peasants and merchants from launching light industries, particularly a cotton industry, within a decade or two of France and Germany. A generally stable currency and a slowly, but steadily, expanding credit system sustained the expansion of manufacturing at mid-century. The emancipation greatly enhanced Russia's potential for economic development. By vastly increasing labor mobility, it made possible a steadily increasing flight from the land. A significant upturn in births supplied more hands for agriculture, which grew not only extensively, but also intensively, as prospering peasants and improving landlords plowed profits back into agriculture. The government ended two decades of ambivalence about railroad construction after the military defeat in 1855 and reformed banking and corporate law in order to promote its growth through private means. The link between joint-stock investment banking and railroads in Russia was typical of the European experience, as was the resulting rapid growth of coal and steel industries. As more Russians and foreigners sought to satisfy the demand for coal, rails, and all kinds of heavy machinery, the number and capitalization of Russia's banks grew apace, while additional capital was supplied by foreign banks and investors, as well as speculators on the new Russian stock exchanges. Demand for textiles and consumer goods expanded through 1914 as the rural population was increasingly divided between those who prospered in the postemancipation atmosphere and those who did not, while the urban population grew slowly. The growth in demand stemmed from a significant increase in per capita income, which came close to doubling between 1900 and 1914, although Russia ranked well behind Germany, France, and England in absolute terms.[31]

Russia often occupied a comparative ranking in the bottom third of the leading seven or eight European countries, but this position still placed Russia among the world's more forward societies. Moreover, Russia followed Europe's nineteenth-century pattern very closely, and can be considered a typical European case, bearing in mind that national peculiarities were a feature of every European society. It is also apparent that the First World War interrupted the period of Russia's most significant economic growth and halted the national government's first serious turn toward improving basic public welfare. It does not seem too far-fetched to speculate that without the cataclysm provoked by the Great War Russia might have continued its rapid economic development and its growing investment in the well-being of its people, leading, perhaps, to steady improvements in its international ranking within Europe.

What does this line of thinking change about our understanding of Russia on the eve of World War I and revolution? It supports the contention, increasingly accepted by economic historians if not by others, that Russia's weaknesses on the eve of the First World War were not primarily economic.[32] If Russia's was not a failed economy going into World War I, economic failures during the war did not stem from the fundamental economic weakness of the empire. Nonetheless, the Russian Empire undoubtedly succumbed to the pressures of war. If its failure by 1917 did not stem primarily from prewar failures to expand its transportation network, its heavy industry, its food supply, and its access to capital, then those seeking to understand its collapse must turn to the political and social weaknesses of the imperial regime.

However, the data supplied here also point to a more fundamental conclusion. The factor that accounts for no small part of Russia's comparative backwardness within Europe is its size. As the figures on railroad density demonstrate most dramatically, in a country so much bigger than all others with whom it sought to compete, even extraordinary increases in capacity had only a modest impact on the economy of individual households and communities. What was so demonstratively true of railroads and means of communication was also true of other kinds of commercial infrastructure, including money supply, credit, industrial and agricultural output, and social investments such as schools and clinics. If the Russian Empire was to be thought of, administered as, and judged as one unit, then the critical lack of commercial and social density, or, conversely, the overwhelming distances and resulting sparseness of people, resources, capital, communications, cities, markets, and goods of all kinds, remained the most central fact of Russian economic life.

To put it another way, in Russia, despite spurts of impressive growth in various indicators, the whole was always much less than the sum of its parts. The limiting economic factor of excessive distances between resources, markets, supplies of labor and capital, and transportation centers helps us to understand Russia's nineteenth century more accurately. Space explains what chronology does not: why did Russia, despite a rough chronological parity with European leaders, and a true parity in many areas of what might be termed elite culture, persistently lag behind the other European states in the impact that economic and cultural growth made on the lives of its people? If "backwardness" continues to seem a useful rubric for understanding Russia's place in Europe, the term should be qualified. In the nineteenth century Russia's famous backwardness was less a feature of chronology than of geography. Imperial Russia was not too late. It was too big.

NOTES

1. Giles Fletcher, "Of the Russe Commonwealth," in *Rude and Barbarous Kingdom: Russia in the Accounts of Sixteenth-Century English Voyagers*, ed. Lloyd E. Berry and Robert O. Crummey (Madison: University of Wisconsin Press, 1968), 170.

2. Stalin's speech of February 4, 1931, is quoted in John Scott, *Behind the Urals: An American Worker in Russia's City of Steel* (Bloomington: Indiana University Press, 1989), 270.

3. Alexander Gerschenkron, *Economic Backwardness in Historical Perspective* (Cambridge, Mass.: Harvard University Press, 1962).

4. A closely reasoned recent article suggests that this notion is incorrect, however. See Steven L. Hoch, "Did Russia's Emancipated Serfs Really Pay Too Much for Too Little Land? Statistical Anomalies and Long-Tailed Distributions," *Slavic Review* 63, no. 2 (Summer 2004): 247–274.

5. Jerome Blum, *Lord and Peasant in Russia: From the Ninth to the Nineteenth Century* (Princeton, N.J.: Princeton University Press, 1961), 330.

6. Stephen Hoch, *Serfdom and Social Control in Russia* (Chicago: University of Chicago Press, 1989), 30–36.

7. Peter Gatrell, *The Tsarist Economy: 1850–1917* (New York: St. Martin's Press, 1986), 139.

8. Gatrell, *Tsarist Economy*, 140.

9. Gatrell, *Tsarist Economy*, 202–203.

10. James Y. Simms, "The Crisis in Russian Agriculture at the End of the Nineteenth Century," *Slavic Review* 36, no. 3 (1977): 377–397.

11. Clive Trebilcock, *The Industrialization of the Continental Powers, 1780–1914* (London: Longman, 1981), 430. The dating of France's industrial spurt is problematic, as it started early (around 1830), but then progressed so slowly that by mid-century it was surpassed by the newcomers among the German states.

12. See Charles P. Kindleberger, *A Financial History of Western Europe* (New York: Oxford University Press, 1993), 49, 53.

13. George E. Munro, "Finance and Credit in the Eighteenth-Century Russian Economy," *Jahrbücher fuer Geschichte Osteuropas*, Band 45, Heft 4 (1997): 552–560.

14. Rondo Cameron, *Banking in the Early Stages of Industrialization: A Study in Comparative Economic History* (New York: Oxford University Press, 1967), 107, 162.

15. Arcadius Kahan, *Russian Economic History: The Nineteenth Century* (Chicago: University of Chicago Press, 1989), 43–44.

16. Gatrell, *Tsarist Economy*, 209.

17. Recently a few important studies of banking-industry links have appeared to supplement older classics. Two that demonstrate bankers' tendency to let Russian managers make key production decisions are Jonathan A. Grant, *Big Business in Russia: The Putilov Company in Late Imperial Russia, 1868–1917* (Pittsburgh: University of Pittsburgh Press, 1999) and V. I. Bovykin, *Frantsuzskie banki v Rossii, konets XIX–nachalo XX v.* [French Banks in Russia at the End of the Nineteenth and Beginning of the Twentieth Centuries] (Moscow: Rosspen, 1999).

18. Trebilcock, *Industrialization*, 445.

19. Gatrell, *Tsarist Economy*, 214.

20. Kahan, *Russian Economic History*, 18.

21. Gatrell, *Tsarist Economy*, 16.

22. Gatrell, *Tsarist Economy*, 150. The first figure covers 1871–1875 and the second 1896–1900.

23. Trebilcock, *Industrialization*, 443

24. Trebilcock, *Industrialization*, 443; the UK, Germany, and France had nearly equally dense networks in 1913; Belgium's was much more dense; and Italy's and Austria-Hungary's were six and seven times denser than Russia's, with far less total track.

25. Trebilcock, *Industrialization*, 432.

26. Besides Grant and Bovykin, cited above, see also Susan P. McCaffray, *The Politics of Industrialization in Tsarist Russia: The Association of Southern Coal and Steel Producers, 1874–1914* (DeKalb: Northern Illinois University Press, 1996).

27. Gatrell, *Tsarist Economy*, 186–187.

28. Kahan, *Russian Economic History*, 36–37.

29. Trebilcock, *Industrialization*, 452.

30. Trebilcock, *Industrialization*, 447.

31. Nicholas V. Riasanovsky, *A History of Russia*, 6th ed. (New York: Oxford University Press, 2000), 432. Riasanovsky cites per capita income in Russia in 1913 at 102.2 rubles, giving ruble figures for the other countries: Germany, 292; France, 355; and England, 463. The United States outpaced the European leaders considerably, at 695 rubles per person per year.

32. See, for example, J. N. Westwood et al., "The Railways," in *From Tsarism to the New Economic Policy*, ed. R. W. Davies (Ithaca, N.Y.: Cornell University Press, 1991), 169–188; and Peter Gatrell, *Government, Industry and Rearmament in Russia, 1900–1914* (Cambridge, UK: Cambridge University Press, 1994).

SUGGESTED READING

Blum, Jerome. *Lord and Peasant in Russia: From the Ninth to the Nineteenth Century.* Princeton, N.J., 1961.

Gatrell, Peter. *The Tsarist Economy, 1850–1917.* New York, 1986.

Gerschenkron, Alexander. *Economic Backwardness in Historical Perspective.* Cambridge, Mass., 1962.

Hoch, Stephen L. *Serfdom and Social Control in Russia.* Chicago, 1989.

Kahan, Arcadius. *Russian Economic History: The Nineteenth Century.* Chicago, 1989.

McCaffray, Susan P. *The Politics of Industrialization in Tsarist Russia: The Association of Southern Coal and Steel Producers, 1874–1914.* DeKalb, Ill., 1996.

——, and Michael S. Melancon, eds. *A Member of the Family: Russia in the European Context, 1789–1914.* New York, 2004.

Trebilcock, Clive. *The Industrialization of the Continental Powers, 1780–1914.* London, 1981.

11

The Trial of Vera Zasulich

Ana Siljak

The trial of Vera Zasulich on March 31, 1878, was one of the most famous Russian trials of the nineteenth century. On the day of the trial, all who held tickets for admission crushed together in their search for seats. Many in Russian high society attended the event, having begged the presiding judge for tickets well in advance. Behind the judges' bench, in a row of specially reserved armchairs, sat the highest-ranking officials in the Russian administration, including the ministers of war, foreign affairs, and finance. And in the nearby press box, foreign and Russian journalists came to observe the trial, including the famous writer Fyodor Dostoyevsky. Outside the courthouse, a large crowd gathered, hoping to catch a glimpse of the accused.[1]

Everyone who attended the event knew, of course, the dramatic story of how Vera Zasulich attempted to assassinate the governor of St. Petersburg, General Fedor Trepov. She had come to his office on January 24, 1878, under the false name of Elizaveta Kozlova, pretending to be an ordinary petitioner. When Trepov asked her for her petition, she meekly gave it to him. Then, after he turned toward the next petitioner, she reached into the folds of the large, black shawl she was wearing and pulled out a small pistol. After firing twice, she threw the pistol into a corner and stood quietly, making no attempt to escape. All of the witnesses to the event were impressed by the calm, cold demeanor she retained throughout the course of events. Even when one of Trepov's guards attacked her and nearly beat her senseless, she never lost her composure.[2]

When asked why she had shot at Trepov, Zasulich answered simply that it was in revenge for the flogging of Bogoliubov in the St. Petersburg House of Preliminary Detention. Zasulich was referring to a nearly forgotten incident that had taken place some six months before her attempted assassination of

Trepov on July 13, 1877. On that hot summer day, Trepov had unexpectedly appeared to inspect the situation at the large, modern House of Preliminary Detention, which mostly contained suspects awaiting trial. There he encountered Bogoliubov (his actual name was A. C. Emelianov), a prisoner convicted of participating in a political demonstration. Trepov was probably irritated by the lax regime he found in the prison—many of the prisoners were strolling aimlessly in the prison yard and others were sitting in the windowsills of their cells. His rage turned on Bogoliubov, for the minor fact that the latter had failed to take off his hat in the presence of the governor. Trepov hit the hat off of Bogoliubov's head, causing an outcry among the prisoners in the yard, which further infuriated Trepov. In anger, Trepov ordered Bogoliubov to be flogged by birch rods, loud enough for everyone to hear. Immediately, a riot swept through the halls of the prison and lasted for three days. Bogoliubov was given twenty-five strokes, though rumors spread that he was flogged unconscious. He later went insane.[3]

At first, Zasulich's attempted assassination of Trepov looked like nothing more than an act of revenge by an angry young woman, and many even surmised that Zasulich was Bogoliubov's lover. But soon investigators discovered that Zasulich was not a lone assassin. The Russian secret police, the Third Department of His Majesty's Secret Chancellery (known simply as the Third Department), found evidence of a wider plot to kill twenty government officials.[4] Threatening letters addressed to Trepov and other officials were found in the mail on the day of the shooting.[5] The Third Department also received reports that, immediately after the incident, brochures and pamphlets praising Zasulich's actions were found in factories and high schools. One of the anonymous pamphleteers declared: "Generations will add your name to the list . . . of martyrs for the freedom and rights of man."[6]

Investigators also unearthed disconcerting facts about Zasulich's past. Zasulich had been arrested and exiled on different occasions for her involvement in socialist revolutionary activity. She was first imprisoned at the age of nineteen, in connection with her involvement with Sergei Nechaev, the infamous revolutionary convicted of conspiracy to murder a member of his own organization. She spent the subsequent four years in and out of exile. Both of her sisters had previously been arrested for revolutionary activity, and both sisters were also married to confirmed revolutionaries. In 1875, she disappeared and successfully hid herself from police surveillance.[7]

In sum, within a month of investigating Zasulich's assassination attempt, the Russian government believed that Vera Zasulich's crime was nothing other than an act of terrorism. Tsar Alexander II, after reviewing one of the documents of the Zasulich case, wrote in the margin: "This perversity is entirely reminiscent of Karakozov," referring to Dmitrii Karakozov, the young student radical who had tried to assassinate the tsar himself in 1866.[8]

Vera Zasulich's trial became the first public jury trial of a Russian terrorist and, as such, had profound consequences both for the future of the Russian judicial system and for the further development of Russian terrorism. The relatively new Russian court system, reformed according to Western models in 1864, was presented with a major challenge: could it withstand the pressures of an increasingly violent terrorist movement, or would its power be curtailed by a regime that feared a system it could not directly control? As the trial date neared, it became clear that neither the prosecution nor the defense believed in the value of due process of law inherent in the reformed courts. Instead, both the Russian regime and the Russian socialist revolutionary movement saw the Zasulich trial as a theatrical event, a performance designed to persuade the public of an ideological point of view. The regime hoped that the trial would prove the dangerous and desperate quality of Russian terrorism. The revolutionaries, including Zasulich, were determined to demonstrate their willingness to become martyrs for the sake of their cause.

The Russian regime's decision to try Vera Zasulich by jury has been one of the most interesting puzzles of the Zasulich case. The regime had another choice—it could have tried Vera in the special, semi-secret courts reserved for those whose crimes had a "political" nature (discussed below). Indeed, when Konstantin I. Palen, the Russian minister of justice, made the decision to try Zasulich by jury, he had to openly ignore all of the evidence of a conspiracy to assassinate government officials. He had to declare that Zasulich was nothing more than an ordinary murder suspect. Anatolii Koni, the judge in the Zasulich trial, remembered the almost conspiratorial attempts to conceal the political nature of Zasulich's crime.[9] It should be kept in mind that the Ministry of Justice in general, and Palen in particular, were usually very eager to try "political" suspects in the special courts.

The most convincing explanation for this peculiar decision is that the Ministry of Justice was convinced that a jury would find Zasulich guilty. She had shot Trepov in front of dozens of witnesses and did not deny that she had done so. And this certain guilty verdict would serve a very important purpose for the regime: the trial would show the Russian revolutionary movement that their actions were repugnant to society. One observer interpreted the decision this way:

> The jurors will deliver a guilty verdict and thereby teach a sobering lesson to the insane coterie of revolutionaries; they will show the Russian and foreign admirers of Vera Zasulich's "heroic exploit" that the Russian people bow before the Tsar, revere him, and are always ready to defend his faithful servants.[10]

For this same reason, Palen decided to allow the Russian press full access to the trial. The crime, he declared, would "disturb the moral sentiments of

everyone," and "necessarily should elicit general indignation and full condemnation."[11] In essence, the Russian regime wanted Vera Zasulich's trial to
become an instructive drama—a show trial.

The idea of a show trial of the revolutionary movement was nothing new
for the Russian regime. Ever since 1864, when the Russian legal system was
completely overhauled, the Ministry of Justice had attempted to utilize one
of the most important principles built into the Russian legal reforms: the
principle of educating the public in civic duty and loyalty to legal authority.

Russia's thoroughgoing legal reforms of 1864 directly followed the liberation of the Russian serfs in 1861. As a result, the authors of Russia's legal
reforms always had two purposes in mind. The first was to provide a more
predictable and evenhanded means of adjudicating criminal and civil matters. The second was to *educate* the recently liberated Russian people in the
concepts of abstract law, the legal process, and faith in tsarist government
and institutions.[12] Although many in the Russian regime feared the legal reforms, believing that former serfs could not participate in a complicated legal system, the reformers argued that participation in a fair and just process
would provide precisely the kind of preparation ordinary people needed.
Even the semi-literate and ill educated could benefit greatly from their encounters with the more open and more regular court system.[13]

The judicial reforms of 1864 were, in intentional and unintentional ways,
the most liberal of Russian reforms of the early 1860s. The structure of the
new courts was almost entirely put together using the examples of Western
European judicial theory and practice. And every aspect of the new system
was to have both a procedural and an educational function. A good example was the insistence on the independence of the judiciary. Judges were appointed for life, and could only be removed if they were convicted of a
crime.[14] According to the reformers, this judicial independence had the important effect of developing "a consciousness of rights," and "a corresponding consciousness of responsibility," in the judges and in ordinary people.[15] For similar reasons, under the new system, most trials were open to
the public. It was hoped that the new system would spread the "feeling of
legality and respect for the law."[16]

One of the most significant of the Russian legal reforms was the institution of a Western-style trial by jury. The Russian jury system was very similar to its European and American counterparts. Each case was decided by
twelve jurors, chosen from an initial list of thirty. Both the prosecution and
the defense had the right to peremptory challenge. The verdict was decided
by ballot, and required only a majority decision.[17]

The jury trial was considered the most important aspect of the legal reforms. According to the reformers, nothing would instill more respect for
legal procedure than participation in the formality and deliberation of a
jury trial. Not only would society be forced to weigh the actions of its own

members, but the outcome would be respected because it would be seen as the result of an open and fair debate. In a memo to the reformers, one former Moscow prosecutor was blunt: only jury trials would help people to "learn about the law."[18]

These liberal judicial reforms did create what one historian has called "an element of disruption" within the Russian government. The Russian regime implemented the reforms, but it never became comfortable with the notion of a judicial process in which formal, abstract justice prevailed, and in which the strict adherence to procedure was more important than the legitimacy of the outcome. The new judicial institutions represented a limitation on autocratic authority—the legal system was designed to be resistant to intervention by the Russian authorities, even in cases where intervention seemed critical to Russian officials. Particularly in the case of jury trials, many in the regime feared that sympathetic juries would too often set criminals free.[19]

But even the most suspicious of the regime officials, like Palen himself, hoped that the educational possibilities of the new system would outweigh the potential dangers. The government increasingly sought to control the outcome of important trials so that a certain message could be delivered to the Russian public. In particular, in the 1870s, the legal system was seen as a potential tool against Russian revolutionary activity.

In 1872, the regime sought to make the outcomes of important trials predictable, while preserving some of the more educational functions of the new courts. A new court was created specifically for "political" trials (or trials of those accused of crimes against the state), called the Special Session of the Senate (Osoboe prisutsviia Pravitelstvuiushchevo Senata, or OPPS). It was composed of senators and representatives from various Russian social classes, all individually chosen by the tsar. But this new judicial tribunal was not a complete departure from the reformed courts. Although there was no jury, the OPPS was still an adversarial system, and the accused could retain independent defense attorneys. The trials were still semi-public, in front of a small audience, and transcripts of the trial (though sometimes abridged) were published in the regime's newspaper, the *Official Messenger*.[20]

In March 1875, the Russian regime explicitly decided to use the OPPS as a means of *publicly* discrediting the revolutionary movement. The regime decided to arrest and to bring to trial hundreds of revolutionaries in front of the OPPS. By making the trial semi-public, they hoped to expose the revolutionary movement as the "delirious ravings of a fanatical imagination."[21] This 1875 decision resulted in the first major Russian "show trials": the famous trials of the "50" and the "193" in 1877–1878. The main purpose of the trials was to expose the apparent revolutionaries who were threatening society with their anti-government, disruptive, and violent activity. Through the trials of Russian revolutionaries, the Russian public would fully come to comprehend the necessity of a respect for the legal system and for a law-abiding citizenry.

But there was one flaw in the regime's plan: the Russian officials who constructed these trials were so assured of the public's immediate condemnation of revolution that they never actually prepared for the "show" in the trials. They believed that it was enough to bring the accused to the courts, and after that, matters would take care of themselves. This was their fatal mistake—they simply did not realize "show trials" were the perfect forum for demonstrating the power of the Russian revolutionary movement.[22] Russian revolutionaries were also aware of the potential educational function of the new court system. And they were quick to exploit the opportunities the new system afforded.

For the Russian revolutionaries of the late 1860s and 1870s, revolution meant many things. In simplest terms it meant the desire to overthrow the existing Russian regime and to overhaul all of Russian society in order to install some form of socialism. Although revolutionaries debated endlessly about how to get the masses to revolt and what to do once revolution occurred, they were united in two important beliefs: the existing system was oppressive and degrading, and therefore no compromise was possible; and only the complete destruction of the existing order would bring about a harmonious future. Many had visions of a postrevolutionary earthly utopia, where all Russians would enjoy a kind of heavenly communal existence.[23]

As a result, a large number of those who joined the Russian revolutionary movement saw it as a kind of religious experience, a cause to which one had to devote one's entire life. For many revolutionaries, the desire for revolutionary activity was even borne out of an early religious fanaticism. Vera Zasulich, for example, recounted her early conversion experience as a young girl, when she read the New Testament account of Christ's passion. In her imagination, his martyrdom became entwined with her own: she even began to dream of rescuing Christ from the cross. After she became an atheist, she said, "The only thing in religion that remained etched on my heart— Christ—I never parted with; on the contrary, I connected with him closer than ever."[24] Her adoration of Christ was entwined with a worship of past Russian revolutionary martyrs. She cherished the example of the poet Kondratii Ryleev, hanged for his participation in the Decembrist plot against the Russian regime in 1825. The twin figures of Christ and Ryleev became associated with the image of a "crown of thorns." She wished to earn this crown as well, by "proving worthy of their struggle."[25] For her, martyrdom was the most beautiful form of self-sacrifice.[26]

This religious desire for self-sacrifice and even martyrdom was common for many revolutionaries. Vera Figner spoke of the influence of Christ's Sermon on the Mount; others spoke of the Christian saints that inspired them to "suffer for the truth."[27] Self-sacrifice and martyrdom took on many forms—many revolutionaries gave up privileged positions in society; others sacrificed careers and personal wealth. In the "going to the people" movement of the mid-1870s, thousands of young revolutionaries left their universities and jobs to live among peasants and workers, to share their back-breaking work, and, in their spare time, to bring the suffering masses to revolt.[28]

After the government arrested thousands of young radicals, some began to argue that the new forum for self-sacrifice could be found in the court-room. During their trials, the revolutionaries would bravely face their accusers and declare their faith in their cause and their willingness to die for revolution. The famous revolutionary writer, Petr Lavrov, developed an entire ethic for revolutionary behavior in court. When facing the judges, Lavrov wrote,

> Revolutionaries should desire nothing more than to be punished for the sake of the cause: you can act forcefully, even if passively, through your suffering, for which you will be written into the roll of martyrs of Russian socialism. Take care that your name inspires others to follow the same path, toward the same goal, to the same suffering. Your martyrology is, perhaps, your final weapon. . . . Your energy may inspire many. Your weakness might discourage an even greater number.[29]

This tract was written in the same year that the Russian government decided to put the revolution on trial.

In essence, by 1875, both the government and the revolutionaries were looking for a confrontation. And the arena for their battle became the courtroom. Neither side was interested in procedure, or due process of law. Instead, as Laura Engelstein has argued, the courts became "tribunals, in which the defendants played dramatic roles in a spell-binding theater of ideas."[30] Both sides saw trials as a theater in which contesting sides would dramatize their ideas for the benefit of the audience—wider Russian society. It was a debate in the form of an educational drama.

The trials in 1877–1878 of the 50 and 193 (these were populists active in the "going to the people" movement) were the first of these show trials. The regime accused the revolutionaries of a Russia-wide conspiracy to commit every kind of crime: "Rejection of religion, family, private property, the destruction of all classes of society through the general assault on all who are above the level of the simple and poor peasant." The very number of defendants was meant to convey the scope and nature of the dangers facing Russian society.[31] The defendants countered with carefully prepared testimonies, using the courtroom as a forum for socialist propaganda. One of the most dramatic moments came during the trial of the 193. The revolutionary defendant I. N. Myshkin, in his prepared statement, declared that the court was "more shameful than a house of prostitution: a woman sells her body out of need, but here the senators, out of vileness and servility . . . sell everything that is valuable to humanity." After the judges repeatedly cried for him to be quiet, he was eventually beaten by the guards in the courthouse. The small audience at the trial began to cry out, thinking that Myshkin was in grave danger of his life.[32]

The trials became a public relations nightmare for the regime. Wild rumors began to spread about the proceedings. Revolutionary groups used illegal presses to publish the texts of the speeches, showing the revolutionaries in a courageous light. Even the judges were unreliable. The sentences handed down were light: ninety were found not guilty, and sixty-one were sentenced to time served.[33] For many, these light sentences became confirmation that the trials were nothing more than scandalous persecution of brave revolutionaries. Sergei Kravchinskii, a revolutionary himself, claimed that the spectators at the trial of the 50 kept repeating, "They are saints."[34]

There is no doubt that the disastrous nature of the trials of the 50 and the 193 weighed heavily on the minds of Palen and others within the Ministry of Justice when they considered the case of Vera Zasulich. More than anything else, they did not want her trial to be plagued by sensational rumors and tales of martyrdom and oppression. This partly led to the decision to give her an open, public, jury trial. No one could protest that her trial was illegitimate or that she was being mistreated.

But if Palen and others were wary of past precedents, they must have also felt optimistic about the case against Zasulich. This time around, the public would certainly condemn revolutionary activity. Zasulich had done something so heinous that no one could see it as justifiable or "saintly." Revolution had degenerated into attempted murder, and the jury would, in Palen's words, "treat the matter severely."[35]

This time, Palen did begin by plotting a prosecutorial strategy with some dramatic elements. He sought to appoint one of Russia's most capable prosecutors, Vladimir Zhukovskii, who was said to look like Mephistopheles and was known for manufacturing entire cases out of a few pieces of evidence.[36] But things did not go Palen's way. Zhukovskii, most likely sensing that the Zasulich case was hopeless, declared that he could not accept it; other candidates similarly refused.[37] Palen ended up forcing the case on a rather hapless and meek assistant prosecutor, Konstantin Kessel.[38]

In frustration, Palen then turned to the judge in the trial, Anatolii Koni. He asked Koni to ensure a guilty verdict. Koni firmly refused to compromise his judicial position, but suggested some effective prosecutorial strategies. At that point, an inexplicable inertia seemed to take hold of the minister of justice. "The prosecutor is not so important," he told Koni in a tired voice. "Despite everything I still will rely on you."[39] Yet again, Palen failed to prepare for the theatrical aspect of what he hoped would be a show trial.

Vera Zasulich and her revolutionary comrades, however, did everything possible to make sure the outcome was a success. They hired one of Russia's best lawyers, Petr A. Aleksandrov, who had so eloquently defended some of the accused in the trial of the 193. Aleksandrov was sympathetic to the revolutionary cause and became well known in radical circles after his eloquent speeches for the defense in the trial of the 193. He knew just how to present Zasulich in the best possible light. Like the regime, he was mindful of the precedent set by the trials of the 50 and the 193. He decided that he would turn Zasulich's trial into a spectacle, and convince the jury that they were persecuting a martyr.[40]

Like Palen, Aleksandrov knew that the Zasulich trial would be high drama—a duel between the regime and Zasulich. Taking this into account, he did his best to choreograph every detail of the trial. For example, he bought Zasulich a brand-new, elegant dress, hoping to cast her in the role of a society lady. Zasulich, already well known in radical circles for her slovenly appearance, simply refused. But she did agree to heed his suggestion not to bite her nails, since he explained that the jurors might consider that a sign of guilt.[41]

On the day of the trial, the courtroom was packed with an audience expecting drama, and the trial provided them with everything they desired.[42] The very entrance of Zasulich caused a stir in the crowd. She was not necessarily what they expected—she was modest, plain, and quiet; "her manner was simple and natural." This helped to create a first impression of a modest, humble woman.[43]

Konstantin Kessel seemed completely unaware of the dramatic dynamics taking place within the courtroom. He restricted his entire strategy to proving that Zasulich shot Trepov and called only four witnesses, each of whom simply testified to seeing Zasulich pull the trigger. Many of the witnesses were Trepov's guards, who had an unsympathetic, official bearing. The prosecutor's case was simply dry and dull. He behaved as if it were an open-and-shut case.

Aleksandrov, on the other hand, played to the audience's desire for spectacle. His primary goal was to twist the entire case around and make it a trial of Trepov for the flogging of Bogoliubov at the House of Preliminary Detention. Alexandrov called witnesses to speak of the events that occurred at the prison.[44] The very appearance of the witnesses to the defense was dramatic. Many of them were young political prisoners, and had been taken to court directly from prison. These sad-looking young people spoke emotionally, with difficulty, sometimes with tears in their eyes. Each told the same story: that Bogoliubov was simply walking in the courtyard of the prison, that Trepov, in a fit of rage, knocked the hat off his head, and that then Bogoliubov was, for no apparent reason at all, sentenced to be flogged. Some declared that they heard Bogoliubov's cries and shouts as he was being flogged.[45] The audience was deeply moved. One woman in the courtroom wrote: "Their pale faces, their voices trembling with tears and indignation, the details of their depositions—all these statements made me lower my eyes in shame."[46]

Aleksandrov next called Zasulich to the stand. She looked younger than her years (she was not quite twenty-nine), and she spoke quietly. She never mentioned her revolutionary activity, but she gave a martyr's account of her actions, a story of being willing to suffer so that others could be saved. She told the courtroom how she had read about Bogoliubov's punishment. She was outraged that one man was powerful enough to vent his "personal spite" on an innocent victim. Such an act "could not go unpunished." But no one punished Trepov—society was silent. There was no other way: "I decided, even at the cost of my own death, to prove that a man should not believe that he is invincible." At this point in her testimony, she became too upset to continue.[47]

At the end of the trial, after Kessel gave his uninspiring summation for the prosecution, Aleksandrov delivered his dramatic coup de théâtre. His summation was a brilliant narrative—so eloquent that some believe Dostoyevsky used it as a model in the courtroom scene at the end of *The Brothers Karamazov.*

Aleksandrov began by telling the sad tale of Zasulich's life in prison and exile. Omitting all reference to her revolutionary activity, he described her as a young woman wronged—an innocent girl seduced into revolutionary activity by the wily Sergei Nechaev and then brutally punished by the Russian regime. Aleksandrov told the jury that Zasulich had spent the "best years of her life" in a dank, dark prison cell, never even aware of the charges against her. Then she was exiled—simply abandoned in a northern Russian city with nothing but the clothes on her back, forced to beg for food.[48]

Aleksandrov then turned to the events of July 13, in the House of Preliminary Detention. Aleksandrov first gave a very detailed, and much embroidered, description of the flogging of Bogoliubov—of his supposed cries and shouts. His retelling of the Bogoliubov story was so moving that at one point—when Aleksandrov declared that Bogoliubov's torturers flogged him until he cried out with pain and shame—the entire courtroom audience began to applaud and shout "Bravo!"[49]

Finally, Aleksandrov put the two tales together. A young woman who had experienced all of the horrors of imprisonment learned of the cruel and vindictive flogging of an unknown young man. She felt all of the sympathy of a fellow sufferer. She prayed that society would punish the torturer, that this horrible crime would be avenged. But nothing happened. She then decided that she would become a defender of the humiliated and abused. Aleksandrov carefully explained that she was not motivated by revenge. She was full of the noble desire to sacrifice herself for the sake of human dignity. Aleksandrov ended with a dramatic statement: Zasulich would gladly accept a guilty verdict from the jury. She would comfort herself with "the knowledge that her suffering, her sacrifice, prevented the repetition of the situation that led her to act."[50]

The effect of Aleksandrov's speech was electrifying. As a lawyer, he had managed to transform Zasulich into what she had always desired to be, a martyr for the good of mankind. Her attempt to kill another human being was, in fact, an act of martyrdom. In his words,

> That which yesterday was considered a crime against the state, today or tomorrow will become a glorious act of civic courage. A crime against the state is often just an expression of a doctrine of premature reform, a preaching of that which is not yet ripe and whose time has not yet come.[51]

The audience was convinced. One journalist remembers that he felt that Zasulich was not on trial; rather it was a trial of Russian society, himself included. Society was entirely to blame.[52]

It did not take long for the jury to pronounce its verdict: "Not guilty." But the foreman could not get past the "Not . . ." before the entire court exploded into a chorus of cheers and shouts. Witnesses reported that even the high-ranking ministers sitting behind the judges in their plush armchairs began to shout for joy.[53] When Zasulich left the courthouse, she was met with an enormous crowd that had gathered to hear the verdict. Shouts of "Bravo!" and "Vera!" were heard everywhere.[54]

Zasulich quickly became an international celebrity. Leo Tolstoy declared the Zasulich case to be a "harbinger of Revolution," French newspapers compared Vera to Charlotte Corday, and in Germany, both Marx and Engels declared that they were impressed by her courage. Famous writers throughout Europe and Russia were inspired by her story: Turgenev wrote a poem about her; Dostoyevsky incorporated components of her trial in *The Brothers Karamazov*; and Oscar Wilde included her story in his first play, entitled *Vera, or The Nihilists*. One Russian émigré made the interesting, if unverifiable, claim that British parents began to name their daughters "Vera" in her honor.[55]

For the Russian regime, the Zasulich acquittal provoked a crisis. The drama in the courtroom did nothing to discredit revolutionaries, but instead humiliated the Russian regime. Some people began to speak of the trial as the "fall of the Bastille."[56] The judicial reforms of 1864 were seen as fundamentally flawed—they were responsible for lenient verdicts and the collapse of the traditional order. The government sought increasingly to curtail the authority of the courts and to restrict access to jury trials. On August 9, 1878, political trials were uniformly to be handed over to military tribunals in cases where there was "armed" action against the government.[57]

In revolutionary circles, on the other hand, the Zasulich acquittal confirmed the power of dramatic acts of terror and martyrdom. Zasulich's subsequent popularity inspired a whole new generation of revolutionaries to turn to terrorism. The only way to truly understand the power she had within the ranks of Russian socialism is to see her as the first socialist terrorist-martyr, the first Russian socialist saint. Years later, when she lived in exile in Geneva, revolutionary activists would make special pilgrimages from Russia to see her and speak with her. Young girls dreamed of following in her footsteps.[58]

The Zasulich trial provided the ultimate precedent for the terrorism that was to follow. Young men and women used bombs, guns, and even knives against Russian officials. The trend reached its peak with the assassination of Alexander II in 1881 and continued to plague Russia even after 1917. Terrorists declared that all forms of corruption and brutality and all perpetrators of oppression would be targets for the swift and severe justice of a small group of revolutionaries. At the same time, most terrorists were themselves willing to pay the supreme price for their actions. They only hoped that, like Zasulich, they would have an opportunity, however small, to declare their faith in a courtroom and show the Russian public their willingness to become martyrs for the cause.[59] Vera Figner, one of the terrorists who plotted the assassination in 1881, declared that she looked forward to her trial. It gave her the opportunity, she wrote, "to confess my faith, to declare before the court the spiritual impulses which had governed our activities, and to point out the social and political ideal to which we had aspired."[60]

In essence, after the Zasulich trial, the Russian judicial system lost much of its power to adjudicate crimes against the state. For both the regime and the revolutionaries, the courts became nothing more than an instrument to be used for achieving political aims. Neither side was interested in the due process of law. In the cycle of violence that followed, an increasingly draconian series of measures were taken against an increasingly violent revolutionary movement.

Even after the Russian Revolution, the aftereffects of her trial continued. The idea of a trial as a spiritual drama, as a revolutionary declaration of the faith, inspired the theatrical spectacles of the Communist courts. Vladimir Illich Lenin, like his tsarist predecessors, believed that the legal system's primary purpose should be educational, not procedural. The courtroom became a spectacle more than a legal institution, in essence, a show trial.[61]

NOTES

1. Margaret Maxwell, *Narodniki Women: Russian Women Who Sacrificed Themselves for the Dream of Freedom* (New York: Pergamon Press, 1990), 3–49. The trial is also analyzed and described in the following books and articles: Jay Bergman, *Vera Zasulich: A Biography* (Stanford, Calif.: Stanford University Press, 1983); Wolfgang Geheiros, *Vera Zasulich und die russische revolutionäre Bewegung* (Munich: R.

Oldenbourg Verlag, 1977); N. A. Troitskii, *Tsarskie sudy protiv revoliutsionnoi Rossii* (Saratov, Russia: Izdatel'stvo Saratovskogo Universiteta, 1976); Iu. S. Karpilenko, *"Delo" Very Zasulich: Rossiiskoe obshchestvo, samoderzhavie i sud prisiazhnykh v 1878 godu* (Briansk, Russia: Izdatel'stvo Brianskogo gosudarstvennogo pedagogicheskogo instituta, 1994); Samuel Kucherov, "The Case of Vera Zasulich," *Russian Review* 11, no. 2 (April 1952): 86–96; A. F. Koni, *Sobranie Sochinenii*, vol. 2 (Moscow: Izdatel'stvo "Iuridicheskaia Literatura," 1966) (also published separately as *Vospominaniia o dele Very Zasulich*).

2. Koni, *Sochinenii*, 66–67. See also the witness testimony on pages 98–105.

3. D. Gertsenshtein, "Tridtsat' let tomu nazad," *Byloe*, no. 6 (1907): 236–257; Sergei Glagol', "Protsess pervoi russkoi terroristki," *Golos minuvshago*, no. 7–9 (September 1918): 147–162; Sinegub, "Vospominaniia chaikovtsa," *Byloe*, no. 10 (1906): 49–54.

4. "Agenturnye doneseniia ob obstoiatelstvakh pokusheniia Zasulich, V. I.," Gosudarstvennii arkhiv Rossiiskoi Federatsii (GARF), fond 109, Sekretnyi arkhiv III-ego otdeleniia, opis' 1, delo 717, listy 10–11; "Vypiski iz pisem Reinberga, . . . i proche o pokushenie na zhizni Gradonachalnika Trepova," GARF, fond 109, Sekretnyi arkhiv, opis' 1, delo 718, listy 1–2, 10. All subsequent archival references, unless otherwise noted, refer to GARF documents.

5. "O dvorianke Very Zasulich," fond 109, 3-ia ekspeditsiia, opis' 163 (1878), delo 68.1, listy 27–30.

6. "O dvorianke Very Zasulich," listy 36, 54, 56. Two of the pamphlets are printed in V. I. Nevskii, ed., *Istoriko-revoliutsionnyi sbornik*, vol. 2 (Leningrad: Gosudarstvennoe izdatel'stvo, 1924), 331–335. Quote on p. 335.

7. "O dvorianke Very Zasulich," listy 5, 11, 13, 40, 42.

8. Fond 109, 3-ia ekspeditsiia, opis' 163 (1878), delo 68.1, list 1. Also printed in Nevskii, *Sbornik*, 329.

9. Koni, *Sochinenii*, 66–67.

10. N. K. Bukh, *Vospominaniia* (Moscow, 1828), 162. Bukh's statement is quoted in Bergman, *Zasulich*, 40 (his translation is slightly modified here), and in S. Volk and M. Vydria's introduction to Koni, *Sochineniia*, 11.

11. Quoted in Karpilenko, *"Delo,"* 28

12. Richard Wortman, *The Development of a Russian Legal Consciousness* (Chicago: University of Chicago Press, 1976), 245, 260.

13. See Joan Neuberger, "Popular Legal Cultures: The St. Petersburg Mirovoi Sud," in *Russia's Great Reforms, 1855–1881*, ed. Ben Eklof, John Bushnell, and Larissa Zakharova (Bloomington: Indiana University Press, 1994), 231–246, esp. 231–232.

14. Samuel Kucherov, *Courts, Lawyers and Trials under the Last Three Tsars* (New York: Praeger, 1953).

15. Wortman, *Development*, 260.

16. Kucherov, *Courts*, 38–39; Wortman, *Development*, 259.

17. Kucherov, *Courts*, 59–60, 62.

18. Gr. Dzhanshiev, *Osnovy sudebnoi reformy: Istoriko-iuridicheskie etiudy* (Moscow, 1891), 126.

19. Wortman, *Development*, 245–270.

20. Troitskii, *Tsarskie sudy*, 101–104, 149; Wortman, *Development*, 281.

21. Troitskii, *Tsarskie sudy*, 158–159. See also Franco Venturi, *Roots of Revolution: A History of the Populist and Socialist Movements in Nineteenth Century Russia* (London: Phoenix Press, 1952), 585.

22. P. I. Negretov, "K sporam vokrug protsessa Very Zasulich," *Voprosy istorii*, no. 12 (1971), 183–189.

23. Andrzej Walicki, *Marxism and the Leap to the Kingdom of Freedom* (Stanford, Calif.: Stanford University Press, 1995); Igal Halfin, *From Darkness to Light: Class, Consciousness, and Salvation in Revolutionary Russia* (Pittsburgh: University of Pittsburgh Press, 2000); and Richard Pipes, *The Russian Revolution* (New York: Vintage Books, 1991), chap. 4.

24. Vera Zasulich, *Vospominaniia* (Moscow: Izdatel'stvo vsesoiuznogo obshchestva politkatorzhan i ssylno-poselentsev, 1931), 13–15.

25. Zasulich, *Vospominaniia*, 15–16.

26. Zasulich, "'Otkrovennye rechi,' vospominaniia o 1870-kh gg . . ." Rossiiskaia natsional'naia biblioteka (RNB), Otdel rukopisi (OR), Dom Plekhanova, fond 1098, opis' 1, delo 29, list 1.

27. Hilde Hoogenboom, "Vera Figner and Revolutionary Autobiographies: The Influence of Gender on Genre," in *Women in Russia and Ukraine*, ed. Rosalind Marsh (Cambridge, UK: Cambridge University Press, 1995), 85.

28. Venturi, *Roots of Revolution*, 504–505.

29. Troitskii, *Tsarskie sudy*, 118–119.

30. Laura Engelstein, "Revolution and the Theater of Public Life in Imperial Russia," in *Revolution and the Meanings of Freedom in the Nineteenth Century*, ed. Isser Woloch (Stanford, Calif.: Stanford University Press, 1996), 340–341.

31. Troitskii, *Tsarskie sudy*, 158–160.

32. A. Iakimova, "'Bol'shoi protsess,' ili 'protsess 193': O revoliutsionnoi propagande v imperii," *Katorga i ssylka*, no. 37 (1927): 27–28; N. S. Tagantsev, "Iz perezhitogo," *Byloe*, no. 9 (1918): 145.

33. Troitskii, *Tsarskie sudy*, 196–197.

34. Quoted in Venturi, *Roots of Revolution*, 586.

35. Koni, *Sochinenii*, 66.

36. Koni, *Sochinenii*, 81; N. P. Karabchevskii, *Okolo pravosudiia* (Tula, Russia: Avtograf, 2001), 656.

37. R. Kantor, "K protsessu V. I. Zasulich," *Byloe*, no. 21 (1923): 89.

38. Koni, *Sochinenii*, 83.

39. Koni, *Sochinenii*, 88.

40. Troitskii, *Tsarskie sudy*, 102–103; "Agenturnye doneseniia," listy 16, 19; Karabchevskii, *Okolo pravosudiia*, 658

41. N. Kuliabko-Koretskii, "Moi vstrechi s V. I. Zasulich," *Gruppa "Osvobozhdenie Truda": Iz arkhivov G. V. Plekhanova, V. I. Zasulicha, i L. G. Deicha*, vol. 3 (Moscow-Leningrad, 1926), 75–76.

42. G. K. Gradovskii in *Golos*, no. 92 (April 2, 1878): 2.

43. Elisabeth Naryshkin-Kurakin, *Under Three Tsars* (New York: E. P. Dutton, 1931), 54; Glagol', "Protsess pervoi russkoi terroristki," 151; Gertsenshtein, "Tridtsat' let," 251.

44. The transcript of the trial is reprinted in Koni, *Sochinenii*, 94–171.

45. Koni, *Sochinenii*, 115–116.

46. Naryshkin-Kurakin, *Under Three Tsars*, 55.

47. Koni, *Sochinenii*, 120.

48. Koni, *Sochinenii*, 136–138. Much of Alexandrov's biographical information on Zasulich was either exaggerated or simply wrong.

49. Gertsenshtein, "Tridtsat' let," 252.

50. Koni, *Sochinenii*, 149–151, 156.

51. Koni, *Sochinenii*, 145–146.

52. Gradovskii, *Golos*, 2; Naryshkin-Kurakin, *Under Three Tsars*, 55.

53. Glagol', "Protsess pervoi russkoi terroristki," 155; Koni, *Sochinenii*, 173; Naryshkin-Kurakin, *Under Three Tsars*, 55.

54. Glagol', "Protsess pervoi russkoi terroristki," 157; Kuliabko-Koretskii, "Moi vstrechi," 76.

55. Bergman, *Zasulich*, 54–55.

56. "Vypiski iz pisem," listy 39, 40, 48, 50, 55; Koni, *Sochinenii*, 180.

57. Troitskii, *Tsarskie sudy*, 105.

58. R. M. Plekhanova, "Stranitsa iz vospominanii o V. I. Zasulich," in L. Deich, *Gruppa "Osvobozhdenie truda,"* vol. 3, 83; L. S. Fedorchenko, "Vera Zasulich," *Katorga i ssylka*, no. 23 (1927): 198.

59. Zasulich, *Vospominaniia*, 65–66.

60. Vera Figner, *Memoirs of a Revolutionist* (DeKalb: Northern Illinois University Press, 1991), 158.

61. Julie A. Cassiday, *The Enemy on Trial: Early Soviet Courts on Stage and Screen* (DeKalb: Northern Illinois University Press, 2000), 37. I would also like to thank Elizabeth Wood for her insights into the links between trials and theater in early Soviet Russia.

SUGGESTED READING

Bergman, Jay. *Vera Zasulich: A Biography.* Stanford, Calif., 1983.

Engel, Barbara Alpern. *Five Sisters: Women against the Tsar.* New York, 1975.

———. *Mothers and Daughters: Women of the Intelligentsia in Nineteenth-Century Russia.* Evanston, Ill., 2000.

Engelstein, Laura. "Revolution and the Theater of Public Life in Imperial Russia." In *Revolution and the Meanings of Freedom in the Nineteenth Century,* edited by Isser Woloch, 340–341. Stanford, Calif., 1996.

Kucherov, Samuel. "The Case of Vera Zasulich," *Russian Review* 11, no. 2 (April 1952): 86–96.

———. *Courts, Lawyers and Trials under the Last Three Tsars.* New York, 1953.

Maxwell, Margaret. *Narodniki Women: Russian Women Who Sacrificed Themselves for the Dream of Freedom.* New York, 1990.

Pomper, Philip. *The Russian Revolutionary Intelligentsia.* Arlington Heights, Ill., 1993.

Venturi, Franco. *Roots of Revolution: A History of the Populist and Socialist Movements in Nineteenth-Century Russia.* London, 2001.

Wortman, Richard. *The Development of a Russian Legal Consciousness.* Chicago, 1976.

12

The *Zemstvo* in Late Imperial Russia

Social and Political Change in the Countryside

Thomas E. Porter

The debacle and final defeat Russian forces experienced in the Crimean War led the new tsar, Alexander II, to accept the necessity of extensive and fundamental reform of Russian society, of which the *zemstvo* was a vital part. On March 25, 1859, an imperial order raised the question of how rural local government would be affected by the emancipation of the serfs, then in preparation and ultimately proclaimed in 1861. The result was the issuance of the statute of January 1, 1864, creating the *zemstvo* at the county and provincial levels. The new institutions of local self-government were based upon the suffrage of the local inhabitants, including the newly freed serfs.[1] Another important aspect of the Great Reforms was the judicial reform, also of 1864, by which equal treatment was to be given to all defendants.

Taken together, the two reforms were part of a policy designed to make the ex-serfs full citizens. The nobles had previously acted as virtual viceroys of the tsar in the countryside and had therefore held full legal and political control over their peasant charges. The intention to make the serfs into "free rural inhabitants" thus made the creation of both judicial and governmental frameworks necessary since the noble serf owners were now removed from their customary role as intermediary between the government and the peasant masses. The *zemstvo* was implemented to bridge this administrative gap. The tsarist government hoped that this single, integrated, and hierarchical bureaucratic apparatus would allow for the deconcentration of particular state functions while the bureaucracy would retain ultimate control and oversight. The *zemstva* were to administer certain specific, circumscribed tasks; there would of course be no independent activity by the organs of local self-government.

Many *zemstvo* activists (*zemtsy*), however, would come to demand not only a devolution of real governing authority, but also the removal of the prohibition of lateral contacts between the provincial or county *zemstva* that was contained in Article 3 of the *Zemstvo* Statute. They also began a protracted campaign for the extension of the *zemstvo* downward to the local level (the so-called small *zemstvo* unit) where the peasantry still lived under customary law. The *zemtsy* hoped to convert the *zemstvo* into a school for the civic education of the isolated and particularistic peasantry. The *zemstvo* would therefore become a vehicle for social and political change that would work to close the yawning gap between Russia's educated and privileged elite society and the peasant masses.

This clash of ideas was instrumental in laying the groundwork for the conflict between elements of the bureaucracy (in particular the Ministry of Internal Affairs) and the *zemstvo* deputies. These dedicated and progressive nobles would come to dominate the *zemstva* assemblies, which met twice a year for several weeks at a time and approved the implementation of programs to provide important local services such as health care, education, public welfare, and economic development. When not in session, executive boards were charged with administering these tasks and managing the many professional technical specialists (such as doctors, teachers, statisticians, agronomists, veterinarians, etc.) that were hired to conduct *zemstvo* business. All of these deputies and specialists would come to see themselves as being public servants and would strenuously resist the government's efforts to make them into mere creatures of the bureaucracy.[2] They believed that the *zemstvo* should be an independent institution standing outside of the governmental apparatus.

The most important result of the establishment of the *zemstvo*, however, was the fact that the elective principle was inaugurated. All males over the age of twenty-five who held (1) rural private property, (2) urban private property, or (3) allotment land (land taken from the nobility at the time of the emancipation and entrusted to the peasant villages in order to keep the peasantry from falling into peonage) were eligible to vote in one of these three curiae. Those few peasants who held private rural property were allowed to vote in the first curia with the nobility; all the peasant delegates elected to the *zemstvo* sat with their former masters as equals and deliberated with them on the myriad issues facing rural Russia. This served to give further legal sanction to the peasants' new status in society; Russia seemed to be emerging from its society of social order, with status being based upon birth, to a nation composed of socioeconomic classes with all of its citizens equal before the law. To be sure, elections to the *zemstvo* were not equal. The number of deputies of noble origin to the *zemstvo* was more than twenty times greater than was warranted by their percentage of the local population. In part this could be attributed to the regime's concern that the nobility be compensated for their lost authority in the countryside. It also reflected a simple reality: peasants could not afford to travel to the county or provincial center two or three times a year for weeks at a time. And one should keep in mind that the statute was promulgated before the second Reform Bill of 1867; thus, even in England only 20 percent of males were eligible to vote.

The vast majority of the nobility, however, was completely indifferent to the problems of local self-government and exhibited little interest in participating in the *zemstvo*. Those that did bestir themselves thought that local societies' interests should be distinguished from the essentially political and administrative interests of the state. Over the next quarter century the *zemtsy* pressed the regime for a widening of the sphere of competence of the *zemstvo* and also vigorously sought to limit the tsarist regime's paternal rule over the countryside. In effect, the *zemtsy* wanted to transform the *zemstva* into legitimate, autonomous organs of local self-government. But the government wanted to ensure that it retained its control over the *zemstva* and tried to integrate them more fully into the bureaucratic apparatus. In 1866 the prohibition on lateral *zemstvo* contacts was reaffirmed.[3] Article 16 of this law forbade discussion of national political issues and reiterated the illegality of any proposals for the *zemstva* to contact one another. Another decree promulgated on June 13, 1867, made the chairmen of the *zemstva* assemblies responsible for the conduct and activities of its deputies. In effect, this law attempted to make these dedicated public servants governmental representatives, thus realizing the bureaucracy's long-standing goal of manifesting its presence at the local level.[4]

But it was only with the assassination of the "Tsar-Liberator" Alexander II and the accession of his deeply conservative son, Alexander III, to the throne in 1881 that the steady social and political progress made by Russia since the era of the Great Reforms was completely frozen. Alexander III considered ideas of *zemstvo* independence to be "unattainable fantasies." He authorized the preparation of a second *zemstvo* statute. An imperial order announced the introduction of the measure on June 12, 1890. This *ukaz* noted that the issuance of a second statute was necessary so that the *zemstvo* "in proper unity with other governmental institutions could carry out with greater success the important state business entrusted to them."[5] The wording of the statute unequivocally delineated the sphere of competence of the *zemstvo*. Once again Article 3 limited the activity of the *zemstvo* to the boundaries of the county or province. All members of the executive boards at both the county and provincial levels were to be confirmed in office by the bureaucracy. All members of the executive boards and the county executive board chairmen had to be approved by the governor of the province; the chairmen of the provincial executive boards had to be confirmed in office by the minister of internal affairs himself.[6]

Even more troubling was the fact the 1890 statute abolished the "non-class" character of the *zemstvo* and curtailed the elective principle insofar as the peasantry was concerned. The peasants could now only vote for deputies to the county *zemstvo* (from which deputies were then elected to serve in the provincial *zemstvo*) through the third, now officially "peasant" curia. It no longer made any difference as to what type of property was held. These delegates were then to be scrutinized by officials of the Ministry of Internal Affairs and only the limited number of those deemed "reliable" would ultimately be permitted to take their seats. The new statute was part of a conscious effort to once again make the nobility into a bulwark for the regime and to freeze Russia's sociopolitical evolution. The "counter-reforms" were also intended to stifle the growing sense of civic consciousness amongst Russia's educated society. That this new ethos of public initiative could not be stifled, and was in fact crucial if Russia was to address the myriad problems that beset her, was made clear during the famine of 1891–1892. The regime was forced to turn to the *zemstvo* when the scope of the disaster became apparent. Lacking both the personnel and the infrastructure to manage relief efforts, it relied instead upon the *zemstvo* to play the major role in the food supply campaign.[7]

The heir to the throne, Nicholas, was placed at the head of the regime's Special Committee on Famine Relief. It acted as a mediator between the government and the *zemstva* as well as the numerous private philanthropic and charitable organizations that were created to deal with the crisis. To Russia's educated society, it appeared that the autocracy had sanctioned the initiatives of the liberal public. Thus, when Nicholas ascended to the throne in 1894 upon the death of his father, many *zemstva* addressed hopeful petitions to the crown requesting a greater degree of autonomy and participation in public life. A historian of the *zemstvo*, Boris Veselovskii, wrote "these were the first signs of the reanimation of *zemstvo* life after a decade of repression."[8] Nicholas II, however, angrily rebuffed these entreaties as "senseless dreams" and promised to continue his father's policies "firmly and unflinchingly."[9] Unfortunately, he kept this promise. For another decade the *zemtsy* were forced to meet furtively and secretly, like criminals planning a bank robbery, as they sought to find a way to convince the regime that it was in its own best interest to permit the development of a strong system of local government. This would allow for the development of a public sphere and ultimately would lead to the creation of the kind of civil society that existed in the West. Only then, the *zemtsy* believed, would it be possible for Russia to meet the myriad economic and social challenges posed by industrialization.

It would be hard to overemphasize the magnitude of the lost opportunity for Russia's social and political development that resulted from the conservatism of the last two tsars. Alexander III's period of repression and counterreform (1881–1894) and Nicholas's stubborn adherence to his father's policies through the first decade of his reign represented nearly a quarter century of misguided efforts to modernize Russia while attempting to maintain its feudal social and political order. The pressure for reform would continue to build until Russia exploded into flames in 1905. Thus, the *zemtsy* were virtually forced underground throughout the 1890s and well into the first decade of the twentieth century whenever they wished to gather in order to discuss their plans for the future of the *zemstvo*. Several prominent *zemtsy* formed their own private club (called *Beseda*, or Symposium), which met two or three times a year. Representing twenty-one of the thirty-four *zemstva*, they called again for the establishment of the "small" *zemstvo* unit, the return to the "all-class" voting procedures, an increase in funding for the education of the peasantry, and the right to form an interregional *zemstvo* union. In other words, they wanted to return to the original intentions of the Great Reforms of Alexander II in order to make the peasantry into free citizens. To be sure, the regime was not interested in these progressive ideas and, as the nineteenth century came to a close, even broke up a meeting of *zemtsy* in Moscow that had hoped merely to dedicate a plaque for Alexander II's statue.

That the regime considered the *zemstvo* a threat to its hegemony was made clear in finance minister Sergei Witte's famous memorandum, *Autocracy and the Zemstvo*. In it, he stated that the primary purpose of the *zemstvo* was to provide the state with "steadfast support and be an absolutely reliable instrument in its administration and be in complete accord with the government."[10] Still further, he wrote, "It is impossible to grant any further expansion of activity to the *zemstvo*; it is necessary to lay down a clear demarcation line for it and it is not to be permitted in any respect to cross that line."[11] Yet when a war with Japan broke out in 1904 the regime would be forced once again to accept the de facto unification of the *zemstvo* in order to care adequately for the tsar's sick and wounded soldiers. In order to get around the prohibition on joint *zemstvo* work, the newly founded General *Zemstvo* Organization drew up a master plan of operations in Moscow and then left it up to the fourteen participating provincial *zemstva* to ratify the necessary legislation and implement their relief operations "independently."[12]

Internal affairs minister V. Plehve thought this organization to be little more than a conspiracy against the throne; he issued an order to his minions which instructed them to block any further meetings that took place without his prior written permission.[13]

Society was shocked when its well-intentioned efforts were once again rebuffed by the bureaucracy. Pavel Miliukov, the famous liberal leader, recounted hearing a military officer complain: "Is not every spontaneous action doomed? Is there any room for conscious patriotism? Has not even the humble attempt of the self-governing assemblies to unite in helping the sick and wounded been denounced as criminal, and forbidden by Plehve?"[14] Prince Georgii L'vov, head of the organization and future minister-president of the Provisional Government upon the collapse of the tsarist regime, was forced to visit the tsar personally to get permission for the *zemtsy* to move forward with their plans.

During the course of the conflict with Japan, the General *Zemstvo* Organization accepted 50,385 soldiers for treatment. They rendered assistance to another 25,698 men for minor ailments and evacuated yet another 9,068 soldiers for treatment by the army's medical corps on *zemstvo* trains. The canteens set up by the organization provided hot meals for 389,579 men and distributed snacks of bread with jam and tea to another 71,493. In the last months of the campaign they supplied boiled water for 107,193 men. Thus, the total number of soldiers who received some form of assistance from the *zemstvo* was 653,416. In order to pay for these endeavors, the organization disbursed the stupendous sum of 2,080,894 rubles.[15] More important, after the cessation of hostilities the union voted to continue its philanthropic endeavors in European Russia, despite the ban on such activities imposed by the *Zemstvo* Statute. The *zemtsy* believed that eventually the regime would be forced to permit independent public initiative to better meet the needs of the people in a rapidly changing Russia. In point of fact, Peter Stolypin, imperial Russia's last great statesman, who served as prime minister from 1906 until his assassination in 1911, largely agreed with these sentiments and "recognized the benefits of the further development of the activity of the General *Zemstvo* Organization."[16]

During the decade of its existence (1904–1914) the organization played a crucial role in famine relief for Russia's hard-pressed peasantry. Repeated crop failures produced not only famine but also outbreaks of diseases such as diphtheria, typhus, and cholera. They also played a key role in the facilitation of peasant resettlement to Siberia. The total amount spent by the *zemtsy* on these philanthropic endeavors was 14 million rubles. They rightly noted that the significance of their efforts could not be found in these figures but instead lay in the fact that society had demanded and won a role in governance and that henceforth "the government would be compelled to accept societal forces in all these affairs."[17] Even more remarkable was the dramatic increase in *zemstvo* activity at all levels. This fact flies in the face of the dominant paradigm in the field which contends that educated society was demoralized and marginalized and unable to play a constructive role in Russian public life, especially after the so-called *zemstvo* reaction set in after the revolution of 1905. The seizure of the *zemstva* by conservatives in the wake of this upheaval has been amply discussed in the scholarly literature. Especial emphasis has been placed on the broad array of programs that were immediately slashed or shut down during the "liquidation." Conservative domination of the *zemstvo* after 1905 has repeatedly been cited as proof that the organs of local self-government could not possibly have fulfilled their mission as agents for change in the countryside.

This, in turn, has led many historians to conclude that the further development of a civil society in Russia during the years before the Great War was impossible and therefore the revolution in 1917 was well nigh inevitable. The problem with this standard view, however, is that it stops with 1907, the very year Veselovskii's magisterial study of the *zemstvo* ceases its chronicle. It does not take into account the historical record from 1908–1914, which shows that the conservative nobles almost immediately realized that their curtailment of *zemstvo* activities would undermine their own political influence and eliminate their ability to shape events in the countryside. They began to reassemble programs that they had cut and implemented a broad-ranging program for educational reform that was even more impressive than that which had originally been instituted by their liberal forebears.[18] To be sure, they jealously guarded their primacy in the countryside and defeated many of Stolypin's proposals to democratize the *zemstvo*. Stolypin did manage to restore the peasantry's right to select their own deputies to the *zemstvo*, and the granting of internal passports to the peasantry finally brought them into full citizenship. But his legislation both to democratize the elections to the county *zemstvo* and to establish the small *zemstvo* unit (which no amount of legerdemain could prevent the peasantry from dominating) were blocked by rightist forces both on the local level and in the State Council.

Taken together, these proposals, along with Stolypin's attempt to break up the commune and create a class of prosperous, property-owning peasants who would be acculturated to the norms of a civil society, represented Russia's best chance to develop into a stable, free, and democratic society. That they were blocked by the newly engaged, conservative nobility was indeed a tragedy, but if one looks deeper there are positive developments in the *zemstvo* during the period 1905–1914. This decade was formerly known as "the lost decade" of Russian history, as many specialists uncritically accepted Trotsky's dictum that Russia's revolution in 1905 was but the "dress rehearsal" for the *Zusammenbruch* of 1917. Many historians and social scientists thus concentrated their efforts upon elucidating the antecedents of that revolution while minimizing or even ignoring countervailing trends. Much ink was spilt chronicling the murders of ordinary policeman or charting the rise in the militancy of the labor movement, which might have been expected given the legalization of such activity in the wake of the 1905 revolution. Putting aside the ideological blinders that accept historical outcomes as being inevitable, one finds that the *zemtsy* implemented an impressive expansion of educational programs in the countryside and also began a remarkable, well-organized campaign to allow society more autonomy and leeway in local governance.

The years after the 1905 revolution saw *zemstva* budgets increase dramatically and by 1914 the total budget was 347 million rubles. In the single most important endeavor, education, the budget increased from a mere 2 million rubles in 1907 to more than 40 million by the beginning of the war. The number of teachers also increased from 24,389 in 1879 to 62,913 in 1911. Of all the areas of *zemstvo* activity, primary education showed the most impressive growth between 1880 and 1914. Thus, on the eve of the First World War, Russia's social and political transformation was well under way. And, again contrary to the standard view, the coming of the war did not derail but instead accelerated this evolution toward a civil society. Russia's educated society responded to the crises that the conflict engendered by assuming myriad burdens that normally would have been the responsibility of the state.

The General *Zemstvo* Organization was replaced by the dynamic, centralized All-Russian *Zemstvo* Union. Again headed by Prince L'vov, the union, along with numerous other organizations established by Russia's increasingly civic-minded entrepreneurial and professional class, virtually ran the war effort. The government soon proved incapable of meeting even its most basic obligations to the Russian people during the war. It was forced to authorize the various organizations to expand the scope of their activities. The voluntary organization's activities grew to include the provision of munitions and matériel to the army, refugee assistance, food supply, vaccination programs, and of course aid to the sick and wounded troops both at the front lines and at hospitals in the rear. Russia's incipient civil society demonstrated its viability by stepping forward and taking on the responsibility, as Prince L'vov noted, "not only for a broad expansion of our sphere of work as formerly planned, not only for the extension of our activity up to the front as far as the advance positions, but also that we take upon ourselves such functions, the fulfillment of which had been undertaken as purely governmental tasks and which in all preceding wars had been fulfilled exclusively by governmental organs."[19]

The government became increasingly alarmed at the significance of the practical work undertaken by the *zemstvo*. Internal Affairs Minister Maklakov warned that, unless constrained, the *zemtsy* "were preparing themselves for work on the reconstruction of public life which must come, they feel, at the conclusion of the war."[20] As official concern deepened, Prime Minister Shtiurmer noted that the activities of the *zemtsy* would inevitably "lead to the transformation of the *zemstva* from institutions dealing with the local economy under the supervision of the government, into organs of local government, independent of the authorities."[21] The *zemtsy* had indeed come to the realization that Russia could no longer afford to delay the modernization of its social and political relations. By 1916 the gloves had come off. As Prince L'vov wrote, "the activity of the unions long ago acquired state significance. . . . The unions have proven that what is unfeasible for the government is feasible when undertaken by the people's organized forces. . . . It has also proven that the government mechanism of state administration is far from conforming with the living force of the country."[22] The government recognized not only the increasing threat posed to it by the Russian *zemstvo* but also the fact that it could not be shut down without an inexcusable increase in human misery. As one minister rightly noted, "It was impossible to liquidate this problem because the administration could not manage without them."[23]

The wartime activities of the *zemtsy* highlight the beginnings of a new political culture, one based on the underpinnings of a civil society. But modern wars require a commitment on the part of all of a country's citizens. Russia's peasants were unfamiliar with the concept of the nation and thus lacked any kind of commitment to the country's war effort. This position is overstated and again is derived from a fundamental ignorance of developments in the countryside both during the prewar years and during the conflict itself. The war with Japan had served to open up the peasant village to the outside world and had introduced the concept of the "nation" through the spread of newspapers and maps. World War I, with its millions of mobilized peasants, accelerated the peasantry's demand for news from outside of their villages and many peasant soldiers wrote letters home urging that their children be sent to school. As a result, by the fall of 1916 *zemstvo* schools were besieged with applicants and many children had to be turned away. But the *zemtsy* understood that schooling alone could not transform peasant culture. Only educational programs beyond the three-year literacy courses, such as lectures, the establishment of libraries, and, most important, the implementation of a wide-ranging program of adult education, could transform peasant culture.[24]

Zemstva had already increased spending on adult education during the prewar years and now seized on the opportunity to expand their offerings. The impetus given to peasant demand for education by the war and the concomitant expansion of available programs and information accelerated their development of a national consciousness and at least the beginning of the end of their particularism. That the elements of a democratic, civil society were in fact beginning to flower can be seen both by the *zemstvo* elections in the fall of 1917 before the Bolshevik coup (and six months after the collapse of the tsarist regime) and by the constituent assembly elections in November of that same year. The turnout for the former was low, which attests to the intransigence and isolation of the peasantry from the political life of the nation. But considering that the *zemstvo* elections were held at harvest time and women (who were eligible to vote for the first time) generally stayed away from the polls, a turnout that ranged from 40 to 50 percent was remarkably high. And the political maturity of Russian society was revealed in the elections to the constituent assembly, as nearly 50 million citizens expressed their will through the ballot box and not in the street.

This chapter has sketched the possibilities and promise that existed for a stable, prosperous, and democratic Russia, if not for the quarter century lost from 1881 to 1904. The *zemstvo* program to establish the small *zemstvo* unit and implement universal schooling had important implications for peasant integration which until now have been little explored. This, along with the expansion of the *zemstvo* sphere of competence, would have served to construct the rudiments of a civil society. After the Bolshevik revolution this prescription for progress and the need for a longer time horizon to accomplish it were acknowledged by the perceptive Russian historian A. A. Kornilov, who wrote in his memoirs:

> At the present time I see quite clearly that had there been no catastrophe on March 1 (the assassination of Alexander II) and the enduring reaction that followed upon it . . . [as] we would have had a broad and solid development of democratic zemstvo self government, and moreover it would have been given the foundation it lacked, in the form of a small zemstvo unit of one kind or another. At the same time we would have seen the free development of popular education, so necessary for Russia.[25]

NOTES

1. *Polnoe sobranie zakonov Rossiiskoi imperii, sobranie vtoroe* (St. Petersburg: Tip. II Otdeleniia Sobstvennoi Ego Imperatorskago Velichestva Kantseliarii, 1867), vol. 39, no. 40457, January 1864. Hereafter this series is referred to as *PSZRI*.

2. Charles Timberlake, "The *Zemstvo* and the Development of a Russian Middle Class," in *Between Tsar and People: Educated Society and the Quest for Public Identity in Late Imperial Russia*, ed. Edith W. Clowes, Samuel Kassow, and James L. West (Princeton, N.J.: Princeton University Press, 1991), 178.

3. B. B. Veselovskii, *Istoriia zemstva na sorok let*, vol. 3 (St. Petersburg: Izdatel'stvo O. N. Popovoi, 1911), 127.

4. *PSZRI Vtoroe*, vol. 42, no. 44690, June 13, 1867.

5. *PSZRI Tret'e*, vol. 10, no. 6922, June 12, 1890.

6. *PSZRI Tret'e*, vol. 10, no. 6927, June 12, 1890.

7. Richard G. Robbins, Jr., *Famine in Russia, 1891–1892: The Imperial Government Responds to a Crisis* (New York: Columbia University Press, 1975), 1–2.

8. Veselovskii, *Istoriia*, 3:375.

9. I. P. Belokonskii, *Zemskoe dvizhenie* (Moscow: Zadruga, 1914), 41.

10. S. Iu. Witte, *Samoderzhavie i zemstvo* (Stuttgart, Germany: J. H. W. Sietz Nachf, 1903), 196.

11. Witte, *Samoderzhavie*, 211–212.

12. *Desiatiletie obshchezemskoi organizatsii blagotvoritel'noi pomoshchi naseleniia, 1904–1914 gg.* (Moscow: Tipografiia Russkogo Tovarichestva, 1914), 4.

13. Veselovskii, *Istoriia*, 3:592.

14. P. N. Miliukov, *Russia and Its Crisis* (New York: Collier Books, 1906), 221.

15. *Obshchezemskaia organizatsiia na dal'nem vostoke* (Moscow: Tipografiia Russkogo Tovarichestva, 1908), 1:19.

16. *Desiatiletie*, 15.

17. *Desiatiletie*, 36.

18. Thomas Porter and Scott Seregny, "The *Zemstvo* Reconsidered," in *Local Government in Russia: Power, Authority, and Civic Participation*, ed. Alfred Evans and Vladimir Gelman (Lanham, Md.: Rowman & Littlefield, forthcoming).

19. *Kratkii ocherk deiatel'nosti vserossisskogo zemskogo soiuza* (Moscow: Gorodskaia Tipografiia, 1917), 8.

20. Gosudarstvennyi Arkhiv Rossiisskogo Federatsii, fond 102, opis' 17, ed. khr. 343, November 18, 1914, list 10.

21. V. P. Semennikov, *Monarkhiia pered krusheniem, 1914–1917* (Moscow: Gosudarstvennoe izdatel'stvo, 1927), 124.

22. *Kratkii ocherk*, 2.

23. *Krasnyi arkhiv*, vol. 2 (Moscow: Gospolitizdat, 1929), 150–151.

24. Scott Seregny, "Zemstvos, Peasants, and Citizenship: The Russian Adult Education Movement and World War I," *Slavic Review* 59, no. 2 (Summer 2000): 290–315.

25. Quoted in Terence Emmons and Wayne Vucinich, eds., *The Zemstvo in Russia: An Experiment in Local Self-Government* (Cambridge, UK: Cambridge University Press, 1982), 442–443.

SUGGESTED READING

Ascher, Abraham. *P. A. Stolypin: The Search for Stability in Late Imperial Russia*. Stanford, Calif., 2001.

Bradley, Joseph. "Subjects into Citizens: Society, Civil Society, and Autocracy in Tsarist Russia," *American Historical Review* 107, no. 4 (October 2002): 1094–1123.

Brooks, Jeffrey. *When Russia Learned to Read: Literacy and Popular Literature, 1861–1917*. Princeton, N.J., 1985.

Clowes, Edith, Edward Kassow, and James West, eds. *Between Tsar and People: Educated Society and the Quest for Public Identity in Late Imperial Russia*. Princeton, N.J., 1991.

Conroy, Mary Schaeffer, ed. *Emerging Democracy in Late Imperial Russia: Case Studies on Local Self-Government (the Zemstvos), State Duma Elections, the Tsarist Government, and the State Council Before and During the First World War*. Niwot, Colo., 1998.

Emmons, Terence, and Wayne Vucinich, eds. *The Zemstvo in Russia: An Experiment in Local Self-Government*. Cambridge, UK, 1982.

Polunov, Alexander. *Russia in the Nineteenth Century: Autocracy, Reform, and Social Change, 1814–1914*. Edited by Thomas C. Owen and Larissa Zakharova. Translated by Marshall S. Shatz. Armonk, N.Y., 2005.

Porter, Thomas, and Scott Seregny. "The Zemstvo Reconsidered." In *The Politics of Local Government in Russia*, edited by Albert B. Evans, Jr, and Vladimir Gelman. Lanham, Md., 2004.

Seregny, Scott. "Zemstvos, Peasants, and Citizenship: The Russian Adult Education Movement and World War I." *Slavic Review* 59, no. 2 (2002): 290–315.

III

SOVIET RUSSIA

The historical signposts of the Soviet "experiment" are easy to delineate, beginning with the emergence of the Soviet Union following the political and social upheavals of 1917 and ending with the unraveling of the Union in 1991. Within these precise bookends are located the establishment of the first ostensibly socialist government in history; war Communism; revolutionary culture (socialist and otherwise); the New Economic Policy (NEP); the rise of Stalin to power; industrialization and collectivization; the Great Purges of the 1930s; the more mundane aspects of Soviet society in the 1930s, or "everyday Stalinism" to quote a recent term; Soviet involvement in the Second World War and its catastrophic effects on the peoples of the Soviet Union; the Cold War; de-Stalinization; the stability (later developing into stagnation, if of a rather vibrant sort) of the Brezhnev era, along with the rise of dissent; Gorbachev, perestroika, and glasnost'; the apparently sudden emergence of concern (at least by Western historians) with the non-Russian nationalities and their particular national histories; and finally, the breakup of what had seemed to be a durable, if increasingly sclerotic, polity. Part III of this volume is intended to give the reader a sampling of recent scholarship on the Soviet Union. The Soviet Union was a complex, enduring, politically seductive, "backward," and yet in part wholly "modern" state that the Bolsheviks imagined into existence in 1917, and which due to overreach and inbuilt limitations, imploded in 1991 with little to no outside assistance.

Rex Wade's entry is an attempt, argued with admirable concision, to explain one of the most analyzed episodes in modern world history: how did the Bolsheviks come to power in 1917? Perhaps the most vexing problem facing the new Soviet regime—and until recently one insufficiently understood—was how the new Union would manage to accommodate its myriad non-Russian ethnic minorities (who eventually made up, of course, a clear majority of the population). Soviet attitudes toward one of these nationalities, the Jews, and Jewish responses to the new, apparently supportive, state, are the subject of Jeffrey Veidlinger's account. Scott Palmer's and Richard Bidlack's contributions examine Soviet efforts to understand and counter (ideologically and later militarily) the fascist threat facing the county. In Palmer's case, his sweeping discussion of Soviet aviation cinema demonstrates that it was a valuable means for the inculcation of "Soviet values." The blockade of Leningrad (1941–1944) was one of the most tragic, and heroic, episodes punctuating Soviet experiences in the Second World War. It is also a valuable prism, as shown by Bidlack, through which to decipher the loyalty of the citizenry to the Stalinist state.

After the war, the difficulties facing the devastated Soviet lands did not recede; rather, with the onset of the Cold War, the dangers facing Stalin's government remained ever present. The regime's response was increased (compared to the very relative laxity of the war years, that is) domestic repression, a topic ably explicated by Kees Boterbloem. William Taubman has condensed selected themes from his recent tome on Nikita Khrushchev, offering morsels from Khrushchev's remarkable life story, posing questions about his personality/psychology, and hypothesizing how these traits might have affected his exercise of power. He offers the reader a compelling portrait of this enigmatic figure: part reformer, part brutal authoritarian. The collapse of the Soviet Union will long remain one of the most debated of historical issues (indeed no persuasive synthetic account exists of the last days of the Soviet Union). Sergei Arutiunov and Martha Merritt offer their perspectives on it. With a perceptive eye on the "periphery," Arutiunov vividly illustrates the corruption and waning of ideological zeal that pervaded late Soviet society (1960s–1980s). Establishing a degree of legitimacy was a pressing need of Gorbachev's, and his failure to accomplish this formidable, perhaps unachievable, task is the subject of Merritt's study.

13

Popular Aspirations, the New Politics, and the October Revolution

Rex A. Wade

The Russian Revolution remains without doubt one of the most important events of modern history, central to the shaping of the twentieth-century world, and its legacy continues to be influential to the present. The history of the Russian Revolution has been fundamentally rewritten in the past four decades. First and most important, the period from the late 1960s through the 1980s saw an enormous expansion of serious academic study of the revolution. This included a new "social history" that opened up new perspectives by focusing attention on social classes and popular aspirations. Prior to that time most studies had focused on political history, especially the main political parties and their leadership (Lenin most of all). There was little social or economic context, and the people were simply "masses" to be manipulated by a few political leaders. Second, the collapse of the Soviet Union has made it somewhat easier to put the Russian Revolution into better historical perspective, while the unlocking of archives in Russia stimulated scholarship generally as well as opened up areas of research that had formerly been impossible or difficult. By the beginning of this century a new history had emerged that combined the new social and old political history, old and new sources, and looked at regions and groups previously largely ignored. In the process, important parts of the history were significantly revised, including the October (Bolshevik) Revolution.[1]

POPULAR ASPIRATIONS

What then is new and important in writing about the revolution? First, there is a recognition of the importance of popular aspirations and actions.

Without such recognition the revolutionary events make little sense. The February Revolution released the pent-up frustrations and aspirations of the population, which put forward long lists of often conflicting expectations from the revolution. The industrial workers, who had begun the revolution, demanded increased wages, an eight-hour day, better working conditions, dignity as individuals, and an end to the war. Soldiers demanded and implemented fundamental changes in the conditions of military service, and then became the most ardent opponents of continuing the war. Peasants laid claim to the land and greater control over their lives and villages. The educated middle classes looked forward to expanded civil rights and a society based on the rule of law. Women demonstrated for the right to vote and better access to education and professions. National minorities demanded expanded use of their languages, respect for cultural practices, and political autonomy within a federal state. Hundreds of groups—soldiers' wives, medical assistants, apartment residents' associations, overage soldiers, and others large and small—expected the government to address their needs. These aspirations, and their fulfillment or nonfulfillment, profoundly shaped the working out of the revolution. For all inhabitants of the Russian state, of whatever class, gender, ethnicity, occupation, or other category, the revolution stood for the opening of a new era and a better future, and they expected those aspirations to be met.

Moreover, the people of the Russian Empire quickly organized to realize their hopes. Within a few weeks they created a vast array of organizations for self-assertion: thousands of factory committees, army committees, village assemblies, Red Guards, unions, nationality and religious organizations, cultural and educational clubs, women's and youth organizations, officers' and industrialists' associations, householders' associations, economic cooperatives, and others. These many organizations and continuous meetings represented genuinely popular movements and gave form to the hopes and aspirations of the peoples of the empire. The intersection of the political parties with these many organizations, and especially the more powerful ones such as factory and soldiers' committees, is a key issue of the revolution. Political leaders struggled to garner the popular support of these organizations, while the populace and their organizations, selecting from a rich buffet of political, social, economic, and cultural ideas, searched for leadership that could articulate and implement their aspirations. Unmet aspirations drove the revolution leftward throughout 1917 as the population sought new leaders—local and central—who would meet those expectations. Recognizing the role of these aspirations and the activities and significance of the new organizations, including how those linked up to political movements, is a central feature of current writing about the revolution. Without them, the activities of "high politics" and leaders make little sense.

THE NEW POLITICAL SYSTEM AND
"ALL POWER TO THE SOVIETS"

Part of the new history of the revolution is a "new political history" that closely integrates social issues into the political story. One part of that is reconceptualizing politics to recognize the role of political blocs rather than parties. The political elites in 1917 had to struggle to create a viable new government and a new political system through which they could work with the new popular organizations, gain control over the population's self-assertiveness, and fulfill popular aspirations. The political elites, however, were in turmoil, caught in a sweeping political realignment that cut across party lines and created political blocs that were in many ways more important than traditional parties. The revolution swept away the old right wing of Russian politics, while the former Left reformed in three blocs—liberals, moderate socialists, and radical Left socialists. Politics after February were dominated by a twofold struggle: an uneasy alliance/rivalry between the liberals and the initially dominant moderate socialist bloc, and by the rivalry of both with the radical Left (Bolsheviks and others). Although parties cannot be forgotten, thinking in terms of these blocs gives a more realistic picture of politics in 1917, and certain developments make sense only from this perspective.

The new political system was unstable from the beginning. Power ostensibly rested with the Provisional Government formed on March 2, which initially was composed of primarily liberal elements of educated society. Alongside it, however, was the Petrograd Soviet, formed on February 27. Led by socialist intellectuals, it claimed to speak for the workers, soldiers, and broad mass of the population and quickly became the real political power (as did local soviets in the cities of Russia). The uneasy working relation between these two bodies created the "February System" that lasted until the October Revolution replaced the Provisional Government with "Soviet power."

This new political system formed after the February Revolution was extremely unstable and buffeted by recurring crises, large and small. This soon gave rise to a call for a radical restructuring of the government and the creation of an all-socialist government. A half step in that direction was taken following the April Crisis, which arose over conflict between the socialists' demand to end the war by negotiation and the liberals' insistence on victory. This led to the collapse of the first Provisional Government and creation of the first "coalition government" in May, in which several moderate socialist and Soviet leaders entered the government (still called the Provisional Government).

The coalition, however, failed to satisfy the aspirations of almost every group. It not only failed to end the war, but instead launched a military offensive in June that was unpopular from the beginning and soon turned into a devastating defeat. This, plus worsening economic conditions, nationality and peasant discontents, crime and public disorders, a foreboding sense of pending social conflict, and other problems, amplified the demand for "All Power to the Soviet," especially among the urban workers and soldiers. On the surface this meant simply that an all-socialist, multiparty government based on the Petrograd Soviet or the All-Russia Congress of Soviets should replace the Provisional Government. Beyond that, however, was an underlying demand for a government that unequivocally advanced the interests of the worker, peasant, and soldier masses against the "bourgeoisie" and privileged society, one that would rapidly carry out radical social and economic reforms and end the war. These yearnings came together in the simple slogan of "All Power to the Soviets," as workers, soldiers, and others turned toward arguments that stressed that citizens could achieve peace and fulfill their aspirations only through a new revolution that would produce a radically different government more attuned to their needs. The concept of "Soviet power" and its growing popularity was, without doubt, one of the most important features of the revolution, although it has been traditionally underestimated. Without grasping its significance, the events of the summer and fall of 1917, especially the October Revolution, are inexplicable.

The demand for Soviet power and the underlying frustrations of the workers and soldiers led first to massive anti-government demonstrations in June and then burst loose with the tumultuous disorders usually called the "July Days." Enormous crowds of workers and soldiers paraded through the city and besieged the Petrograd Soviet headquarters, where they demanded that the Soviet take power. The moderate socialists, mostly Mensheviks and Socialist Revolutionaries (SRs), who controlled the Petrograd Soviet, rejected the demand for Soviet power and refused to take power. As a result, workers, soldiers, and others turned toward the radical Left—Bolsheviks, left SRs, Menshevik-Internationalists, and anarchists—who had supported the call for Soviet power. The radicals, at the same time, articulated the vision of a new and more radical revolution that promised fulfillment of the aspirations of the revolutionary masses, accompanied by vigorous criticism of the government and moderates. From August to October, organization after organization replaced its moderate socialist leadership with radical, most importantly Bolshevik, leadership. In September, a Bolshevik-led radical majority took control of the Petrograd Soviet, by election, with Leon Trotsky as the new chairman of the Soviet (arguably the most powerful position in Russia by this time).

By September, the question was not whether the Provisional Government (now in its fourth incarnation) would be replaced again, but how and by whom, and in what manner. Ever-larger segments of the political elite, as well as the general population, believed that the time had come for some type of new, all-socialist government. This came close to implementation in late September by agreement among socialist party leaders, but failed. The question, however, would not go away. By mid-October, amid rising social and political tensions, the question ever more was not so much *would* the Bolsheviks and their allies attempt an overthrow of the Provisional Government by the Congress of Soviets, but the details. Exactly how would it happen? What would be the exact nature of the new government? To what extent and how successfully might the government, headed by Alexander Kerensky, resist? (Kerensky, the popular hero of the early days of the revolution, by this time was isolated politically and unpopular.) Would this spark civil war, as the moderate socialists feared?

THE OCTOBER REVOLUTION

"What are the Bolsheviks planning to do?"—that was the question debated on street corners, in newspapers, and in public meetings. This question tormented Lenin as well. From his Finnish hiding place—an order for his arrest dating from the July Days still existed—Lenin feared that the Bolsheviks would do too little, too late. He already had turned away from any idea of cooperation with the moderate socialists in some kind of shared Soviet power. Ignoring the debates going on in Petrograd about what kind of broad socialist government to form, Lenin in mid-September shifted to a strident call for an immediate armed seizure of power by the Bolsheviks. For him, Soviet power had come to mean a new type of government dominated by the Bolsheviks, a rather different meaning than was usually associated with the term. From Finland he wrote a series of letters to the Bolshevik Central Committee insisting that the time was ripe for a seizure of power and that the party must organize and prepare for it. Lenin believed that the fall of 1917 offered a unique opportunity for a radical restructuring of political power and, for a man such as himself, one unlikely to come again.

Lenin's call divided the party leadership. A minority supported Lenin's call to arms. Another group, led by Grigorii Zinoviev and Lev Kamenev, urged caution and favored a broad coalition of socialists in a democratic left government, probably created at the Constituent Assembly.[2] An intermediate position, increasingly identified with Leon Trotsky and probably representing a majority of the party's leadership, looked to the forthcoming Second All-Russia Congress of Soviets as the vehicle for the transfer of power. The Bolsheviks and other parties supporting Soviet power would have a majority at the Congress, and the Congress could then declare the transfer of power to itself. Although this itself would be a revolutionary move, Trotsky and those of like mind believed that Kerensky's government would be unable to resist. Despite Lenin's demands, therefore, the party's political efforts focused on the forthcoming Congress of Soviets and the selection of deputies to the Congress who would support a transfer of power.

Frustrated and fearing that an irretrievable opportunity was slipping by, Lenin took the chance of moving from Finland to Petrograd. On October 10 he met, for the first time since July, with the Central Committee of the party. After an all-night debate the Central Committee seemingly gave in to Lenin's passionate demands for a seizure of power. It passed a resolution stating "the Central Committee recognizes that . . . [follows a long list of international and domestic developments] all this places armed uprising on the order of the day."[3] This resolution later became central to the myth of a carefully planned seizure of power carried out under Lenin's direction. It was, in fact, something different and more complex than that. First of all, it did *not* set any timetable or plan for a seizure of power. Rather, the resolution was a formal reversion of Bolshevik party policy to the idea that an armed uprising was a revolutionary necessity, but did not commit the party to a seizure of power *before* the Congress of Soviets or at any other specific time or by any specific means. Nor did it start actual preparations for a seizure of power, as many within the Bolshevik leadership would point out in discussions in the following days. Despite Lenin's bullying, the party leadership continued to focus on the Congress of Soviets as the time, place, and vehicle for the transfer of power. This would be the new "revolution" called for in the Bolshevik resolution of October 10 as well as in hundreds of local workers' and soldiers' resolutions for Soviet power. The Bolsheviks' left SR allies also were aiming at the Congress to take power and form an all-socialist government.

At this point Lenin was the recipient of a series of unforeseeable lucky breaks that made possible the violent seizure of power that he wanted and gave rise to the durable myth of a secretly- and well-planned Bolshevik seizure of power. First, on October 18 the moderate socialists decided to postpone the opening of the Congress of Soviets from the twentieth to the twenty-fifth. This was momentous, for the Bolsheviks were totally unprepared for and could not have attempted any seizure of power before the twentieth even if they wished to do so. The five extra days changed everything.

Between October 20 and October 24 were days of furious popular debate over numerous issues (preparation to send garrison troops to the front, fears of German invasion, threat of moving the capital, a severe economic and food crisis, factory closings, the acknowledged instability of the government, etc.). These had Petrograd in turmoil. Moreover, both sides undertook during these days to mobilize supporters because a declaration of the transfer of power at the Congress of Soviets, however much expected, would after all be an insurrectionary action that Kerensky presumably would resist. Bolsheviks and left SRs worked to take away the government's last bits of authority over the garrison of Petrograd, thus destroying any ability of the government to use its soldiers against the seizure of power by the Congress of Soviets. Seen in this light, as a growing confrontation between the Provisional Government and the Petrograd Soviet, and as preparation by the latter to defend a transfer of power at the Congress of Soviets, the actions by the government, the Bolshevik and left SR leaders, other political figures, and local factory activists have a logic that they do not have if one holds to the old myth of careful planning for a Bolshevik seizure of power *before* the Congress.

Shortly before the Congress, Lenin's second piece of luck fell into place: Kerensky decided to act, however tentatively, against the Bolsheviks. All along Bolshevik leaders in Petrograd had been warning Lenin that the workers and soldiers would not come out on behalf of an action by the Bolsheviks, but would in defense of the Soviet and the Congress of Soviets. As most of Petrograd slept in the predawn hours of October 24, a small detachment sent by the Provisional Government raided the press where two Bolshevik newspapers were published. Bolshevik and left SR leaders at Soviet headquarters (not including Lenin) quickly branded the press closure a counterrevolutionary move "against the Petrograd Soviet, . . . against the Congress of Soviets on the eve of its opening, against the Constituent Assembly, against the people," and appealed for support.[4] Unbeknownst to anyone, including the Bolshevik leaders, the October Revolution had begun. Kerensky's simple but ill-conceived act provided the very "counterrevolutionary" action against which the Left had been warning, precipitating the October Revolution and unexpectedly handing Lenin his ability to seize power before the Congress of Soviets.

Despite some radical leaders who wanted to respond to Kerensky's action with an immediate attack on the government, most of those present at Soviet headquarters on the morning of October 24 focused on defensive measures to guarantee that the Second Congress of Soviets would meet the next day. Throughout the twenty-fourth, the Soviet leaders (Lenin was still absent) called on workers and soldiers to defend the Congress and the revolution, while some radicalized army units and the workers' Red Guards took to the streets to defend the Soviet and the revolution. In confused, largely uncoordinated struggles that involved mostly push and shove, bluff and counterbluff, Red Guards and pro-Soviet soldiers gradually took control of bridges and key buildings. There was little shooting: few were willing to die for either side and what enthusiasm and hard support existed rested on the side of the Soviet. By nightfall pro-Soviet forces controlled most of the city.

About two o'clock the morning of the twenty-fifth, Bolshevik and Soviet leaders shifted from the defensive to an offensive drive to seize power. Two things came together to cause this. One was a growing realization that the government was much weaker than had been thought and that the city was coming under the physical control of soldiers and Red Guards rallying to the defense of the Soviet. The second was the arrival of Lenin at Soviet headquarters. Lenin had been in hiding on the city outskirts but, realizing that important events were taking place in which he was not involved, he left his hiding place to go to Smolny (Soviet and Bolshevik party headquarters). Lenin's arrival, coinciding with the dawning realization of the success of pro-Soviet forces, dramatically changed the equation. Lenin had not been part of the cautious defensive reaction of the twenty-fourth, and he was the one leader who had consistently urged an armed seizure of power before the Congress of Soviets met. Under his pressure and the reality of their growing strength, the Soviet leaders shifted from a defensive posture to the offensive. By the time a cold, gray, windy day dawned on the twenty-fifth, pro-Soviet forces had extended their control to almost all of the city. Lenin took advantage of this to achieve his goal of proclaiming the overthrow of the Provisional Government before the Congress of Soviets met. About ten o'clock that morning, Lenin finished a hastily written proclamation of the overthrow of the Provisional Government and handed it over for immediate printing and distribution.

By the evening of the twenty-fifth it appeared that Lenin had obtained his goal of a transfer of power by a violent act of seizure before the Congress of Soviets. It is worth noting, however, that the transfer of power was in the name of the Petrograd Soviet and affirmed by it. It was not a revolution in the name of the Bolshevik party, and the multiparty Congress of Soviets was still to be the ultimate legitimizing institution. Transforming a seizure of power in the name of the Soviet into a Bolshevik regime would depend on yet a third unforeseeable stroke of luck.

The Second Congress of Soviets that opened the evening of the twenty-fifth had, as expected, a radical, Bolshevik-led majority that favored the transfer of power to the Soviets. Everything was in place for creating a multiparty, all-socialist government—what "Soviet power" had meant throughout 1917—and the first motions and speeches pointed in that direction. Then, suddenly, the right and center wings of the Menshevik and SR parties denounced the Bolsheviks and walked out in protest. That walkout left the Bolsheviks in a majority rather than merely a plurality, and hardened political positions. As a result, Lenin was able to form an all-Bolshevik government, something completely unforeseen. Lenin had his Bolshevik seizure of power.

In emphasizing the unexpected strokes of luck, or opportunities, if one prefers, that came Lenin's way during October, I do not want to leave the impression that this was all an accident. The October Revolution was a complex mixture of powerful long-term political and social forces moving toward a radical government of some type, of the actions of individuals, and of unpredictable events of the moment that shaped its specific form and outcome. The nature of the October Revolution should remind us of the complexity of history, of the intermingling of long-term "causes," of the chance of the moment, and even of personal actions.

The Russian Revolution does not end with the October Revolution. Indeed, many in October 1917 saw it as merely another political crisis, punctuated with the usual street disorders and producing yet another "provisional" government (a term the new government in fact used at first). Instead, the dispersal of the Constituent Assembly on January 6, 1918, is a better point to take as the end of the revolution in the precise usage of the term and as the transition to civil war. During the period from October 25 to January 6, Lenin successfully turned a revolution for Soviet power into Bolshevik power and pushed the country to civil war and the new regime toward dictatorship. The immense popularity of the idea of Soviet power allowed the new government both to defeat the initial armed opposition and to witness the successful spread of "Soviet power" across much of Russia and through the army by the beginning of the new year. However, the meaning of Soviet power and the purposes of power had not yet been fully defined. Only with difficulty did Lenin overcome a serious effort during the first week after the October Revolution to force him to share political power through formation of a broad multiparty socialist government, which it had been commonly assumed Soviet power involved. At the same time Lenin and Trotsky worked to polarize opinion and parties and to strengthen the Bolshevik hold on power. They did this in part through swift movement to meet popular aspirations, including a decree distributing land to the peasants, an armistice with Germany, an extension of workers' authority in management of factories, and other measures. At the same time they tightened control through censorship, the formation of the Cheka (political police), repressive measures against the Kadet Party, and other actions to suppress opposition. The resort to use of armed force against political rivals was an important turning point in the history of the revolution and marked the beginning of the descent toward dictatorship and civil war. It was here, incidentally, that Lenin provided effective leadership and really came into his own in "leading" a political revolution.

The final act in marking the end of the revolution and the onset of civil war was the dispersal of the Constituent Assembly. The elections to the Constituent Assembly and its forthcoming convocation kept alive the notion not only of a future broad, multiparty socialist government, but also that Lenin's government was just another temporary—provisional—government. This sense muted early opposition to the new government. It also presented Lenin and the radical Left with their great dilemma. Throughout 1917 they had criticized the Provisional Government for delay in convening the Constituent Assembly. For Lenin, however, it now was an obstacle to retaining political power.

As predicted, the elections in November gave the SRs a majority that, however unstable, would control the Constituent Assembly in its opening stages. Any government coming out of the assembly would be a coalition, probably the broad socialist coalition that the slogan "All Power to the Soviets" was thought to mean. Accepting it meant yielding power, and this Lenin was unwilling to do. His unwillingness led him and other Bolsheviks, and some left SRs, to prepare action against the assembly. This came on January 6 when the Constituent Assembly was forcibly closed after one meeting. Dispersal of the assembly was not essential for maintenance of a socialist government, or even "Soviet power," but it was necessary if Lenin and Trotsky were to hold power and realize such a radical government as they envisioned.

NOTES

1. The following draws upon arguments and narratives developed more fully in Rex A. Wade, *The Russian Revolution: 1917* (Cambridge, UK: Cambridge University Press, 2000).

2. The Constituent Assembly was to be elected on a universal ballot. It was generally accepted that the assembly would create a new, fully legitimate government for Russia and resolve the basic political and social issues. Elections were scheduled for November.

3. Robert H. McNeal, ed., *Resolutions and Decisions of the Communist Party of the Soviet Union*, vol. I, edited by Ralph Carter Elwood (Toronto: University of Toronto Press, 1974), 288–289.

4. *Petrogradskii voenno-revoliutsionnyi komitet: Dokumenty i materialy* (Moscow, 1966), 1:84.

SUGGESTED READING

Acton, Edward, Vladimir Iu. Cherniaev, and William G. Rosenberg, eds. *Critical Companion to the Russian Revolution, 1914–1921*. Bloomington, Ind., 1997.

Figes, Orlando, and Boris Kolonitskii. *Interpreting the Russian Revolution: The Language and Symbols of 1917*. New Haven, Conn., 1999.

Hasegawa, Tsuyoshi. *The February Revolution: Petrograd 1917*. Seattle, 1981.

Holquist, Peter. *Making War, Forging Revolution: Russia's Continuum of Crisis, 1914–1921*. Cambridge, Mass., 2002.

Koenker, Diane, and William G. Rosenberg. *Strikes and Revolution in Russia, 1917*. Princeton, N.J., 1989.

Rabinowitch, Alexander. *The Bolsheviks Come to Power: The Revolution of 1917 in Petrograd*. New York, 1976.

Raleigh, Donald J. *Revolution on the Volga, 1917 in Saratov*. Ithaca, N.Y., 1986.

Smith, S. A. *Red Petrograd: Revolution in the Factories, 1917–1918*. Cambridge, UK, 1983.

Wade, Rex A., ed. *Revolutionary Russia: New Approaches*. New York, 2004.

——. *The Russian Revolution: 1917*. Cambridge, 2000.

White, James D. *Lenin: The Practice and Theory of Revolution*. London, 2001.

Wildman, Allan K. *The End of the Russian Imperial Army*. 2 vols. Princeton, N.J., 1980, 1987.

14

The Jewish Question in the Soviet Union, 1917–1953

Jeffrey Veidlinger

The Soviet government under Stalin struggled throughout its existence with the "Jewish question." Lacking a territorial homeland, the Jewish population of the Soviet Union did not fit into Stalin's model of national minorities. Yet due to its demographic size, geographic dispersion, and prominence in the revolutionary movement as a whole, the Jewish population could not be ignored. Although the Jews failed Stalin's litmus test for nationhood, the Bolsheviks chose to treat them as though they were a national minority. As with all national minorities, the Soviet government hoped eventually to assimilate them, but in order to do so Stalin believed that in the short term they should be accorded limited national rights and be subjected to the policy of nativization. This included the right to use their own language in official matters and the right to be administered by co-ethnics. This policy continued relatively uninterrupted until after the Second World War. Popular anti-Semitism flared up during and after the war, while Jewish national sentiments increased as well. In the aftermath of the Holocaust and the establishment of the State of Israel, though, the Soviet government became convinced that the Jews were unlike other national minorities. With the founding of a Jewish state beyond the borders of the Soviet Union, Stalin began to question the loyalty of Soviet Jewry. Beginning in 1948, Stalin decided that the Jewish population was a fifth column, and began a long-term series of deliberately anti-Semitic attacks to intimidate and persecute Soviet Jewry.

THE JEWISH POPULATION

According to an 1897 census there were nearly 5.2 million Jews living in the Russian Empire: nearly 25 percent lived in Poland, 5 percent in Russia, and the remaining 70 percent were confined by law to the Pale of Jewish Settlement, a region including much of Ukraine, Belorussia, and Lithuania. Nearly half of the Jewish population lived in large cities, many of which became part of independent Poland after World War I. Almost a third of the population lived in small towns (shtetls), and the remaining fifth lived in rural villages. Moscow had a Jewish population of approximately 8,000; St. Petersburg had approximately 21,000. Due in part to restrictions on Jewish landholding, the vast majority of the Jewish population supported itself through petty trade (39 percent) and handicrafts (35 percent). The February Revolution of 1917 removed all restrictions on the Jews, including the residency restrictions of the Pale of Jewish Settlement, and occupational restrictions. Nevertheless, in 1926 over three-quarters of all Soviet Jews still lived in the regions of the former Pale of Jewish Settlement. According to the 1926 census, there were nearly 2.6 million Jews in the Soviet Union, of whom 21 percent lived in Russia, 61 percent lived in Ukraine, and 16 percent lived in Belorussia. The decline in overall population of Jews was due both to large-scale emigration, mostly to America, and to the independence of Poland, where some 2.8 million Jews lived. The Jewish populations of large Russian cities, though, had grown exponentially during this period: Moscow had a population of approximately 130,000 Jews, constituting 6.5 percent of the total population of the city, and the Jewish population of Leningrad (St. Petersburg) had grown to 85,000, constituting 5 percent of the population. Throughout the 1930s, the Jewish population continued to trickle out of the former Pale of Jewish Settlement into the large cities of the Russian Federation, and within the provinces to larger urban centers. In 1939 there were approximately 3 million Jews in the Soviet Union. Over half of them lived in Ukraine (1.5 million), nearly one-third in the Russian Soviet Federated Socialist Republic (RSFSR), and just over one-tenth in Belorussia. The Jewish population of Moscow had grown to 250,000 (6 percent of the total population) and Leningrad to 201,000 (6 percent). By this time, the largest group of Jewish breadwinners was engaged in white-collar work, although certain blue-collar enterprises, such as the textile and metal industries, continued to draw large numbers of Jews. Although they still only comprised a tiny fraction of all agrarian workers, some Jews were beginning to farm the land.[1]

JEWS IN THE REVOLUTIONARY MOVEMENT

The accusation that Bolshevism was a Jewish phenomenon has been made by counterrevolutionaries during the Russian Civil War, Hitler's propaganda machine during World War II, and others with an anti-Semitic agenda. The libel still proliferates today in the bowels of the Internet. In fact, a reasonable estimate of Jewish membership in the Communist Party in 1917 is that of the twenty-three thousand members of the party, one thousand (4 percent) were Jewish. Thus, Jewish party membership was slightly greater than the proportion of Jews in the overall population, but less than the proportion of Jews living in the large cities, from which most Communist Party members were recruited. As the Communist Party grew in size, the proportion of Jewish membership remained relatively steady. Jews were overrepresented, though, in the party leadership. Among delegates to the Eleventh Party Congress in 1922, there were seventy-seven Jews, or 15 percent of the Congress. At the very top echelons of the party, the Politburo, Jews were even more active: 20 percent of the 1926 Politburo, for instance, was composed of Jews.

By and large, prior to the revolution, Jews were not attracted to Bolshevism. Instead Jews concentrated themselves in other socialist parties, such as the Mensheviks, where about half the central committee was Jewish, and the Jewish Bund, a social democratic party that recognized Jewish national-cultural autonomy and boasted a membership of nearly thirty-four thousand in 1917. Taken together, about 10 percent of the revolutionary elite in all parties were Jewish. That is, of about three thousand individuals who could be counted among the elite, about three hundred were of Jewish heritage, although many, if not most, of these were completely assimilated into Russian society. This includes the leaderships of the Bolshevik Party, the Mensheviks, the Socialist Revolutionaries, and the leftist Constitutional Democrats. Although these figures are disproportional to the general Jewish population of the Soviet Union, they do not sustain the claim that revolutionary politics was primarily a Jewish phenomenon. Further, the success of the various Zionist parties, which boasted a combined membership of three hundred thousand, also indicates that revolutionary politics could not even claim the loyalty of the majority of politically engaged Jews.[2]

There are several reasons why Jews were overrepresented among the revolutionary parties. The primary reason is that, as we have seen, they were overrepresented among the socioeconomic group most prone to revolutionary politics: the urban working class. Secondly, Jews had a great deal to benefit from a revolution. Jews suffered terribly from tsarist policies that forced them to live under repressive restrictions and humiliating legislation. Among the most notorious of such restrictions was the Pale of Jewish Settlement, which confined the vast majority of the Jewish population to the western provinces of the Russian Empire. With exceptions only for the elite, Jews were denied freedom of movement and were barred from entering the central cities of the empire. Further, quotas were placed on Jewish admission to the universities, to the legal bar, and to the medical profession. Anti-Jewish violence and slander had also been increasing throughout the Russian Empire since the 1880s, leading to a series of pogroms (anti-Jewish massacres) that periodically flared up in Jewish-populated regions. As the Russian liberal press largely looked the other way, many Jews began to feel that their only salvation lay in revolutionary politics. Finally, Jews tended to be highly educated: elementary religious education was still mandatory for most Jewish boys and at 70 percent, the Jewish literacy rate was nearly double that of the general population. Since extensive legal restrictions still barred these highly educated Jews from professional satisfaction, many became frustrated and itinerant intellectuals who saw revolutionary politics as a potential panacea.

As it turned out, it was not the Bolshevik government that removed restrictions on the Jewish population, but rather the Provisional Government, established in February 1917. Thus, in October 1917 most Jews were sympathetic to the Provisional Government and did not initially welcome the Bolshevik revolution. However, the Civil War that engulfed the new Soviet empire was accompanied by a resurgence of bloody pogroms throughout Ukraine and Belorussia that resulted in between 150,000 and 200,000 Jewish casualties. The Red Army's reluctance to join in such anti-Jewish atrocities and its sometimes defense of Jews in the face of violence led many Jews to develop a trust in the Bolsheviks, or at least to regard them as the lesser of evils.

SOVIET POLICIES AND THE JEWS

In 1913 Stalin defined a nation as "a historically evolved, stable community of language, territory, economic life, and psychological make-up manifested in a community of culture." Stalin explicitly excluded the Jews, who, he wrote, "do not, in our opinion, constitute a single nation."[3] As is made clear at the end of his essay, Stalin was motivated to write about nationality issues for reasons of internal tactical politics within the Russian Social Democratic Worker's Party (Bolshevik). The coalition between the Jewish Bund and the Bolsheviks that was forged in 1906 had broken down as a result of the Bund's insistence that the autonomy of the Jewish socialist party be recognized. In order to bolster the Bolshevik argument for what Stalin called "the principle of international solidarity of the workers" he denied the Jews nationhood. Nevertheless, Stalin declared anti-Semitism to be a punishable offense and a "phenomenon profoundly hostile to the Soviet regime." Although anti-Semitic outbreaks and discrimination against Jews continued throughout the Soviet Union, the government punished anti-Semitic acts and made its opposition to anti-Semitism clear.

Although Stalin never officially reversed his opinion that Jews did not constitute a nation, once the Bolsheviks seized power they recognized the Jews as a de facto national minority. The Jews were accorded the same rights as other national minorities within the Soviet Union and were crippled with the same restrictions. The first admission that Jews should be treated as a national minority came with the foundation of Jewish organizations within the state and party structures, the most important of which were the Jewish Sections of the Communist Party established in 1918. The Jewish Sections were responsible for spreading Bolshevik ideology and policies to the Jewish population and for taking administrative control of Jewish communities throughout the Soviet Union.[4]

The primary means of accomplishing these tasks was through the use of a language accessible to the Jewish masses. Thus, like other national minorities, the Jews were permitted to use one of their own languages in official business. The only question was which language would be deemed the "Jewish national language": Hebrew or Yiddish. Hebrew was at the time predominantly a liturgical language, used by Jews around the world in synagogue and in religious writings, while Yiddish was the spoken language of most Eastern European Jews. Notably, the Zionist movement, which sought the establishment of a Jewish national homeland in Palestine, had adopted Hebrew as its language. The Jewish Sections, in opposition to the Zionists, joined the proponents of Yiddish, arguing that Yiddish was the language of the common people. Indeed, according to the 1897 census of the Russian Empire, 97 percent of Jews declared Yiddish as their mother tongue. The Jewish Sections were also motivated by the fact that Hebrew was associated with their two most ardent opponents: Zionists and the religious establishment.

Once Yiddish was recognized as the official language of Soviet Jews, the Jewish Sections and other state and party organizations set about creating a Yiddish infrastructure for the purpose of infiltrating the Jewish street. Yiddish courts, Yiddish party cells, Yiddish theaters, Yiddish libraries, Yiddish printing presses, Yiddish newspapers, and Yiddish schools were established throughout the Soviet Union. As a result of the state's support for Yiddish cultural activities, the Soviet Union under Stalin became one of the major centers in the world for Yiddish culture. The most visible sign of this Yiddish renaissance was the Moscow State Yiddish Theater. The Moscow State Yiddish Theater, based in the heart of Moscow's theater district, presented both prerevolutionary Yiddish plays by prominent writers, such as Sholem Aleichem and Yitshak Leyb Peretz, and modern Soviet plays glorifying the revolution and the Bolshevik victory in the Civil War. The theater, along with the Yiddish printing press, helped promote a new generation of Soviet Yiddish writers, including Yekhezkel Dobrushin, Avrom Veviurka, and Shmuel Halkin. Later in the decade these writers were joined by numerous Yiddish writers, such as Peretz Markish, Moyshe Kulbak, and Dovid Bergelson, who came to the Soviet Union from Poland, Germany, and other countries under the tragically mistaken belief that the Soviet Union offered a bright future for Yiddish writers.[5]

Throughout the 1930s, Yiddish secular culture continued to flourish in the Soviet Union with Stalin's support. In 1937 the Moscow State Yiddish Theater presented Shmuel Halkin's version of the classic Yiddish play, *Shulamis*, set in biblical Judaea, and the next year Solomon Mikhoels, the director of the theater, starred as Tevye the Dairyman in the highly acclaimed Sholem Aleichem play of the same name. Yiddish fiction also flourished. Dovid Bergelson published his two-part novel about Jewish life in the Ukraine, *At the Dnieper*, and in 1939 the Soviet Yiddish writer, Der Nister (the Hidden One), the pen name of Pinhas Kaganovich, published his epic novel of Jewish life in the shtetl, *The Family Mashber*. Yiddish music performance also flourished, with popular Yiddish singers, such as Zinovii Shulman and Mikhail Aleksandrovich, filling concert halls throughout the country. Scholarship on Yiddish folk music reached world stature under the leadership of Moyshe Beregovskii, who headed the Kiev Institute of Jewish Culture (after 1936, the Cabinet of Jewish Culture). Beregovskii conducted extensive ethnomusicological work through the shtetls of Ukraine and Belorussia, transcribing and recording Jewish folk music. Nevertheless, as a result of assimilationist tendencies, Yiddish language usage declined in the first two decades of the Soviet Union. By 1939 only 40 percent of Jews declared Yiddish their mother tongue, compared with 97 percent forty years earlier. The shift was most dramatic in the Russian Republic, where 73 percent declared Russian their mother tongue.

In addition to fostering the development of a secular Sovietized Yiddish culture, the Jewish Sections were also responsible for destroying those aspects of Jewish national identity that they regarded as hostile to Communist ideals. Chief among their targets were the Zionist movement, Jewish religious practice, and the Hebrew language.

The propaganda campaign against Zionism began in 1919, when many Zionist activists were arrested and the Central Bureau of the Zionist Organization was closed and its funds and archives seized by local police. Many Zionist organizations, though, continued to exist underground or in a semilegal situation and attracted supporters in large numbers for the next five years. In 1923 the government began a new, more repressive campaign against Zionism, this time led by the Soviet Secret Police. Between 1923 and 1926 tens of thousands of right-wing Zionist activist were arrested. Over the next two years, the left-wing socialist Zionist parties were also liquidated, culminating in the dissolution of the Poalei-Zion labor Zionists in 1928.

The 1920s also saw a campaign against the Jewish religion. Of the 447 synagogues that were officially recognized in the Russian Federation before the revolution, 257 were closed by 1933. In total some 650 synagogues were closed throughout the Soviet Union in the 1920s. In addition to the simple closing of synagogues, the Jewish Sections embarked upon a massive anti-religious campaign designed to discredit religion and to mock rabbinical authorities. Books of anti-clerical jokes were published in Yiddish and schoolchildren were taught songs mocking Jewish religious practice. Mock courts were established to put the Jewish religion "on trial," and "Red Haggadahs" were published, retelling the Passover story as deliverance from tsarist oppression rather than Egyptian slavery. Although the Jewish Sections claimed success in eradicating religious practice, the picture is much more complicated. Certainly few Jews in Moscow or St. Petersburg attended synagogue or maintained Jewish rituals, but these were always the most assimilated groups of Jews. In the provinces of Ukraine and Belorussia, where the majority of Jews were concentrated and where the Jewish population tended to be more grounded in religion, the anti-religious campaigns had limited effects. Despite the closure of their synagogues, many Jews in the provinces continued to pray together in private homes. Jewish rituals, such as the Passover seder and the giving of Hanukkah gelt, continued, sometimes celebrated alongside modern Soviet festivals. With the destruction of formalized Jewish education, though, the continued practice of Jewish rituals was severely threatened and would eventually be decimated by the Holocaust.

The Jewish Sections regarded the Hebrew language as an instrument of both Zionism and religious Judaism, and so silenced it as well. Most Hebrew-language education came through the *kheyders*, the Jewish primary schools at which Jewish boys were educated. Throughout the 1920s about one thousand *kheyders* were closed. Many of the leading Hebrew writers of Russia, including its preeminent poet Haim Nahman Bialik, were encouraged to emigrate soon after the revolution; most settled in Palestine. Among those who remained, such as Chaim Lensky, most were arrested in the purges of the 1930s; Lensky perished in a labor camp after his second arrest in 1941. The Hebrew-language theater Habimah achieved world fame in the early 1920s with its production of S. An-sky's mystical play *Dybbuk* in Bialik's Hebrew translation, and was even in favor with some members of the party elite. Yet the troupe saw the writing on the wall and in 1926, while on a European tour, defected to Palestine. It was not only the Hebrew language itself that was targeted, but even Hebrew-language root words and orthography that appeared in the Yiddish language were removed from dictionaries and from Soviet Yiddish writings.[6]

In addition to encouraging the use of Yiddish as the national language of the Jews, the Soviet government also sought to normalize the Jews by providing them with the other criterion for nationhood they lacked: a territorial homeland. The Jews were anomalous among national minorities in that they did not possess a territorial homeland either within the Soviet Union (as did the republic national minorities) or abroad (as did the diaspora nationalities, such as Far East Koreans, Volga Germans, and Soviet Finns). Several attempts were made to establish a territory (if not an actual homeland) for Soviet Jews. Most of these efforts were coupled with the goal of inducing Jews to leave the shtetls and their "petty-bourgeois" lifestyles and encouraging them instead to farm vacant land and join the industrial proletariat. Some members of the Jewish Sections of the Communist Party hoped initially that a Jewish territorial unit could be established in Belorussia, the traditional Jewish heartland. By 1924, however, attention had shifted to the underpopulated Crimea, where the idea of establishing a Jewish autonomous region was supported by several leading Bolsheviks, including Leon Trotsky, Lev Kamenev, and Nikolai Bukharin. Despite the migration of tens of thousands of Jews to the region in the mid-1920s, ultimately the Peoples Commissariat of Agriculture rejected the proposal for fear of antagonizing the native populations of the region. Instead of the autonomous republic envisioned, five Jewish national districts were established in the Crimea and south Ukraine, and over two hundred Jewish collective farms were established in the region. Funding for the establishment of Jewish communities in the Crimea came, in part, from foreign, and particularly American, Jewish charities.

The idea of concentrating Soviet Jews in a single territory, however, stayed alive. In 1924 Mikhail Kalinin and others in the Kremlin began promoting Jewish settlement in a region of far eastern Siberia near the Mongolian border, called Birobidzhan. In addition to providing Soviet Jews with what the government regarded as a national territory, Jewish settlement in Birobidzhan would also serve to populate the barren regions of the Far East and to exile Soviet Jews to the outer reaches of Siberia. In 1928 the region was officially reserved for Jewish colonization and in 1934 was designated as the Jewish Autonomous Region. Over the next five years, a massive propaganda campaign was launched to attract Jewish settlers from around the world to this region that until then had no Jewish population. Within the next few years, nearly forty thousand Jews were attracted to the region. But colonizers were not provided with adequate housing, food, medical care, or working conditions, and were forced to combat fierce mosquitoes, massive floods, and unhelpful local officials. As a result, over half of the new immigrants left within their first few years. By 1939, Jews comprised fewer than 20 percent of Birobidzhan's population; despite continued propaganda, the region never attracted a significant Jewish population.[7]

THE GREAT TERROR

Owing to their disproportionate representation among the intellectual community and the party elite, the Jews bore a special fate during the Great Terror. Many of the most prominent Jewish members of the party were the first to be accused of "anti-Soviet sabotage," most notably Leon Trotsky, Lev

Kamenev, Grigorii Zinoviev and Karl Radek. The latter three were executed after dramatic show trials, in which the tortured prisoners were forced to confess to outrageous crimes against the state they had helped found. Within the next two years the purges spread through the lower ranks of the party. Both prominent and rank-and-file members of the Jewish Sections fell victim to the purges. In 1937 Moyshe Litvakov, the editor of *Der emes* (*The Truth*), the Yiddish party newspaper, was arrested. He died in prison several weeks later. Within a year, the entire Jewish party apparatus had been liquidated and its leading members arrested: Moyshe Rafes, Mikhail Levitan, Semën Dimanshtayn, Aron Vaynshtayn, and Aleksandr Chemeriskii, along with many others, all shared Litvakov's fate. At the same time, those Jewish institutions attached to the party and its organs were shut down, including the Yiddish party paper that Litvakov had led.

Although party functionaries were targeted over cultural figures, the latter were not immune to the purges. As accusations of foreign espionage engulfed the cultural intelligentsia, the Jews, with their notorious international contacts, became an easy target. Over the summer of 1937 Soviet prosecutors fabricated a center of Jewish terrorism in Minsk, purportedly aimed at the revitalization of the Bund with the support of foreign powers. Among the first victims of this purge were the Yiddish literary critics Yashe Bronshtein and Max Erik. Soon after, Izi Kharik, a prominent poet and editor of the Yiddish literary periodical *Shtern*, was arrested, as was the poet Moyshe Kulbak, who died three years later in a Siberian labor camp. Although numerous centers of Jewish culture survived the purges, the Jewish political apparatus had been decimated and many prominent Jewish cultural activists had been murdered. Jews suffered disproportionately during the Great Terror, primarily because of their overrepresentation among the party apparatus and the intelligentsia rather than due to any outright discrimination on the basis of religion or nationality. Although the Terror was not motivated by official anti-Semitism, the troubled times did unleash latent anti-Semitic attitudes among large segments of the population and individual officials, who blamed their woes on the Jews.

WORLD WAR II

The twenty-two-month alliance between the Soviet Union and Nazi Germany that began with the Molotov-Ribbentrop Pact and ended with the German invasion of the Soviet Union was a slap in the face of Soviet Jewry. By allying with Hitler, Stalin, who had presented himself as a defender of Jewish national rights to the world, demonstrated that he was willing to sacrifice the Jews for the preservation of power. After the Nazi invasion of Poland, the Soviet Union annexed eastern Poland, bringing another 2 million Jews under Soviet rule. Initially viewing the Red Army as their liberators from Nazi rule, many Jews in the annexed territories greeted the Soviet government enthusiastically. The newly incorporated Soviet Jews, though, soon found the Soviet government unsympathetic to their plight. Further, their initial enthusiasm and support for Soviet rule tainted them as traitors in the eyes of their Polish, Ukrainian, and Belorussian neighbors. Local animosities against the Jews would soon explode violently when the region fell under Nazi rule.

In June 1941, the German army entered Soviet territory and quickly engulfed Ukraine, Belorussia, and other regions with large Jewish populations, including the newly annexed territories. Soviet Jews suffered unprecedented atrocities under Nazi rule, which ultimately led to the murder of about 2.5 million Jews who had lived on Soviet territory. Most of these were murdered by German Mobile Killing Units in ravines or forests on the outskirts of their hometowns. In Babi Yar, on the outskirts of Kiev, for instance, over thirty thousand Jews were massacred over two days in September 1941. Others were forced into ghettos where they starved to death or died of disease. Still others were killed in forced labor camps. About 1 million Jews survived by evacuating Nazi-occupied territories for the east, settling in Tashkent and other eastern cities. Despite the obvious targeting of Jews under Nazi rule, official Soviet propaganda downgraded Jewish suffering and refused to acknowledge the extent of the Holocaust.[8]

The tendency among some segments of the population to blame difficult times on the Jews increased dramatically during the Second World War. During the war, Stalin promoted patriotism and national exuberance as a means of inspiring the population toward war. He not only promoted Russian patriotism, but also allowed for a resurgence of Jewish patriotism, epitomized by the Jewish Anti-Fascist Committee and its Yiddish newspaper, *Eynikayt* (Unity). The Jewish Anti-Fascist Committee (JAFC), headed by Solomon Mikhoels, was formed in order to garner international support, primarily from British and American Jewry, for the Soviet war effort. The JAFC was the first Jewish political organization to be permitted in the Soviet Union since the liquidation of the Jewish Sections, and *Eynikayt* the first Yiddish newspaper since the 1937 demise of *Der emes*. As part of its international propaganda campaign, the JAFC called for unity between Soviet and world Jewry, and in 1943 Solomon Mikhoels and the poet Itsik Fefer traveled to North America and Britain to make personal appeals for aid and support. After the war, the JAFC became the de facto representative of the Jewish people to the Soviet government. *The Black Book: The Nazi Crime against the Jewish People* was compiled by the JAFC and became one of the first documentary sources on the Holocaust. Although its publication was forbidden in the Soviet Union, the book was published in New York in 1946. The JAFC also received numerous appeals for help from Jewish refugees after the war, and struggled to petition for assistance from the Soviet government on behalf of these refugees. The Soviet government, though, no longer had a use for the JAFC and regarded its continued existence as a potential threat and its appeals on behalf of Jewish war victims as meddling, leading the way toward the 1948 liquidation of the committee and the subsequent arrest of many of its leading participants.[9]

Popular anti-Semitism also flourished during the war and in its immediate aftermath. Anti-Semitic propaganda had been spread widely in regions that had been under Nazi control and reached beyond as well. Further, many Soviet citizens in Ukraine and other Nazi-occupied territories had benefited from the Nazi extermination of the Jews—they had taken over abandoned Jewish houses, stolen Jewish property, or replaced Jews in the workforce. Some had even been active collaborators with the Nazis, helping round up Jews for extermination or even killing Jews themselves. Others had simply been silent as their Jewish neighbors were murdered. Many of these people feared retribution if the Jewish refugees were permitted to return, felt guilt about their wartime behavior or the behavior of their neighbors, and feared the loss of the benefits they had reaped from the Jewish absence. As a result, the postwar period witnessed a renewal of pogroms in parts of Ukraine and a general rise of anti-Semitic incidents throughout the Soviet Union. Further, although Jews fought valorously at the front—they were awarded a disproportionately large number of military honors and played particularly prominent roles in the partisan movement—rumors spread that Jews were avoiding military service, and that the Jews were to blame for Soviet involvement in the war altogether.

The experience of shared persecution under Nazi rule united and galvanized a bourgeoning national movement among Soviet Jews. The Holocaust taught many Jews and non-Jews around the world that the Jewish people could only be safe from persecution in a state of their own. Thus, in November 1947 the United Nations, with the support of the Soviet Union, voted to establish a Jewish state in Palestine. The prospect of becoming a "normal" people with an independent nation-state unleashed a wave of enthusiasm among world Jewry, including Soviet Jewry. Hebrew study groups began to emerge throughout the Soviet Union, especially in Ukraine, to train Jews to function in a Hebrew society (the language of the State of Israel). Many Soviet Jews also sent letters to the JAFC asking to be dispatched to Israel to fight in its War of Independence, asking the JAFC to coordinate aid to the new Jewish state, or simply expressing support.

OFFICIAL ANTI-SEMITISM

The Soviet government, though, had voted in favor of the establishment of the State of Israel not out of any sympathy for the Jewish population or the

Zionist position, but rather as a means of enhancing Soviet geopolitical power against the West in the Near East. The continued Soviet opposition to Zionism and Jewish nationalism was evidenced when Solomon Mikhoels was murdered by the Soviet Secret Police in January 1948, probably for having expressed support for the future State of Israel a few weeks earlier. The murder of Mikhoels heralded the beginning of official anti-Semitism and Stalin's outright persecution of Soviet Jewry.

The May 1948 establishment of the State of Israel and the September 1948 arrival in Moscow of the first Israeli diplomatic legation unleashed spontaneous celebrations among some Soviet Jews. In an article in *Pravda*, the prominent Russian Jewish writer Ilya Ehrenburg warned Soviet Jews against identifying too closely with the State of Israel, but his warning went unheeded. Golda Meyerson (Meir), the first Israeli minister to the USSR, recalls that when she and the Israeli legation attended Moscow's Choral Synagogue during the Jewish New Year in October 1948, a crowd of "close to 50,000 people was waiting for us. . . . They had come—those good, brave Jews—in order to be with us, to demonstrate their sense of kinship and to celebrate the establishment of the State of Israel."[10] The following week, as the legation returned for the Day of Atonement, the scene was repeated. The manifest identification of many Soviet Jews with the State of Israel roused Stalin's suspicions of the Jewish people. Further, the Soviet government had long discriminated against "diaspora nationalities," those national minorities whose territorial homeland lay outside the borders of the Soviet Union. Until 1948 Jews were excluded from this category. But as the State of Israel came into being, the Jewish population of the Soviet Union was transformed into a diaspora nationality and as such became subject to Soviet purification drives.[11]

The new official anti-Semitism and Stalinist attacks against the Jews, which had begun with the murder of Mikhoels, intensified in late 1948 and early 1949.[12] During this time, the last remaining Jewish institutions in the Soviet Union were closed down, beginning with the Jewish Anti-Fascist Committee and its Yiddish newspaper in November 1948, followed by the Yiddish Printing Press and finally the Moscow State Yiddish Theater in February 1949. Additionally, the anti-cosmopolitan campaign that had been brewing in the Soviet press was transformed into a deliberately anti-Semitic crusade. On January 28, 1949, *Pravda* published an article that used anti-Semitic motifs to accuse a group of theater critics, most of whom were Jews, of "anti-patriotic" activity. During this same period dozens of leading Jewish political, cultural, and intellectual personalities were arrested, followed by a long-term campaign of persecution against Jewish journalists, academicians, artists, politicians, students, military personnel, and ordinary citizens on charges ranging from cosmopolitanism to bourgeois nationalism. Meanwhile tortuous interrogations were being conducted of many of the arrested Jewish personalities in preparation for the secret trial of the JAFC, conducted in the spring of 1952. Although the trial was probably originally intended as a show trial along the lines of the show trials of the 1930s, the defendants' unwillingness to participate, and their sometimes open repudiation of the charges, probably enticed Stalin to conduct the trial in secret. On August 12, 1952, on a night known as the "Night of the Murdered Poets," thirteen defendants associated with the JAFC were executed, including the Yiddish writers Leyb Kvitko, Peretz Markish, Dovid Bergelson, Dovid Hofshteyn, and Itsik Fefer.[13] In November of that same year, Stalin arranged for a show trial in Communist-controlled Czechoslovakia. Secretary general of the Czech Communist Party Rudolf Slansky and ten other Jewish politicians were tried in Prague on trumped-up charges of encouraging Zionism, espionage, and plotting to murder Czech president Klement Gottwald through his physician. Slansky and seven others were executed the following month (along with three non-Jewish defendants). Finally, on January 13, 1953, an article entitled "Arrest of Group of Saboteur-Doctors" appeared on the front page of *Pravda*, announcing the arrest of a group of mostly Jewish doctors who were accused of collaborating with Jewish organizations abroad to poison leading Kremlin officials. The article made no secret of its anti-Semitic implications. The "Doctors' Plot" was intended as a final purge against Soviet Jews, rumored to include the complete exile of all Soviet Jews to Siberia. They were saved only by Stalin's death two months later.[14]

CONCLUSION

Stalin's theory of nations as developed prior to the revolution denied that the Jews were a nation because they lacked a territorial homeland and a common language. Nevertheless, once the Bolsheviks seized power, they realized that in order to propagandize effectively among Soviet Jews, they needed to treat the Jews as a national minority. Thus, the Soviet government encouraged the use of Yiddish and helped develop a secular Yiddish culture that would cultivate Communist values and loyalty. State support of the Yiddish language led to a renaissance of Yiddish culture in the Soviet Union. The Soviet government also sought to establish a territorial homeland for the Jews in Birobidzhan. The project ultimately failed, mostly because of the inhospitable climate, leading many Jews to regard the plan as a cynical attempt to exile them to eastern Siberia. At the same time, the Soviet government worked to destroy elements of Jewish identity it regarded as hostile. Zionism, the Hebrew language, and the Jewish religion were all attacked, as were those individuals who identified with them. Jews also suffered disproportionately during the Great Terror, mostly as a result of their overrepresentation in targeted groups. The Soviet-German nonaggression pact of 1939 was a distressing blow to Soviet Jewry, who regarded any alliance with Hitler as anathema.

When the Second World War began, Soviet Jews suffered unprecedented atrocities at the hands of Nazi troops and collaborators. The final postwar years of Stalin's reign saw an intensification of popular anti-Semitism, bolstered by official governmental anti-Semitism. As Soviet Jews struggled to come to terms with the Holocaust and embraced the newfound State of Israel, Stalin deemed Soviet Jewry to be an unreliable and suspect group and began a drawn-out and deliberate policy of persecution and intimidation. Thus, having just survived the greatest atrocities ever witnessed by humanity in the form of the Holocaust, Soviet Jews were then forced to confront renewed anti-Semitism from the very state that defeated the Nazi enemy.

NOTES

1. For more on the Jewish population in tsarist Russia and the Soviet Union see Zvi Y. Gitelman, *A Century of Ambivalence: The Jews of Russia and the Soviet Union, 1881 to the Present*, 2nd ed. (Bloomington: Indiana University Press, 2001).

2. For more on Jewish participation in the revolutionary movement see Erich Haberer, *Jews and Revolution in Nineteenth-Century Russia* (Cambridge, UK: Cambridge University Press, 1995).

3. Joseph Stalin, *Marxism and the National and Colonial Question* (New York: International Publishers, 1936), 8.

4. For more on early Soviet policies toward the Jews and the establishment of Jewish Sections of the Communist Party of the Soviet Union see Zvi Y. Gitelman, *Jewish Nationality and Soviet Politics: The Jewish Sections of the CPSU, 1917–1930* (Princeton, N.J.: Princeton University Press, 1972).

5. See Jeffrey Veidlinger, *The Moscow State Yiddish Theater: Jewish Culture on the Soviet Stage* (Bloomington: Indiana University Press, 2000).

6. See Yehoshua A. Gilboa, *A Language Silenced: The Suppression of Hebrew Literature and Culture in the Soviet Union* (East Brunswick, N.J.: Associated University Presses, 1982).

7. For more on Birobidzhan see Robert Weinberg, *Stalin's Forgotten Zion: Birobidzhan and the Making of a Soviet Jewish Homeland; An Illustrated History, 1928–1996* (Berkeley: University of California Press, 1998); and Allan Laine Kagedan, *Soviet Zion: The Quest for a Russian Jewish Homeland* (New York: St. Martin's Press, 1994).

8. For the Jewish experience in the Soviet Union during World War II see Lucjan Dobroszycki and Jeffrey S. Gurock, eds., *The Holocaust in the Soviet Union: Studies and Sources on the Destruction of the Jews in the Nazi-Occupied Territories of the USSR, 1941–1945* (Armonk, N.Y.: M. E. Sharpe, 1993).

9. On the Jewish Anti-Fascist Committee see Shimon Redlich, *Propaganda and Nationalism in Wartime Russia: The Jewish Antifascist Committee in the USSR, 1941–1948* (Boulder, Colo.: East European Quarterly, 1982) and Shimon Redlich, ed., *War, Holocaust and Stalinism: A Documented Study of the Jewish Anti-Fascist Committee in the USSR* (Luxembourg: Harwood Academic Publishers, 1995).

10. Golda Meir, *My Life* (Camberwell, UK: Futura Publications, 1976), 205.

11. See Jeffrey Veidlinger, "Soviet Jewry as a Diaspora Nationality: The 'Black Years' Reconsidered," *East European Jewish Affairs* 33, no. 1 (2003), 4–29.

12. See Gennadi Kostyrchenko, *Out of the Red Shadows: Anti-Semitism in Stalin's Russia* (Amherst, N.Y.: Prometheus Books, 1995); and Yehoshua Gilboa, *The Black Years of Soviet Jewry* (New York: Little, Brown & Company, 1971).

13. See Joshua Rubenstein and Vladimir P. Naumov, eds., *Stalin's Secret Pogrom: The Postwar Inquisition of the Jewish Anti-Fascist Committee* (New Haven, Conn.: Yale University Press, 2001).

14. On the Doctors' Plot see Jonathan Brent and Vladimir P. Naumov, *Stalin's Last Crime: The Plot against the Jewish Doctors, 1948–1953* (New York: HarperCollins, 2003).

SUGGESTED READING

Dekel-Chen, Jonathan L. *Farming the Red Land: Jewish Agricultural Colonization and Local Soviet Power, 1924–1941.* New Haven, Conn., 2005.

Gilboa, Yehoshua. *The Black Years of Soviet Jewry, 1939–1953.* Boston, 1971.

Gitelman, Zvi. *A Century of Ambivalence: The Jews of Russia and the Soviet Union, 1881 to the Present,* 2nd ed. Bloomington, Ind., 2001.

Kostyrchenko, Gennadi. *Out of the Red Shadows: Anti-Semitism in Stalin's Russia.* Amherst, N.Y., 1995.

Levin, Nora. *The Jews in the Soviet Union since 1917: Paradox of Survival.* London, 1988.

Pinkus, Benjamin. *The Jews of the Soviet Union: The History of a National Minority.* Cambridge, UK, 1988.

Roi, Yaacov, ed. *Jews and Jewish Life in Russia and the Soviet Union.* Essex, 1995.

Rubenstein, Joshua, and Vladimir P. Naumov, ed. *Stalin's Secret Pogrom: The Postwar Inquisition of the Jewish Anti-Fascist Committee.* New Haven, Conn., 2001.

Schwarz, Solomon M. *The Jews in the Soviet Union.* Syracuse, N.Y., 1951.

Shneer, David. *Yiddish and the Creation of Soviet Jewish Culture: 1918–1930.* Cambridge, UK, 2004.

Shternshis, Anna. *Soviet and Kosher: Jewish Popular Culture in the Soviet Union, 1923–1939.* Bloomington, Ind., 2006.

Slezkine, Yuri. *The Jewish Century.* Princeton, N.J., 2004.

Vaksberg, Arkady. *Stalin against the Jews.* New York, 1994.

Veidlinger, Jeffrey. *The Moscow State Yiddish Theater: Jewish Culture on the Soviet Stage.* Bloomington, Ind., 2000.

Weinberg, Robert. *Stalin's Forgotten Zion: Birobidzhan and the Making of a Soviet Jewish Homeland; An Illustrated History, 1928–1996.* Berkeley, Calif., 1998.

15

Aviation Cinema in Stalin's Russia

Conformity, Collectivity, and the Conflict with Fascism

Scott W. Palmer

Of the many technologies that transformed human experience in the first half of the twentieth century, none were more significant than aviation and cinema. As mountains were conquered and continents traversed, the airplane overturned traditional notions of time and space, compelling citizens and statesmen alike to reconsider their relationship to the natural world. Accompanying the physical changes that it effected, aviation contributed to the formation of a new aesthetic in which ideas of power and authority were communicated in terms of speed and altitude, flight duration, and technical proficiency. Cinema, for its part, contributed to the expansion of human sensibilities by capturing motion on film, creating fantastic, imaginary worlds, and allowing audiences to participate publicly in the presentation of preserved spectacle. Cinema was a collective experience, ideally suited to communicating ideas and emotions to audiences otherwise divided by cultural and linguistic differences. As such, it would emerge as the medium of choice for states intent on cultivating popular legitimacy and instilling collective values among the ranks of their citizenry.

In the years that followed October 1917, Soviet leaders established a symbiotic link between cinema and the airplane, enjoining these two modern technologies in support of their quest to construct a new socialist order. Throughout the decade of the 1920s, when airplanes were scarce and the perceived need to introduce them to the populace was pressing, cinema brought the reality of flight to mass audiences in the forms of newsreels and short features.[1] Projected images of light and shadow substituted for the reality of canvas and metal as moving pictures provided the aeronautically uninitiated with initial glimpses of the technological changes sweeping their land. During the 1930s, the relationship between cinema and aviation was transformed as flying dreadnoughts ventured into the Soviet countryside to bring cinema to citizens unable to experience the metropolitan movie hall. Equipped with onboard projectors and scores of state-produced films, these "fly-in theaters" were essential components of Soviet propaganda, assisting party leaders' efforts to modernize the nation by mobilizing citizens for the tasks of socialist construction.

The link between aviation and cinema in the Soviet Union extended, as well, to the thematic content of motion pictures. Between the launch of the first Five-Year Plan in 1928 and the start of the Second World War in 1939, Soviet studios released more than two dozen films involving aviation. The appearance, on average, of one new feature every seven months during a period when movies were expensive to produce and film was often in short supply testifies to the importance attached to aviation cinema by official Soviet culture. Still, while these films doubtless appealed to their audiences thanks to well-developed plots, sympathetic characters, and exciting aerial scenes, their production had less to do with popular entertainment than political education. Set in flight schools, airplane factories, modeling circles, and airfields, these films capitalized upon widespread public interest in airplanes to convey party-mandated messages of civic obedience, social conformity, and loyalty to the state.

Gogi: The Courageous Flier was the first full-length aviation film to appear in Stalinist Russia.[2] Released in March 1929, the film employed aeronautical themes in an attempt to impart to audiences the need for personal discipline and obedience to party authority. Celebrating the values of cooperation and collectivism, *Gogi: The Courageous Flier* decried spontaneous, uncontrolled initiative as detrimental to both individual citizens and Soviet society as a whole. In doing so, the film established what would become the central message of almost every flight feature released during the decade of 1929–1939.

The production concerned the adventures of a small band of boys, Gogi, Leva, Kolia, and Alik, who dream of becoming pilots. In the hope of mastering airplane construction, the determined Gogi inspires his friends to build their own airplane. Instructed by Gogi to secure construction materials for the airplane, the gang members obtain the necessary parts through less-than-respectable means. Alik and Leva steal from the local cooperative while Kolia strong-arms a younger child into surrendering the wheels from his wagon. When he learns of his comrades' misdeeds, the honorable Gogi decries their "criminal ways" and compels them to promise to return the materials once they have accomplished their aeronautical mission.

The boys complete construction of their soapbox airplane and the day arrives for its inaugural flight. Local children gather at a nearby hill to witness Gogi's daring attempt to fly. His efforts are thwarted by the laws of gravity and aerodynamics: the jerry-rigged plane is dashed to pieces and the "courageous flier" is gravely injured. Gogi awakens, bruised and battered, in the town's hospital. There, he and his friends are lectured by a local party representative on the importance of joining the party-sponsored aviation society, Osoaviakhim. Chastened by their unfortunate experience, Gogi and his gang resolve to continue their interests in airplane modeling only within the framework of the officially sanctioned organization.

The didactic and moral lessons imparted by *Gogi: The Courageous Flier* were revisited in the subsequent 1929 release *I Want to Be an Aviatrix*.[3] Focusing on the efforts of children to contribute to society through the mastery of aviation technology, *I Want to Be an Aviatrix* reinforced the official message that individual initiative in the absence of strict guidance could be dangerous to one's life. The film likewise encouraged young citizens to assist in the construction of socialism by joining officially sanctioned organizations which would help shape and direct their energies towards productive labor.

Thirteen-year-old Tanya and her infant brother live in the Moscow suburbs with their mother, a seamstress. Tanya, a voracious reader and irrepressible daydreamer, is kept busy at home raising her sibling and undertaking numerous chores while her mother works. Despite her outgoing personality and impressive organizational talents (in Taylorist fashion she "rationalizes" her chores, doing homework and washing dishes while rocking her brother's crib with her foot), Tanya is ignored by her male contemporaries because she is a girl.

The organization of a local modeling circle sparks Tanya's imagination. Ignoring her mother's admonitions that she "would do better learning how to sew," she joins the group as it is preparing to enter an airplane design competition. Tanya's entry into the modeling circle is met with the great mistrust of the all-boy group. Vovka, one of the circle's more outspoken members, brusquely informs her that "we don't allow girls," and he warns Tanya to "stay out of men's matters." The Communist Party representative who supervises the circle allows Tanya to participate over the objections of the boys. The young girl's status in the group suffers a setback, however, when her first model airplane performs poorly on its maiden flight. Returning home, the dejected Tanya encounters the shadowy figure Ian Burinskii. Burinskii, a "businessman" who specializes in marketing toys, tempts the young girl with an offer to sell her a working model which, he promises, will assure her first place in the upcoming competition. Tanya resolutely refuses and informs the crass speculator that she is quite capable of building her own airplane.

Circle members Vovka and Vitya observe Tanya's discussion with Burinskii and make note of the model merchant's address. They return to his workshop a few days later. There, thanks to a tip from Tanya, the circle's remaining members catch the boys in the shameful act of purchasing models. In response to this transgression, the collective publicly censures the two renegades, condemning them for "substituting their own hard work with the services of a speculator." Thus chastised, Vovka and Vitya resolve to work through the night constructing their own planes for the next day's competition.

The day of the competition finally dawns. Tanya's new airplane flies well, promoting the success of the circle as a whole. As a result, she wins the acceptance and admiration of her modelist comrades. The film ends with the transmission of a valuable lesson to the audience: "Each and every dream, even the most audacious, will someday be achieved, if only through persistence and labor."

The role of the collective as the cornerstone of Soviet society was given still greater emphasis in the 1935 feature *One Stop to the Moon*, which, like other aviation films, used the story of a young child's aeronautical adventures to communicate the officially sanctioned values of discipline, obedience, and social conformity.[4] Hailed by the Soviet press as a "serious and fascinating children's film," *One Stop to the Moon* was understood to contain social and political messages suitable for adult audiences as well.[5]

Young Lenia Glebov dreams of flying to the moon. He spends his days at school working on the equations he will require to navigate the stars. In his free time he labors to complete a miniature "Starflyer" which, he hopes, will provide him with the experience he needs to undertake a manned expedition into space. Late one evening, Lenia and some local children secretly gather to launch the rocket ship. With great fanfare, the fuse to the gunpowder-propelled craft is lit. The Starflyer takes off like a winged bottle-rocket straight up into the air. "In no time," Lenia proudly proclaims, "it will be on the moon." To Lenia's surprise, however, the Starflyer, having reached the apex of its flight, turns back toward the earth and crashes on the roof of the kolkhoz granary. The detonation of the model ignites a fire. As the town's citizens rush to douse the flames, the children scatter. The granary is engulfed in flames.

In the wake of the fire, young Lenia is summoned to meet with the local political officer, Andrei Vestovoi. To the boy's great surprise, the party representative expresses little anger over the accident. A veteran aviator who defended Petrograd from the Whites during the Civil War, Vestovoi appreciates Lenia's fascination with flight and the initiative that he demonstrated in building his Starflyer. Nonetheless, the political officer lectures the youngster on his need for discipline, education, and guidance if he is ever to realize the dream of one day reaching the moon. "Our nation," Vestovoi intones, "requires educated flyers, engineers, and constructors." But, he notes, it is imperative that Lenia study diligently if he is to contribute to the advance of the Soviet Union. "Nothing ever comes one's way 'nonstop,'" Vestovoi admonishes. Before an individual can walk, he must learn how to crawl, and before Lenia can fly, he must learn how to construct models.

To assist Lenia in his quest to reach the moon, Vestovoi announces that he will organize an aviation circle for the town's children. There, Lenia and his comrades will receive the education they will need to contribute to the country's development. Vestovoi promises Lenia that following the arrival of his sister Natasha (an accomplished pilot who is coming to the collective farm to assist with agricultural operations), the circle will have an energetic leader willing to work with the local youth.

Natasha's arrival inaugurates another adventure for the precocious and incorrigibly wayward Lenia. True to the political officer's word, Natasha assists the newly organized circle. She offers the children expert guidance and an abundance of literature concerning the laws of aerodynamics and the proper methods by which airplanes are constructed. In no time, the children are well on their way toward becoming true aviators. Lenia's curiosity, however, remains unfulfilled. He resolves to subject his glider to a personal test flight in order to finally realize his dream of flying. Late at night, while the village is asleep, Lenia secretly attaches his glider to the tail of Natasha's plane using the coverage of some shrubbery to mask his mischief. The following morning, as Natasha departs, her plane lifts off, carrying Lenia and his glider into the air. The horrified collective farmers watch as the force of the launch rips Lenia's glider apart, dashing the plane and its young pilot to the ground. Lenia is hospitalized. Miraculously, he is not seriously injured.

While recovering in the hospital, Lenia receives a letter. In it, a representative from the regional Osoaviakhim council informs the boy that one of his airplane designs (previously forwarded to the council by Natasha) has caught the attention of a renowned aeronautical engineer. Owing to the unusually advanced nature of the designs, the council has decided to invite Lenia to participate in an upcoming glider competition in the Crimea. The invitation spurs Lenia's speedy recovery. He arrives at the competition as a member of the kolkhoz's Osoaviakhim circle. There, he is allowed to pilot the circle's entry. The movie ends with a beaming Lenia flying the circle's glider through the sky.

Contemporary press coverage of *One Stop to the Moon* emphasized Lenia's role as a prototypical model for Soviet youth. In the same way that Soviet art and literature of the 1930s created iconographic images of "new" Soviet men and women, transformed by the party into politically conscious and socially responsible participants in socialist construction, Lenia was upheld as the archetypal "new child" from which the new Soviet citizen would mature. According to one reviewer, Lenia was a model for others to follow as his talents were uncovered "in the Soviet way, among other children, in the middle of his comrades." His individualism, this review concluded, was properly realized through participation in the collective.[6]

The emphasis placed by the press upon Lenia's personal development within the community of the aeronautical circle reaffirmed officials' intentions that aviation films like *One Stop to the Moon* underscore the role of the collective in shaping Soviet society. In the absence of strict supervision, Lenia's intelligence, inquisitiveness, and spontaneity prove dangerous to himself and the residents of the kolkhoz. These exceptional characteristics, like those possessed by Gogi in the earlier production, are not, in themselves, negative qualities. They do, however, demand the discipline, guidance, and structure proffered by authority if they are to contribute to the development of society. Lenia, ultimately, is made aware of this reality and attains a higher level of consciousness (as do all of the heroes within this cinematic genre) through the tutelage of the Communist Party.

The themes of discipline, consciousness, and the importance of the collective also framed what historian Peter Kenez has called "the most successful of all Soviet aviation films," the 1935 production *Fliers*.[7] Conforming both in style and thematic structure to other productions within the aviation film genre born of the cultural revolution, *Fliers* reiterated the official line regarding the centrality of social conformity, the suppression of unregulated spontaneity, and the need for unwavering obedience to the party.

Fliers' contribution to Soviet aviation cinema is best revealed through an examination of the relationship between the film's three major protagonists: the air base commander Rogachev, the experienced stunt flyer Beliaev, and the young female pilot Bystrova. These three individuals are less autonomous, fully developed characters than they are idealized types, the likes of which Soviet audiences had seen before. As the stern flight school commander and spokesman for collective discipline, Rogachev is a cinematic successor to the political officers, party members, and representatives of state authority that had appeared in previous aeronautical productions. He is the on-screen personification of the ideal Soviet military pilot and party member. Experienced, courageous, and resolute, Rogachev is unwavering in his loyalty and dedication to the party. As the film's principal representation of Soviet authority, Rogachev was the most celebrated of *Fliers'* three protagonists. The actor who portrayed the air base commander on screen, Boris Shchukin, received unending praise from reviewers for bringing heroism and honor to his portrayal of a party stalwart.[8]

Sergei Beliaev is the commander of one of the airfield's aviation squadrons. Dashing, debonair, and supremely self-confident, he is a fearless stunt flyer and the best pilot the base has to offer. He is also an incurable show-off who lacks the discipline and sense of responsibility expected of a Soviet pilot. Beliaev "is reckless in his bravery, careless in his concern for the technical condition of his airplane, and he values, above all else, meaningless displays of daring and dangerous air stunts."[9] In one of the film's defining scenes, Beliaev ignores a direct order from Rogachev not to test-fly an airplane that has a faulty fuel line. As a result of his "aeronautical hooliganism," the plane crashes, landing the pilot in the hospital. Beliaev's disobedience is upheld as an example not to be followed by the school's cadets. When he returns to the base after being released from the infirmary, the pilot is met by the stony glares of his comrades and a large banner urging all pilots, engineers, and aeronautical workers to "Fight against Beliae-vism." The unperturbed and unrepentant flyer refuses to abandon his cock-sure ways. In the end, he is forced to answer for his insolence. Beliaev is permanently grounded by Rogachev.

In contrast to the disciplined Rogachev and reckless Beliaev, Galia Bystrova is an intermediary figure. She is awed by Rogachev's personality and looks to the commander for inspiration and guidance. Following Beliaev's crash, Bystrova admonishes the pilot to seek atonement by publicly confessing that he lacks discipline. Despite her advice, Bystrova secretly admires Beliaev's heedless spirit and, for a time, contemplates the possibility that she may be in love with him. Torn between the two men, Bystrova falls under the influence of the charismatic Beliaev. She takes off on her own unauthorized stunt flight. In response, Rogachev delivers a stern lecture in which he reprimands her for lacking discipline: "Youth, heroism, this is our country, our life. This is who we are. But when youth is transformed into foolhardiness and heroism into tricks, we call it philistinism. In the West, they earn their bread that way, but we recognize it as philistinism." Bystrova's transgression proves to be only a temporary lapse. Following a brief grounding, she regains her discipline and is allowed to fly again. In the end, her controlled daring garners her the privilege of test-flying a new airplane. She performs brilliantly, wins the accolades of Rogachev, abandons any feelings for Beliaev, and is awarded a commission flying an air route over the Pamir Mountains.

Ultimately, *Fliers* is best understood as a cinematic triptych in which the three main protagonists provide the audience with a highly stylized version of Soviet reality. The film is the quintessential cinematic adaptation of Socialist Realism.[10] In the absence of a linear plot, *Fliers* unwinds through the dialectical interactions of its three characters. The disciplined Rogachev (consciousness) is challenged by the careless Beliaev (spontaneity). Each man exerts influence upon the impressionable Bystrova, who, in realizing her own potential, resolves the antitheses of her two comrades and emerges as the true "heroine" of the film. The dialectical progression of the film, in turn, underscores its fundamental message of collectivity. The movie is built upon the threefold unity of Rogachev, Beliaev, and Bystrova. Each is essential to the film's internal structure. In the words of one contemporary reviewer, "There are no negative personalities in the film. In all of the heroes on the screen, one can see [at different stages of development] our own Soviet people."[11]

Alongside films that focused on modeling circles and flight schools, a number of Stalin-era aviation features addressed military themes. In part a response to the ideological challenge posed by the fascist regimes in Italy and especially Germany, these films reflected the growing militarism of 1930s Soviet culture. Although these films exhorted viewers to support the state through depictions of the country's battle against unrepentant revanchists, amoral capitalists, and warmongering fascists, they continued to emphasize the importance of social conformity, discipline, and collectivity.

The first cinematic feature to portray prominently military aviation was the ominously titled 1933 release *City under Siege*.[12] The film exploited contemporary fears (consciously fed by party authorities) of the possibility of a surprise chemical attack on Soviet soil by a squadron of foreign aircraft. The sinister chemist Professor Runge has been laboring for some time on a powerful new gas weapon. The evil fruit of his research, "Runget-88," promises to be the most deadly chemical agent known to the world. The concoction, which has the scent of fresh rose blossoms, can kill any living organism in less than twenty seconds. In search of potential customers for "Runget-88," the professor entertains foreign representatives at his research laboratory. There, a number of agents witness a graphic demonstration of the gas weapon's potency. A cat is placed inside of a sealed glass container. "Runget-88" is slowly released through a tube into the test compartment. As the gas fills the container, the shrieking cat convulses violently and dies. A wry smile is visible on Runge's face. The gathered foreign agents begin bidding on the gas. The screen fades to black.

The scene shifts to a new Soviet electrical station located in the center of a large city. Built in accordance with the most modern standards of world technology, the station, nevertheless, is situated in a precarious position not far from the border with a hostile foreign state. "One good high-explosive bomb and the whole region would be paralyzed!" Inside, a foreign consultant hired to bring the station online is conducting an inspection of the station's equipment. The consultant is Karl Runge, son of the creator of "Runget-88." The younger Runge is angry with the Soviet workers who man the station. "The most recent technology demands exact precision!" he tells the station's chief engineer Arkad'ev. "You were late with your adjustments by more than an hour." In truth, however, Runge is not really concerned. His contract has expired and he is due to depart for his homeland. Runge's return, however, is unexpectedly delayed when the station receives word that the fascist government of a neighboring state has launched a surprise attack upon the Soviet Union. The nation's borders are closed, preventing the young engineer from leaving. He is indignant. Like his father, Karl Runge is "apolitical" and he claims disinterest in the conflict. He protests the order that prevents him from departing, but to no avail. Furious with his Soviet hosts, Runge storms off.

The fascist forces, meanwhile, organize their assault. At an enemy air base, a group of pilots await instructions. Their general announces the plan: white-guardist forces, allied with the fascists, will parachute behind Soviet lines. They will capture the new electric station and, from there, provide the coordinates needed for a great attack upon the Soviet population. The assault will be accompanied by "destructive explosive devices and the scent of fresh rose blossoms."

Soviet defense forces prepare to counter the fascist air assault. A reconnaissance station informs the general staff of the approach of the first wave of enemy planes. A squadron of Soviet aircraft is dispatched to meet the invaders. A second and then a third squadron follow as more and more enemy planes approach the city. With the civilian population in danger, the Soviet commander Ognev orders the last of his reserves into the battle. At a crucial moment, a lucky hit by the fascist bombers damages the control center of the electric station. Without the station, the Soviet command cannot coordinate the region's defenses. The station's technicians send for Karl Runge, but the engineer obstinately refuses to assist with the repairs. "It isn't my station," he demurs. "My contract has expired. Besides, I am not obliged to go running around on the streets when there are bombs falling from the sky!" In the face of Runge's cowardice, the Soviet technicians repair the command center themselves.

In the hope of diverting the enemy planes from the populated areas, Commander Ognev orders that the city be immersed in darkness save for the electric lights that adorn a recreational area on the outskirts of town. His ruse succeeds. The fascist bombers harmlessly empty their payloads of "Runget-88" upon the abandoned park. The strategy provides the defenders with time to reorganize their fighter squadrons. Reinforcements arrive and annihilate the fascists.

The destruction wrought on the power station by the enemy raid is completely repaired by the Soviet engineers in just one night. As the defenders of Soviet freedom rest, Karl Runge timidly enters the command center. He now wishes to be of service and acknowledges that he made a grave mistake in not coming to their aid when called upon. He is warmly greeted by the Soviet technicians and informed that the path to his homeland is now open. Runge is thankful and very glad, but not for long. An economic crisis has beset his nation. Electricity to his hometown has been cut off. His fellow countrymen "now live under conditions not seen since the Middle Ages." In contrast, the Soviet electrical station is flooded in light while "day and night the station labors to guard the peace of the land of the Soviets."

The defeat of the invading fascist forces also underscored messages concerning Soviet self-reliance and invulnerability. Despite the younger Runge's abandonment of his post during a critical moment in the battle (an allusion to the contemporary axiom that the Soviet Union would be abandoned by the West in its fight against fascism), the electric station's Soviet personnel demonstrate their ingenuity by quickly mastering this "most advanced technology" and returning the station to operational status. Meanwhile, the damage wrought by the surprise invasion proves to be minimal. The fascist bomber squadrons are tricked into releasing their payloads on an abandoned park before they are annihilated. The damage to the power station is credited to an incidental stray bomb. This apparent paradox, which would be repeated in subsequent films, indicated the party's contradictory efforts to communicate the gravity of fascism's threat while downplaying the possibility that enemy forces could actually do damage to the Soviet Union.

The 1936 production *The Motherland Calls* likewise used the scenario of a surprise attack as the vehicle for communicating broader messages concerning Soviet self-reliance, and citizens' need for discipline and vigilance.[13] The famous flier Sergei Novikov and his capable crew return home following the completion of a long-distance test flight aboard an advanced aircraft. The mission has run smoothly and the aircraft has demonstrated the unmatched technical mastery of the Soviet aviation industry. As the airplane begins its descent, Novikov and his crew encounter an unexpected fog bank. The pilot's vision is obscured and the safety of the plane's final approach is threatened. Novikov steers the craft sharply to the side to avoid hitting a radio tower shrouded by the fog. In the process, some of the cockpit's equipment is jarred loose and a heavy metal canister strikes the pilot on the leg, aggravating an injury that he suffered during the Civil War. The steadfast Novikov overcomes this unforeseen challenge and lands the aircraft safely despite his pain. He and his crew are rapturously greeted by the workers of the factory, who organize a grand reception in honor of the "proud falcons." The celebration of the air crew's return is interrupted by news that a treacherous surprise attack on the Soviet Union has been launched by the enemy.

The Soviet people meet the news of the insidious attack with disciplined resolve. They rally to the support of the nation's leaders. Newsreel footage of Joseph Stalin, Kliment Voroshilov, and Mikhail Kalinin appears on the screen, followed by scenes of Soviet tanks, airplanes, soldiers, and citizens mobilizing to repulse the foreign invader. The members of the factory collective fall into line. They quickly and efficiently organize themselves into shock brigades and labor battalions. The enemy is thrown on the defensive. Radio announcements (which are interspersed with battle scenes of advancing Soviet forces) update the audience on the progress of the wider war. The invasion has been halted. The Soviet Red Army will now launch a massive counteroffensive.

Inspired by the groundswell of love for the Soviet Union, Novikov's young son, Iurka, decides that he, too, must join the battle against fascism. He pens a note informing his family that he is leaving for the war, packs up some belongings, and sets out to fight the fascist menace. Novikov arrives home soon thereafter to inform his loved ones that he must return to active duty. He will leave for the front immediately. As good-byes are said, the scene is interrupted by another radio announcement. A squadron of enemy bombers, flying in the direction of the local aviation factory, has been intercepted by a detachment of Soviet fighter planes. During the ensuing melee, the Soviet planes routed the aggressor's forces. All enemy aircraft were annihilated save for a single bomber, identified by its markings as "W-22." This aircraft managed to elude destruction by taking cover in a cloud bank. Citizens are instructed to be on the lookout for the lone enemy plane as "it may release its destructive payload in an effort to expedite its return flight home."

The scene now shifts to the young Iurka, who walks along a desolate road in the direction of the front. High overhead the low drone of an airplane engine is faintly audible. The noise grows in intensity as the aircraft nears. It is the enemy bomber W-22! Recognizing the airplane's fascist insignia, the alert boy rushes to take cover from the approaching craft, but to no avail. The enemy bomber discharges its deadly cargo. As the poisonous toxins contained in the plane's chemical bombs are released into the air, Iurka fumbles with his gas mask. He is too late. Overcome by the lethal fumes, the young boy convulses and dies, an innocent victim of fascist brutality.

The young lad's lifeless body is returned to the distraught Novikov family by a group of Red Army soldiers. Only now, in the wake of the tragedy, is the note left by Iurka discovered by the boy's grandmother. Hardened by the personal loss that he has suffered, Commander Novikov resolutely answers the call of his motherland. He departs for battle. There, he leads a squadron of Soviet fighters assigned to annihilate the enemy's air force. Novikov's mission is a brilliant success. The fascist air force is completely destroyed and the way is cleared for the Soviet counterinvasion. Novikov is now free to pursue his personal vendetta against the fascists. He flies out in search of the W-22. When he discovers the enemy airplane, the pilot turns his fighter loose upon the hated instrument of fascist barbarism. The bomber is destroyed and, as the end of the war approaches, Soviet forces quickly advance into enemy territory.

The Motherland Calls reiterated the collectivist themes that had been so prominent in earlier aviation productions. Novikov's family was intended to serve as a microcosm of the Soviet nation. The retribution that the pilot exacted for the death of his son was a transparent metaphor for the vengeance that the state would seek against those attempting to harm the Stalinist "Great Family." This collectivist spirit of *The Motherland Calls* earned the praise of the movie's many reviewers.[14] One commentator gave the film particularly high marks for its depiction of "our Soviet patriotism, our loyalty to our motherland, and the willingness of Soviet laborers and citizens to sacrifice their lives in defense of their country." *The Motherland Calls*, according to this reviewer, was less a military production than it was a celebration of the collective spirit of Soviet socialism.[15]

The final military aeronautical film made before the onset of the Second World War, *Deep Strike* (1938), reiterated themes identical to those developed in *City under Siege* and *The Motherland Calls*.[16] Like its predecessors, the film was intended to depict "the readiness of the valiant Red air force" and the "rapid, successful counteroffensive" that would follow any surprise attack attempted by hostile fascist powers.[17]

Red Army pilot Aleksandr Kosykh has recently been awarded the prestigious Order of Lenin for his contributions to the defense of the Soviet Union. Friends and family gather at his house to celebrate the honor that has been bestowed upon him. Under the watchful gaze of a portrait of Stalin, the assembled guests convene around a piano to sing the Soviet national anthem. The phone rings. Kosykh and his comrades must leave at once for their air base. A surprise attack on the Soviet Union has been launched by a hostile neighboring state!

Kosykh and the other aviators take to the air to repel the foreign invaders. Their fast-flying airplanes quickly intercept the approaching bombers and, in no time, the enemy squadrons are completely destroyed. All that remains of the invading force is a lone high-altitude dirigible that has somehow managed to evade the Soviet fighter planes. As the airship slowly sails above Soviet territory, it releases a handful of small, ineffective bombs that strike the earth, causing only inconsequential damage. Alert to the presence of the enemy aerostat, a brave Soviet pilot ascends higher into the sky, pushing his airplane to the limits of its ability in order to overtake the craft. He finally attains the proper altitude and quickly dispatches the ponderous zeppelin with his airplane's machine gun. The flaming airship plummets to the earth. The initial assault has been repelled.

The scene now shifts to the opposition's military headquarters, located behind the front lines. The general in charge of the fascist air fleet informs his aviation officers of the mission now before them: a secret air assault on an important Soviet air base. Before the general is able to conclude his briefing, however, air raid sirens and the sound of exploding bombs are heard from outside. A surprise Soviet air strike has preempted the fascists' plans! Enemy pilots scramble to launch their aircraft as the Soviet Red Air Fleet bombards the command center. By the time that the air strike is completed, all that remains of the fascist air corps are the smoldering chassis of incinerated planes.

Soviet scout planes advance over enemy airspace. They are the lead element of a massive counterstrike directed at the enemy's military-industrial center, the city of Fort. The scout planes encounter the enemy's anti-air defenses and several are shot down by enemy guns (although their crew members are able to parachute to safety). One scout ship, damaged in the fracas, has lost the use of its starboard engine. As the aircraft's pilot, Ivan, searches for a location to set down his plane, he spies the underground air base from which the enemy will launch its own aerial counterstrike. Ivan instructs his crew to release the plane's bomb load. Although the air base is damaged, enemy planes begin to take to the sky. The brave pilot knows what must be done. He orders his crew to abandon the plane. Once they have parachuted free from the aircraft, Ivan directs his aircraft downward, toward the mouth of the cavern in which the base is hidden. The enemy airfield is paralyzed by the fiery crash that consumes Ivan and his plane. Thanks to the pilot's selfless sacrifice, the path of the Soviet air assault is now clear. Fort is pummeled by an unrelenting air assault, the fascists are routed, and Soviet ground troops advance deep into enemy territory.

Deep Strike echoed the strident patriotism and martial pomposity characteristic of other aviation features such as *City under Siege* and *The Motherland Calls*. Like these films, it employed the standard story line of a surprise enemy attack followed by the swift response of the Soviet military and the utter annihilation of the fascist aggressors to foster public unity and to instill confidence in party officials. Contemporary reviewers praised the production for portraying the "power of Soviet aviation, the nation's unconquerable might, and the people's love for their brave falcons."[18] As a result of the film, they concluded, the everyday labors of Soviet airmen were placed within proper perspective, enabling them to serve as models of discipline, courage, and sacrifice for ordinary citizens.

In elevating the hagiography of the nation's pilots to such an extraordinary level, *Deep Strike* anticipated the heroic mythmaking that would be realized fully during the Second World War. As the Red Army weathered the brunt of the German Wehrmacht's offensives during the years 1941–1945, the Soviet state undertook to create a new generation of heroes more suitable to the realities of wartime Russia. In place of the youthful modelists and daring aviators that had graced the screen during the 1920s and 1930s, the party created legends out of real-life heroes whose wartime exploits were upheld as inspirational models for Soviet citizens to emulate. Individuals such as the legless pilot Aleksei Maresev and the partisan fighter Zoia Kosmodem'ianskaia were exploited by state officials to motivate citizens to acts of bravery and to unite the nation behind the party and its ideology.[19] Another such hero was the military pilot Nikolai Gastello. On June 26, 1941, Gastello, the commander of a Soviet bomber group, elected to crash his damaged plane into a column of enemy tanks in an effort to delay the German advance on Moscow. Had Gastello seen *Deep Strike*, a film that had premiered just three years prior to the German invasion? Was he aware of the example set by the Russian "everyman," Ivan, who sacrificed himself to ensure Soviet victory? Was Gastello's decision motivated, at least in part, by a desire to realize the standards of the nation's on-screen martyrs? Whatever the answer, this extraordinary incident, in which life imitated art, provided more propagandistic fodder for a political system committed to creating art that appeared larger than life.

Throughout the decade of the 1930s, Communist Party officials exploited cinema and aviation to generate public support for their regime. Glorifying Soviet technical accomplishments and communicating the need for citizens' civic consciousness, Stalinist aviation films celebrated the virtues of collectivism, conformity, and loyalty to the party. These films were essential tools for state propagandists who endeavored to fabricate new social myths that would serve state interests by uniting citizens behind the party and its leaders. Aviation films featuring young modelists, heroic "falcon-flyers," and stalwart party representatives were instrumental in advancing the fiction of the Soviet "Great Family," ensuring that metaphors of kinship and collective family assumed increasing prominence in Stalinist Russia. Likewise, in the years that followed Hitler's rise to power in Germany, Soviet military aviation films reinforced the importance of collectivity and patriotism by playing to public fears of an impending confrontation with the forces of fascism.

NOTES

1. Scott W. Palmer, "Peasants into Pilots: Soviet Air-Mindedness as an Ideology of Dominance," *Technology and Culture* 41, no. 1 (January 2000), 8–10.

2. *Gogi: Otvazhnyi letchik*, directed by N. Kakhidze, Goskinprom Gruzii, 1929.

3. *Khochu byt' letchitsei*, directed by K. Gertel', Kollektiv "Kinofilm," 1929.

4. *Na lunu s peresadkoi*, directed by N. Lebedev, Lenfil'm, 1929.

5. "Isskustvo i fantastika," *Kino*, January 10, 1934.

6. "Na lunu s peresadkoi," *Kadr* 1, no. 104 (January 1935), 2.

7. Peter Kenez, *Cinema and Soviet Society, 1917–1953* (Cambridge, UK: Cambridge University Press, 1992), 162; *Letchiki*, directed by Iu. Raizman, Mosfil'm, 1935. The movie was released in the United States under the title *Men on Wings*.

8. *Komsomol'skaia pravda*, April 9, 1935; "Molodost' nashei strany," *Kino*, March 28, 1935; and "Legkaia ritmichnost', bodrost', um," *Kino*, April 17, 1935.

9. "Lirika optimizma," *Kino*, April 4, 1935.

10. Katerina Clark, *The Soviet Novel: History as Ritual* (Chicago: University of Chicago Press, 1981), 15–24.

11. "Okrylennye liudi," *Vecherniaia Moskva*, April 10, 1935.

12. *Gorod pod udarom*, directed by Iu. Genika, Soiuzfil'm, 1933.

13. *Rodina zovet*, directed by A. Machert, Mosfil'm, 1936. The film was released in the United States under the title *Call to Arms*.

14. See *Kino*, September 5, 1935; *Izvestiia*, March 18, 1936; *Vecherniaia Moskva*, April 19, 1936; and *Pravda*, May 12, 1936, among others.

15. S. Ginzburg, "Rodina i ee geroi," *Isskustvo kino*, June 6, 1936, 4.

16. *Glubokii reid*, directed by P. Malakhov, Mostekhfil'm, 1938.

17. "Glubokii reid," *Pravda*, February 4, 1938.

18. "Patrioticheskii fil'm," *Kino*, February 5, 1938, 1.

19. Rosalinde Sartorti, "On the Making of Heroes, Heroines, and Saints," in *Culture and Entertainment in Wartime Russia*, ed. Richard Stites (Bloomington: Indiana University Press, 1995), 176–193.

SUGGESTED READING

Higham, Robin, John T. Greenwood, and Von Hardesty. *Russian Aviation and Air Power in the Twentieth Century*. London, 1998.

Kenez, Peter. *Cinema and Soviet Society, 1917–1953*. Cambridge, UK, 1992.

Lawton, Anna, ed. *The Red Screen: Politics, Society, Art in Soviet Cinema*. London, 1992.

McCannon, John. *Red Arctic: Polar Exploration and the Myth of the North in Soviet Russia, 1932–1939*. Oxford, 1998.

Palmer, Scott W. *Dictatorship of the Air: Aviation Culture and the Fate of Modern Russia*. Cambridge, UK, 2006.

Stites, Richard, ed. *Culture and Entertainment in Wartime Russia*. Bloomington, Ind., 1995.

Wohl, Robert. *The Spectacle of Flight: Aviation and the Western Imagination, 1920–1950*. New Haven, Conn., 2005.

Youngblood, Denise J. *Movies for the Masses: Popular Cinema and Soviet Society in the 1920s*. Cambridge, UK, 1992.

16

Political Loyalties in Leningrad during the "Great Patriotic War"

Richard Bidlack

The 872-day siege of Leningrad[1] was one of the largest life-and-death struggles in history. No city suffered greater loss of life over a comparable period of time. According to recent estimates, during World War II roughly 1 million Leningrad civilians died within the city or while being evacuated from it, and close to another million military personnel perished defending territory nearby. Most of the civilian deaths occurred in the winter of 1941–1942. Leningrad's defense held strategic importance for the USSR. It was the nation's second-largest city, and its six hundred factories accounted for about 10 percent of the nation's industrial output. Leningrad's numerous military industries manufactured tanks, warships, artillery guns, fighter aircraft, and other weaponry, as well as many types of ammunition. Had Germany taken the city in the latter half of 1941, it could have linked up with Finland, consolidated its position on the Baltic, and directed additional hundreds of thousands of troops to the offensive against Moscow. In turn, had Germany then quickly seized Moscow (and perhaps Stalin), Soviet resistance might have ended.

Leningrad's first year of war represents an important period for gauging the extent to which its inhabitants supported the Communist state following years of brutal dictatorship, which had left an indelible mark on Leningrad. When German Army Group North was camped less than three miles south of Leningrad, the prevailing uncertainty compelled supporters of the party-state to rally to its defense. It also gave opponents with pent-up grievances their best chance since the Civil War to overthrow the government, although all realized that political revolution would result in enemy occupation of the city.

215

This chapter attempts to describe the kinds of political loyalties that Leningrad's broad masses demonstrated during the first year of the war, to show how strong those bonds were, and to explain reasons for those allegiances. Analyzing political mood is inherently difficult. Individual political viewpoints were often complicated, even contradictory, and subject to change. Moreover, the Stalinist party-state modified its image at the very start of the war, and it is not always clear to which image of authority people were reacting. When Molotov broke the news about the German invasion in a national radio broadcast at noon on June 22, he portrayed the struggle as a "patriotic" war and drew a parallel to Napoleon's failed campaign of 1812. That name for the war stuck and continues to be used by Russians today. The Soviet leadership never cast the war in predominantly Marxist terms. After about the first week of the war, Leningrad's main newspaper, *Leningradskaia pravda*, quit expressing the hope that the German proletariat and soldiers would not tolerate the invasion of the world's first socialist state. Instead, the war was depicted as a life-and-death struggle to defend the "motherland" or "fatherland." To be sure, from the mid-1930s, Stalinism had included a large dose of patriotic rhetoric; it grew at an exponential rate, however, once Germany invaded. On June 26, the war also officially became a "holy" one as Leningrad's metropolitan of the Russian Orthodox Church, Aleksei, publicly called on believers to defend the homeland in a statement that made no mention of the Soviet government or Stalin. Except for brief and ritualistic praise, Stalin's name rarely surfaced in Leningrad's periodicals early in the war.

This study focuses on four distinct crisis periods during the first year of the war and examines one key aspect of popular political attitudes for each.

THE FIRST DAYS OF THE GREAT PATRIOTIC WAR

Molotov's announcement of the German invasion came as a near total surprise to Leningraders, as it did to the nation at large, and jolted them from their enjoyment of the first Sunday of summer. Men born between the years 1905 and 1918 were immediately called up for active military service. The most remarkable demonstration of spontaneous enthusiasm for the war effort in Leningrad (and probably in the entire USSR) was massive volunteering for military service among those not subject to the draft. Some one hundred thousand Leningraders volunteered for service during the first twenty-four hours of the war, before Soviet officialdom could exert much pressure on them to do so and before they had knowledge of German atrocities. By the end of the first week of war, 212,000 had volunteered, out of a total civilian population of approximately 3 million. Many of the volunteers were subsequently rejected for various reasons; nevertheless, by the beginning of October, 156,000 were selected for what became officially known in early July as the people's militia (one of several possible translations for *narodnoe opolchenie*).[2] Male defense-plant workers, who generally were exempt from the mobilization decree, accounted for a large percentage of the early volunteers. But they were not the only ones who signed up. Teachers, writers, artists, scientists, and others joined them, as did teenagers and pensioners. Whole families signed up together. Women comprised about one-quarter of those selected for the volunteer service. Leningrad became the first city in the nation to form a civilian auxiliary army, and the Central Committee made the Leningrad divisions the model for other cities, including Moscow, to follow.

It is unclear, however, for what exactly the *opolchentsy* thought they were volunteering. Because the fighting was far from Leningrad during the war's first several weeks, during which time little was divulged by the state-controlled media about the enemy's rapid advance, and because Soviet propaganda in the years preceding 1941 had confidently stated that any invader would be quickly repulsed, it is hard to believe that the volunteers imagined they would end up fighting on front lines, in some cases within just a few days of the formation of their divisions. Their fate proved tragic. Hurriedly trained and equipped with hunting rifles, grenades, and gasoline-filled bottles, *opolchenie* units were smashed by armored German divisions.

The rate of volunteering subsided for four days after the initial surge of the first day of the war. On June 27, Leningrad's party leader Andrei Zhdanov requested permission from the main command of the Red Army to form seven volunteer divisions. He received authorization on the twenty-ninth, and the process of assembling units commenced in every district the following day. Hence, between June 27 and 30, the mass volunteering changed from being mainly a spontaneous movement to one that was encouraged and organized by the city's party leadership. Enlistments, particularly among male workers, increased at the same time that the movement became "official." The number of volunteers at the mammoth Kirov Factory, which supplied most of the members of the first *opolchenie* division, rose quickly at this time. Up to June 26, some nine hundred members of the plant's total workforce, which numbered over thirty thousand, had volunteered. By the end of the month, the number of volunteers had soared to at least fifteen thousand.

On July 3, Stalin spoke on national radio for the first time during the war and ordered the formation of *opolcheniia* in all cities threatened by enemy attack. He thereby lent the movement his personal imprimatur. Stalin's endorsement of the *opolchenie* made it easier for party and trade union recruiters to use pressure tactics. One eyewitness stated that a recruiter assigned especially to him said that it was necessary to volunteer "to show political face." The recruiter tried to convince him to join the *opolchenie*, "which is organized," the recruiter emphasized, "by the directive of comrade Stalin."[3]

Stalin's speech was a clear signal for party personnel to enlist. They responded accordingly. For example, all remaining party members in one workshop of the Ordzhonikidze Baltic Shipyard and every member of the Komsomol (the party's youth section) at the Vulkan machine-construction plant joined the *opolchenie* right after Stalin's speech. The Komsomol contingent of the city's Primorskii district volunteered en masse only after the radio address. It is clear that there was some reluctance among party personnel to volunteer prior to Stalin's speech.

ENEMY AT THE GATES!

Most Leningraders did not know that their city was directly threatened until August 21, when *Leningradskaia pravda* published a letter by Zhdanov, front commander Kliment Voroshilov, and chairman of the City Soviet Piotr Popkov which finally revealed that the enemy was closing in and might attempt to seize the city. Over the following month Leningrad's situation was precarious. In mid-September secret police (NKVD) sappers mined several defense plants and other key locations in the city's southern districts in anticipation of an expected German ground assault. On September 16, *Leningradskaia pravda*'s headline screamed: "The Enemy is at the Gates! We Will Fight for Leningrad to the Last Beat of Our Hearts!" These words provided no assurance that the city's defenses would in fact hold. On September 22, Hitler decided (in his words) "to erase the city of Petersburg from the face of the earth" through blockade and heavy bombardment—but not by attempting to occupy it first—as he had turned his primary attention to an all-out offensive for Moscow.[4]

At the start of the blockade on September 8, many, perhaps most, Leningraders thought that their city could not be defended. After all, up to that time no European city had withstood the advance of the Wehrmacht. It was widely presumed that if the city fell, the occupiers would liquidate party personnel and the large Jewish population, but opinions were divided over what would happen to the rest of the inhabitants. Some were not alarmed at the prospect of German occupation. A worker at the Kirov plant named Efimov was overheard saying: "The Germans will not shoot everyone but sift them through a sieve."[5] Others hoped for a German victory, especially those who had been victims of collectivization or purges. Swastikas occasionally appeared on courtyard walls, and anonymous letters decrying Soviet power and Stalin and calling for a Paris-style surrender of the city were mailed to the city's party leaders. Although such actions were deemed "counterrevolutionary" and could carry the death penalty, criticism of Soviet power increased during this pivotal period. (Arrests for suspected military desertion also rose sharply in Leningrad at this time.) However, anti-Soviet sentiment did not coalesce into anything approaching an organized opposition movement.

A key concern for Leningrad's leaders when the city was most vulnerable to attack was the depth of loyalty of Communist Party members and how well the party would fare in recruiting new members. Ordinary party workers were increasingly shrinking back from denouncing "defeatist" sentiment. Professional agitators and other visible agents of party authority often were reluctant in large meetings to chastise hecklers or respond to threats of reprisal, probably fearing that scores would be settled if the city fell. On September 2, L. M. Antiufeev, the secretary of the City Party committee in charge of gathering and assessing informants' reports on political mood, wrote to Zhdanov and other top leaders:

> At many factories Communists do not unify or lead the nonparty masses, nor give a rebuff to disorganizers, panickers, and anti-Soviet elements, but frequently lag behind in a backward state of mind. Several communists show themselves to be cowards and panickers . . .[6]

Nor could the party recruit many replacements for the large numbers that had been sent to the front or been evacuated, despite repeated admonitions from party higher-ups. Many factory party committees were unable to fill vacancies, in part because they had more pressing demands. Recruitment was further complicated by the fact that party records were disorganized, as reams of materials had been destroyed or sent out of the city during the summer. However, there was also another explanation. Many chose not to join the party out of fear that Germany would take the city and hunt down and kill party members. Of the first nine months of the war, the one in which the smallest number of Leningraders became party candidates was the critical month of September. Even during February 1942, when several thousand starved to death on individual days and thousands of others were being evacuated over frozen Lake Ladoga, more Leningraders joined the party than had in September 1941.

The Leningrad party organization, therefore, was faced with a very real survival crisis in the latter half of 1941. Unable to replenish its ranks, its membership dropped almost exactly in half from 122,849 at the start of the war to 61,842 on January 1, 1942. The city's Komsomol lost 90 percent of its members. Leningrad's experience reflected an extreme version of the national trend as party membership across the USSR dropped from about 4 to 3 million over the same period.

Many party candidates and full party members in Leningrad chose to dissociate themselves subtly from the party without severing ties altogether. There was much political fence-sitting when the city's defense was most in doubt. Candidate members in overwhelming numbers did not attain full membership within the defined candidacy period. In some cases, candidates were simply unable to advance, because the local party cell had collapsed when members had left the city. However, some candidates themselves did not want to become full members. Full members often refrained from paying their dues. Some chose to hide their party cards and party literature, and the number of party cards reported as "lost" rose in the autumn of 1941, although in the general chaos of the time there undoubtedly were party members who genuinely misplaced their cards. Very few, however, took the open and extreme step that an employee named Kondratenko at the Okhtenskii Chemical Factory did. He approached the secretary of the local party organization and said: "Please do not write my name in the membership list, for then it would be easy to find out that I am a communist."[7]

ALL FOR THE FRONT!

Even though the expected German assault did not materialize, October, November, and the first half of December was a time of growing terror and desperation for Leningrad. German artillery and aircraft continued to bombard the city. Few supplies reached Leningrad from the east across Lake Ladoga. Reserves of food, fuel, and raw materials diminished rapidly. The blockade proved most effective for Germany between November 8 and December 9, when its forces occupied the rail junction city of Tikhvin to the southeast of Leningrad, which forced Soviet transport to lengthen its circuitous supply route to Lake Ladoga by about eighty miles. The ration for bread, the only food that was reliably available, was cut three times between October 1 and November 20. Between November 20 and December 25, the daily bread ration for most workers, engineers, and technicians was 250 grams, or a little over one-half pound. Most everyone else got only 125 grams. These rations were too small to be life sustaining, and, to make matters worse, the bread often contained inedible additives as filler.

In the fall of 1941, about one-third of Leningrad's population was classified as workers (*rabochie*) of some sort. A large percentage of them were employed in defense plants, most of which continued to employ the eleven-hour work shift which had been introduced at the start of the war. Some shifts were longer. The Kremlin continued to order Leningrad to supply Moscow with much of its manufactured weapons and ammunition. A ubiquitous propaganda slogan during autumn was "All for the front!" and, indeed, Leningraders had to put the needs of the front ahead of their own. Industrial production was complicated by a host of other urgent tasks. Many factories that had produced goods for the local economy prior to the war with Germany were continuing the process begun in the summer of changing over to manufacturing munitions. The transition meant that supply relationships among factories were in continual flux. Other factories were dismantled for evacuation (approximately 164,000 employees and 472,000 dependents were evacuated before the start of the siege), while still others were relocated to safer regions within Leningrad. Employees also had to prepare their work areas to become a war zone and were required to undergo military training during nonworking hours. As a result of all of this activity, during the autumn Leningraders made virtually no preparations for the coming winter.

The level of popular frustration and disdain for authorities peaked as food rations were cut. Large meetings were convened in factory workshops to explain the reductions. Official "agitators" had to respond to many angry comments and questions. A commonly expressed view was "If you demand more work, give us more food." Dissatisfied workers at times hurled official promises and propaganda back at the authorities. For example, agitators were asked repeatedly at mass meetings what had happened to the ten-year supply of food, which officials had claimed existed before the war.

Reactions to cuts in food rations took various forms. Many employees tried to protect themselves and family members in ways they hoped would remain unnoticed, such as by spending a little extra time in factory cafeterias, leaving work early, or even not showing up for work at all. In some factories enforcement of strict work rules had weakened significantly by late autumn as the generation of electrical power diminished and the first starvation deaths occurred. On occasion, groups of workers refused to complete long work shifts without receiving extra food. On October 19, twelve workers in one workshop left two hours early, claiming that "one bowl of soup did not give them enough strength for twelve hours of work." A group of eighteen workers at another factory walked off the job on November 16. They said: "They feed us poorly, we have no strength for more work, we worked as much as we could." When told that their salary would be docked by 15–20 percent, one responded: "I could give up more. I don't need more as there is nothing to buy." What is as noteworthy as the insubordination itself in these instances is the fact that no one tried to prevent these workers from leaving, even though their actions might be construed as desertion in a war zone, which was a serious offense. (Managers and workers alike in these instances, however, may have subsequently been arrested after their actions were criticized in informants' reports.)[8]

One particularly vulnerable group was teenagers enrolled in industrial trade schools. Although they trained for up to eleven hours each day, these growing youths received only the "dependent," or lowest, category of food rations. According to one account, the large majority of those who attended trade schools perished during the blockade.[9] An NKVD investigation of sixty-four trade schools in November found them to be filthy dens of gambling, theft, and hooliganism. A starving trade school student snatching someone's bread allotment or ration card was not an uncommon sight, even though apprehended pickpockets were liable to be shot. Trade school students also attempted to defect to enemy lines where they believed they would find a "better life." The NKVD discovered 270 students who tried (whether successfully or not is unclear) to reach German lines in October and November.

Some workers who eagerly awaited the city's fall were emboldened enough to threaten their superiors with reprisals. In the first week of October a communications worker named Efremov at the Kirov plant was stopped from entering a factory cafeteria by its manager, Gurev. Their exchange was recorded as follows:

> Efremov: "Soon . . . you will be on your knees begging to eat."
> Gurev: "You won't live to see such a day."
> Efremov: "There will be such a day, and it's coming soon."[10]

Between October 15 and December 1, a total of 957 Leningrad civilians were arrested by the NKVD for "counterrevolutionary" activity, or on average, twenty per day. Their crimes generally consisted of displays of anti-Soviet or pro-German sentiment.[11] A number of small and isolated groups were convicted of conspiratorial activity, although overly zealous NKVD officials fabricated at least some of those cases. The combined efforts of anti-Soviet activity in wartime Leningrad never came close to posing a serious threat of insurrection.

THE HUNGRY WINTER

By the middle of December, essential services in Leningrad were ceasing to function. Trams quit running, homes and most enterprises lost electricity as only one city power plant barely continued functioning, and heating pipes froze and burst. The city was entering an apocalypse of cold and starvation unprecedented in history. How did Leningraders react to their leaders' inability to protect them? Arrests for counterrevolutionary activity dropped during December to eleven per day, then rose once again to twenty per day from January 1 to February 15, 1942. In the first half of March, counterrevolutionary arrests would drop to fifteen per day.[12] What is significant here is that despite the fact that the death rate soared and reached its peak in late January and early February, the detected level of anti-Soviet activity and support for the enemy did not surpass that of late October and November.

Political loyalties during the winter were shaped by several factors, including the horrific circumstances that the blockade produced. Leningraders devoted their ebbing physical and mental faculties to searching for the life-sustaining essentials of water, food, and warmth. In general, most other considerations, including political ones, were of secondary importance. Realizing as they did by the autumn that the food rations alone would probably not sustain them, people tried to acquire more food. Some means were legal (such as securing employment at a food-processing plant and obtaining permission to leave Leningrad over frozen Lake Ladoga), and others not (theft of food and ration cards and even murder and cannibalism).[13]

During the coldest weeks of winter, people became increasingly isolated and endured prolonged periods without any detailed news from the front. Elena Kochina, an employed mother in her mid-thirties, noted in her diary on January 9 that "in our room we live as if we were on an ark, seeing nothing and meeting no one. We don't even know what's going on at the front. Only by chance do we learn something while standing in line."[14] This loneliness, like the single-minded effort put into survival, served to numb people, both literally and figuratively, to political matters.

Germany and, to a lesser extent, Finland were responsible, of course, for the blockade. Leningraders came to view their tactic of trying to subdue the city by starvation as monstrously barbaric. Popular hatred and contempt for the enemy grew during the winter. In overheard speech and in newsprint as well as in printed cartoons and posters, Germany's leaders were increasingly portrayed as despicable beasts, rodents, and vermin, as subhuman and demonic, for the suffering they imposed. The surging animosity engendered a widespread desire for revenge. For example, members of the party committee of the Kirov factory took a pledge in early January that repeated the words "we demand revenge" several times and described "Hitler's plundering army" as "a pack of fascist beasts, whose real face has been exposed by their wild barbarian evil acts."[15] Moreover, the Wehrmacht's retreat before Tikhvin and Moscow in December discouraged German sympathizers in Leningrad from taking the risk of openly expressing their views.

A change in manufacturing goals also served to dampen anti-Soviet sentiment. By late December, Leningrad's most important defense plants had to cease working on large production orders due to the power shortage. At this point, employees were allowed at last to turn their attention squarely to their own problems, to trying to turn workshops into survival enclaves and assisting others in the city. Industrial employees divided up responsibility for such essential chores as cleaning up living quarters, repairing shoes and clothing, taking meals to the apartments of starving workers, placing orphaned children in homes or establishing their own orphanages, setting up clinics, and arranging for burial of corpses. They also made repairs at nearby hospitals and supplied them with stoves, towels, soap, lamps, buckets, utensils, and other items.[16] Efforts at mutual support focused people's attention on their immediate circle of work colleagues, friends, and family members and thereby helped ease political tension. The bread ration was raised four times during the winter. If cuts in rations during the fall sparked protest, the first increase in the bread ration on December 25, 1941, produced temporary jubilation. While party informants overheard people criticizing Stalin when rations were lowered ("If Stalin received 300 grams of bread a day, we would see how much he would work"), praise for Stalin was noted following the first increase in the bread ration. But this sense of relief, optimism, and gratitude proved fleeting when the siege did not quickly come to an end. "If in the first days after the increase in the bread ration the hopes of the city's population were raised," Secretary Antiufeev wrote on January 9, "then in the last few days, those hopes have fallen into despondency for a large part of the population."[17] The bread ration was increased on January 24; yet, within three days, when the temperature had dropped to about -40°F and many stores received less than a third of their usual bread supply, sentiment sharply critical of the city's leadership had become widespread. Informants' reports include numerous examples of caustic comments from people standing for several hours in the pitch dark early in the morning of January 27 in food lines of seven hundred to eight hundred people. A common complaint was that city leaders lived a privileged existence and lacked for nothing, while the population starved:

I myself saw them bringing the bread to Smolny [party headquarters]. They're probably sitting there stuffed. . . . Our rulers, of course, are full. They get not only bread, but also lunch and dinner. So they don't care about us, about starving people.[18]

Smolny's food supply was indeed abundant throughout the winter. One high-ranking party official later recalled that throughout the month of March, one special cafeteria at party headquarters offered "meat, mutton, chicken, goose, turkey, sausage (all kinds), fish, caviar, cheese, pies, chocolate, coffee, and tea" in addition to generous servings of bread and butter.[19] Fresh food was regularly flown in to Zhdanov, who was continually in a poor state of health during the siege. To be sure, few party members ate as well as Zhdanov did; nevertheless, party members as a group fared better than did the rest of the population. During the first half of 1942, 15 percent of all party members in Leningrad starved to death, which was approximately half of the city's overall percentage of starvation victims.

CONCLUSION

During the spring, Leningrad's death toll declined but still remained high. Leningraders proceeded to clean up their city and plant gardens in practically every open patch of soil they could find. Others prepared to join the evacuation across Lake Ladoga. The most dangerous part of the war had passed for Leningrad, although the city remained under siege until January 1944.

From the four crisis periods studied, two predominant characteristics of political mood emerge. First, attitudes fluctuated significantly over time. Secondly, Leningraders displayed considerable shrewdness and subtlety in their political words and deeds. Although some one hundred thousand Leningraders volunteered for military service on the war's first day, thousands of others signed up only when it became politically expedient to do so. Similarly, masses of party members and candidates tried to keep their political options flexible in September when Leningrad's fate was impossible to predict. In October and November, some emaciated and exhausted factory workers rejected overtime work, but they generally did not refuse to work altogether. And their verbal protests were at times carefully couched in the language of official propaganda.

Perhaps the most important determinant of political loyalty (or, more precisely, lack of expressed disloyalty) was the leadership's ability to defend the city during a time of extreme crisis. Conversely, when Leningrad's security was most in doubt, from late August to early October 1941, the rate of arrests for counterrevolutionary activity was the highest. Overheard expressions of support for the enemy reached their peak when it appeared the city might fall. Political dissent was also a function of the food supply. Arrests for political disloyalty ran nearly as high from mid-October through the end of November and in the middle of winter, when the main threat was the reduction in food rations followed by the onset of widespread starvation.

Nevertheless, most Leningraders continued to obey their leaders, and opposition sentiment never assumed a massive and organized character. Acts of genuine heroic self-sacrifice were common, and pride in Leningrad, which no enemy had ever conquered, was widely felt, especially among intellectuals. There were still other important factors that help explain the city's generally resolute response to total war at its gates. The level of surreptitious support for Germany, which had been the USSR's wartime ally from 1939 to 1941, declined as the devastating effects of the siege shattered the myth of the Germans as victorious emancipators and provoked an intense fear and loathing of them during the winter, when Leningraders were forced to concentrate otherwise on simple survival.

The retooling of city factories during the winter to produce more consumer goods probably translated into support for city leaders; although, as noted above, Leningraders were quick to blame the leadership for shortages of food and other necessities. All the while, the knowledge that Germany kept the blockade intact only by holding a narrow strip of land along Lake Ladoga's southern shore continually fueled Leningraders' hope that the liberation of their city was potentially imminent, and, therefore, further inspired them to persevere. Soviet victories on other fronts in the winter raised these hopes further.

A final, but not necessarily least, important reason for the maintenance of relative calm was that Leningrad's leaders never signaled an intention to evacuate the city, despite some document burning and the secret evacuation of families of the elite in the summer of 1941. City leaders made every effort to retain control of the population. By contrast, in Moscow when party and state officials began a massive evacuation to Kuibyshev in October of 1941, four days of rampant looting and unauthorized flight from the city ensued. Order was restored only when it was announced that Stalin had remained in the capital and that it would be defended. Although the Leningrad party organization shrank in size during the summer and autumn of 1941 and became less effective, the NKVD and city police maintained a large and formidable presence and devoted enormous resources to ferreting out all forms of dissent. Between July 1, 1941, and July 1, 1943, a total of 3,799 Leningrad civilians were convicted of counterrevolutionary crimes (and 759 of them, or 20 percent, were executed).[20] Anyone overheard ridiculing Stalin, Zhdanov, the Communist Party, or the Red Army, or praising Nazi Germany might be denounced, arrested, and even shot. If Leningrad's leaders themselves had begun to evacuate, or if the city's control apparatus had noticeably faltered, order in the city might have rapidly dissolved.

NOTES

I wish to thank the International Research and Exchanges Board (IREX) and the Dean's Office of Washington and Lee University for supporting travel to Russia to gather materials for this chapter. I am also indebted to my Russian colleague and friend Nikita Lomagin for his help in research. Finally, I would like to express my deep gratitude to Marianna Viktorovna Korchinskaia, a survivor of the siege of Leningrad, who was my host during two research trips to St. Petersburg in the 1990s. This chapter is a revised and updated version of "The Political Mood in Leningrad during the First Year of the Soviet-German War," which appeared in the January 2000 issue of the *Russian Review*.

1. Leningrad reverted to its original name of St. Petersburg in 1991.

2. Tsentral'nyi gosudarstvennyi arkhiv istoriko-politicheskikh dokumentov Sankt-Peterburga [Central State Archive of Historical-Political Documents of St. Petersburg] (TsGAIPD SPb), fond 24, opis' 2v, delo 4819, list 45.

3. Konstantin Kripton, *Osada Leningrada* [The Siege of Leningrad] (New York: Izdatel'stvo im. Chekhova, 1952), 85–86.

4. David M. Glantz, *The Battle for Leningrad, 1941–1944* (Lawrence: University of Kansas Press, 2002), 85–86.

5. TsGAIPD SPb, fond 1012, opis' 3, delo 53, list 173.

6. TsGAIPD SPb, fond 24, opis' 2v, delo 4819, list 3.

7. TsGAIPD SPb, fond 24, opis' 2v, delo 4819, list 36.

8. TsGAIPD SPb, fond 24, opis' 2v, delo 4819, listy 1–4, 48; delo 4921, list 2.

9. See the documentary film *Blokada*, produced in 1994 by Fauna Films of St. Petersburg.

10. TsGAIPD SPb, fond 1012, opis' 3, delo 53, listy 42, 153.

11. Arkhiv Upravleniia Federal'noi Sluzhby Bezopastnosti Leningradskoi Otde- lenii [Archive of the Administration of the Leningrad Branch of the Federal Security Service] (Arkhiv UFSB LO), fond 21/12, opis' 2, poriadkovyi nomer 11, tom 1, delo 4, list 69.

12. Arkhiv UFSB LO, fond 21/12, opis' 2, p. n. 11, tom 1, delo 4, listy 82, 95, 97.

13. For a description of methods employed to survive the starvation, see my arti- cle on "Survival Strategies in Leningrad during the First Year of the Soviet-German War," in *The People's War: Responses to World War II in the Soviet Union*, ed. Robert W. Thurston and Bernd Bonwetsch, 84–107 (Urbana: University of Illinois Press, 2000).

14. Elena Kochina, *Blockade Diary*, trans. Samuel C. Ramer (Ann Arbor, Mich.: Ardis, 1990), 70.

15. TsGAIPD SPb, fond 1012, opis' 3, delo 138, list 16.

16. Richard Bidlack, "Workers at War: Factory Workers and Labor Policy in the Siege of Leningrad," *The Carl Beck Papers in Russian and East European History* (Pitts- burgh: University of Pittsburgh, 1991), 20–22.

17. TsGAIPD SPb, fond 24, opis' 2v, delo 5760, list 8.

18. TsGAIPD SPb, fond 24, opis' 2v, delo 5760, list 35.

19. Marius Broekmeyer, *Stalin, the Russians, and Their War*, trans. Rosalind Buck (Madison: University of Wisconsin Press, 2004), 84.

20. A. R. Dzeniskevich, ed., *Leningrad v osade: Sbornik dokumentov o geroicheskikh oborone Leningrada v gody Velikoi Otechestvennoi Voiny, 1941–1944* [Leningrad in the Siege: A Collection of Documents on the Heroic Defense of Leningrad in the Great Patriotic War, 1941–1944] (St. Petersburg: Liki Rossii, 1995), 461.

SUGGESTED READING

Barber, John, and Mark Harrison. *The Soviet Home Front, 1941–1945: A Social and Economic History of the USSR in World War II.* New York, 1991.

Bidlack, Richard. "Survival Strategies in Leningrad during the First Year of the Soviet- German War." In *The People's War: Responses to World War II in the Soviet Union*, ed- ited by Robert W. Thurston and Bernd Bonwetsch, 84–107. Urbana, Ill., 2000.

———. "Workers at War: Factory Workers and Labor Policy in the Siege of Leningrad." *The Carl Beck Papers in Russian and East European Studies.* Center for Russian and East European Studies, University of Pittsburgh. Pittsburgh, 1991.

Glantz, David M. *The Battle for Leningrad, 1941–1944.* Lawrence, Kans., 2002.

Goure, Leon. *The Siege of Leningrad.* Stanford, Calif., 1962.

Kirschenbaum, Lisa A. *The Legacy of the Siege of Leningrad, 1941–1995: Myths, Mem- ories, and Monuments.* Cambridge, UK, 2006.

Kochina, Elena. *Blockade Diary*. Translated by Samuel C. Ramer. Ann Arbor, Mich., 1990.

Mawdsley, Evan. *Thunder in the East: The Nazi-Soviet War, 1941–1945*. New York, 2005.

Overy, Richard. *Russia's War: A History of the Soviet War Effort: 1941–1945*. New York, 1998.

Salisbury, Harrison E. *The 900 Days: The Siege of Leningrad*. New York, 1969.

Simmons, Cynthia, and Nina Perlina, eds. *Writing the Siege of Leningrad: Women's Diaries, Memoirs, and Documentary Prose*. Pittsburgh, 2002.

Skrjabina, Elena. *Siege and Survival: The Odyssey of a Leningrader*. Translated by Norman Luxenburg. Carbondale, Ill., 1971.

17

Empire Besieged: Postwar Politics (1945–1953)

Kees Boterbloem

Foreign and domestic policies in the Soviet Union were intrinsically linked in Stalin's and other Soviet leaders' Marxist-Leninist perception of the past, present, and future. Although we will discuss politics at home and abroad separately in the following pages, comprehensively disentangling their complex interaction during Stalin's last years (1945–1953) will be artificial.

From early 1939 Stalin had begun to concentrate much more on foreign policy than he did during the inward-looking previous decade that saw crash industrialization, massive social upheaval, the bloody implementation of collectivized agriculture, and the massacre of the Great Terror. Since the Second World War led to an enormous expansion of the Soviet "sphere of influence," this focus on foreign affairs was preserved after 1945. Until the second half of 1947, Stalin and foreign minister Vyacheslav Molotov (1890–1986) attempted to maintain the Soviet wartime alliance with the West, but mutual distrust and misunderstanding led to a tense situation of armed peace or, as it came to be known, Cold War. During the Cold War (1945–1991), the Soviet Union and the United States exchanged hostile rhetoric, engaged in a (conventional and nuclear) arms race, and supported opposite sides in the many local conflicts that erupted in the post–Second World War era, but never went openly to war against each other.

By the middle of 1947, Soviet foreign and domestic policy vehemently re-emphasized the long-held Bolshevik idea that the Communist bastion was besieged by the forces of world capitalism. This perception led to a return to Communist isolationism, a turn inward, and a sealing off of the "Eastern Bloc" from the West. After a brief hesitation in 1944 and 1945, between 1945 and 1948 the states of East-Central Europe and North Korea all adopted Communist regimes that were based on the Stalinist model. In 1949, they were joined by Communist China. Even though Stalin committed a host of errors in his foreign policy during the postwar period, he could look back at the end of his life with some satisfaction at having forged a huge Communist empire. But international Communist unity was shaken by the Sino-Soviet conflict for which Stalin laid the groundwork and which erupted soon after his death (of which the Yugoslav defection from the Soviet Bloc can be seen as a sort of prelude). And in erecting a superpower (i.e., a country that can deploy nuclear arms), the leadership had exposed the Soviet population to continued starvation and poverty, while denying it most human rights and freedoms as codified in both its own constitution and the United Nations' charter (the Soviet Union joined the UN at its founding in 1945).

During the war, the Soviet Union lost one-sixth of its prewar population; in its European territory west of Moscow as far north as Leningrad and the Caucasus mountain range in the south, most of its public buildings, factories, houses, roads, bridges, and livestock were obliterated. Attempts at reconstructing this devastated country were hindered by lack of (state) investment in light industry and agriculture during its fourth and fifth Five-Year Plans (respectively 1946–1950 and 1951–1955). Rather than concentrating on the rapid rebuilding of housing, infrastructure, or collective farms, great expenditure and effort went toward defense, especially to the Soviet project to build an atomic bomb. It is unlikely that the postwar famine which affected most of the USSR's European region in 1946–1947 could have been prevented entirely, but it is further testimony to Stalin's merciless style of rule that he preferred allocating substantial means to the bomb project and even ordered the export of some grain to East-Central Europe while his own population was starving (perhaps 2 million died of hunger). Meanwhile, the last years of Stalin's life saw a fundamental return to prewar patterns in most areas of domestic politics.

One of the main props upholding Stalin's autocracy continued to be the use of brutal coercive means, although the detention and prosecution of putative political enemies and criminals were generally more selective in the postwar period than in the years of the Great Terror of 1937–1938. Occasionally, nevertheless, Stalin ordered massive arrests of alleged or real Soviet foes, evoking memories of similar persecution waves during the prewar period. Thus, in 1949, Stalin ordered the arrest of a number of higher party and government leaders who had been connected at one time or another with the Leningrad party organization. They were accused of plotting against the state, espionage, and other treasonous activities. The putative ringleaders, Politburo (PB) member and State Planning Bureau chief Nikolai Voznesensky (1903–1950) and Central Committee (CC) secretary Aleksei Kuznetsov (1905–1950), together with four others, were sentenced to death in a closed trial in October 1950. In connection with this "Leningrad

Affair," hundreds of others were arrested, tried, and sentenced to death or to long stints in labor camps. In the last years of his life, Stalin may have also been preparing the elimination of some of his other lieutenants, such as former secret police chief Lavrentii Beria (1899–1953), former foreign minister Molotov, and trade tsar Anastas Mikoyan (1895–1978), all three both PB members and vice premiers in the late 1940s and early 1950s. By such persecutions or threats, Stalin kept all of his closest collaborators off balance and forced them to show utter loyalty to him alone.

But Stalin also resorted to purges for other reasons than settling personal political scores. In 1948, he initiated an anti-Semitic campaign within the Soviet Union, partially the result of his suspicion about Soviet Jews' loyalty to the USSR after the creation of the State of Israel in that year. Jews were attacked in the press and dismissed from their jobs in the government and party, various Soviet research centers, educational institutions, hospitals, and elsewhere. In 1952, members of the wartime Jewish Anti-Fascist Committee were tried in Moscow for espionage on behalf of the Americans, while in early 1953 the Soviet press announced the discovery of a plot by Kremlin doctors, most of whom were Jewish, to assassinate the leadership. Within weeks of Stalin's death, this "Doctors' Plot" was announced to have been a hoax, but state-sponsored anti-Semitism never quite disappeared in the Soviet Union thereafter.

Starting in 1949, Stalin ordered the organization of public trials against former Communist bosses in the "satellites," usually on accusations of Titoism (see below), Zionism, and espionage on behalf of the Americans. The conviction of the putative capitalist spies Traicho Kostov (1897–1949) in Bulgaria, Laszlo Rajk (1909–1949) in Hungary, and Rudolf Slansky (1901–1952) in Czechoslovakia was accompanied by a multitude of arrests of their alleged followers in the various East-Central European countries. Those tried and convicted joined thousands of others who had been sentenced in the earlier postwar political persecutions of non-Communists, from extreme rightist Nazi collaborators to Catholic or Orthodox priests, social democrats, and university professors, in Poland, Czechoslovakia, Hungary, Romania, Bulgaria, Albania, or Eastern Germany.

Between 1944 and 1950, Soviet secret police and regular armed forces met widespread anti-Soviet armed resistance in the newly (re-)annexed areas of the Baltic countries and western Ukraine with determined reprisals. On both sides, thousands died in this struggle, while tens of thousands of Ukrainians, Lithuanians, Estonians, and Latvians were sent to labor camps for participation in or support for this anti-Soviet resistance. Particularly thanks to this influx, the concentration camps and jails of the "Gulag Archipelago" (as famously coined by Alexander Solzhenitsyn) had more inmates than ever between 1945 and 1953 (between 2 to 3 million convicts). For years after the war the Soviets also confined hundreds of thousands of especially German and Austrian, but also Romanian, Finnish, Italian, and Hungarian prisoners of war. Like the Soviet convicts, they were assigned to various labor projects to aid the rebuilding and growth of the Soviet economy.

Finally, secret police detachments deported entire ethnic groups (Chechens, Ingushetians, Kalmyks, Crimean Tatars, Volga Germans, Kabardino-Balkars) between 1941 and 1946 from their native regions to inhospitable areas of Siberia and Kazakhstan on the accusation of wartime collaboration with the Germans. Many succumbed while resisting deportation, during the railroad transport, or in their place of exile. With the exception of the Crimean Tatars (who have never been given back their land and property on the Crimean peninsula), these "Punished Peoples" (Alexander Nekrich's evocative label) were only allowed to return to their ancestral land after Stalin's death.

Terror thus remained a key component of Stalin's regime in the immediate postwar period, but it was accompanied by attempts at persuasion by other means. The massive growth of party and Komsomol (Young Communist League) membership during the war is partially indicative of how Stalin's regime and personal popularity dramatically increased during the war. Stalin's rule acquired a new legitimacy in the eyes of many Soviet citizens, for he and his cronies were credited with the steadfast defense of the country and the ultimate victory over the "Hitlerites" (Soviet propaganda was silent about their responsibility for the lack of preparedness in 1941 or their poor generalship during the early phase of the war). But it proved much more difficult to make politically conscious and erudite Communists out of this raw material.

The Soviet Communist Party had grown significantly during the war, when many soldiers had entered the party under special dispensation. On January 1, 1946, its membership stood at 5.5 million (of a total population of approximately 170 million), almost 2 million more than on the eve of the war, and more than twice the size of the party in early 1939. Over half of these members had joined the party during the war. The political education of many of these new Communists was rudimentary. A huge network of study circles and party schools was set up between 1945 and 1949 to inculcate the basics of Marxism-Leninism in these novices, who studied especially intensively the *Short Course* of the Communist Party's history, the foremost best seller of Stalin's rule. When soon after the war the careful selection procedure for new members was restored (and several party purges were conducted), membership increase slowed, reaching 6.8 million at the time of the Nineteenth Party Congress in October 1952.

Study circles and party schools were used to instill ideological orthodoxy into society's vanguard, the Communist Party, while young people belonging to the Komsomol also enrolled in political courses. The political sophistication of the Komsomol members was, however, much less rigorous than that of the party members, and their paltry political education vexed the Soviet leaders. Meanwhile, the Komsomol's membership burgeoned to encompass about half of all Soviet teenagers and young adults at the end of the war, when numbers began to decline again. A new membership drive began in 1949, leading to a Komsomol membership in late 1952 of 16 million, which superseded the 1945 level by 1 million.

Among Soviet leaders, Stalin was the central figure until his death in 1953. By 1945, the dictator was in his late sixties, and in the autumn of that year he likely suffered the first of a series of minor strokes that ended with a fatal brain hemorrhage in March 1953. Despite his health problems, during most of the postwar period Stalin personally drafted or edited the outlines of key policies in the fields of foreign affairs, defense, culture, and security matters, while keeping a watchful eye on areas of policy in which he was generally less interested, such as industry and agriculture. Few major decisions made by the Soviet leadership in the postwar period can be identified in which Stalin played no part, even if before 1950 he spent several long holidays in his Black Sea retreat, and from 1950 onward he increasingly lived and worked on his country estate near Moscow rather than in the capital's Kremlin. When not in the city himself, he used a variety of lines of communication (information reached him both via the secret police couriers and other channels, such as through conversations with his PB colleagues who either met him at his country house or phoned him there) to keep a watchful eye on the country's affairs until his last days. But Stalin did leave the more pedestrian day-to-day management of the enormous party and state bureaucracy to his assistants, whom he rotated regularly in order to stop them from becoming too entrenched in their positions.

Within the paramount ruling instrument in the Soviet political system, the Communist Party, Stalin occupied the post of first or general secretary, the position which he had been appointed to for the first time in 1922 and which he held until his death. Since he was also prime minister[1] (and for some months after the war even remained defense minister), however, he was forced to delegate some of his tasks in ruling the party to the three or four other secretaries of its Central Committee. Because of Stalin's retirement from the day-to-day affairs of the party, the position of its second secretary became particularly important, even if such a position formally did not exist (from 1941 to 1946, G. M. Malenkov [1902–1988] was in this position, from 1946 to 1948, Andrei Zhdanov [1896–1948], and from 1948 to 1953, again Malenkov).

Key decisions were issued in the name of the Politburo (elected by the CC from its own ranks), but although it consisted of no more than a dozen or so voting and nonvoting members, within it an even smaller leading group was cultivated, made up of Stalin and his favorites of the moment, usually no more than a handful of men. At the Nineteenth Party Congress in 1952, the Politburo was replaced by a much larger Presidium, but within it, too, a leading group was distinguished during Stalin's last months. Immediately upon Stalin's death in 1953, those key courtiers reduced the size of the Presidium to that of the earlier Politburo.

In theory, the Communist Party was to concentrate primarily on ideological indoctrination (agitation and propaganda, or agitprop) of Communists and non-Communists, selection of party and government personnel (cadres), checking up on the execution of decisions made by party bodies, monitoring the behavior of party officials (which was mostly the terrain of the Party Control Commission), and, at the Central Committee level, maintenance of contacts with sister parties abroad. Although the party and government administration were formally separate, the leading party bodies of all-Union, republican, provincial, city, and rural districts, which included the ranking leaders of government of the respective territories, were responsible for important political decisions (at least, if they had not been imposed by a higher party organization) rather than any government body. And, like in Moscow, the first party secretaries of republics, provinces, or cities towered high above their colleagues in the party bureaus. In Moscow after the war, just as before it, several government ministers belonged to Stalin's inner circle (such as Molotov, Beria, Mikoyan, and K. E. Voroshilov [1881–1969]), but their power was likewise contingent on their membership in the Politburo and especially Stalin's favor, rather than on their post as government minister.

The pretense of a democracy, based on the 1936 Constitution, continued to be observed in the Soviet Union, and elections for municipal, republican, and all-Union soviets (councils) were staged regularly in the postwar period. These legislatures officially elected the government at all levels (thus the Supreme Soviet chose the Council of Ministers). In reality, however, government officials were selected by the Communist Party's committees and their bureaus (at the highest level, by the Central Committee and the Politburo); frequently it was the individual party secretaries who alone picked officials in the state and party hierarchy of their region.

The CC secretaries and PB members made thousands of appointments to the higher posts in the hierarchy by way of the *nomenklatura* system, which was copied as well at lower levels. This appointment mechanism originated in the early days of Stalin's leadership over the party, and was supervised by the CC Cadres Directorate (from July 1948, by the Department of Party, Trade Union, and Komsomol Organs). It carefully maintained personnel files for thousands of leading politicians in the Soviet Union's party and state apparatus, upon which basis the CC Secretariat hired, transferred, promoted, demoted, or fired people such as provincial and district party secretaries, regional secret police chiefs, newspaper editors, planning specialists, and diplomats. The secretaries and bureaus of higher-level committees thus appointed lower-level committees throughout all levels of the party's hierarchy, even though local and central party organizations held formal meetings in which committees, bureaus, and secretaries were elected, too (usually, lists of preselected candidates were submitted to delegates who could vote for no one else but those candidates presented on the election sheet).

When in Moscow (and sometimes at the republican level) conflicts arose between (the chiefs of) the party and government bureaucracies, these were not always resolved to the advantage of the party apparatus and its bosses, despite the paramount position of the Communist Party within the Soviet system. For example, immediately after the war, high-level officials of the Ministry of Foreign Affairs (MID),[2] led by Molotov, could sometimes successfully defy the CC's Department of Foreign Policy.[3] Throughout the entire postwar period, especially, the two security ministries, the Ministry of Internal Affairs (MGB) and the Ministry of State Security (MVD),[4] and the various defense ministries bypassed lesser party chiefs in reporting directly to Stalin. In general, government bureaucrats at all levels could only risk resisting the wishes of party officials if protected by a high-level patron. Thus MID bureaucrats could hold out against CC *apparatchiki* because they were sheltered by PB member Molotov, and MGB chief V. S. Abakumov (1894–1954) could safely withhold materials from Beria (who was formally responsible for the security police among PB members) because he was shielded by Stalin.

Once more relying heavily on tried-and-true prewar models, Stalin was the mastermind behind the postwar campaigns in culture and ideology which began in 1946. Its main public spokesman was CC secretary Andrei Zhdanov, who led a three-pronged campaign, one part of which was to improve the political literacy of the many new Communists that had joined during the war. A second part was an attempt to narrowly circumscribe the parameters of Soviet literary and artistic production. In highly publicized speeches (in which he explicated CC resolutions condemning the artists and their art) in August 1946 and January 1948, Zhdanov heavily criticized poets, prose writers, film directors, and composers for not properly celebrating Soviet life, and for indulging in political themes and individualistic introspection. The works of the poet Anna Akhmatova (1889–1966), the writer Mikhail Zoshchenko (1895–1958), the film directors Leonid Lukov (1909–1963) and Sergei Eisenstein (1898–1948), and the composers Vano Muradeli (1908–1970), Dmitrii Shostakovich (1906–1975), Sergei Prokofiev (1891–1953), and Aram Khachaturian (1903–1978) were pilloried and those responsible for allowing the diffusion of their oeuvre dismissed in this Zhdanovshchina.[5] As a result, in the late Stalinist period almost no art of great interest was produced (except several works which the artists kept secret from the authorities, such as *Dr. Zhivago* by Boris Pasternak [1890–1960]). Perhaps the period's most striking artifacts are the five high buildings that were erected in Moscow, of which those of the Foreign Ministry and Moscow State University are the most renowned.

The third component of the postwar campaign was an offensive to improve vigilance regarding state secrets, which began in earnest in early 1947. Within a couple of years, it led to the virtual prohibition of any contact by Soviet citizens with the non-Communist world. Like the other two parts of the campaign, this offensive seems to have been triggered both by Stalin's renewed suspicion of subversive capitalist activities and by his discontent regarding the Soviet citizenry's mood at the end of the war. Many among the creative intelligentsia (artists, scientists, and scholars) appear to have expected the continuation of the somewhat greater wartime freedom of expression and the maintenance of the more intensive wartime communications with their academic and artistic counterparts in the Western world. Toward the end of 1946, with the rift between the Soviet Union and the West growing ever wider, however, several incidents of supposed careless divulgence of state secrets by Soviet citizens made Stalin decide to seal off his empire hermetically (particularly the transfer of a supposedly breakthrough anti-cancer treatment to the Americans in 1946 irked him).

Marriages between Soviet citizens and foreigners were prohibited in early 1947, and special trials were staged of scientists and bureaucrats accused of having carelessly allowed state secrets to fall into the hands of the West. By June 1947, a new law drastically increased penalties for treason or espionage. Some of those convicted under its statute received twenty-five years at a labor camp. Discipline was further heightened by another law of June 1947 mandating long jail sentences for those convicted of stealing public property. By 1949, the culture, secrecy, and ideology campaigns had acquired a sometimes absurd anti-Western guise. Many Western scientific inventions (such as the lightbulb) were claimed as Russian and recent Western cultural achievements were denounced as "decadent" (such as jazz or atonal music), while any praise for the West by Soviet citizens was labeled as "kowtowing before the West."

Considering the antagonistic essence of the Marxist-Leninist worldview, the growing hostility between the Soviet Bloc and the West after May 1945 might have been inevitable. The British in particular had already voiced strong objections to the Soviet actions toward Poland at the Yalta Conference of February 1945. At Yalta, Stalin promised to have his country join the United Nations' organization and have his army come to the aid of the British and American forces against Japan after the victorious conclusion of the war in Europe. In July 1945 the Big Three met for the last time at Potsdam near Berlin. Here irritation between Stalin, on the one side, and now American president Harry Truman (1884–1972) on the other, became more palpable. Stalin was dismayed to find out (while travelling to Germany) from his spies that the British-American atomic project (to which the Soviets had never been invited) had succeeded in detonating an atomic bomb. This added to his displeasure with the immediate postwar cancellation by the American government of the Lend-Lease program (which had substantially aided the Soviet war effort). Although Stalin reiterated at Potsdam his promise to have free elections staged in East-Central Europe, he proceeded to prohibit the establishment of pluralistic liberal democracies in countries bordering the Soviet Union in Europe (with the exception of Finland). Despite several conferences of the foreign ministers of the allied countries subsequent to Potsdam, the Soviets made few concessions to their Western counterparts regarding the postwar settlement in Europe. The future status of Germany and Austria thus remained moot, although in 1947 the Soviet Union and the Western Allies concluded official peace treaties with Finland, Italy, Hungary, Romania, and Bulgaria.

In the course of 1947, the "sovietization" of East-Central Europe neared completion. Opponents of the local Communist parties were forced to submit. Some of those who refused managed to go into exile, while others were jailed. Protest was muted due to the presence of the Red Army in all countries of the region (except Yugoslavia), while Soviet secret police and political advisors aided the local Communist bosses in suppressing the protests that did sporadically erupt. Non-Communist parties survived but were led by Communist straw men, such as Otto Grotewohl (1894–1964) in the German Democratic Republic (Eastern Germany), Jozef Cyrankiewicz (1911–1989) in Poland, or Zdenek Fierlinger (1891–1976) in Czechoslovakia.

In early 1947, the Truman administration decided to contain the further spread of Communism into the Mediterranean area by announcing massive military aid to the Greek and Turkish governments. In June, secretary of state George Marshall (1880–1959) announced a comprehensive package of American loans for European governments seeking to overcome the devastation of the Second World War (the Marshall Plan). The Soviet Union and its East-Central European satellites refused this aid when conditions for eligibility appeared to constitute an infringement of their national sovereignty. It added to the Soviet suspicion that the West was committed to destroying the USSR and Communism and that it was willing to use any means toward this goal.

In September 1947, the Soviet leadership orchestrated a meeting of the major European Communist parties in Poland, where a coordinating organ was agreed to, the Communist Information Bureau or Cominform. It was to be a further instrument to make the European Communist parties do the Soviet bidding. At its inaugural meeting, it was again Andrei Zhdanov who gave the key speech, announcing that the world had split into "two camps," one peace loving and democratic, the other imperialist and aggressive. But within a year of its creation, the most zealous Soviet partner of the early postwar years, Yugoslavia, defected from the Cominform and the Communist Bloc. In early 1948, the Yugoslav leader Tito (Josip Broz: 1892–1980) provoked Stalin's displeasure by taking too independent a posture in his support of the Communists in the Greek civil war and by engaging in unauthorized conversations with the Bulgarian leader Georgii Dimitrov (1882–1949) about a Communist Balkan federation. Tito refused to apologize for his insubordination to Stalin and led his country out of the Soviet Bloc in mid-1948, even though Yugoslavia remained a Communist dictatorship. The Cominform died a quiet death toward 1950, by which year Stalin appeared to prefer to monitor the fraternal Communist parties by having their leaders visit him in Moscow rather than communicating with them through the mediation of the Information Bureau. In 1949, a Communist Economic Confederation (Comecon) was created with the aim of coordinating the economies of the Eastern Bloc. It formalized a situation by which the East-Central European countries bought Soviet goods dearly and sold their own goods cheaply to the Soviet Union.

At exactly the time the Yugoslavs defied Stalin, the Soviets blockaded their occupational zone of Berlin (June 1948) in reaction to the Western allies' permission to have a new West Germany currency introduced in West Berlin. The Berlin blockade was the culmination of the process of estrangement between the former wartime allies that had started in 1945. It made permanent the division of defeated Germany into a liberal democracy in the West and a Soviet-type dictatorship with a planned economy in the East. But this first major crisis of the Cold War did not lead to war, even if the blockade lasted almost for a year. The Soviet pressure failed to persuade the Western allies to return to the negotiation table to find a postwar settlement for Germany and Berlin different from the permanent division of the country and its former capital. The British, French, and Americans helped the Berlin population to survive the Soviet attempt to starve them out by supplying West Berlin through the air. The Berlin crisis hastened the foundation of a Western military alliance in the spring of 1949, the North Atlantic Treaty Organization (NATO). By May 1949, Stalin called off the blockade.

The successful detonation in 1949 of the Soviet atomic bomb, which had been developed under the lead of Lavrentii Beria and the physicist Igor Kurchatov (1903–1960), compensated for the failures of the Berlin blockade and the Cominform. Another noteworthy success was the Communist triumph in the Chinese Civil War under the lead of Mao Zedong (1893–1976), which meant that in the fall of 1949 one-third of the global population was ruled by Communist regimes. Stalin, perhaps slightly dizzy with this success, agreed unwisely to the North Korean Communist leader Kim Il Sung's (1912–1994) plan to invade South Korea in 1950. The Korean War involved Chinese "volunteers" fighting on the North Korean side (and, secretly, Soviet fighter pilots) and a UN expeditionary army under

American lead defending the South Koreans. It ended with a truce concluded only after Stalin's death in 1953. The armistice divided Korea along the thirty-eighth parallel, which was more or less the same dividing line between North and South that had existed before fighting broke out in 1950. While hundreds of thousands of Koreans and others suffered in what was therefore a largely futile armed conflict, the Korean War also damaged the international image of the Soviet Union as an "anti-imperialist" and "peace-loving" country (particularly among many newly independent countries who gained their independence in the post–World War II decolonization wave), for Stalin's support of Kim Il Sung's aggressive venture was suspected by observers outside the Soviet Bloc.

While Stalin in his last years appeared worried about his intellectual legacy (he published two theoretical essays, one on linguistics, the other on economics), he also grew morbidly suspicious of his longtime lieutenants. At the Nineteenth Party Congress of October 1952 (the first one since 1939), Stalin only gave a short speech, leaving the major speeches to Malenkov and Nikita Khrushchev (1894–1971), who thus appeared as leading contenders for Stalin's succession. At the first Central Committee meeting after the end of the Congress (when the Politburo was replaced by a much enlarged Presidium), Stalin singled out Molotov and Mikoyan for heavy criticism, which has led some scholars to suggest that Stalin may have been preparing a new cleansing of the party's leadership. This hypothesis will likely never be proven, for Stalin's death in March 1953 prevented any purge from unfolding.

Stalin's death in March 1953 was followed by an uncertain transition period in domestic and foreign policy, during which the leadership wavered between liberalization of the ruling system and an unreconstructed continuation of the administrative-command system,[6] the top-down autocracy of Stalin's quarter century at the helm of the Soviet Union. Some hesitation about the direction of domestic policy was linked to the struggle for Stalin's succession, a battle finally won by Nikita Khrushchev in 1957. In its vacillation between hard-line and soft-line, this contest found some reflection in foreign policy, too. Soviet leaders disagreed on which concessions to make to the United States (although a truce was concluded in Korea in 1953), while the American response to the Soviet suggestion of a "peaceful coexistence" between the two blocs was tepid and thus made the effort seem hardly worth the while. Quarrels broke out between Molotov and Khrushchev about a rapprochement with Yugoslavia. Ultimately, any fundamental Soviet concessions aiming at a comprehensive agreement between East and West on the many issues that had not been resolved since the end of the Second World War (such as the fate of Germany or the restoration of full self-determination to the countries of East-Central Europe) were never offered before the second half of the 1980s. Before that time, Stalin's heirs could not (or did not seem to want to) contemplate such bold steps, for they could be construed by rivals, both within the Soviet leadership and in the Communist world (China), as a revisionist denial of a fundamentally hostile view of the non-Communist Other.

Stalin's shadow loomed over most of the next thirty-five years of Soviet history. Only by the 1980s had a new generation of Soviet leaders emerged that was at least willing to consider both substantial domestic reforms and imaginative foreign policy initiatives toward ending the Cold War.

NOTES

1. In March 1946 the Council of People's Commissars was renamed Council of Ministers, and individual people's commissars were henceforth called ministers. In some of the English-language literature, the Russian contraction for Council of Ministers is used (Sovmin, i.e., *Sovet Ministrov*), as Sovnarkom (*Sovet narodnykh komissarov*) is used for Council of People's Commissars, and *narkom* for people's commissar.

2. MID: *Ministerstvo inostrannykh del.*

3. OVP: *Otdel vneshnei politiki.* It had taken over much of the personnel of the former Communist International, the Comintern, which had been dissolved in 1943.

4. MGB: *Ministerstvo gosudarstvennoi bezopasnosti*; MVD: *Ministerstvo vnutrennykh del.*

5. Zhdanovshchina: "The Zhdanov Thing"; the ending *-shchina* in Russian connotes a negative phenomenon.

6. During the late 1980s and early 1990s the Russians would increasingly use this term to describe the Soviet regime.

SUGGESTED READING

Boterbloem, Kees. *Life and Death under Stalin: Kalinin Province, 1945–1953*. Montreal-Kingston, 1999.

———. *The Life and Times of Andrei Zhdanov, 1896–1948*. Montreal-Kingston, 2004.

Djilas, Milovan. *The New Class: An Analysis of the Communist System*. New York, 1957.

Fainsod, Merle. *How Russia Is Ruled*. Cambridge, Mass., 1955.

Gorlizki, Yoram, and Oleg Khlevniuk. *Cold Peace: Stalin and the Soviet Ruling Circle, 1945–1953*. New York, 2004.

Holloway, David. *Stalin and the Bomb*. New Haven, Conn., 1994.

Khrushchev, Nikita. *Khrushchev Remembers*. Vols. 1–3. Boston, 1970, 1974, 1990.

Montefiore, Simon Sebag. *Stalin: The Court of the Red Tsar*. London, 2003.

Nekrich, Alexander. *The Punished Peoples*. New York, 1978.

Pollock, Ethan. *Stalin and the Soviet Science Wars*. Princeton, N.J., 2006.

Solzhenitsyn, Alexander. *The First Circle*. Chicago, 1997.

———. *The Gulag Archipelago, 1918–1956*. Vols. 1–2. New York, 1973.

Volkogonov, Dmitrii. *Stalin: Triumph and Tragedy*. New York, 1991.

Zubkova, Elena. *Russia after the War: Hopes, Illusions, and Disappointments, 1945–1957*. Armonk, N.Y., 1998.

Zubok, Vladimir, and Constantine Pleshakov. *Inside the Kremlin's Cold War*. Cambridge, Mass., 1996.

18

Khrushchev

The Impact of Personality on Politics

William Taubman

The monument at Nikita Khrushchev's grave in Novodevichy Cemetery, designed by Ernst Neizvestny, whom Khrushchev excoriated during outbursts against the artistic intelligentsia in 1962 and 1963, consists of intersecting slabs of white and black stone. On one sits a bronze head of Khrushchev with a pained expression on his face. The memorial captures the contradictions that were so striking in his life and career.

Born into a humble peasant family in the southern Russian village of Kalinovka in 1894, he received no more than two or three years of formal education in a village school. Yet he managed not only to climb into Stalin's inner circle, but to survive the *vozhd* (leader) and then to succeed him.

An accomplice in Stalin's crimes, Khrushchev turned against Stalin and denounced him in a secret speech to the Twentieth Party Congress in February 1956. A true believer in Marxism-Leninism, he aimed to cleanse socialism of its Stalinist stain, but his de-Stalinization campaign began the long process of unraveling the Soviet system that culminated several decades later in 1991.

Khrushchev tried to ease East-West tensions and to restrain the arms race, but he also provoked the most dangerous crises of the Cold War in Berlin and Cuba. He meant well and he cared about his people and country, but by the time of his ouster in 1964 he was unappreciated and even despised.

What explains these contradictions? The answer lies at the intersection of history and personality, of Khrushchev's character, on the one hand, and the circumstances that shaped him and that he shaped in turn. The role of individual leaders (of "great men," as it used to be said in the prefeminist era) in history is itself a controversial issue. According to Thomas Carlyle, "History is the biography of great men." But others prefer to emphasize the impact of deeper, more impersonal forces, whether economic, social, political, or ideological. Moreover, this larger issue of historical determinants is particularly pertinent in Russia, whose former ruling Marxist ideology insisted on the primacy of economic determinism, but where individual leaders and their personalities have had the greatest impact on events that can possibly be imagined. Absent Lenin's maniacal insistence on seizing power in October 1917, the Bolshevik revolution would not have occurred, at least not when and how it did. Although Stalin's "revolution from above" was supported by many in his party, it was he who transformed it into a reign of terror that lasted for nearly two decades.

Khrushchev, who succeeded Stalin and served as party leader from 1953 to 1964 and as head of the Soviet government from 1958 to 1964, may not seem such an all-important, larger-than-life leader. His rivals for power, men like Lavrentii Beria, Georgii Malenkov, and Vyacheslav Molotov, underestimated him—virtually until the moment he defeated them all. By October 1964, when he was suddenly and ignominiously ousted by his former allies in the Kremlin, he had alienated practically all his own supporters. In the West, he may be best remembered for banging his shoe at the United Nations in October 1960, although recent research has revealed that he may have only brandished his shoe and not actually banged it.[1]

In fact, however, Khrushchev represents a classic case of the influence of personality on history.

Not all political leaders have a great impact on their time. Nor can it be said of all those who do that their personalities, rather than, say, their views and opinions, made a difference. Three qualities characterize those whose characters count for a great deal.

First, such leaders have great power. That may seem obvious, but some leaders are more powerful than others, and the Soviet system placed more power in the hands of its leaders (or better to say that those leaders grabbed more power themselves) than do other forms of government, especially liberal democratic regimes in which leaders are limited by constitutional guarantees, separation of powers, independent political parties, and active, energized civil societies.

The second criterion that justifies claiming that a leader's personality makes a difference is "uniqueness," that is, the fact that such a leader does not do what any other would do in his or her place. The point, in other words, is to establish that the leader in question is more than a carrier of values widely shared in his or her society, and is not simply responding to the dictates of situations with which he is confronted.

A third mark of a leader whose character counts is that he acts in strange, seemingly irrational ways that can subvert his own cause and career. For this suggests that he may be in the grip of internal drives and compulsions that help to account for his political behavior.

Khrushchev qualifies on all three counts. That he possessed great power needs little demonstration. The fact that he was so readily removed might seem to suggest that there were distinct limits on his power, but one reason he was ousted, according to those who conspired against him 1964, was that he had acted arbitrarily and unilaterally, failing to consult with his Kremlin colleagues who, until they mustered the courage to mount a conspiracy, feared to challenge him.

In some ways, Khrushchev was the archetypical Soviet man. Countless workers and peasants rose through the ranks after the revolution. Nor was he the only one with humble origins who reached the very top; Kliment Voroshilov and Lazar Kaganovich, for example, came from backgrounds almost as lowly as his. And some of the reforms associated with Khrushchev were supported by many of his colleagues. Even arch-Stalinists like Molotov, Kaganovich, and Voroshilov wanted to end the arbitrary mass terror that threatened to destroy even them, and to reduce the isolation in which the Soviet Union found itself (except for its Communist allies and satellites) when Stalin died. But would anyone besides Khrushchev have denounced Stalin at the Twentieth Party Congress? Strange as it may seem, Beria might have done so had he not been arrested and executed in 1953, for although he was thoroughly complicit in the terror, he was cynical enough to denounce his former master so as to increase his chances to succeed him. But all the other leaders either had no desire to launch a de-Stalinization campaign, which might undermine their own power, or were too cautious to do so even if tempted. Of all of them, Anastas Mikoyan seems to have been most supportive of Khrushchev, but even if he was willing, he was not able to act unless Khrushchev took the lead.

Or take the Caribbean crisis of 1962. Would anyone else in the Central Committee Presidium have sent rockets capable of striking the United States to Cuba? For that matter, would anyone else have pulled those rockets out as quickly as Khrushchev did, when president John F. Kennedy threatened to wipe them out and to invade Cuba? Other Soviet leaders might have been willing to retreat in the face of American resistance, but it is virtually certain that none of them would have triggered the crisis in the first place.

As for the third criterion listed above, the existence of an irrational self-destructive pattern of action, this is only one-half of the Khrushchev profile. The other half is a series of remarkable successes to go along with a devastating set of mistakes.

Khrushchev's rise from the humblest of origins into Stalin's inner circle is a stunning success story—provided, of course, one does not count the cost in blood to so many whose victimization he authorized or approved, or to which he at least acquiesced. Just to survive Stalin took some doing when so many other Politburo members did not, likewise in winning the Kremlin battle to succeed Stalin. When the new party Presidium was chosen after Stalin's death, Khrushchev was listed fifth behind Malenkov, Beria, Molotov, and

Voroshilov. Malenkov was the heir apparent, Beria the power behind the throne. Molotov, who had been Stalin's close collaborator longer than anyone else, also seemed a contender. Virtually no one in the USSR or abroad imagined that Khrushchev had a chance of besting them all. Yet two and half years later, Beria had been arrested and executed, Malenkov demoted, and Molotov subjected to withering criticism. If Khrushchev foresaw his own triumph, he was the only one who did. Yet the way he pulled it off was utterly predictable. Like Stalin in the 1920s, he identified his cause with that of the Communist Party apparatus, manipulated the party machine against his rivals, wielded domestic and foreign policies for political purposes, and made and betrayed allies. The real puzzle is not how Khrushchev did it, but why his colleagues allowed him to. The answer is that they all underestimated him.

The elimination of Beria was a particular accomplishment. Beria was smart, calculating, and in charge of the secret police. Khrushchev led the conspiracy against him.[2] Defeating Malenkov and Molotov was easier; Khrushchev enlisted the latter against the former, and then turned against Molotov himself. But the two men survived to fight another day. Allowed to remain in the ruling Presidium, they joined with Voroshilov and Kaganovich, recruited Nikolai Bulganin, Mikhail Pervukhin, Maksim Saburov, and Dmitry Shepilov, and in June 1957, forming a majority in the Presidium, they attempted to oust Khrushchev. Of course, Khrushchev prevailed in a marathon, eleven-day showdown, and so dramatic was the duel and so decisive the victory, that the main point has seemed to be the way he won. In fact, however, the real question is how he almost managed to lose. Part of the answer was the logic of power in the Kremlin: Khrushchev's rivals were bound to try to get him before he got them. But another answer is the way another of Khrushchev's achievements, his "secret speech" denouncing Stalin, helped to provoke turmoil at home, unrest in Poland, and revolution in Hungary.

Khrushchev's speech at the Twentieth Party Congress was the bravest and the most reckless thing he ever did. The Soviet regime never fully recovered, and neither did he. Of course, political calculations were partly behind it: by denouncing Stalin, Khrushchev could cleanse his own reputation while tarnishing those of rivals who had been closer to Stalin than he. But the speech also reflected Khrushchev's sense of guilt and shame about his own complicity in Stalin's crimes, and anger at the *vozhd* who had forced him to take part in them. As early as 1940, he privately denied to a friend from childhood that he was involved in the killing of men like Kirov, Tukhachevsky, and Yakir, and swore that someday he would "settle with that 'Mudakshvili' in full."[3] Asked late in life what he most regretted, Khrushchev answered, "Most of all the blood. That is the most terrible thing that lies in my soul."[4] Mikoyan later claimed that he pressed Khrushchev to denounce Stalin, and complained that Khrushchev took all the credit in his memoirs, refusing "to share the glory with anyone else."[5] But whatever advice he received, it was Khrushchev who acted: he who insisted on the speech, he who delivered it, he who spurred the process of releasing and rehabilitating prisoners and giving back their good names.

The trouble was that, as in so many of his major decisions, he did not think through the possible consequences of his action. In this case, he did not foresee the reaction, did not prepare for the process of "de-Stalinization from below," did not equip party officials and propagandists with ways to cope with the flood of questions and criticisms that followed when his speech was read to millions of party members and others throughout the USSR. After a while, he was forced to retreat, particularly in a June 30, 1956, Central Committee resolution which virtually retracted much of what he had told the Twentieth Party Congress. But that resolution was not enough to calm the unrest building in Eastern Europe, and when that turmoil exploded in Hungary, Soviet intervention to crush the Hungarian revolution sparked more protests in the USSR. In early 1957 several hundred Soviet citizens were convicted as criminals and sentenced to prison.[6] For the rest of his time in power, Khrushchev zigzagged back and forth between encouraging and discouraging de-Stalinization, between supporting and attempting to restrain its champions, especially in the intelligentsia.

After the long night of late Stalinism, with its pogrom against great artists like Anna Akhmatova and Sergei Prokofiev, the post-Stalinist "thaw" felt "like a great holiday of the soul," film critic Maya Turovskaya recalled.[7] Khrushchev himself did not initiate the thaw (between 1953 and 1955, the party leadership seemed to have no firm position on the limits of party control over the artistic intelligentsia, and even after the Twentieth Party Congress uncertainty continued to reign until 1957),[8] and at times he seemed to be trying to stop it. But while his reign was marked by tirades against liberal artists and writers (in 1957, 1959, 1962, and 1963) and the vicious 1958 campaign against Boris Pasternak after the publication in the West of *Dr. Zhivago*, Khrushchev personally authorized the publication of works like Aleksandr Tvardovsky's long poem, "Distance beyond Distance," Yevgeny Yevtushenko's "The Heirs of Stalin," and Solzhenitsyn's *One Day in the Life of Ivan Denisovich*. The artistic and scientific intelligentsia was a natural constituency for the leader who tied his own fate to de-Stalinization, but by the time of his ouster, they, like so many others of his former supporters, had lost faith in him.

Agriculture was yet another area in which failures came to overshadow Khrushchev's successes. In 1953, first Malenkov and then Khrushchev proposed reforms (increased procurement prices, reduced taxes, encouragement for individual peasant plots) that gave hope to peasants beaten down by years of Stalinist exploitation. But although practical enough to see what needed doing, and bold enough to do it, Khrushchev was ideologically opposed to the very principle that underlay his own recommendation—namely, that peasants should be freed from the most severe constraints of collectivism. The crash program to develop the Virgin Lands, which Khrushchev forced through the Presidium against Molotov's opposition, promised rapid results by ideologically pure means; instead of bribing peasants with "individual material incentives," it beckoned idealistic youths to a great socialist adventure, or so it seemed before they encountered the bitter hardships that awaited them in western Siberia and Kazakhstan. But after a fast start, Virgin Lands' harvests declined while leaving an ecological disaster in their wake. Meanwhile, Khrushchev steadily retreated from his initial encouragement of the private plots which produced so much of the nation's milk and vegetables; launched an ill-advised corn campaign that led to its being planted in far northern regions where it could not grow; and continually reorganized party and state agencies supervising agriculture, going so far as to actually split the party apparatus itself into industrial and agricultural branches, a move that violated the party's long-standing practice of protecting its monopoly of power by centralizing its own ranks.

In foreign policy, too, Khrushchev's record boasts successes, but also devastating failures. His efforts to ease Cold War tensions involved several East-West summits (in Geneva in 1955, an abortive session in Paris in May 1960, a meeting with president John F. Kennedy in Vienna in 1961), and innumerable trips overseas, including a tumultuous two-week tour of the United States in September 1959, and resulted in a 1963 partial nuclear test ban. But in November 1958 he sparked a crisis in Berlin (by giving the Western powers six months to recognize the German Democratic Republic or face abrogation of rights granted to them by the postwar Potsdam accords) without being clear in his own mind as to exactly what he wanted to accomplish and how he was going to accomplish it, or about the obstacles in his way, especially West German chancellor Konrad Adenauer and French president Charles de Gaulle. When Sergei Khrushchev asked what his father would do if the West still rejected Soviet terms when the six-month ultimatum expired, Khrushchev answered that "he intended to act in accord with circumstances and depending on our partners' reactions." He added that he hoped to get them to negotiate. What would happen if the negotiations did not produce results, Sergei asked. "Then we'll try something else," his father answered with a tone of irritation in his voice. "Something will always turn up."[9]

Khrushchev's decision to send missiles to Cuba was not thought through either. He later claimed that the decision was "worked out in the collective leadership" because he was determined that it "should not be forced down anyone's throat."[10] In fact, he barely consulted with foreign minister Anatoly Gromyko, did not consult at all with those of his aides best equipped to predict Washington's reaction (his foreign policy assistant Oleg Troyanovsky and ambassador to Washington Anatoly Dobrynin), and ignored a warning not to proceed from Anastas Mikoyan, who had spent more time in the United States than any other Soviet leader. When the party Presidium and the Soviet Defense Council finally met, Khrushchev led off by announcing that he favored the missile deployment, with the result that no one dared express doubts about whether the missiles could really be delivered and deployed without being detected—as in fact they were on October 14, 1962. In the end, Khrushchev agreed to withdraw the missiles from Cuba in return for an American promise not to invade Cuba (and for a secret U.S. pledge to remove American rockets from Turkey), and interpreted this result as a triumph. But as his Kremlin colleague Pyotr Demichev later recalled, "He made show of being brave, but we could tell by his behavior, especially by his irritability, that he felt it was a defeat."[11]

In Sino-Soviet relations, too, early successes gave way to eventual failures. Khrushchev resolved to manage Mao better than he thought Stalin did. Between 1953 and 1956, Moscow provided Beijing with what the Harvard University historian of China, William Kirby, has called "the greatest transfer of technology in world history," while offering diplomatic and military support as well.[12] But by the end of 1956, Mao concluded that Khrushchev had mishandled the Stalin question, and the two leaders quarreled bitterly during two meetings in Beijing in 1958 and 1959. Khrushchev had hoped to play the benevolent tutor to Mao, so it was all the more devastating when, instead of expressing gratitude and respect, Mao started condescending to him, not just denying him the satisfaction of outdoing Stalin, but returning Khrushchev to his former role of an upstart mortified by a new master. Khrushchev got his revenge in 1960 by pulling out Soviet advisors from China, tearing up hundreds of contracts, and scrapping hundreds of cooperative projects, all in less than a month. Soviet ambassador to China Stepan Chervonenko was amazed and distressed by the decision, as was Central Committee official Lev Deliusin. "I consider this one of Khrushchev's most flagrant mistakes," Deliusin recalled. "Of course, it led to a further worsening of relations. He thought it would improve them."[13]

Grant, then, that Khrushchev's personality shaped his domestic and foreign policies. The next question is how to analyze his character. One thing to notice is the sharp contrast between his behavior when he was seeking power, and how he conducted himself after seizing and consolidating it. As a power seeker, Khrushchev was much more successful than as a power holder. Until 1957, when his defeat of the "anti-party group" seemingly eliminated his last rivals for power, numerous personal qualities served him extremely well: driving ambition, which he managed to disguise even as it propelled him forward and upward; apparently unquenchable energy and a willingness to take risks; a seemingly straightforward democratic nature, along with an activist, populist approach, which won him the support of common people as well as party colleagues; and boldness, daring, and an aptitude for innovating. But beginning in 1957, he began to change for the worse. According to Presidium colleague Gennady Voronov, Khrushchev's "innately democratic approach, which couldn't but win you over when you first met him, gradually gave way to estrangement, to an attempt to close himself off in a narrow inner circle of people, some of whom indulged him in his worst tendencies."[14] Mikoyan recalled: "After 1957 [he] got conceited," as if feeling that "he didn't have to reckon with anyone, that everyone would just agree with him."[15] Khrushchev's daughter Rada Adzhubei remembered: "At an earlier stage, he would hear you out even if you were telling something that included criticism. But at a certain stage he said, 'That's enough! Don't tell me that sort of thing. I'm sick and tired of it. I don't want to hear it.' He wanted to distance himself from anything unpleasant. When did these changes occur? Toward the end of the 1950s, I think."[16]

Until 1953 Khrushchev's behavior was constrained by his terrible boss, and for the next four years by the demands of the struggle to succeed Stalin. After 1957, it was his freedom to be himself that got him into trouble. Part of the problem was that the very qualities that had suited an earlier, simpler era, such as his nonstop activism and willingness to take huge risks, became liabilities when he tried to lead a more developed, complicated society as the second-most-powerful man in the world. Equally problematic, he could now freely indulge his tendency to take on too much and to fail to think things through, to be supersensitive to slight and to overreact to failure.

In 1961 the United States Central Intelligence Agency commissioned some twenty psychiatrists and psychologists to study Khrushchev's personality in preparation for President Kennedy's upcoming summit with the Soviet leader in Vienna. Their conclusions focused on his "hypomanic" character.[17] A standard psychology manual defines hypomania as a "syndrome that is similar to, but not as severe as that described by the term 'mania.'" As with full-fledged mania—accompanied by its bipolar opposite, depression—hypomania is commonly associated with "lability of mood, with rapid shifts to anger or depression."[18] Psychoanalyst Nancy McWilliams's listing of hypomanic characteristics describes Khrushchev almost perfectly:

> Elated, energetic, self-promoting, witty and grandiose. . . . Overtly cheerful, highly social, given to idealization of others, work-addicted, flirtatious and articulate while covertly . . . guilty about aggression toward others, incapable of being alone . . . corruptible and lacking a systematic approach in cognitive style. . . . Grand schemes, racing thoughts, extended freedom from ordinary physical requirements such as food and sleep . . . constantly "up"—until exhaustion eventually sets in.[19]

Or as Khrushchev's wife Nina Petrovna put it more simply to U.S. ambassador Llewellyn Thompson's wife, Jane, as the Soviet delegation flew toward the United States in September 1959: "He's either all the way up or all the way down."[20]

One must be careful not to reduce big and complicated political decisions to what may be their psychological roots. Khrushchev obviously had many reasons to denounce Stalin, to declare a Berlin ultimatum, and to dispatch rockets to Cuba. But one also suspects that he was in a manic mood when he decided to gamble in these and other cases, and that he was depressed when, confronted with the unexpected consequences of his choices, he cut himself off from his colleagues and retreated into a small inner circle in which no one dared tell him he was wrong.

Besides his hypomania, if that is what it was, various features of his early life and career help to explain his later behavior. After his minimal formal schooling, he tried to resume his education in a Stalino *rabfak* (a worker's training program that prepared its students for more specialized technical education) in the early 1920s and at the Industrial Academy in Moscow in 1929, but he was quickly distracted by his role as party leader in both institutions. Yet, despite being, as sculptor Ernst Neizvestny later put it, "the most uncultured man I've ever met,"[21] Khrushchev was hugely ambitious, spurred on initially by his adoring mother, and by a village teacher in Kalinovka who admired him. The very fact that Khrushchev was so primitive facilitated his miraculous rise into Stalin's inner circle: trading on his image as a simple peasant, he became a kind of jester in Stalin's court. If he played the *prostak* (simpleton) so well that even a paranoid like Stalin came to trust him, and his rivals to fatally underestimate him, that was partly because in some ways he was a *prostak*—and therefore all the more mortified to have to play up that fact in order to survive and advance.

Although Khrushchev reached the very top, he was ill equipped to lead a vast transcontinental country coping with Stalin's terrible legacy. It was but a matter of time, therefore, until troubles in domestic and foreign affairs closed in. As they did, he resorted to ever more desperate gambles seeking to turn the tide, only to have them backfire, deepening his predicament, and prompting him to take even greater risks, until he was unceremoniously ousted in 1964.

The black and white monument at Khrushchev's grave sums up the man in whose character so many contrasts were so starkly intertwined. He was both a true believer and a cold-eyed realist; an opportunist yet principled in his own way; fearful of war while all too prone to risk it; the most unpretentious of men even as he pretended to power and glory exceeding his grasp; complicit in great evil, yet also the author of much good. Toward the very end of his life, when he was in retirement, he said, "After I die, they will place my actions on a scale—on the one side evil, on the other side good. I hope the good will outweigh the bad."[22] Between 1938 and 1940, in Ukraine alone where he was in charge, more than 160,000 were arrested, of whom more than 50,000 are said to have been executed.[23] Yet Khrushchev not only denounced Stalin and released millions from the Gulag, but began the unraveling of Communism. Does the good he did indeed outweigh the bad? Readers will have to judge for themselves.

NOTES

1. See William Taubman, *Khrushchev: The Man and His Era* (New York: Norton, 2003), 657.

2. Both Molotov and Mikoyan give Khrushchev this credit: Molotov in F. Chuev, *Sto sorok besed s Molotovym* (Moscow: "Terra," 1991), 343–345; Mikoyan in *Tak bylo* (Moscow: Vagrius, 1999), 586.

3. Stalin's real Georgian name was Dzhugashvili. Khrushchev altered it by playing on one of the many Russian words for "prick." Author's interview with Khrushchev's friend's daughter, Olga I. Kosenko, Donetsk, June 1991.

4. *N. S. Khrushchev (1894–1971): Materialy nauchnoi konferentsii posviashchennoi 100-letiu so dnia rozhdeniia N. S. Khrushcheva* (Moscow, 1994), 39.

5. Mikoyan, *Tak bylo*, 590–591.

6. Vladimir P. Naumov, "Repression and Rehabilitation," in *Nikita Khrushchev*, ed. William Taubman, Sergei Khrushchev, and Abbott Gleason (New Haven, Conn.: Yale University Press, 2000), 109.

7. Author's interview with Maya Turovskaya, Amherst, Massachusetts, March 1995.

8. As demonstrated in Vladislav M. Zubok, "Stalin Dies, Zhdanov Stays: Soviet Writers Respond to De-Stalinization, 1956," paper presented to the convention of the American Association for the Advancement of Slavic Studies, Toronto, November 2003, pp. 6, 9–10, 20.

9. Sergei N. Khrushchev, *Nikita S. Khrushchev: Krizisy i rakety*, vol. 1 (Moscow, 1991), 416.

10. Nikita S. Khrushchev, *Khrushchev Remembers* (Boston, 1970), 498–499.

11. Author's interview with Pytor N. Demichev, Moscow, August 1993.

12. Kirby spoke at the International Symposium on Sino-Soviet Relations and the Cold War, Beijing, October 1997.

13. Deliusin spoke at the Beijing symposium in October 1997.

14. Author's interview with Gennady Voronov, Moscow, June 1991.

15. Mikoyan, *Tak bylo*, 601–602.

16. Author's interview with Rada Adzhubei, Moscow, June 1991.

17. One of the psychiatrists, Dr. Bryant Wedge, described the study in "Khrushchev at a Distance: A Study of Public Personality," *Trans-action* (October 1968): 24–28.

18. *Diagnostic and Statistical Manual of Mental Disorders*, 3rd ed. (Washington, D.C.: American Psychiatric Association, 1980), 206–207.

19. Nancy McWilliams, *Psychoanalytic Diagnosis* (New York: Guilford Press, 1994), 248. McWilliams is quoting S. Akhtar, *Broken Structures* (Northvale, N.J.: Jason Aronson, 1992), 193.

20. Author's interview with Jane Thompson, Washington, D.C., March 1983.

21. Ernst Neizvestny, "Moi dialog s Khrushchevym," *Vremia i my* (May 1979): 182.

22. Cited in the preface to Nikita S. Khrushchev, *N. S. Khrushchev: Vospominaniia—vremia, liudi, vlast'*, vol. 1. (Moscow: Moskovskie novosti, 1999), 4.

23. The figure of 165,565 arrested between 1938 and 1940 is in a report to the Central Committee by a Politburo commission headed by Aleksandr Yakovlev. The report is in "Massovye repressii opravdany byt' ne mogut," *Istochnik*, no. 1 (1995): 127. The figure of 54,000 killed is recalled by Molotov in Chuev, *Sto sorok besed*, 443.

SUGGESTED READING

Filtzer, Donald. *The Khrushchev Era: De-Stalinization and the Limits of Reform in the USSR, 1953–1964*. London, 1993.

Fursenko, Aleksandr, and Timothy Naftali. *One Hell of a Gamble: Khrushchev, Castro and Kennedy, 1958–1964*. New York, 1997.

Khrushchev, Nikita S. *Khrushchev Remembers*. Translated and edited by Strobe Talbott. Boston, 1970.

———. *Khrushchev Remembers: The Glasnost Tapes*. Translated and edited by Jerrold L. Schecter with Vyacheslav Luchkov. Boston, 1990.

———. *Khrushchev Remembers: The Last Testament*. Translated and edited by Strobe Talbott. Boston, 1974.

Khrushchev, Sergei N. *Khrushchev on Khrushchev: An Inside Account of the Man and His Era*. Translated and edited by William Taubman. Boston, 1990.

———. *Nikita Khrushchev and the Creation of a Superpower*. University Park, Pa., 2000.

McCauley, Martin, ed. *Khrushchev and Khrushchevism*. Bloomington, Ind., 1987.

McMillan, Priscilla Johnson. *Khrushchev and the Arts*. Cambridge, Mass., 1965.

Miller, R. F., and F. Feher, eds. *Khrushchev and the Communist World*. London, 1984.

Taubman, William. *Khrushchev: The Man and His Era*. New York, 2003.

Taubman, William, Sergei Khrushchev, and Abbott Gleason, eds. *Nikita Khrushchev*. New Haven, Conn., 2000.

Tompson, William J. *Khrushchev: A Political Life*. New York, 1995.

Zubok, Vladislav, and Constantine Pleshakov. *Inside the Kremlin's Cold War: From Stalin to Khrushchev*. Cambridge, Mass., 1996.

19

Late-Soviet Prerequisites for Post-Soviet Disasters

Reflections

Sergei Arutiunov

The collapse of the Soviet Union resulted in many disasters for its former citizens in all of its constituent republics and territories, but perhaps the most devastating effects were felt in the Caucasus. A sharp drop in the gross national product (GNP) in 1990–1992 was ubiquitous. However, while in Russia proper, the Baltic states, and Central Asia, the drop was 20–30 percent, it was 30–40 percent in the Northern Caucasus (within the Russian Federation), 40–50 percent in Azerbaijan and Armenia, and nearly 80 percent in Georgia. Unemployment, which during the Soviet era was virtually nonexistent, grew approximately by the same percentage.

This difference was predetermined by a number of factors, some of which were quite obvious and expectable. It was clear that among all regions of the former Soviet Union, the Caucasus was the least autarchic and the most dependent on other Soviet regions for both resources and markets. The Baltic states possessed a highly developed modern economy—in relative terms—with a considerable amount of autarchy. The main product of Central Asia was and is cotton, for which in the world market there is a fairly reliable demand. On the contrary, the economy of the Caucasus, both in the North and in the South, was formed in the Soviet era as an appendage to the economy of central Russia, being a) strategically important and a militarily developed territory, with many bases, location stations, airstrips, and related auxiliary infrastructure, b) an important recreational area, with health resorts, beaches, spas, clinics, sanatoriums, and even a more or less tolerated business sector of small private hotels, and c) a vital producer of such warm-climate products as tobacco, tea, wines, fruits, flowers, early vegetables, canned products, etc. In addition, there was a labor surplus, with said labor force both cheap and sufficiently well skilled to favor the development of military-oriented industry, like the production of chips for electronic equipment (Armenia), sophisticated navy machinery (Dagestan), trucks and aircrafts (Georgia), and chemical products and instrumental devices (North Caucasus).

On the other hand, with exception of the Kuban and Stavropol territories, most Caucasian regions were not able to satisfy the demand of the growing urban population for grain, meat, dairy products, and other basic foodstuffs, which had to be largely imported from the North and were in constant short supply. Therefore an abrupt breakaway from the central Russian market would result in, among other things, drastic reductions in exports and imports, a (temporary) halt in the tourist flow, the closing of military-oriented industries, and a stoppage of energy supplies, all of which would be irrespective of any specific social and psychological conditions. Only blindfolded nationalists and political adventurers could disregard the inevitably deleterious consequences of severing seventy-year-old ties between the constituent parts of the Soviet Union. But then, in the early 1990s, it seemed to many as if it was Russia which was fatally ill, and legions of non-Russians believed that their particular nation might be saved only if it was able to separate itself from the decaying heart of the empire. But there were other social, psychological, and moral preconditions that aggravated the consequences of the collapse, and these had been prepared, if not by the previous seven decades of Soviet life, then at least by the last twenty-five years of the precollapse (or rather post-Khrushchev) Soviet developments.

The iron grip of Stalinism, which used a heavily barbed whip and a rather emaciated carrot on every nation, more or less indiscriminately, did not allow any local or ethnic/national elite to form firmly, let alone to show any degree of disobedience and independence. Everybody was a docile slave, only some slaves did have a few slaves of their own, while others were bereft of any such advantages.

After the death of Stalin, followed by the short power struggle between Khrushchev and an array of rivals, most prominently Beria and Malenkov, from which Khrushchev emerged victorious, the political situation changed considerably. Khrushchev was very inconsistent; he did his best to be liked by everybody and in the end was, perhaps inevitably, despised by many. Apart from his rather foolishly spontaneous moves in the international arena, in the domestic sphere he permitted, indeed encouraged, the genie of criticism to escape out of the bottle by dismantling the Stalinist Cult of Personality, only to make a vain attempt to create a new, though less bloodthirsty, and certainly less universal, cult of personality around his own rule. He launched a multitude of economic and administrative changes, many of them, perhaps incorrectly, viewed as failures; he both encouraged and insulted the intelligentsia, ultimately humiliating and embittering many poets, authors, playwrights, painters, artists, and scholars. When he tried to be harsh, as when he ordered an attack on a "rioting" crowd in Tbilisi in March 1956, as well as in Novocherkassk in 1962, he only made his subjects rather more angry than frightened. After Stalin, the people would no longer play the role of obedient slaves, plebeians, yes, but helots, no. Even when being the frightened and obedient slaves of Stalin, however, not all Soviet citizens were also blindfolded slaves in their day-to-day life.

Many Russians (and formerly Soviet citizens), coming for the first time to the United States, are often quite shocked by the naiveté with which Americans seem to have imbibed a pervasive set of myths about their own nation's history (themes such as the wisdom of the founding fathers, the greatness of American democracy, equal opportunity for all, the glorious achievements and virtues—and yes, there have to be virtues, usually moral—of the former presidents, and so on). Perhaps many Americans would not classify these notions as myths or propaganda at all, but most Russian—indeed foreign—observers of American life, as a result of their own experiences, think of them in this way. Americans may, in fact, be far less naive than they appear. Still, the gap between these national myths and their blind acceptance was and is certainly narrower in the United States than it was in the Soviet Union even during the Stalin era.

The number of Communist true believers was perhaps larger in the 1920s than in later years. However, after the Stalinist purges of the 1930s and 1940s, the contrast between slogans and reality became too pronounced to go unnoticed by the majority of the population. I am aware of two main categories of "red" true believers, that is, the ardent supporters and official propagators of Communist (or rather Soviet) ideology. The first group consisted of young people in their late teens, mostly beginning university students, recruited into the leading strata of the cells of the Komsomol (the Young Communist's League). Although some stayed with the Communist Party into adult life, many of these young men and women often became the most determined dissidents, overtly or covertly, by the time they had to write their M.A. theses.

The second group comprised numerous petty instructors in district party committees and the innumerable lecturers and teachers of Marxist-Leninist theory and the history of the Communist Party. Mostly from the poorest peasant families, and often only modestly educated, these people stuck to the official dogma instinctively, since it was the only available means for them to rise in society, or even to make a decent living. The core of today's demonstrators seen at the celebrations on the first of May and the seventh of November, brandishing red flags and portraits of Stalin, comes from these two categories of people. The remainder of the population constituted a broad spectrum of political belief. This ranged from a pinkish red group, who believed most of the slogans of official government propaganda, with just a few secret exceptions and reservations, to a lily white group of those who rejected Communism completely, but never said so in public.

As for top party functionaries, officers of the police and secret services, almost all those who had any real ideology vanished in the purges and trials of the 1930s. By the end of the Second World War, most people in the Soviet elite were inspired by only a very fungible ideology or perhaps none at all. They were ready to support any slogan pronounced by the supreme power, especially if complicity would increase their chances to move one step further toward the top rungs of power. Margaret Mead correctly viewed this readiness to shift one's ideological position as being typical of Soviet Russia. However, this tendency, of course, predates the Soviet system, and may reflect cultural patterns that transcend those we see as specifically Soviet.

Similar shifts are easily observed in Russian history. Among such examples is the fact that between 1796 and 1825, Paul succeeded Catherine the Great on the throne, Alexander I succeeded Paul, and Nicholas II succeeded Alexander I, all in less than thirty years. By stark contrast, no repression or threat of execution could break the stoicism of Old Believers in the seventeenth and eighteenth centuries, or of SRs (Socialist Revolutionaries) in tsarist and Soviet prisons. In fact, extreme prowess in adapting to changing conditions and heroic stoicism in defending one's homeostasis are probably two sides of the single coin of the so-called Russian character. We see this depressingly today, when about 90 percent of the politicians in the party of power, most of the bureaucrats, and the successful managers of private businesses are the same former important Communist Party functionaries, or Komsomol leaders, or ex-KGB officers who ruled so incompetently over the late Soviet Union. We find them today quite sincerely denouncing Communist dogmas and advocating the market economy. But there are, however, certain ethnic or national differences.

What do a Belorussian and a Tajik have in common? Or a Don Cossack and a Saha-Yakut? The question is decidedly difficult, and must be considered dynamically over time. When Brezhnev announced the creation of a new historical community, the Soviet people, or when Communist "ethnopolitologists" wrote about the formation in the Federal Republic of Germany and the German Democratic Republic of two distinct German nations, many dissident critics considered these notions to be laughable nonsense. It is no longer so easy to dismiss such nation-building notions. It is sobering to realize that although it has been nearly two decades since the collapse of the Soviet Union and since the two Germanys were merged, the demarcation between Ossies and Wessies in Germany remains evident, while Kazakhs, Tajiks, Chechens, and Abkhazians speak with nostalgia about good old Soviet times. Derogatory nicknames like Homo Sovieticus or the colloquial "Sovok" continue to exist, obviously reflecting some objective reality, a certain set of commonly shared features, even when these features are viewed only as negative.

At the other end of the spectrum we have the overwhelming majority of people in the titular Baltic nations (Latvians, Lithuanians, Estonians), who never considered themselves part of the Soviet community, believing themselves to be suffering from a temporary, albeit prolonged, Soviet occupation. At the same time, a handful of overtly or covertly dissident-minded members of the metropolitan intelligentsia (including myself and a rather narrow circle of like-minded friends) discussed in our Moscow kitchens the scenarios and timings of the inevitable collapse of the USSR.

However, rank-and-file Soviet citizens in Kiev, Kazan, Novosibirsk, and elsewhere perceived something very different. They did not dream of this collapse, and in no way anticipated it. To them, as to the majority of outside observers, it seemed that the USSR would continue to exist for an indefinite time.

This shared (though illusory) feeling of a common destiny produced some of the common features prevailing among Soviet people. Another factor that led to a shared pattern of attitudes was the universal understanding that any commercial private initiative was, if not completely impossible, then at least very risky. The safest and surest way to vertical social mobility, to an improvement of one's material wealth and social status, was through education and, preferably, through membership in the Communist Party. These circumstances could not fail to create a certain set of shared values and orientations, however fragile the foundations. Still, stark differences also prevailed.

I never had an opportunity to observe from within any of the big Muslim societies of the Soviet Union, such as those of the Tatars or Uzbeks. As far as the period from the 1930s to the 1950s is concerned, I can speak only of Russians, Georgians, and Armenians, all of whom belong to very similar Orthodox Christian faiths. The differences between these Christian ethnic communities seen as a group and those of the former Soviet Muslim nations are probably more marked than among these three communities compared with each other. However, even the differences among these three Orthodox communities were very significant. Referring to the above-mentioned red-white spectrum, I would identify people in Georgia as mostly concentrated in the whitish, non-Communist part of the spectrum. Russians and especially Armenians (who constituted the majority of the working class in Transcaucasia) displayed more pinkish overtones, but not too noticeably. Georgians, mostly peasants and intelligentsia recruited from the former gentry, were probably 90 percent white, though an exceptional ability at successful mimicry in support of the Communist party line was regarded more often with admiration than contempt. A totally red person in Georgia, that is, a sincerely devoted believer in the official Communist ideology, was usually regarded as a fool. When in 1950, at the age of eighteen, I first went to Moscow to study at Moscow University, I was definitely shocked by the fact that so many rank-and-file Russians, including the intelligentsia, seemed to be rather red. Because of my youthful experiences in the Caucasus, I was surprised to see that they indeed felt some filial piety and sympathy for Stalin, and that they accepted a good deal of Communist propaganda at face value.

Accordingly, when at the Twentieth Party Congress Nikita Khrushchev in his famous secret speech (February 24–25, 1956) exposed Stalin and his Cult of Personality, many Russians and Soviets (not to mention foreign Communists) felt disoriented and embarrassed. The shift of loyalty demanded of them at that moment was too enormous to execute easily. For people with a Transcaucasian background, Khrushchev's speech was by no means a revelation. But many Georgians reacted in a rather peculiar way. Consider the peasants in Kardanakhi, the native village of my grandfather, and in many other villages from whom I had learned certain truths about the Gulags already in the early 1940s. These people never referred to Stalin in other terms than "the moustached one," or more explicitly, "that moustached beast" (*es ulvashiani mkhetsi*) when in a circle of trusted people. Now, they promptly displayed portraits of Stalin on the windshields of their tractors and trucks. In Tbilisi, spontaneous rallies of protest were held on the third anniversary of Stalin's death, in 1956, and police and Russian troops killed scores of people in the ensuing riots. This was a surprising diametrical shift. However, while among Russians it was a shift from one sort of conformity to another type of conformity, in Georgia the shift was from one style of nonconformity to another kind of nonconformity.

Thus, while attitudes of the authorities toward the masses were more or less the same throughout the USSR, the attitudes of the masses toward the authorities were rather different in different parts of the country. Even if one limits the scope of such analysis to Russians only, significant differences among such groups as Don and Kuban Cossacks, Siberian Old Believers, St. Petersburg's working class, Pomor fishermen of Archangel, peasants of the black-earth belt of central Russia, and other groups of the "Great" Russian population were still apparent.

No doubt, such differences were far more apparent between the Caucasus area and the Slavic-speaking parts of the Soviet empire than among various ethnic groups of the Caucasus itself. Even within the latter group, however, the differences were becoming deeper and deeper over time, due to the fact that what had been a more or less equally impoverished and hungry beginning to the Soviet project, marked by uniform Bolshevist party policies in the years after the end of the Civil War, evolved into more and more diversifying trends of economic developments, along with the emergence of local ethnic party elites, especially after the Second World War. During the war itself, the centralized command structure as well as common military needs largely obliterated local variations. The emergent elites mightily increased their importance by being apparently devoted supporters of Khrushchev's power (in fact they were rather unreliable and untrustworthy supporters, as it soon turned out), and became the pivotal actors in all ethnoterritorial units of both the Northern ("Russian") and Southern Caucasus during the Brezhnev era (1965–1985). It is these two decades, plus the five years of Gorbachev's attempts at perestroika that constitute "late Soviet" in this chapter.

Two trends broadly characterize the social and psychological developments of the Brezhnev era. One was a diminishing fear of the authorities. The late Soviet regime was much less repressive than Stalin's. Dissidents were never shot and only rather rarely imprisoned; most often they were forced into exile, like the physicist Andrei Sakharov or the writer Alexander Solzhenitsyn. It could not be otherwise in a time of attempts at détente and related global human rights campaigns. And while out-of-serfdom Russian peasants and Buddhist Kalmyks were still showing some signs of fearfulness and apathy, the Caucasus highlanders, with their long-standing traditions of revolts and free communes, more and more felt rather fearless, or at least ready to take risks. The second trend was a growing discontent with the senile imbecility of the aging Kremlin leadership.

This readiness to take risks and to show their discontent was brilliantly revealed in the spring of 1978, when Tbilisi students organized a mass protest march against the absence of the Georgian state language in the new draft of the Georgian constitution. The march was peaceful, but Eduard Shevardnadze (first secretary of the Georgian Communist Party), afraid of widening disturbances, immediately called Brezhnev and easily persuaded him to grant him permission to at least partially meet the demands of the students. The inclusion of corresponding concessions in the constitutions of Azerbaijan and Armenia followed almost automatically, while neither in Ukraine nor even in the Baltic republics, let alone those of Central Asia, did local leaders dare to do this—but then again there were no demonstrations "threatening instability" in these areas. Meanwhile, the Abkhazian constitution got three state languages—Abkhazian, Russian, and Georgian. There can be no doubt that Stalin, in a similar situation, would have plainly ordered the demonstrators to be shot, while Khrushchev would have ordered, at the very least, their dispersal.

The general well-being of the population was undoubtedly rising in the late Soviet era, although with a much slower tempo than the populace expected, and also rather unevenly.

Mountain villages high above sea level were usually crushingly poor. Some people fled from them voluntarily, seeking a more exciting life and/or better-paid employment (or simply employment). In many cases whole villages were forcibly relocated to the lowlands, mainly to compensate for the shortage of manpower in geranium and coriander plantations and similar agricultural enterprises. In Stalin's era this was done with extreme brutality, accompanied by the burning of peasants' houses so as to make impossible any attempt at return. In Brezhnev's time methods were milder; relocations were mainly conducted with persuasion and administrative pressure. The majority of the population, however, did not want to be resettled, preferring scarce means of subsistence in a healthy environment to the perhaps higher income marking the flatlands, with its hot climate and endemic diseases that decimated new settlers lacking adaptive immunity. Nevertheless the pressure by the authorities was strong, and as a result, the rich pastoral lands and other resources of the highlands today lie abandoned and many villages are practically uninhabited.

Forced resettlements have also sown the seeds of many ethnic conflicts today. New settlers were usually of entirely different ethnic roots and traditions, and the local population often regarded them with enmity. Land claims and conflicts over water and other resources, which are traditional in the Caucasus, were more and more structured along ethnic lines. On the other hand, the majority of peasants ("collective farmers"; but they were putting much more labor into their small though highly productive quasi-private plots than into largely neglected "collective" vineyards, orchards, and fields) were quite well-to-do. Their yearly income could often amount to ten thousand to twenty thousand rubles or more. To compare, my yearly professor's salary was six thousand rubles, and it was considered quite a high income in Moscow. Some of my colleagues in the Caucasus were earning much more, for the reasons described below.

At that time, the buying capacity of a ruble was in fact nearly equal to that of a U.S. dollar (the official rate was 1 dollar = 0.67 rubles). In the pervasive black market, however, one dollar could easily be sold for two and even three rubles (selling dollars in the USSR was, needless to say, an illegal and risky business, though it was also a practice that many Soviets engaged in). To give an idea of the prices in the 1960s and 1970s (the price differences from the 1960s to the late 1970s were negligible), I offer some excerpts from my diary of 1979: lunch at an inexpensive restaurant in Vladivostok, 2 rubles; lunch in a students' canteen in Moscow, 1 ruble; an "average" book, 3 to 5 rubles; a monthly ticket (bus, tram, metro) within Moscow, 7 rubles; a bottle of vodka or some decent wine, 3–4 rubles; monthly rent on an apartment in Moscow, 50 rubles; an air ticket from Tbilisi to Yerevan, one way, 10 rubles; an air ticket from Tbilisi to Moscow, one way, 40 rubles; an average taxi drive in Moscow, 5 rubles; one kilogram of sugar, 1 ruble; one kilogram of "fresh" meat in the farmer's market, 4 rubles; and for those who wished to splurge, tickets on a Volga cruise for two, deluxe cabin, 17 days, Moscow–Astrakhan–Moscow, all food included, 500 rubles.

From this admittedly random price list, it can be seen that in the last years of the Soviet period a yearly income of twenty thousand rubles was quite a princely sum. How did various Georgian, Armenian, and North Caucasian farmers earn it? First of all, by selling their flowers, fruits, fresh and pickled vegetables, etc., to private mediators who would then take said goods to the large cities of central Russia to trade. Local canneries would give a cheaper price, but harvests were usually big and maintenance costs (fuel, chemicals, etc.) low. In other places, like, in Balkaria, the source of income was Angora goat wool and the knitwear made from it. In many areas, tourist services, such as renting rooms, catering, and the like also made for sizable incomes. Thus, there was a constant flow of money from central Russia to the Caucasus.

Conspicuous or ostentatious consumption was nearly unheard of in Stalin's time, and rather rare in Khrushchev's time, but by the late Soviet era, Soviet society was becoming more and more consumerist. Compared to Western consumer society it made, of course, for a rather pale reflection in the bleak socialist mirror, but it was a beginning, and as ostentatious consumption began to matter, it began to have a profound effect on society. Nearly everybody now wanted fashionable shoes and clothes, some china, and stylish furniture; more and more people wanted to buy televisions, stereos, and, most spectacularly, automobiles. At first, however, all of this was accessible to only the very few. There was much more money than things to buy with it. It was an economy of planned socialist distribution, and only low-quality goods, produced by an increasingly creaky Soviet socialist industry, could be bought with ease. For better things, especially imported, you had either to overpay tremendously on the black market, or to use whatever "connections" to which you had access. The attitudes of the relevant authorities to the fast-growing demand for consumer goods were, to put it mildly, contradictory. On the one hand, the official party line discouraged this "petty-bourgeois consumerism"; on the other hand, the government spent lavishly in the 1970s to import scarce "luxury" goods (most of the money for these purchases was amassed from oil sales—the Soviet Union was awash with oil money throughout most of the 1970s).

Besides an array of basic household goods and that most prized of possessions, a car, what many farmers (those who found themselves suddenly burdened with newfound wealth, that is) craved the most was to build a new, modern, and rather luxurious house. Building materials, however, could not be purchased on the market. They were distributed by the state to state-owned civil and military construction firms (all according to the still-adhered-to plan). Farmers were ready to pay a good price for them, but they were not available. So all the constructors had to do was overestimate requirements for necessary building materials, use much less than the officially established norms, and sell the rest to those with the means to pay a premium price for them.

As for the money "earned" in these endeavors, the middlemen were not only lining their own pockets, but also paying the workers far above their meager official salaries. And so it was across the Soviet Union; party functionaries closed their eyes to these abuses and everybody was happy. Unhappy events did, however, have a troubling tendency to emerge later, events that highlighted some possible repercussions of Soviet economic practices. When the Spitak earthquake in Armenia in December 1988 killed twenty-five thousand people, for example, many of these people were killed only because the concrete panels of recently built houses turned out to contain two times less cement and two times more sand than was allowed by the supposed norms. Older houses stood undamaged. The old name of the city of Leninakan was Giumri, and the new proverb said: "Leninakan kanwets baits Giumri mnats"—Leninakan fell but Giumri remained. Other incidents of a smaller scale, but of the same type, were numerous across the crumbling Soviet infrastructure.

The demand for good-quality shoes, clothes, and other everyday necessities was often met by a curious phenomenon called *tsekhoviks* (from *tsekh*— a workshop). Some entrepreneurially smart people would organize, behind the front of some legal, state-owned factory, *tsekhs*, in fact privately owned factories, with better equipment, better-paid workers, and a higher level of production than was attained in state-owned factories. While this was a form of "true" capitalism, the raw materials for these factories, which theoretically were supposed to come from recycling, or "waste," in fact had to be largely stolen from the government. Such supplies as metal, leather, wool, and textiles were acquired through elaborate schemes, which were possible only with the aid and consent of state and party functionaries. These officials would, of course, receive often lavish bribes from the *tsekhoviks*. While during the Stalin era these would-be capitalists would be shot, and under Khrushchev they were also often harshly punished, neither Brezhnev nor Gorbachev took systematic actions against such apparent malfeasance.

This phenomenon was common for all regions of the Caucasus, though rather less common in central Russia. I do not have any reliable data about Central Asia, but there, as well as in central Russia, farmers were mostly quite poor and the wealth of the emerging semi-criminal middle class must have come through some other schemes. All such schemes, naturally, could work only in the atmosphere of "planned socialism," and as the planned economy collapsed, so did the *tsekhoviks*, because now there was neither a solvent demand nor an accessible supply.

Farmers and better-paid workers wanted not only new houses; they wanted adequate medical care for themselves and their families and a decent education for their children. Both were theoretically free according to the Constitution, though quite inadequate in fact. But doctors could pad their salaries with private consultations and schoolteachers and university professors with private lessons. While it is possible that these latter individuals would teach their students something useful, at the same time the tutor's connections were indispensable for access to universities, and many simply took bribes at exam time. Like forms of bribery were the main source of income for lawyers, judges, policemen, and petty bureaucrats, among others with "skills" and connections to sell, and were usually taken for granted by the citizenry. Education and Communist Party membership remained the main preconditions for access to sought-after positions in the Soviet Union. Education, as we have seen, could be bought, whether in terms of admission to a university or just a fake diploma. But party membership, too, not only *could* be bought, but often *was* bought. The standard price for admission to the party in Adzharia in 1982 was two thousand rubles. The rates might differ from one republic to another, but not considerably.

Corruption, thus, was all permeating. The ruling strata in central Russia were gradually catching up to the realities of doing business in the Caucasus and elsewhere, not least due to the fact that Caucasian and other provincial officials of all sorts were constantly visiting Moscow with rich "presents," lobbying to secure their interests. The Central Committee of the CPSU and Central Headquarters of the KGB are said to have remained relatively free of corruption the longest, but with perestroika and its developing embryos of free enterprise, they also started to be permeated by corruption.

As one can easily see, society in the Caucasus, once famous for its integrity, was losing this integrity under the socialist regime, and by the late Soviet era had lost it completely. This situation continues today because the collapse of the Soviet Union, unlike that of Eastern Europe, was not followed by any lustration. On the contrary, nearly 70 percent of the current bureaucracy across the former Soviet Union are former CPSU members, having occupied the same or similar positions in the Gorbachev and even Brezhnev eras. Today although there is not a CPSU or related party cells, connections, often based on family ties, remain the precondition for getting things done in a timely and sufficient manner.

The economic base is different, of course. Farmers are quite poor today. Their production rarely is successful on the Russian market. But millions of Georgians, Armenians, Azeris, and North Caucasians work successfully in central Russia, which experiences a serious labor shortage, and they send home a good deal of the money they earn. Another source of income is a great number of formerly state-owned enterprises—including shops, small factories, and gasoline stations, indeed whole chains of them—which were privatized and bought by various "oligarchs." In Dagestan, with a population of 2.5 million, two hundred families, less than six thousand people, control about 80 percent of the national wealth. They pay salaries (much lower than those in Soviet times), they maintain their private little armies of "bodyguards," and they subsidize a large clientele. The socialist-era pyramid remains, but now the money flow goes not from the bottom to the top, but from the top to the bottom. Bribery and corruption are, of course, at epidemic levels in Dagestan and in other regions of the Caucasus. Anyone who is in a position to demand bribes does so. If someone is desirous of becoming a policeman, a doctor, or a teacher, the procedure is rather simple. He must give a certain sum of money to some well-placed bureaucrat, very often directly to the minister or vice minister of justice, of health, of education, and so on.

The collapse of the Soviet Union was followed by the squeezing out, humiliation, and deprivation of the ethnically Russian segments of the population in not only the non-Russian republics of the former Soviet Union, but in many areas of the Russian Federation itself where Russians are in the minority. In Dagestan, their number has dropped from 20 percent to a meager 4 percent. Almost all Russians have left Azerbaijan, a majority have left or are leaving Armenia, many, especially members of religious sects, are leaving Georgia, and the number of Russians in Abkhazia since 1992 has been halved and continues to shrink. The shrinking of the Russian community is, it would seem, a feature everywhere in the former Soviet Union (even in Russian-majority areas of the Russian Federation, emigration and disastrous health factors have served to startlingly reduce the population). In the period of "total privatization" the members of the leading (titular) ethnic communities were in the most favorable position, because all leading posts became quickly occupied by their ethnic "compatriots." Smaller groups with a high ethnic cohesion could also partly defend their interests. But ethnic Russians, who long ago lost whatever feeling of ethnic solidarity they once had, were the last to be accorded any consideration and in consequence they received little in the way of political or economic spoils in the newly independent states of the former Soviet Union. From rebellious Chechnya, practically all Russians simply had to flee, abandoning all their property. It is hard to imagine any of these refugees will ever return.

The more or less ubiquitous negative attitude toward ethnic Russians is partly the result of the arrogant, and self-defeating, policy of forced Russification carried out not only by "viceroys" (i.e., first party secretaries) appointed from Moscow, but also by native party potentates, who in their fervor to prove their loyalty to the Kremlin, tried to be, as it were, more Catholic than the pope. Now, in a not-so-surprising series of twists, former "internationalists" have become committed ultranationalists, and former militant atheists have become the most pious parishioners of churches and mosques.

It must be admitted that much of the corrosive character of ethnic, economic, and social life in the former Soviet Union has its roots in the hypercontradictory nature of Soviet existence itself. These contradictions were most glaring—to observers both internal and external—in the last twenty-five years of the Soviet era. Theoretically, the often negative consequences of regime (Soviet and immediate post-Soviet) policies could have been lessened with better policymakers. Then, perhaps, the course followed by some of the former republics after the dissolution of the Soviet Union might have led to rather more peaceful and civilized conditions. However, for better policymakers to have come to the fore it was also necessary that a system be in place that could have produced and nurtured them. Said conditions, as is depressingly clear, were entirely absent across the vastness of Soviet space. Neither the Soviet masses nor their rulers were predisposed to establishing a responsible and effective polity. Such polities, after all, are rarely conducive to either absolute rule by the authorities or to the utter avoidance of responsibility by the populace.

SUGGESTED READING

Derluguian, Georgi M. *Bourdieu's Secret Admirer in the Caucasus: A World System Biography.* Chicago, 2005.

Jowitt, Ken. *New World Disorder: The Leninist Extinction.* Berkeley, Calif., 1992.

Kapuscinski, Ryszard. *Imperium.* New York, 1994.

Kornai, Janos. *The Socialist System: The Political Economy of Communism.* Princeton, N.J., 1992.

Ledeneva, Alena V. *Russia's Economy of Favours: Blat, Networking and Informal Exchange.* Cambridge, UK, 1998.

Lieven, Anatol. *Chechnya: Tombstone of Russian Power.* New Haven, Conn., 1998.

Scott, James C. *Seeing like a State: How Certain Schemes to Improve the Human Condition Have Failed.* New Haven, Conn., 1998.

Suny, Ronald. *The Revenge of the Past: Nationalism, Revolution, and the Collapse of the Soviet Union.* Stanford, Calif., 1993.

Yurchak, Alexei. *Everything Was Forever, Until It Was No More: The Last Soviet Generation.* Princeton, N.J., 2005.

Zinoviev, Alexander. *Homo Sovieticus.* New York, 1986.

20

Gorbachev and the Soviet Collapse

Stirrings of Accountable Government?

Martha Merritt

Though the Soviet Union was far from experiencing a renaissance when Mikhail Gorbachev became general secretary of the Communist Party in 1985, his country was one of two global superpowers and the regime seemed firmly in charge. Certain problems were clear: much of the Soviet population by the 1980s had ceased to believe in any kind of vision associated with Communism, the economy was under duress, and, perhaps most critically, the political elite languished between cynicism and malaise. Gorbachev saw his mission as one of transforming the party into a legitimate and effective ruling organ by making members accountable for their work.[1] The more Gorbachev pushed for accountability for others, however, the more these efforts compromised his own ability to govern the Soviet Union. Ironically, in Gorbachev's achievements lay the seeds of his ultimate political failure.

The creation and use of accountability forums during the Gorbachev era provide a vehicle for understanding the Soviet collapse and its lessons for Gorbachev's successors. When Gorbachev at the end of 1991 resigned from the newly created Soviet presidency, he had been undermined by conservatives, whose political power was under threat, and by his anti-Communist opponents, who came to see his reform efforts as ill conceived or half-hearted. Gorbachev's struggle all along had been to avoid responsibility for past and, increasingly, present decision making even as he sought to introduce accountability for other political actors. In the end, only his rival, Russian president Boris Yeltsin, understood that a popular mandate and the willingness to judge other Soviet-era power holders harshly was the recipe for political survival in the upheavals of the early 1990s.

GORBACHEV'S AGENDA IN HISTORICAL CONTEXT

Few would turn to Soviet history for a primer on political accountability, but one way to understand why Gorbachev placed political change at the center of his reform efforts is to consider the Soviet leadership's ongoing struggle to institute accountability for the rank and file. The Politburo had long sought to keep party officials answerable while they themselves retained the maximum ability to exercise power—and thus to minimize their own accountability. Throughout Soviet history, what the leadership perceived as opposition movements seeking to curtail Kremlin-based power were often also stirrings of a call for accountable government, promptly stifled. Although we are primarily concerned here with the latter half of the 1980s and Gorbachev's efforts to shake the Communist Party from its Brezhnev-era lethargy, all progressive constituencies saw the admission of the crimes of the Stalin era as a precondition for reform. If Stalin's repressions could be acknowledged, including the incredible death tolls of the purges and resettlements of peoples, then presumably the Communist Party could rebuild its authority on a more enduring foundation. Contemporary power holders could reestablish their authority and at the same time alter the state-centered dynamic of the Communist system to incorporate individual initiative and to reinvigorate the economy.

Gorbachev tended to reach back to Lenin's time to retrieve what he portrayed as the flexibility of early Communism and to suggest that the relatively relaxed New Economic Policy of the 1920s provided an ideological foundation for political liberalization and economic reform in the 1980s. The tensions in Soviet Marxism in Lenin's time did provide some sense of historical antecedent for Soviet thinkers regarding accountability in the Gorbachev era, as the early Bolsheviks paid a great deal of attention to questions of who was responsible for what, and to whom. Their motivation in doing so, however, was similar to Gorbachev's: the ongoing challenge of keeping lesser officials on their toes and loyal to the Kremlin.

The Lenin-era precedents for accountability were thus not very encouraging. Though Lenin tolerated disagreements among his inner circle as long as loyalty quickly prevailed, he used force more often than persuasion when ruling on a wider scale. One of the earliest insurrections faced down by the leading Bolsheviks came soon after their seizure of power in 1917, fomented by party members who protested Lenin's brand of political terror for fear it would lead to unaccountable government. The Bolsheviks did adopt a constitution, unlike their tsarist predecessors, and over time set up elaborate systems of supervision and discipline. But the reliance of the early Bolsheviks on personal networks and their failure to set up strong institutional safeguards against abuse of power made a mockery of constitutional authority and set the scene for Stalinism.

Under Stalin, the secret police were able to substitute a system of terror for government in any regular sense. Stalin's successors had the task of building authority for the Communist Party as a ruling organ without the overt use of terror. With no institutional power greater than itself—including the rule of law—the Communist Party became its own organ of accountability after the terror of the Stalin years. The mechanism through which the party could "answer to itself" became a hollow norm of self-criticism and permitted a multiple-tier system of privilege for party members, stoking the anger of a population encouraged to sacrifice for the country's defense. Reform-minded leaders came to prioritize personnel change as a symbol of their desire to cleanse party ranks and practices, and they had some leeway in bringing at least this about. Nikita Khrushchev and Mikhail Gorbachev heralded their intention of far-reaching change through personnel turnover.

Khrushchev struggled mightily with the legacy of Stalinism, perhaps because of his own sense of personal responsibility. Although it is true that Khrushchev never seemed to understand the fundamentals of power sharing, his recognition that an inclusive system was preferable to an overtly coercive one was linked with a conception of a Communist Party that would *prove* itself useful through its work. Among the many reasons for Khrushchev's unprecedented ouster was his insistence that the party adopt mandatory personnel rotation, an accountability measure reintroduced only some thirty years later when Gorbachev became general secretary.

Yet even Khrushchev understood consultation with the people to be an unfortunate symptom of leaders who would follow public whim. Toward the end of his rule he gave a series of rambling and regret-laden public speeches, but the apologetic tone was for his having failed to solve the country's problems, not a recognition that a more responsive and consultative political system might have helped with the process. Khrushchev had no intention of relinquishing the last word.

Under Brezhnev the party and state apparatuses became increasingly focused on indicators rather than actions. For example, officials were required to make decisions on letters from the public within a specified time frame, a typically formalistic indicator of regime responsiveness. The jailed dissident Vladimir Bukovsky put the system to the test by launching a massive letter-writing campaign. The denials from Communist bureaucrats came to be quite efficient. Bukovsky received one letter that consisted of a single sentence: "During the past month 187 complaints have been received from you and refused."[2]

Gorbachev introduced more substance into the formulaic language of party communication, permitted discussion of the party's past, and opened up especially the print media. Within only a few years, given that the party apparatus remained unresponsive and focused on its own well-being, Gorbachev's repertoire of assault on party norms came to include altering the means of personnel selection through competitive elections and creating a new legislative structure, as well as a Soviet presidency. These new political institutions were potentially important venues in which to hold power holders accountable and brought unprecedented checks on executive power.

THE DUAL EDGE OF GLASNOST'

Gorbachev's campaign of *glasnost'* (loosely translated as "openness"), as with all of his reform efforts, was fraught with ambiguity. On the one hand, Gorbachev tolerated increasingly far-reaching criticism of the Stalin era and gradually even the contemporary scene. He permitted the publication of long-banned books and essays. One of his earliest initiatives as general secretary of the Communist Party was to order the removal of enormous signs with propaganda slogans along the Moscow River, a gesture that irritated conservatives and gave the first flicker of hope to long-suffering Khrushchev-era reformers. Gorbachev sought to move the party from vacuous sloganeering to more substantial engagement and understood that this process had to include robust differences of opinion. The realm of the possible in terms of debate and criticism changed so rapidly in a few years that virtually no one—including Gorbachev—could have anticipated the consequences.

On the other hand, Gorbachev tended to let others move the debate along and thus left his own role open to question. He met regularly with editors of the leading press organs. Although these meetings were used initially to encourage the expansion of the boundaries of expression, as the press became increasingly critical, Gorbachev's role was more often to scold. Television remained under state control and was far more conservative in its coverage than the print media. And where disasters were concerned, such as the devastating nuclear accident at Chernobyl' in 1986 or the violent seizure by government troops in 1990 of the television center in Vilnius, Lithuania, the Gorbachev regime exhibited classic Soviet-style silence, denial, and refusal to take responsibility for the event or its consequences. Gorbachev ushered conceptual richness into what had been a barren political scene, but then often appeared to be uncomfortable in the new landscape.

For a critique of the party itself, reform-minded newspaper editors came to understand that they could stretch the limits of the possible if they stayed within traditional forms but allowed daring content. The most secure vehicle for doing so was through public voice. Letters to the editor became the forum of choice for heartfelt criticism, sometimes followed, after a few weeks of testing the waters, by an investigative article seeking "answers for the people." By 1990, many letters went to the heart of deep and abiding anger about the "haves" in society and the majority's continued "have-not" status, including the quest for simple consumer goods that periodically went missing:

> Esteemed editorial board! Take a discreet look to see whether or not [prime minister] N. I. Ryzhkov and his ministers are wearing socks. If they are, where did they find them?[3]
>
> I heard our party leaders say on television, "Our privileges are and will be only in accordance with the law." Publish that law in your newspaper, please.[4]

The latter request was published in a column called "Questions without Answers."

Back in 1975 *Izvestiya*, a daily newspaper and official organ of the state apparatus, received an average of 1,500 letters per day.[5] Under conditions of glasnost', those media that were in the forefront of critical journalism found tremendous reader response. The weekly *Argumenty i fakty* in 1989 received an average of 2,500 letters per day,[6] or 17,500 letters per issue. With 22 million subscriptions purchased by individual readers that year, the formerly dry fact sheet had become the largest circulation newspaper in the world. The reform-minded editor published letters that targeted the leadership rather than faceless scoundrels and charged that corruption was widespread. Political conservatives were rattled as criticism crossed the line from chastizing underlings for mistakes to indicting the leadership for abuse of power.

Young journalists became skilled at capturing the surreal quality of the clumsy machinations of the Communist Party in the disintegrating political world. Much of the reporting marking the "new" journalism provided a Dali-esque juxtaposition of the still-common abacus in bread shops with computers in sleek new offices, Soviet tractors with Mercedes-Benz convertibles, the melting clock of Communist time with an apparently linear and quite rapid Western pace. Even the clumsy and short-lived coup attempt of August 1991, led by Gorbachev's conservative cabinet, included a press conference. Although the bravado of the question resonated around the world, it was a seemingly world-weary twenty-four-year-old Russian journalist who asked the visibly shaken vice president Gennady Yanayev if he and his compatriots were aware that they were committing a crime. Party-based discipline in the media was effective only so long as the Communist Party maintained an atmosphere of fear and a stranglehold on information. The media, in demonstrating the regime's loss of control over information, sent the message that Communist domination of political power was also eroding.

ELECTIONS AND THE PRESIDENCY

Three years after his selection as general secretary, Gorbachev launched electoral reform to assist with his struggle to hold party members accountable.

He seemed to believe initially that calls for "invigoration" of the system and a "speeding up" of the economy would have a greater effect.[7] As it became clear that changes were mostly cosmetic and party members were yet again resisting initiative from the Kremlin by dragging their heels, Gorbachev became willing to enlist multiple-candidate, secret ballot elections in his struggle, as well as term limitations. The guaranteed sinecure of a party position was coming to an end.

Multiple-candidate elections were approved by party members and then resisted by some of them, as they nevertheless ran unopposed or squeezed out potential contenders. The party, to Gorbachev's dismay, thereby lost any claim to progressive behavior. In previous elections an unmarked ballot meant a positive vote, and citizens were usually too intimidated to cross off the single name on the ballot (which was the only reason to enter the private voting booth provided). In 1989 during the popular election for members of the Congress of People's Deputies, the newly constituted legislature, some voters publicly and gleefully crossed off the single name in constituencies where party members had defied the announcement that these elections would, "as a rule," be competitive.

Though he oversaw the most significant electoral reform in Soviet history, what Gorbachev did not do was stand for popular election in 1990 for the newly established office of Soviet *president*. Gorbachev instead was elected as head of state by the Congress of People's Deputies once it convened. Though the statutes for the presidency established that the next presidential election would be by popular vote, Gorbachev's failure to provide a "demonstration effect" of his commitment to reform by standing for election himself was a mistake.[8] He left himself open to charges of being yesterday's politician and was bested as a reformer by Boris Yeltsin, who later that year created and ran for the office of president of the Russian Federation.

As it was, Gorbachev could have faced serious political contestation even for election by the new legislature, which he won with less than the customary automatic support. Fellow Politburo member and prime minister Nikolai Ryzhkov claimed ten years later that he had nearly opposed Gorbachev for the presidency and was confident at the time that he could have won.[9] If Ryzhkov was correct, his election would have offered further proof that the party had little understanding of society's desires or needs. Ryzhkov of all people was among the least popular officials, given a disastrous series of economic reforms (such as the confiscation of fifty- and hundred-ruble notes) launched under his management. But Gorbachev's unwillingness to subject himself to the electoral test of public support at that time meant his historical legacy could be seen as that of a determined power holder rather than a champion of the leadership's obligation to the public.

A party monopoly on accountability was especially strained by the Congress of People's Deputies' initial session, which bypassed the usual filters to bring sharp and lively debate into nearly every household in May and June 1989. So many millions watched the televised proceedings that worker productivity in the country fell during those weeks. Even reformers who participated in the proceedings were astonished to see members of the Politburo sitting in the audience rather than on the stage, listening to "strangers from the Far East with chests full of medals" criticize the army.[10]

But the amazement of viewers, many of whom witnessed the first public criticism of the regime at that time, was lessened as the legislature's successes seemed to peak with debate. The new body proved no more effective than any other institution in providing a steady supply of goods to the public, nor was it able to address another vast shortage: public confidence in the regime's willingness to redress grievances. A legislative commission was formed to investigate responsibility for the civilian deaths, including those of women and children, during a protest in Tbilisi in April of 1989. Gorbachev saw to it that Politburo members and the commanding officer in Tbilisi, General Igor Rodionov, gave testimony, and he appeared before the commission himself. This was a landmark moment, in one sense, but testimony from high-level officials was the result of Gorbachev's decisions and not because of any formal powers held by the commission. The resulting report cast grave suspicion upon high-ranking political and military figures; in its aftermath no party member faced charges, the party secretary for the Georgian Republic having already resigned with full pension, and Rodionov was reassigned to Moscow to head the Voroshilov Military Academy (he later served as minister of defense under Yeltsin). The struggle for unmediated accountability for party members would not be resolved in favor of the legislature.

Typical of the positive and negative attributes of the Gorbachev era was the late career of Andrei Sakharov, a stalwart seeker of regime accountability who in a few years shot from internal exile to the Congress of People's Deputies. A prominent physicist who helped to develop nuclear weaponry for the Soviet Union, Sakharov first came to a politics of protest when he encountered official indifference to the damage—including deaths—resulting from nuclear bomb testing conducted too close to cities. After alerting the Soviet leadership to this danger, Sakharov was put in his place in the crudest possible terms: the message was essentially "you build the bombs, we decide what to do with them."[11] Finding this unacceptable, Sakharov used his fame and rank in order to petition for government that would be answerable to its citizens: a dangerous message given the Soviet Union's anemic relations between citizen and state.

Sakharov's trajectory of protest evolved over thirty years, from proposals to limit weapons testing, to a call for increased civil liberties (especially regarding the availability of information), and, finally, to the need for a law-governed state. He was sent into internal exile in 1980 when he criticized the Soviet-Afghan war in an interview on American television. Sakharov was freed in 1986 and became a presence at the Congress of People's Deputies session in 1989 only because Gorbachev personally authorized his release and subsequently facilitated his rise to political power. But Sakharov's frequent lengthy speeches and insistence on repeating his points at the Congress finally led Gorbachev, who was chairing the proceedings, to turn off the microphone. This act, shown repeatedly on Soviet television, suggested to viewers and especially to the increasingly disillusioned liberals that Gorbachev was no more interested in contradictory opinions than other party leaders, that he also retained the right to silence opponents. Denying Sakharov "voice" in a representative forum lingers in post-Soviet memory rather than Gorbachev's efforts to return Sakharov to public life in the first place.

MINISTERIAL REVIEW

A potentially critical sea change for Soviet power was marked by the legislative review of ministerial appointees in 1989, a process that abruptly gained meaning after decades of ritualized approval (under Article 129 of the 1977 Constitution). Although there had been discussion among legal scholars in the late Soviet period concerning a parliamentary right to review at least some appointments, most political actors were surprised at how vociferously the newly constituted Supreme Soviet, a smaller body elected from the Congress of People's Deputies, seized its first meaningful weapon against the executive branch.

Since over 60 percent of the ministerial candidates in the first-ever review were incumbents, many were grilled on their departmental and occasionally personal records, with charges of nepotism causing particular controversy. The prime minister himself was subject to Supreme Soviet approval, and in the course of answering deputies' questions he confirmed that "if the Supreme Soviet does not confirm a minister, then the Chairman . . . should agree with this. If he is convinced that the minister can fulfill his function, then he is required to prove this to the deputies."[12] The administration intervened in a few cases in which rejection seemed imminent, and in one instance pulled a rejected candidate out of the dustbin of history, but the legislature proved to have a sharp bite.

Ministers could scarcely countenance the questions they were asked and expected to answer. Gorbachev saved several of his own administration's appointments, most notably defense minister Dmitry Yazov, after more than four hours of fierce questioning, but his own appointees were not much safer than "lifers." Ultimately, the Supreme Soviet rejected nine candidates. Any country's executive would be shaken by the rejection of so

many ministerial nominees, and the significance of this check by the legislature was clear to political elites. The Communist Party leadership's domination of decisions on key appointments, first shaken by the 1989 general
elections, was on the wane.

Ministerial review is the single most significant example of a new forum
for accountability that was actually used. Many of the other developments
marked potential accountability or "accountability next time," as with the
promise of future Soviet presidential elections. By January 1991, when the
confirmation of new cabinet ministers again came before the legislature,
the country was in profound crisis. The use of violence by special government troops against unarmed civilians in Lithuania caused a storm of
protest and pushed all three Baltic states into rejection of Soviet power.
Events had moved so far past regular government control and management
that appointments and even policy decisions seemed irrelevant. Just over a
year after the Soviet Union adopted the convention of ministerial review it
was superseded by state and party crises so profound that the survival of the
regime—and of the country itself—was in serious doubt.

LEGAL REFORM AND THE PROMISE OF ACCOUNTABILITY

The evolution of legal reform under Gorbachev featured impressive
changes. For a brief time, law had the potential to stick. Key for party accountability was Article 6 in the Soviet Constitution, which specified that
the Communist Party played a "leading and guiding role" in society but did
not specify its powers or, of primary import here, restrictions on its powers.
Gorbachev's resistance to calls to delete this amendment from the Constitution in 1989 offers another opportunity to see him in a positive or negative light. Certainly Gorbachev needed some kind of governing apparatus in
order to execute his policies and to maintain order in the country. His new
role as president came without any sort of enforcement mechanism (a
problem that would become painfully clear to Boris Yeltsin in a few years).
The party, flawed and recalcitrant as it was, penetrated to every village in the
country and had a tradition of exercising authority. But for some critics, preserving the constitutional basis for party authority meant also maintaining
party impunity. By 1990, Gorbachev agreed to drop Article 6 and called for
the party to be a "democratically acknowledged force" without "legal and
political advantages."[13] This move was shocking to some, and too little, too
late to others. Gorbachev was increasingly alone in the center.

The Gorbachev era also brought the formation in 1990 of the Committee of
Constitutional Supervision, the first nonparty entity charged with interpretation of the Constitution. In contrast to the presidentially appointed Constitutional Court in today's Russia, the Committee consisted of twenty jurists

elected by the Congress of People's Deputies. It had substantial powers—for example, the power to suspend or to move the repeal of formal legal acts of legislatures where they were found to contradict existing laws of the Constitution—but its scope was limited to "juridical norms" and thus left party actions to other authority. And as with its successor Constitutional Court, the Committee of Constitutional Supervision had insufficient powers to implement decisions that faced stiff executive-level resistance.

The Committee's historic moment came when it crossed Gorbachev's wishes and declared unconstitutional a March 1991 presidential decree regulating demonstrations in central Moscow. Gorbachev accepted the defeat. Other events soon conspired to render the Committee and its short burst of activity obsolete, but Russia for the first time had an example of executive authority bound by a constitutionally based counterweight. Most importantly, the Committee could interfere if the president strayed outside the law, and it could not be dismissed by him. Perhaps this precedent will bear fruit in time, but the legal checks and balances that functioned briefly in the Gorbachev era have not yet prevailed in the distribution of power between the executive and judiciary in contemporary Russia.

GORBACHEV AND THE COLLAPSING CENTER

Gorbachev's attempts to maneuver between ideological camps, now making concessions to liberal forces, then to conservative ones, help to explain why his admirers and critics focus on different aspects and periods of his rule. Even with this dichotomy, the Gorbachevian ideal came across as a paternalistic participatory system, in which the executive responds to demands deemed sensible but otherwise is responsible for impressing upon the citizenry that the government knows best. Gorbachev's views could accommodate the need for the party to account for certain past actions, but he understood the efforts of others to hold the contemporary Politburo and general secretary accountable as bald power plays.[14] The tension between Gorbachev's support of accountability in principle and his lack of support for personal accountability of top party officials identifies the crucial difficulty for a reformer in Russia: he struggles to protect his own position while endorsing change.

Part of the problem for the last Soviet leader by 1989 was the unraveling of party discipline at precisely the time he was trying to assert his personal control of the situation. What he continued to perceive as "a crisis—not of the party, but of its old functions"[15]—became a breakdown. Gorbachev's eternal search for the middle ground, even as it shifted, was particularly infuriating for liberals, as was his acceptance in real time of new mechanisms of accountability for nearly everyone but himself. Ultimately he lost support among political liberals and helped to launch the reincarnation of Boris Yeltsin, a member of the Communist Party until 1990, as a democrat.

The very significant concessions to political pluralism Gorbachev introduced usually left open the power of executive review, leaving the final say at first with the Politburo and eventually with himself (or, more charitably, with the Soviet president). Thus, media representatives received a prod forward and then were chastised in party venues if they went too far; members of the party *apparat* who failed to earn "the confidence of the people" and a seat in the new legislature might or might not lose their party position; the force of legislative resolutions was left unclear. Whether Gorbachev's behavior reflected generally liberal intent struggling against tremendous opposition or an internally dissonant reform agenda that unleashed pent-up social forces, he struggled valiantly to keep the leash in his hand while the Soviet system was choking. However enlightened the statesman, politicians in power the world over resent, and try to avoid, being called to account in practice even when they may favor accountability in theory. Gorbachev moved between support for leadership answerability and retreat behind party discipline in a way that prolonged his political survival but resulted in alienating both progressive and conservative camps.

The leadership's understanding of reform or institutional changes can cease to be the most relevant interpretation of their significance. While politicians bickered about who was responsible for what, sought to avoid being held accountable for past and present mistakes, and staked out increasingly polarized points of view, the public seized every opportunity to affect the most important shift of all: holding institutional power holders and entire structures to account. This is why the great political survival tactic of Gorbachev would have been a willingness to participate in competitive popular elections for the Soviet presidency. The boldness of asking the public for power when he could merely have assumed it would have provided democratic inspiration well beyond whatever Gorbachev's tenure in power proved to be. Gorbachev's focus in 1990 was instead to acquire further security for himself as the top executive, through dual posts in the party and the new Soviet presidency. Drawing on the lessons of the Khrushchev era, Gorbachev could not be dismissed by the Communist Party alone. His attention should have been on the emerging power of the public, however, and his rival's ability to tap into vast anger regarding party corruption and abuse. Yeltsin's early seizure of this issue and understanding of its role for the public yielded an electorate anxious to vote for him as a way to stand up against Communist Party privilege. Gorbachev, in attempting to hover above the maelstrom of accountability forces which he helped to release, came to be seen as out of touch and ineffective.

Gorbachev's apparent confidence that the combination of obedience bred by Communist Party norms and the appeal of his own ideas would prove sufficient to see reform through let him take risks and expose executive power to opposition forces in a manner new to Soviet, and indeed, imperial politics. Many who lived under Gorbachev's rule saw him as indecisive and, eventually, weak; when the electorate finally had the chance to vote on Gorbachev as leader, in 1996 when he ran for president of Russia, they gave him a humiliating .52 percent of the votes cast.

SUMMING UP THE LAST SOVIET REVOLUTION

Gorbachev's political reforms came in tandem with two crucial countervailing tendencies that lessened the ability of accountability to stick: the introduction of alternative forms of political and economic power for elites, and the erosion of central authority's ability to maintain order in the country. Among the first to take advantage of new opportunities were political elites who sought personal profit and aggrandizement of their own power. Gorbachev's rule was distinct from the Soviet norm in that he permitted elites to build alternative power structures and allowed opposition movements to challenge him. Public outrage over party privilege and a declining standard of living found champions among the political elite, who were able to move to newly created positions, leave the Communist Party altogether, and then challenge Gorbachev from a safer distance.

Gorbachev can be credited with continuing to tolerate unanticipated results of his policies, including wide-open public debate and political opposition. He had set in motion a complex dynamic of unprecedented vulnerability for executive, that is, party, authority through the press, elections, and membership in the new legislature. The collapse of Communist power in the Soviet Union demonstrated the unprecedented vulnerability of the party to an opponent who was willing to hazard everything—including the empire—if he could banish his enemies and gain power. The most significant aspect of Gorbachev's struggles against Yeltsin was Gorbachev's refusal to use his political and strategic advantages in settling them.

Similarly, Gorbachev exhibited a reluctance to sanction the use of decisive military force against opponents to Soviet power, chiefly in the escalating conflict between Armenia and Azerbaijan and other nationalist conflicts focused on independence. His restraint came under question on two occasions already mentioned here, the deaths of civilians in Tbilisi in 1989 and in Vilnius in 1990; these flashbacks to typical Soviet repression had such a powerful negative lesson for Gorbachev's potential liberal allies that he lost any chance of their support. They largely abandoned him and were prepared to believe that the 1991 coup attempt was a sham, with Gorbachev himself pulling the strings. Strange though a "self-coup" may seem to outsiders, this particular charge against Gorbachev shows the depth of uncertainty about his political convictions toward the end of Soviet power.

The tragedy of the transformation in the climate of political accountability during the Gorbachev era is that it occurred without enduring and significant concessions of power to democratic structures. A fear of the struggle for power then and now leads rulers to prefer reform initiatives that can be centrally managed. In the Putin era we see that competitive elections are easier to manipulate than strong rival political parties. In trying to hold others accountable but to keep himself above the fray, Gorbachev exercised the preference of his predecessors—and his successors—to monitor rather than to be monitored. He had trouble avoiding party constraints, however, a condition that has not yet fettered Russian presidents.

Gorbachev's eventual triple assault through media, electoral, and legislative checks intended to reform a corrupt and ineffectual Communist Party blossomed instead into an alternative politics. These decisions precipitated the Soviet collapse and appear to have provided unfortunate lessons in avoiding accountability for Gorbachev's successors. Gorbachev's resignation marked the first—and to this day, only—peaceful surrender of power to the opposition in Russian history.

NOTES

1. Gorbachev gave speeches for public consumption that were clearly critical of the way the Communist Party exercised power, but after his fall archival records revealed his even sharper—and more historically unusual—criticism in closed forums such as Politburo meetings (*Stenograficheskii otchet*, September 8, 1988, "O razgranichenii Partii" at Tsentr khraneniia sovremennoi dokumentatsii [TsKhSD] fond 89, opis' 42, delo 22).

2. Vladimir Bukovsky, *To Build a Castle: My Life as a Dissenter* (New York: Viking Press, 1978), 35–40.

3. Letter published in *Argumenty i fakty* 41 (1990).

4. *Argumenty i fakty* 52 (1990).

5. Ksenia Broder, *Readers Write to Their Newspapers* (Moscow: Novosti, 1976), 5.

6. *The Independent*, March 31, 1989.

7. For analysis of this point, see Graeme Gill, *The Collapse of a Single-Party System* (Cambridge, UK: Cambridge University Press, 1994), 31.

8. See Archie Brown's discussion of the dilemma for Gorbachev: *The Gorbachev Factor* (Oxford: Oxford University Press, 1996), 202–207.

9. Interview with Nikolai Ryzhkov on "S'ezd pobezhdennykh," an NTV television retrospective on the Congress of People's Deputies viewed by the author in Moscow, May 25, 1999.

10. Author interview with Iurii Afanas'ev, Moscow, June 1990.

11. Andrei Sakharov, *Memoirs* (New York: Knopf, 1990), 194.

12. Nikolai Ryzhkov, quoted in *Izvestiya*, June 9, 1989.

13. *Pravda*, February 6, 1990.

14. Mikhail Gorbachev, *Zhizn' i reformy*, vol. 1 (Moscow: Novosti, 1995), 551.

15. Mikhail Gorbachev, *Partiinaia zhizn'*, no. 15, 1989, 5.

SUGGESTED READING

Breslauer, George W. *Gorbachev and Yeltsin as Leaders*. Cambridge, UK, 2002.

Brown, Archie. *The Gorbachev Factor*. New York, 1996.

———. *Seven Years That Changed the World: Perestroika in Perspective*. New York, 2007.

Chernyaev, Anatoly. *My Six Years with Gorbachev*. University Park, Pa., 2000.

Cohen, Stephen F., and Katrina vanden Heuvel, eds. *Voices of Glasnost': Interviews with Gorbachev's Reformers*. New York, 1989.

Connor, Walter D. "Soviet Society, Public Attitudes, and the Perils of Gorbachev's Reforms." *Journal of Cold War Studies* 5, no. 4 (Fall 2003): 43–80.

Gill, Graeme. *The Collapse of a Single-Party System: The Disintegration of the CPSU*. Cambridge, UK, 1994.

Hauslohner, Peter. "Politics before Gorbachev: De-Stalinization and the Roots of Reform." In *Politics, Society, and Nationality: Inside Gorbachev's Russia*, edited by Seweryn Bialer, 41–90. Boulder, Colo., 1989.

Service, Robert. *Comrades! A History of World Communism*. Cambridge, Mass., 2007.

Sharlet, Robert. *Soviet Constitutional Crisis: From De-Stalinization to Disintegration*. Armonk, N.Y., 1992.

Index

About the Contributors

Sergei Arutiunov is professor emeritus at the Russian Academy of Sciences, Moscow. The author of dozens of books and articles, he was formerly the director of the Caucasus Department, Institute of Ethnology and Anthropology, Russian Academy of Sciences.

Richard Bidlack is associate professor of history and Russian area studies at Washington and Lee University. A much-published specialist on the siege of Leningrad, he is now completing a book on the siege, with Russian historian Nikita Lomagin, for Yale University Press's Annals of Communism series.

Kees Boterbloem is associate professor of history at the University of South Florida. *Life and Death under Stalin: Kalinin Province, 1945–1953* and *The Life and Times of Andrei Zhdanov, 1896–1946* are among his recent works.

James Cracraft is professor of history at the University of Illinois at Chicago, where he has taught courses in Russian and European history for over thirty-five years. He is the author of numerous works in Russian history, including a three-volume account of the Petrine revolution in, respectively, Russian architecture, Russian imagery, and Russian culture.

Chester S. L. Dunning, a fifth-generation Californian, is Eppright University Professor and professor of history at Texas A&M University, where he teaches courses in Russian history and early modern European history. His publications include *Russia's First Civil War: The Time of Troubles and the Founding of the Romanov Dynasty*, *A Short History of Russia's First Civil War*, and *The Uncensored* Boris Godunov: *The Case for Pushkin's Original Comedy*, with annotated text and translation by Chester Dunning, with Caryl Emerson, Sergei Fomichev, Lidiia Lotman, and Antony Wood.

Colum Leckey is assistant professor of history at Piedmont Virginia Community College. His work has appeared in *Russian History/Histoire Russe*, *The Russian Review*, and *Slavic Review*.

Alexander M. Martin is associate professor of modern European history at the University of Notre Dame. His publications include *Romantics, Reformers, Reactionaries: Russian Conservative Thought and Politics in the Reign of Alexander I* and *Provincial Russia in the Age of Enlightenment: The Memoir of a Priest's Son*. An editor of the journal *Kritika: Explorations in Russian and Eurasian History*, Martin is currently working on a social history of early nineteenth-century Moscow.

Susan P. McCaffray received her Ph.D. from Duke University. She has taught at Marquette University and Wake Forest University and is currently professor of history at the University of North Carolina at Wilmington. She is the author of *The Politics of Industrialization in Tsarist Russia*, and, along with Michael Melancon, the co-editor of *Russia in the European Context: 1789-1914; A Member of the Family*. Her current research focuses on economic thought and policy in early nineteenth-century Russia.

Martha Merritt is associate dean for International Education at the University of Chicago. She received her D. Phil from Oxford University in 1994, and is a specialist in Soviet and Russian politics.

Patrick O'Meara is professor of Russian and a master of Van Mildert College, Durham University. A former fellow of Trinity College Dublin, he has held visiting fellowships at the Kennan Institute in Washington, D.C., the Australian National University in Canberra, and Fitzwilliam College at Cambridge. He is author of *The Decembrist Pavel Pestel': Russia's First Republican* and *K. F. Ryleev: A Political Biography of the Decembrist Poet*, and the editor-translator of S. M. Soloviev's *History of Russia: Empress Elizabeth, 1741–1744*.

Scott W. Palmer is associate professor of history at Western Illinois University. He is the author of *Dictatorship of the Air: Aviation Culture and the Fate of Modern Russia*.

Jelena Pogosjan is associate professor in the Department of Modern Languages and Cultural Studies at the University of Alberta. She received her M.A. (1992) and Ph.D. (1997) in Russian literature from Tartu University in Estonia. Her principal teaching areas are Russian language, Russian literary criticism, and the history of Russian culture and literature of the seventeenth and eighteenth centuries. A prolific author on eighteenth-century Russia (*Peter I: The Architect of Russian History* [in Russian] is her latest work), Pogosjan is currently researching "official culture" and the Russian Empire in the eighteenth century, the history of the Russian imperial calendar, Mikhail Lomonosov, and themes and poetics of the Russian ode.

Thomas E. Porter is professor of modern European and Russian history at North Carolina A&T State University in Greensboro, North Carolina. Porter has authored nearly two dozen articles on topics ranging from local self-government, politics, and education in late imperial Russia to the development of civil society and Russian national identity in the post-Soviet era. Several of these articles have been translated and republished in Russian journals. He is currently working on a project for the U.S. Holocaust Memorial Museum in Washington, D.C., on the fate of Soviet POWs during the Second World War.

Ana Siljak teaches European and Russian history at Queen's University, Canada. Her study, *Angel of Vengeance: Vera Zasulich and Russia's Age of Assassins*, is forthcoming in 2008.

Douglas Smith, a resident scholar at the University of Washington's Jackson School of International Studies, is the author of *Working the Rough Stone: Freemasonry and Society in Eighteenth-Century Russia* and *Love and Conquest: Personal Correspondence of Catherine the Great and Prince Gregory Potemkin*.

William Taubman is Bertrand Snell Professor of Political Science at Amherst College. He is the author of *Khrushchev: The Man and His Era*, which in 2004 won the Pulitzer Prize for biography, the National Book Critics Circle Award for biography, the Wayne J. Vucinich Prize of the American Association for the Advancement of Slavic Studies, and the Robert H. Ferrell Book Prize of the Society of Historians of American Foreign Policy. Taubman is also editor and translator of *Khrushchev on Khrushchev* by Sergei N. Khrushchev and co-editor (with Sergei N. Khrushchev and Abbott Gleason) of *Nikita Khrushchev*.

Steven A. Usitalo, assistant professor of history at Northern State University, previously taught Russian and modern European history at McGill University and Concordia University in Montreal. He is the author of a forthcoming study of the myth of Mikhail Lomonosov in Russian culture.

Jeffrey Veidlinger is associate professor of history and Jewish studies, and associate director of the Borns Jewish Studies Program at Indiana University, Bloomington. His first book, *The Moscow State Yiddish Theater: Jewish Culture* *on the Soviet Stage*, won a National Jewish Book Award and the Barnard Hewitt Award for Outstanding Research in Theatre History. Veidlinger is currently completing a monograph on Jewish public culture in late imperial Russia.

Rex A. Wade is professor of history at George Mason University. He is the author of *The Russian Search for Peace, 1917; Red Guards and Workers' Militias in the Russian Revolution; The Russian Revolution, 1917;* and *Revolutionary Russia,* along with other books and numerous articles on revolutionary-era Russia.

William Benton Whisenhunt is professor of history at the College of DuPage. He is the author of *In Search of Legality: Mikhail M. Speranskii and the Codification of Russian Law,* and is co-author (with Marina Swoboda) of *A Russian Paints America: Pavel P. Svin'in's Impressions of Early Nineteenth-Century America,* forthcoming from McGill-Queen's University Press. In 2006, he was a J. William Fulbright Senior Scholar at Ryazan State University, Russia.